ISBN 978-1-333-48609-9
PIBN 10510456

1 MONTH OF
FREE
READING

at

www.ForgottenBooks.com

By purchasing this book you are eligible for one month membership to ForgottenBooks.com, giving you unlimited access to our entire collection of over 1,000,000 titles via our web site and mobile apps.

To claim your free month visit:

www.forgottenbooks.com/free510456

THE GIRLHOOD OF QUEEN VICTORIA

A SELECTION FROM HER MAJESTY'S
DIARIES BETWEEN THE YEARS
1832 AND 1840

PUBLISHED BY AUTHORITY OF
HIS MAJESTY THE KING

EDITED BY VISCOUNT ESHER, G.C.B., G.C.V.O.

IN TWO VOLUMES

VOL. I

LONDON
JOHN MURRAY, ALBEMARLE STREET, W.
1912

In the preparation of this book much is due to the ungrudging help given to the Editor by the late Mr. Hugh Childers in the tedious and complicated task of tracing the numerous references to persons and places mentioned in the Queen's Journals.

Mr. Hugh Childers rendered valuable service to the Editors of *The Letters of Queen Victoria*, and in the preparation of this book his labour and trouble were no less freely expended under trying circumstances of failing health. His loss is deeply regretted by the Editor.

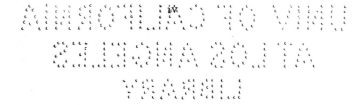

PREFACE

THESE extracts from the early Journals of Queen Victoria have been edited by command of her son, King Edward VII., and under the gracious auspices of her grandson, King George V.

The Editor feels bound to express his humble gratitude to the King, and his deep obligation to the Queen, for the encouragement and assistance he has received from their Majesties in the preparation of these volumes.

Without the Queen's help and exact historical knowledge of the period covered by the Journals, many imperfections in the editing of them would have passed unnoticed.

The Editor must also return his warmest thanks to H.R.H. Princess Christian of Schleswig-Holstein, whose retentive memory of the persons mentioned in the text has been unreservedly and generously brought to bear upon the notes to these volumes, and to H.R.H. Princess Henry of Battenberg, to whose pious regard for her Mother's memory, as Executrix of Queen Victoria's Will, the publication of the Journals may be ascribed.

Furthermore, he is anxious to thank Lord Rosebery for his friendly co-operation in having read the proofs, and for many valuable suggestions.

v

And, finally, he cannot sufficiently acknowledge the care lavished upon the publication of this book by his friend John Murray, junior, whose inherited gifts have been placed unreservedly at the disposal of the Editor.

CONTENTS

vii

CONTENTS

CHAPTER VI

1837

CHAPTER VII

1837 (*continued*)

CHAPTER VIII

January and February, 1838

CHAPTER IX

March, April, and May, 1838

CHAPTER X

June, July, and August, 1838

LIST OF ILLUSTRATIONS

VOL. I

NOTE.—The illustrations marked * are taken from the Queen's private albums, in which she kept portraits of relations and friends, specially painted for her.

INTRODUCTION

I

APART from the onward surge of Empire during both epochs, apart from the flow of scientific thought and the breeze of literary enthusiasm characterising them, there is much in the atmosphere of Victoria's advent to the Throne, and her long and glorious tenure of it, to remind us of the central figure of the Elizabethan age.

Both princesses were reared and educated, although for very different reasons, in the uncertain glory of succession to the Throne. Both mounted the Throne early in life alone and unprotected, at a moment of reaction against the abuses of monarchy. Under George III. as under Henry VIII. this country had been subjected to violent commotion consequent on the struggle for national freedom against a foreign power. The Reformation in England and the Napoleonic wars owed their successful issue to the persistent determination of the English people to be free. The hated marriage of Mary and the matrimonial scandals of George IV. had cast a gloom over the temper of the nation. Even the triumph of the popular cause, due to the grudging support given by William IV. to his Whig Ministers, had not restored the forfeited prestige of the Monarchy.

Reaction was the corollary against the fear inspired by Philip in the one case and the humiliating memories of Queen Caroline in the other. That reaction came in the shape of the popular enthusiasm inspired by a young and attractive Tudor princess, who at Hatfield on a late November afternoon in 1558 heard from Cecil that she was Queen of England. Three centuries later a similar outburst followed the accession of another youthful princess only just eighteen years old, looking scarcely more than a child, when she received the homage of Lord Melbourne at Kensington Palace on a June morning of 1837.

It is tempting to follow this seductive pathway through the devious alleys of historical comparison and contrasts. The troubles of Elizabeth's childhood at Hunsdon, the pitiful laments of her excellent governess at the poverty of her ward's surroundings, and the hostile atmosphere surrounding her person were reflected in a minor degree within the precincts of Kensington during the early years of Princess Victoria's life.

Our concern, however, is not with Elizabeth but with Victoria, with the England into which she was born, and with the influences which helped to give her character and bearing a certain strength and dignity, and attuned her heart, not perhaps to deep tenderness, but to much compassion.

The pen recoils from an attempt to tell again the story of Princess Victoria's birth and early life, or to describe once more the political events of her first years upon the Throne. Moreover, these volumes tell their own tale. They set forth in the young Princesses' own artless words the daily facts of her existence at Kensington, or when making some provincial royal progress in the company of her mother.

The reader can catch many a glimpse here and there of the soul of a Princess, proud and head-strong, affectionate and sometimes perverse, seated on the lonely heights of the Throne. The portrait is here, within these pages. It is not unskilfully drawn, when the youth of the artist is borne in mind. At the time when the first entries in these Journals were made, the writer was thirteen years old. The last page was written on the day of her marriage. She had been two years a Queen, and she was in her twenty-first year.

Princess Victoria, the only child of the Duke and Duchess of Kent, and the ultimate heiress in direct succession of George III., was born on May 24, 1819. In 1819 the aspect of English country life was not very different from that of to-day ; if the roads were not so well surfaced, and if woodlands were rather more plentiful, the fields and hedgerows, the farmsteads with cottages grouped around them, the Tudor manor-houses, the Georgian villas, the church spires, and the village greens have remained unchanged. Except for lines of railway and telegraph poles, the hop-fields of Kent and the Surrey commons have kept their shape and contours. So that, in spite of the miracles wrought by machinery in the minutiæ of life, any one of our grandparents cruising in an airship at an elevation of some hundreds of feet over the lands where he hunted and shot, or even the great town in which he spent his summer months, would probably be unconscious of much distinctive change.

Young people, however, think it odd when they read that when Princess Victoria was taken from Kensington to Claremont—a journey now accomplished with as little thought as would then have been given to a drive between the Palace and Hyde Park—it was considered a " family removal " of such moment as to require all the provision and precautions associated to-day with an autumn holiday.

To those still young, but old enough to remember Queen Victoria, it may seem hardly credible that she was born into a world devoid of all the marvels of steam and electric contrivance that appear to us the necessities, and not merely the luxuries, of life. How much more difficult it must be for them to realise that when the young Princess (whom they remember a great and mysterious figure, welcoming back only the other day her soldiers from South Africa, and rejoicing in their victories) was carried into the saloon of Kensington Palace to be received by Archbishop Manners Sutton into the Church of Christ, the mighty spirit of Napoleon brooded still behind the palisades of Longwood, and George III.'s white and weary head could still be seen at the window of his library at Windsor!

The Victorian era covers the period of the expansion of England into the British Empire. The soldier, still young to-day, who put the coping-stone on the Empire in Africa in 1900 is linked by the life of the Queen to his forbears, who, when she was born, were still nursing the wounds gloriously earned four years before in laying its foundation in a Belgian cornfield.

That year 1819, however, was a year of deep despondency in England. In Europe it was the " glorious year of Metternich," then at the height of his maleficent power. Europe was quit of Napoleon, but had got Metternich in exchange, and was ill pleased with the bargain. Great Britain, it is true, was free, but our people were overwrought by poverty and suffering. The storm-swell of the great Napoleonic wars still disturbed the surface of English life, and few realised that they were better off than they had been during the past decade.

At Holland House, its coteries thinner but still talking, Lady Holland—old Madagascar—was still debating what inscription should record the merits of Mr. Fox upon his monument in the Abbey for the edification of future ages. In St. James's Place Sam Rogers's breakfasts had not lost their vogue. Tommy Moore was still dining with Horace Twiss, and meeting Kean, and Mrs. Siddons, " cold and queenlike," on her way to view Caroline of Brunswick's " things " shortly to be sold at Christie's, or to criticise Miss O'Neill's dress rehearsals. On the very day that Princess Victoria was born, Byron was writing to John Murray from Venice " in the agonies of a sirocco," and clamouring for the proofs of the first canto of *Don Juan*. In that year *Ivanhoe* was finished, and in the hands of eager readers; whilst Scott was receiving at Abbotsford a certain Prince Leopold of Saxe-Coburg, uncle of the baby

at Kensington, destined thereafter to play a large
part in her early life. Keats had just published
Endymion. It was his last year in England before
going south to die. And it was Shelley's *annus
mirabilis*: the year in which he wrote *Prometheus*
and *The Cenci*—an achievement, some have since said,
unparalleled in English poetry since Shakespeare
lived and wrote.

The Excursion had been published five years
before, but Wordsworth was at Rydal Mount com-
pleting *The White Doe of Rylston.* Southey was
Poet Laureate. Three years before, in the " wild
and desolate neighbourhood amid great tracts of
bleak land enclosed by stone dykes sweeping up
Clayton heights," Charlotte Brontë's eyes had opened
upon her sad world. Carlyle, then a young teacher
in Edinburgh, was passing through that stormy
period of the soul which comes sooner or later to
every one whose manhood is worth testing by God.
And half-way between Horncastle and Spilsby, on
the lower slope of a Lincolnshire wold, Alfred Tenny-
son was reading Pope's *Iliad* and himself " writing
an epic of 6,000 lines *à la* Walter Scott." At Shrewsbury School under Dr. Butler, Charles Darwin, then
a boy of ten, had already begun to develop a taste
for " collecting," manifested in " franks " and seals
and coins. Robert Browning, a turbulent and de-
structive child of seven, had already commenced
making rhymes less complicated, but not less am-
bitious, than those which puzzled his readers sixty
years later. Goethe, who had grown to manhood
within earshot of Frederick the Great and of the

Empress Maria Theresa, was living at Weimar with many years of life still before him, corresponding with the boy Mendelssohn, later to be a welcome guest, at Windsor, of the little Princess, then in her cradle in Kensington Palace.   Mazzini, aged fourteen, was at the University in Genoa, a rebellious lad, but already affecting the deep mourning dress he never altered later in life. Cavour, aged nine, was at school in Turin.   Sir Thomas Lawrence was in that year engaged in finishing his magnificent series of historical portraits afterwards to find a home at Windsor Castle, illustrating for all time the Congress of Vienna and the story of the Great Coalition against Napoleon.

Under this galaxy of stars, some slowly sinking below the horizon, and others just rising above it, Princess Victoria was born.

In the year following, King George III. died. Historians, mostly partisans of the Whig party, have not done this King justice.   Of all Sovereigns who have ever reigned in England, none so completely represented the average man among his subjects.   The King's blameless morals, his regular habits, his conservative instincts and narrow obstinacy, were characteristics which he shared with the people he ruled.   Of the House of Hanover he was the first King born in England, and he spoke his native tongue without a foreign accent.   If he could have reconciled it to the family tradition, he would have married an English wife.   He was essentially British in character and sentiment.   Had he not been overborne by his Ministers, he would have fought out to a finish the war with America, and peace with Washington would not have been concluded. He never for a moment contemplated abandoning the struggle against Napoleon. No party whip could have taken more trouble to keep his chief in office than did George III. to support Mr. Pitt throughout that Minister's first administration. He has been called despotic, but that adjective can only be used, in speaking of him, in the sense that he wished to see his views prevail. He was a good partisan fighter, and this, in the main, his subjects never disliked. A close and impartial examination of the character of George III. discloses a temperament strongly resembling that which her Ministers were destined in the middle and later years of her reign to find in his granddaughter. Strong tenacity of view and of purpose, a vivid sense of duty, a firm though unrevealed belief in the transcendental right of the Sovereign to rule, a curious mingling of etiquette and domestic simplicity, and a high standard of domestic virtue were marked characteristics of George III. and of Queen Victoria. Both these descendants of Princess Sophia had little in common with the Stewarts, but, like Elizabeth and the Tudors, they had intense pride in England, and they showed a firm resolve to cherish and keep intact their mighty inheritance.

When George III. died at Windsor in 1820, and during the ten following years, Princess Victoria's uncle, George IV., reigned as King. For the previous ten years he had reigned as Prince Regent. If his father has been misjudged, this Sovereign too has

been misrepresented by those who have made it
their business to write the political history of our
country. He is generally described as being wholly
bad, and devoid of any decent quality as a man
and as a Sovereign. Decency perhaps was not his
strong point; but though it is not possible to esteem
him as a man, George IV. was not a bad King. In
his youth, as Prince of Wales, in spite of glaring
follies and many vices, he possessed a certain charm.
When a boy he had broken loose from the over-strict
and over-judicious watchfulness of his parents. Kept
in monotonous seclusion, cloistered within the narrow
confines of a Palace, fettered by an Oriental system
of domestic spies, cut off from intercourse with the
intellectual movement of the outer world, the royal
children, warm-blooded and of rebellious spirit, ran
secret riot after a fashion which modern memoirs
have revealed in Borgian colours. It was a natural
reaction of young animal life against unnatural and
unhealthy restraint. The Prince of Wales, when
he was eighteen years old, was unwillingly and
perforce liberated. It followed, simply enough, that
he became a source of constant grief and annoyance
to his royal father. Not only were the canons of
morality violated by him with little regard for the
outward decorum due to his great position, but the
young Prince plunged into a turgid sea of politics,
and it was not long before he stood forth as the
nominal head of a faction bitterly opposed to the
King's Ministers, and the head and front of personal
offence to the King himself.

In the eyes of high society he was a Prince

Charming, vicious if you will, a spendthrift and a rake, the embodiment of a reactionary spirit against the dulness and monotonous respectability of the Court. He was known to appreciate beautiful objects as well as beautiful faces. He was not altogether without literary culture. He appeared to be instinctively drawn to the arts and sciences with a full sense of the joy of patronage, and he made it clear to every one that he welcomed the free intercourse of men of all ranks, provided that they possessed some originality of character or some distinction of mind. In Mr. Fox he found a willing mentor and an irresistible boon companion. Among that little group of Whigs, of whom Sheridan was the ornament and the disgrace, he found precisely the atmosphere which suited him, so completely was it the antithesis of that in which his boyhood had been spent. As he grew older, the rose-tinted vices of his youth became grey and unlovely, while the shortcomings of his mind and his heart were more readily discerned; but much of his personal charm remained. In his most degenerate days, in the years of his regency and kingship, when he dragged into the public eye the indecencies of his domestic misfortunes and paraded his mistresses before the world, he still managed to retain a curious and genuine hold upon the affections of his Ministers. Although he possessed none of their regard, he was not altogether without some following among the people.

George IV.'s merits were a certain epicurean kindness of heart and a not ungenerous desire to

give pleasure, coupled with a true sense of his constitutional position and a firm-drawn resolve to
distinguish between his private predilections and
his public duty. The nation owes him very little,
but in any case it owes him this, that he was the
first Sovereign since Charles I. who showed a blun-
dering reverence for beautiful things. He enlarged
and consolidated the artistic wealth of the nation.
A life-long patron of artists, he fostered the growth
of national art. He added largely to the splendid
collections which now adorn Windsor and the metropolis. Whatever the final judgment passed upon
him may be, both as a man and as a Sovereign, he
must in strict justice be spared the unqualified contempt with which superior spirits, taking their cue
from Thackeray, have treated him. It should weigh
with every man who reads *The Four Georges* that
King George IV. was certainly liked, and was certainly not despised, by Sir Walter Scott. In his
later years the old King displayed some little kindness
to his niece, the young Princess Victoria, who had
succeeded his own daughter as prospective heiress
of England. If he saw her but rarely, he now and
again betrayed knowledge of her existence, and once
took her for a drive in his pony-carriage. There are
still extant some short letters which she wrote to
him in a large baby hand. In 1830 he died, and was
succeeded by his brother the Duke of Clarence.

William IV. was the most fortunate of the children of George III. Thanks to his profession as a
sea-officer, he escaped early from the stifling atmosphere of the Court, and had the glorious privilege

of serving under the command of Hood and of Nelson. His sea service ended when he was only twenty-five years old. It left the usual dominant sea-mark upon his character. Like so many gallant sailors, his mind was untrained and ill-disciplined. His sense of duty was strong, though undiscerning. He was courageous and truthful. He had ten children by Mrs. Jordan born out of wedlock, but they were all well cared for and never disowned. He realised his constitutional duty sufficiently to see that he must yield to the expressed will of the nation, but he yielded so clumsily that all men believed him to be coerced. Wisely anxious to be well known and popular among his subjects, he chose the curious method of walking down St. James's Street dressed in long boots and spurs during the most crowded hour of the afternoon. His predecessor had lived the last years of his life in seclusion and silence; he determined therefore to give full scope to his naturally garrulous disposition. He talked in season and out of season with an irresponsibility which savoured of the quarter-deck, but wholly without the salt of the sea. By his Ministers he was regarded with kindliness, although it cannot be said, in spite of Lord Grey's panegyric, that they held him in much respect. By the middle classes he was looked upon with amused and not unfriendly amazement. In the eyes of the masses he was " Billy," their sailor-King, and among monarchical safeguards there are few stronger than a nickname and the aureole of the Navy.

William IV. married late in life Princess Adelaide

of Saxe-Coburg-Meiningen, but the fates left him
with no surviving children when he ascended the
Throne in 1830. During his reign of seven years the
King showed much kindness to the little niece who
was clearly designated as his successor. Her mother,
however, contrived to irritate him by giving too
much prominence to the obvious fact of her daughter's
heirship to the Throne. By " progresses " made on
different occasions and undertaken with considerable
ceremonial, the Duchess of Kent excited the wrath
of the King, who made no attempt to conceal his
annoyance, and took evident pleasure in the display
of it at embarrassing moments in public. It was
partly owing to the friction between her mother
and King William and to the unpleasant atmosphere
created in consequence of these quarrels, and partly
to the presence in her mother's household of Sir John
Conroy and his family—persons very distasteful to
the young Princess—that Queen Victoria was in the
habit of saying that her childhood had been a sad
one. These Journals, begun in her fourteenth year,
betray no sense of childish sorrow, and no reader can
glean from them any confirmation of her statement
that her early life was unhappy. It must be remembered, however, that this Journal was not a sealed
book. It was not privately put away under lock
and key and reserved only for the eye of the writer.
The young Princess's Journals were commenced in a
volume given to her by her mother for the express
purpose that she should record the facts of her
daily life, and that this record of facts and impressions
should be open to the inspection of the child's gover-

ness as well as of her mother.   It is natural, therefore, that the earlier volumes should contain very little beyond the obvious and simple things which any girl would be likely to write down if she were attempting to describe her life from day to day.   When the Princess ascended the Throne and assumed her queenly independence, the tone of the Journals changes at once.   It becomes immediately clear to the reader that while the Princess's Journal was written for her mother, the Queen's Journal was written for herself.   One of her earliest entries after her succession was to state her intention of invariably seeing her Ministers alone; and she might have added, had she thought it worth stating, that her Journal also would in future be seen by her alone.

Journals are often said to be useful to the historian.   This theory is based on the assumption, hardly borne out by experience, that he who writes a journal writes what is true.   A journal is supposed to record events, great or small, which are happening at the moment, and to convey impressions about personages with whom the writer comes in contact, or who loom sufficiently large to justify their being mentioned.   When, however, it is remembered how inaccurate our information generally is, and how mistaken we often are about the character and motives even of those we know intimately, it is not surprising that the most brilliant diarist should frequently state facts which cannot be verified from other sources, and colour the personality of his contemporaries in a manner quite unjustifiable unless truth be deliberately sacrificed to the picturesque.

The Journal of Charles Greville, perhaps the most famous of English modern journals, is full of gross inaccuracies in matters of fact and still grosser distortions of character. It is, nevertheless, a striking picture of the political and social world haunted by that persistent eavesdropper, and, like any well-written journal, throws a vivid and interesting light upon the character of the writer.

Similar criticisms apply to most famous memoirs, like Saint-Simon's or Lord Hervey's, written with a view to serving the historian of the future, and with the distinct purpose of giving bias to history.

They do not apply to these diaries of Queen Victoria. The Queen makes no attempt to analyse character or the meaning of events. She never strives after effect. Her statements are just homely descriptions of everyday life and plain references to the people she meets at Kensington or at Windsor. If the young Princess sees a play that pleases her or hears a song that touches her, she says so. If the Queen hears something said that strikes her as original or quaint, the saying is put on record. She is not writing for the historian. She writes for her own pleasure and amusement, although there is always present to her mind a vague idea, common enough at the time, that to " keep a journal " is in some undefined way an act of grace.

The reader should not lose sight of the fact that these Journals are the simple impressions of a young girl, not twenty years old, about her own life and about the people she met. This constitutes their charm. She writes of her daily movements, and of the men and happenings that gave her pleasure. Either by nature or design, she avoided the mention of disagreeable things, so that these early Journals give one a notion of a life happily and simply led.

If they throw no new light on the history of the period, they will give to future generations an insight, of never-failing interest, into the character of the young Queen.

II

Princess Victoria's first Journal was commenced on August 1, 1832. She was thirteen years old. The first entry is made in a small octavo volume half bound in red morocco, of a very unpretentious kind.[1] On the first page there appear the words, " This book Mamma gave me, that I might write the journal of my journey to Wales in it.— Victoria, Kensington Palace, July 31."

The Duchess of Kent was at this time forty-six years of age. She had been a widow for twelve years. She was the fourth daughter of the Duke of Saxe-Coburg-Saalfeld, and was first married to the Prince of Leiningen-Dachburg-Hadenburg. He was twenty-three years her senior. By him she had one son, Charles, often mentioned in these Journals, and one daughter Feodorowna, subsequently married to Ernest, Prince of Hohenlohe-Langenburg.

Two years after her second marriage, to the fourth son of George III., the Duchess of Kent was left a

[1] In later years the volumes of the Queen's Journals were of larger size, but they were always simply bound in half calf or half morocco.

widow for the second time.　Crippled by the Duke's debts, that she was quite unable to pay,[1] with three young children on her hands, she was miserably poor. Her jointure yielded her an income of under £300. Her brother Leopold, then living at Claremont, came to her assistance, and made her an allowance of £3,000 a year.

In 1825, when it became evident that her daughter Princess Victoria would in all probability succeed to the Throne of England, Parliament voted an annuity of £6,000 to the Duchess, for the maintenance and education of her child, and this was subsequently increased after the accession of William IV.

The upbringing of her daughter became her absorbing occupation, and, shutting herself up in Kensington Palace, she devoted herself to the child's education.

The lessons of Princess Victoria's childhood were superintended by the Dean of Chester.　Her education, judged by the standards of to-day, was not of an exceptionally high order.　It would be interesting to know what old Roger Ascham would have thought of the Dean of Chester's curriculum.　So far as can be gathered from her own childish records and from the correspondence and memoirs of those who had access to Kensington, she was taught the ordinary things which children are supposed to learn. Fortunately, perhaps, no effort of any special kind was made to train her mind or mould her character, with a

---

[1] They were ultimately paid by the Queen immediately after her accession.

view to the responsibilities which lay before her or
to the position she appeared destined to fill. When,
at a later stage, the Bishops of London and Lincoln
were requested to draw up a report, for presentation
to Parliament, upon her moral and intellectual attainments, they found no difficulty in giving credit to
the Duchess of Kent for the conscientious manner in
which she had endeavoured to educate the heiress
to the Throne. We may, however, take leave to
doubt whether those entrusted with the Princess's
education were teachers endowed with any special
aptitudes; and it is certain that the outlook of the
Duchess herself, although practical and wise, was
not of that discerning character which enabled her
to differentiate between a commonplace education
and its more subtle forms. It was precisely what
might have been expected from one whose youth had
been spent in a small German Court, and whose later
opportunities had not brought her into contact
with highly trained and thoughtful minds.

A foreign observer and critic once suggested a
doubt whether the Queen could have maintained
through life her admirable mental equilibrium if
education had developed in her high intellectual
curiosity or fantastic imagination. It is an interesting speculation. Soundness of judgment possibly
rests upon the receptive rather than upon the creative
faculties, and upon physical rather than upon intellectual activities. It may, as has been said,
require a rare type of intelligence—that of Disraeli—
to combine ideas and dreams with the realities of
public life. In the domain of learning, Queen

Victoria had very little in common with Elizabeth or with any Sovereign of the Renaissance. Her mother and the worthy Dean, who watched over her youth, were content to foster the quality of good sense, and to inculcate high standards of private and public virtue. Her future subjects, could they have been consulted, would have strongly approved. In after-years the English middle-class recognised in the Queen a certain strain of German sentimentality which they affectionately condoned, and a robust equilibrium of mind which they thoroughly admired.

It is as well, therefore, that events took the shape they did, and that the mind and character of the Princess were trained upon simple lines in accordance with the practice of the average citizen families subsequently to be her subjects. In years to come the Queen was perhaps better able to look at events and persons from the point of view of the majority of her people than would have been possible if her education had given her a high place among the intellectuals. It was a saving grace throughout her long reign that while she could recognise intellect and capacity, her sympathies were with average people, whose feelings and opinions she more readily understood and in reality represented.

In these days, when Accomplishments, as they were called in the first half of the nineteenth century, are no longer esteemed in young people, and their place has been usurped by athletic exercises, it is difficult to describe, in a way that appeals to the serious imagination, the girlish tastes of Princess

Victoria. Perhaps the world has not lost much because young ladies to-day learn to play golf and have ceased to sing duets.

In the thirties, music and painting and a knowledge of modern languages were the necessary equipment of a girl destined to move in Society. It mattered little how reedy and small the voice, she was expected to vocalise like Grisi and to sing duets with Mario.

The Queen had been well trained musically, according to the lights of those days. She could appreciate the simpler forms of melody, especially Italian opera, while she could sing and play sufficiently well to give much pleasure to herself and mild pleasure to others. As a linguist, as a reader, and as a writer of letters and memoranda she had no pretensions to pre-eminence; but she could speak modern languages as well as any Queen is called upon to do, she could read and appreciate high literature, although not without effort, and she could express herself with pungency and vigour, although not with any marked literary skill or distinction of style.

Her drawings and water-colour sketches were through life a constant source of happiness to the Queen. There are at Windsor literally hundreds of small sketch-books, containing reminiscences of her journeys and sojournings in Scotland and in Italy, again not of high artistic merit, but sufficiently vital to suggest the reflection that a young lady of to-day is possibly no gainer by having substituted the golf-club for the pencil.

The Queen's teachers were excellent, commonplace people, and they left precisely those traces on her mind that might have been expected. Her character was another matter. They could not and did not influence that, and it is the character of the Queen that places her in the small category of rulers who have not only deserved well of their country, but have left an indelible stamp upon the life of their people.

III

These Journals were commenced in the year 1832, a year memorable in our history for the fruition of hopes deeply cherished by the political party that had arisen, under the auspices of Canning, after the close of the struggle with Napoleon.

During the year when the first Reform Bill became the law of the land, the passions of men had been deeply stirred throughout Great Britain. The political struggle, begun seventeen years before, had come to a head. The classes still paramount had found themselves face to face with the desires and aspirations of classes hitherto subordinate to have a share in the government of the country. These feelings had grown fiercer year by year, and, encouraged by the Whig party headed by Earl Grey, had found ultimate expression in the Reform Bill of 1832, framed under the ægis of that Minister. All over Europe the stream of change and reform, loosed by the French Revolution and subsequently checked by the Congress of Vienna, began once more to flow. During the sixteen years that followed Princess

Victoria's first entry in these Journals, the waters of Revolution had flooded Europe. Thrones and institutions in every European country were shaken, many of them to their foundations, and some with disastrous results. Fortunately for Great Britain, her statesmen had anticipated the events of 1848, and the Reform Bill had so far satisfied the aspirations of the hitherto unenfranchised classes as to render innocuous the frothing of agitators during that tragic year of revolution. In aptitude for anticipating social and political change and avoiding violent manifestations of popular will, the English race stands pre-eminent. Our people as well as our statesmen have from the earliest times proved themselves to be experts in the art of government, and the history of Europe is a commentary upon that gift of the British nation.

There have, of course, been moments when the atmosphere of politics has been highly charged with electricity. Such a moment occurred in 1832. A storm broke with unusual violence over the head of William IV. The House of Lords was bitterly hostile to a Bill, accepted by the House of Commons and supported with enthusiasm by the majority of his subjects. There was no machinery existing under the Constitution for adjusting these differences except that of creating a sufficient number of Peers to ensure the passage of the Reform Bill through the House of Lords. The King therefore found himself in the unpleasant position of having to place his prerogative of creating peers in the hands of his Ministers, or else by his own act to dispense with

their services. The choice found him undecided and
left him baffled. He was not acute enough to see
that in the existing state of public opinion he had
no choice. If he had possessed wit to read the signs
of the times, it is doubtful whether he would have
had sufficient single-minded courage to take immediate action in accordance with the opinion he had
formed. Penetrating vision the King lacked, and
responsibility was distasteful to him. Consequently
he was not only weak, but he showed weakness. It
was clear that the Government of Lord Grey held
unimpaired the confidence of the House of Commons
and possessed the full approval of the country.
Every intelligent observer realised that the Reform
Bill, in spite of its aristocratic foes, in spite of the
prophets of evil, and in spite of its inherent defects,
was bound to be passed into law. King William,
however, conceived it to be his duty to endeavour
to find an alternative Government. It was as certain
as anything could be in politics, that Sir Robert
Peel would not, and that the Duke of Wellington
could not, come to his assistance. There was something pitiful about the spectacle of the old sailor-
King casting about for a safe anchorage, and finding
one cable parting after another. Security was only
to be found in the Ministers who had advised him,
in the last resort, to use his prerogative for the
purpose of swamping a majority in the House of
Lords that hesitated to bow to the will of the people.
Ultimately he was constrained to accept their advice, but it was only after a loss of personal dignity
and a distinct weakening of the authority of the

Crown. The King, men said, had touted about to find Ministers to serve him, and had failed to find them. This humiliation, at least, King William might have avoided, had he possessed a clearer vision of possibilities and greater firmness of character.

The political storms of 1832 appear to have broken noiselessly against the walls of Kensington Palace, for in the little Princess's Journals there is no sign that she was aware of them. The King's worries, however, so affected his temper, that it was impossible for the Princess and her mother not to feel its reflex action. In the Journals no mention is made of the domestic troubles which have been described elsewhere, and we know, from expressions of Queen Victoria's in later years, that she had purposely refrained, in compiling her Journals, from referring to her mother's worries and her own.

During the four years that immediately preceded Princess Victoria's accession to the Throne, from 1832 to 1836, these Journals give us the picture of a young life passed amid the tranquil surroundings of Kensington Palace, its educational monotony only varied by attendance at the opera or the theatre, by autumnal trips into the provinces, or by welcome visits from foreign cousins. These autumnal trips were the " royal progresses," as he called them, against which King William was wont to protest in vehement language. They evidently gave intense pleasure to the Princess. Her Journals contain records of them all. Some examples have been given, in these extracts, of her method of describing her visits to provincial cities and towns, to seaside summer resorts, and to a few of the great homes of those who were afterwards to be her Ministers or subjects.

It was during this period that she got her first glimpse of the Isle of Wight, where so much of her life was afterwards to be spent. The fact that Sir John Conroy, whom she disliked, lived for many years at Osborne Lodge seems not to have prevented her from subsequently becoming deeply attached to that quiet home amid beautiful surroundings created by her and Prince Albert upon the site where Osborne Lodge had stood. Whippingham Church, to be so closely connected with her and her children, was first visited in the year 1833.

Enough has been included in these extracts to show her liking for the opera and for the theatre, her pleasure in music, her devotion to the pursuit of riding, and that love for animals which characterised her through life.

When she was sixteen she went to Ascot for the first time, and figured in the royal procession. It began to be recognised that the young Princess had passed the threshold of girlhood. In that year her Confirmation took place at the Chapel Royal, St. James's, and Archbishop Howley, believed to be the last prelate who wore a wig, officiated. During the autumn she visited Yorkshire and stayed with Archbishop Harcourt at Bishopthorpe and with Lord Fitzwilliam at Wentworth. Coming south, she was the guest of the Duke of Rutland at Belvoir, of Lord Exeter at Burghley, and of Lord Leicester

at Holkham.   In the following year, 1836, she met
for the first time her cousin Prince Albert of Saxe-
Coburg.   He and his elder brother Ernest visited
Kensington Palace at the instance of her uncle
Leopold.   The fact that Prince Albert had been
thought of years before by the King of the Belgians
as a possible husband for Princess Victoria was
sufficient to set King William IV. against the match.
The King, however, was not uncivil to the brothers
when they visited London, but he had ideas of his
own about the future of his niece, and he tried hard
to lay the foundations of an alliance between the
young Princess and the younger son of the Prince of
Orange.   Prince Albert on this occasion made no
deep impression upon Princess Victoria's mind or
heart, but her loyalty to her uncle Leopold and
her regard for his opinion led her to show the graceful young Coburg Prince marked preference over the
somewhat ungainly candidate of King William.   Her
heart was clearly untouched, but she was willing to
be guided by the advice of that counsellor and friend
to whom in preference to every one she had already
begun to turn for help and guidance.   As this became
obvious to King William, his jealousy and dislike for
the Duchess of Kent increased; and in the autumn
of this year, 1836, having invited his sister-in-law to
a state banquet, he scandalised Society by delivering
an after-dinner speech charged with recrimination
and insult to his guest.

This was the Princess's penultimate year as a
minor.   King William had for a long time been
haunted with the fear that he would die before his

niece came of age, and that a regency would devolve upon his hated sister-in-law. He was spared what he would have considered this final humiliation, for on May 24, 1837, the young Princess came of age, just a month before the King died at Windsor.

During the final years of her minority she was thrown freely into the society of many of the eminent and distinguished persons soon to be her subjects. The Duchess gave a series of entertainments at Kensington Palace, and the Princess was brought into contact with her mother's guests. Accounts of these dinners and concerts, and full lists of the guests, are all minutely recorded in the Journals. Comments, however, beyond an occasional expression of delight at the music and admiration for its performers, are excluded. Her life was still the life of a child, and her days were mostly spent with her preceptors, under the auspices of the Duchess of Northumberland, her official governess, and of the Dean of Chester, her tutor.

She had been parted some years before from her half brother and sister by the usual exigencies of time. Prince Charles of Leiningen had become a sea-officer, and Princess Feodore was married. Into the inner orbit of her young life there penetrated only Sir John Conroy, whose person was odious to her, and Baroness Lehzen, the daughter of a Hanoverian clergyman, who had been the Princess's governess since 1824, and to whom she was deeply attached. Lablache, her singing-master, a man of some originality and charm, was a constant source of interest and amusement to the young Princess, and she preferred his lessons to all others.

It was during these last few years before her accession that the final touches were given to her character by the subtle influences of her environment. The position occupied by Sir John Conroy in her mother's house inspired and fortified her subsequent resolve to avoid intimacies with members of her household. She became distant and reserved to those about her, and her relations with her mother were chilled. Her mind acquired an impression that family ties, however binding from the point of view of duty, might be superseded by those of friendship. It is undoubtedly the case that Baroness Lehzen occupied at this time the first place in her pupil's thoughts and affections; while the dawning necessity felt by Princess Victoria for sympathy, and for those intimate communings so attractive to sentimental natures, had a very distinct influence upon the mind and conduct of the Queen in subsequent years. Her Journals afford proof, if proof had been wanting, that, in spite of the opinions of her attainments vouchsafed by eminent clerics, the Princess had not been afforded an education specially designed to fit her for the situation she was to occupy.

She was, at eighteen, as moderately and indifferently equipped as the average girl of her age. If her conversation was not brilliant, her heart was kindly and her judgment sound. She was shrewd and eminently truthful. In spite of her small stature, she was curiously dignified and impressive. Her voice was musical and carried far. And above all things, her rectitude was unassailable, and her sense of duty so keen and high that it supplied any lack of imagination or spiritual deficiency. She was humble-minded, but not, perhaps, very tender. She was passionate and imperious, but always faithful. She was supremely conscious of the responsibilities and prerogatives of her calling, which she was convinced, then and always, were her appanage by the gift of God.

There is nothing in her Journals or elsewhere to show that before she was eighteen years old she had ever talked seriously and at any length to any man or woman of exceptional gifts. It was only when her uncle King Leopold heard of the illness of William IV. that Stockmar was instructed to speak with due gravity upon important matters to the young girl whose accession to the Throne appeared imminent. Her mind at that time was a blank page in so far as questions of high politics or of administration were concerned. In point of fact, this was a fortunate circumstance, and rendered easier the task of those who were bound in the nature of things, and under the constitution of these islands, to use this youthful Princess as one of the chief instruments of government. Her mind was free from any political bias or complexion, and ready to receive the impress of her constitutional Ministers. When, within less than a month of her eighteenth birthday, King William died, and when on June 20, 1837, the Queen found herself face to face with those Whig statesmen in whose hands the destinies of the country had been placed for the time being,

their task was unhampered by preconceived ideas or
by foregone prejudice in their pupil. For the Queen
a new chapter of life was opened. She at once threw
off the trammels of pupilage. Not only was she
able immediately and without effort to shake herself
clear of the domestic influences she had resented
and disliked, but for the first time she was enabled
to meet and to question distinguished men, with
whose names she was familiar, but whose standards
of thought and conversation were far higher than
any to which she had been accustomed.

IV

It was " in a palace in a garden, meet scene for
youth and innocence," as one in later years to be
her favoured Minister wrote, that Princess Victoria
received the news of her accession to a Throne
overlooking " every sea and nations in every zone."
The scene and the circumstances in which her accession was announced to her by the Archbishop
of Canterbury and Lord Conynghame are described
by the Queen in her Journal. She has also recorded
her impressions of what followed when for the first
time she met the Privy Council. What the Queen
has not described is the effect produced upon those
present by her personality, her youthful charm, her
self-possession and perfect modesty, in such strong
contrast to everything which her Privy Councillors
had been accustomed to find in their former Sovereigns. The Queen was not aware of the interest

and curiosity she then excited in the minds of her
subjects. She had been brought up in such com-
parative seclusion, that both to " Society " and to
the great world outside her character was an enigma
and even her appearance very little known. Her
sex and youth rendered her personality exciting to
a public satiated with the elderly vagaries of her
uncles. It was noticed at her first Council that her
manner was very graceful and engaging. It was
particularly observed that after she had read her
speech in a clear and singularly firm voice, when the
two surviving sons of George III., the Dukes of
Cumberland and Sussex, knelt before her, swearing
allegiance, she blushed up to the eyes as if she felt
the contrast between their public and private relations, between their august age and her inexperienced youth. It was also noticed that she spoke
to no one, and that not the smallest difference in
her manner could be detected, even by sharp watching
eyes, between her attitude towards Lord Melbourne
and the Ministers on the one hand, and towards the
Duke of Wellington and Sir Robert Peel on the
other. The Queen does not mention, for she was not
then aware of it, that Lord Melbourne was charmed
and Sir Robert Peel amazed at her demeanour.
They spoke afterwards with emotion of her modesty,
firmness, and evident deep sense of her situation.
She did not know then, although she knew later,
that the Duke of Wellington said that had she been
his own daughter he could not have desired to see
her perform her part better.

These Journals only accentuate what is already

known from many sources, that the Queen showed in difficult circumstances not only good taste and good feeling, but admirable good sense. Her attention to details, which some might consider trifles, but which differentiate the careful from the thoughtless mind, was noticed with approval and surprise by her Ministers. She exhibited caution in her treatment of those persons who had been about her since childhood, and she made no appeal to any of them for advice or guidance. Nor did she permit advice to be proffered. Sir John Conroy was dismissed at once from her surroundings. Baroness Lehzen she retained, as before, about her person, and she speaks of her, throughout these Journals, with deep feeling. It was noticed, whenever she was asked to decide some difficult matter, her customary reply was that she would think it over, and give her answer on the morrow. Onlookers, knowing that she relied on the advice of Lord Melbourne, generally assumed that she referred to him in the interval. He, however, declared that to many of his questions a similar reply was given. In point of fact, she was obeying one of the precepts of her uncle, the King of the Belgians.

It will be obvious to the readers of this book that a potent influence over the mind and actions of the young Queen was exercised by Lord Melbourne. It was the natural outcome of the business relation between a very charming and experienced man of the world who happened to be her Prime Minister and a very young girl isolated in the solitary atmosphere of the Throne.

From the Queen's accession to the day of her
marriage the table-talk of Lord Melbourne fills the
largest space in her journals. Her description of
their intercourse confirms what we know from
other sources, that Lord Melbourne became absorbed
by the novel and striking duty that had fallen to
his lot. His temperament and his antecedents rendered him peculiarly sensitive to the fascinating
influences of the strange relation in which he stood
to this young Queen. Lord Melbourne's life had
been chequered by curious experiences, and his mind
had been thoroughly well trained, for a man of his
station, according to the lights of those days. A
classical education, the privilege from youth upwards
of free intercourse with every one worth knowing,
the best Whig connection, and an inherited capacity
for governing men under oligarchic institutions, had
equipped his intellect and judgment with everything
that was necessary to enable him carefully to watch
and safeguard the blossoming of the character of the
girl who was both his pupil and his Sovereign.

He was no longer young, but he was not old.
His person was attractive. According to Leslie, no
mean judge, his head was a truly noble one, and he
was a fine specimen of manly beauty in the meridian
of life. Not only were his features handsome, but
his expression was in the highest degree intellectual.
His laugh was frequent and the most joyous possible,
his voice so deep and musical that to hear him say
the most ordinary thing was a pleasure; and his
frankness, his freedom from affectation, and his
peculiar humour rendered almost everything he said,

however easy and natural, quite original. Chantrey's bust and the well-known portraits of Melbourne corroborate the descriptions given by his contemporaries.

The Queen's Journals afford us some illustrations of the extent of his memory and reading. In his knowledge of political history he was unsurpassed by any living Englishman, and among the statesmen of that day there were none by age, character, and experience so well qualified for the task of making the Queen acquainted with the art of government, or better able to give her a correct interpretation of the laws and spirit of the constitution. He understood perfectly the importance of training her to work straightforwardly but secretly with that small committee of active politicians, representing the parliamentary majority of the day, which goes by the name of the Cabinet. Sir Robert Peel and the Duke of Wellington, the Leaders of the Opposition, felt and admitted that for her initiation into the mysteries of Kingcraft, the Queen could not have been in wiser hands. It will be obvious from these Journals that the Queen drifted into political partisanship. She lived in dread of losing her Whig Ministers, and she got " to hate " the Tories. This only meant—and under all the circumstances it was natural—that she ardently desired to retain her mentor at her side. It is to the credit of Lord Melbourne that he was constantly discouraging his Sovereign's bias towards the Whig Party, of which he was the head, and that he never lost an opportunity of smoothing the way for the advent of Sir Robert Peel which he knew to be inevitable. He was, not inaptly, called a Regius Professor with no professorial disqualifications, and it was precisely from this point of view that the Tory leaders recognised the indispensable nature of his task, and approved his manner of performing it. He was a Whig no doubt, says his biographer, but at any rate he was an honest-hearted Englishman, and, in no merely conventional sense, a gentleman on whose perfect honour no one hesitated to place reliance.

He treated the Queen with unbounded consideration and respect, yet he did not hesitate to administer reproof. He consulted her tastes and her wishes, but he checked her inclination to be headstrong and arbitrary. He knew well how to chide with parental firmness, but he did so with a deference that could not fail to fascinate any young girl in a man of his age and attainments. The Queen was completely under his charm. The ease of his frank and natural manners, his quaint epigrams and humorous paradox, his romantic bias and worldly shrewdness, were magnified by her into the noblest manly virtues.

He saw her every day, but never appeared to weary of her society. She certainly never tired of his. Yet he was fifty-eight years old, a time-worn politician, and she was a girl of eighteen. He was her confidential servant and at the same time her guardian. She was his ward and at the same time his Sovereign. The situation was full of the possibilities of drama, yet nothing can be more delightful than the high comedy revealed in the passages of the Journals that refer to Lord Melbourne. That he should have happened to be First Minister of the Crown when King William died was a rare piece of good fortune for the new Sovereign and for the country. With all the immense powers of head and heart which the Queen came later to discover in Sir Robert Peel, we may take leave to doubt if he could so lightly and so wisely have assumed and fulfilled the duties imposed upon his predecessor.

It is impossible to exaggerate the effect produced upon the mind and character of the Queen by the apostolic letters of her uncle. Even the sound constitutional dogma of Stockmar might have failed to influence one naturally inclined to be autocratic. Those, however, who were to reap the profit in later years of the shrewd daily culture of the Queen's mind, of the skilful pruning away of ideas dangerous in a British Sovereign, of the respectful explanation of her duties, of the humorous rallying upon slight weaknesses which might have developed into awkward habits, were deeply indebted, as these Journals show, to the sagacity of Lord Melbourne.

V

Two Queens Regnant, Queen Mary and Queen Anne, both of Stewart blood, lived much at Kensington Palace, and both died there. As a place of residence it had no attractions for the Sovereigns of the House of Hanover. Queen Victoria was fond of the old wing in which her youth had been spent, and which was subsequently occupied for many years by the Duchess of Teck and her children. Built on piles, those portions of the Palace that were uninhabited, and therefore indifferently looked after, had towards the end of the Queen's reign fallen into such disrepair that their demolition had been decided by the Treasury. The Queen disliked intensely the idea of removing any part of the old building. Ultimately a bargain was made with the Chancellor of the Exchequer of the day. It involved a certain exchange of houses in the gift of the Crown and some shifting of financial responsibility. Kensington Palace was saved, and a considerable sum was voted by Parliament for its restoration, on condition that the public should be admitted to certain rooms of historic interest.

King George's dream, and no one knows better its visionary character, is to pull down Buckingham Palace, to round off St. James's and the Green Parks at Constitution Hill and Buckingham Gate, and then, with the money obtained by the sale of the Gardens of Buckingham Palace, to reconstruct Kensington Palace as the town residence of the Sovereign.

For Queen Mary the place is full of memories and, because of her keen historic sense, full of interest.

Compared with most of the great European capitals, London is poor in palaces. The homes of the Tudor Sovereigns in and near the metropolis, Nonsuch, Greenwich, and Whitehall, have disappeared. London contains no single palace residentially associated with our long line of Sovereigns. The Court of St. James was housed, in the eighteenth century, in the Palace of that name. It seems to have been adequate for the needs of the Hanoverian Princes, who had none of the amplitude of the Tudors or the fine taste of the Stewarts.

The memories of Windsor, however, are long memories. Although Queen Victoria never liked Windsor, perhaps because she was never in good health there, it is with Windsor Castle that the principal events of her reign are associated. The thoughts of the few, the very few, comparatively speaking, of her subjects who were admitted to the seclusion of Court life during two-thirds of the Queen's reign may carry them back to quiet days at Balmoral or Osborne, but it was round Windsor that the political interest of the Victorian era centred. There the links of the chain have remained unsevered between the Sovereigns of Great Britain to-day and their Plantagenet ancestors.

If the Queen's attachment to Windsor was not deep, she was more indifferent still to Buckingham Palace. There is not a word in her Diaries or correspondence to show that she in any way looked upon it as a home or even a residence in any degree interesting or attractive. No attempt was made, after the death of the Prince Consort, to improve or beautify it. The magnificent objects of art and the splendid collection of pictures were badly displayed and quite unappreciated. Few, outside the circle of the Court, knew of their existence. The Palace was judged by its mean façade, and the nation was rather shamefaced about the home of its Sovereign, and certainly took no credit for the really

noble rooms and their contents which Buckingham
Palace contains.

Yet, through the picture-gallery of this Palace
hung with masterpieces of the Dutch School, through
the throne-room and the drawing-room resplendent
with the royal portraits of Reynolds and Gainsborough, or through the matchless corridor at Windsor,
have passed nearly all the great figures of the nineteenth century, practically the whole of which was
spanned by the life of the Queen.

It is an imposing array, worthy of its setting.
Heroes and statesmen, men of science and letters,
artists and scholars, all moved, with a feeling of awe,
into the presence of the Queen whose girlhood is
recounted by herself in these pages.

To those accustomed to the easier manners of
more recent times it is difficult to convey a sense
of the atmosphere of Windsor during the reign of
the Queen. Her extraordinary aloofness was its
determining cause, but the effect was that of a
shrine. Grave men walked softly through the rooms
of the Castle, and no voice was ever raised. The
presence of the Sovereign brooded, so to speak,
over the Palace and its environment. The desire
to be negligently at ease never entered the mind.
The air was rarefied by a feeling that somewhere, in
a region unvisited by any but the most highly privileged, was seated, not in an ordinary arm-chair,
but on a throne, the awe-inspiring and ever-dignified
figure of the Sovereign. The proud intellect of
Gladstone and the rugged self-sufficiency of Bright
bent before the small, homely figure in widow's weeds.

In spite of this homeliness of appearance, notwithstanding her love of simplicity and her dislike of
tawdriness and display, her spirit never put aside the
regal habit. How rarely the Queen extended her
hand ! It was a great privilege, and only on special
occasions vouchsafed to her Ministers. Men and
women bent very low to kiss that hand. This was
not due to her small stature, but to the curious, inde-
finable awe that she undoubtedly inspired during
the later portion of her life in all who approached
her. Will the reader find, in these records of her
girlhood, intimations of that moral ascendency she
afterwards acquired over her subjects ?

It was unquestionably a triumph of character.
Even now to attempt a serious estimate of the intellectual capacity of Queen Victoria is a difficult
task. There are too many still among us the
greater part of whose lives were spent under her
sway. It is a fault in nearly all recent biographies
that they attempt appreciations which only the
lapse of time can enable a writer to draw in true
perspective.

A venerable Sovereign, in full possession of his
great powers of intellect and character, who was
almost an exact contemporary, still rules a European
people as proud of him as were her subjects of the
Queen. At least one of her faithful servants, who was
present at her Coronation seventy-four years ago and
at every great ceremonial throughout her reign, is still
alive and full of manly vigour. Her children are
in the prime of life, and her favourite grandson is
the beloved Sovereign of the people she governed.

Unqualified praise is always distasteful, and critical analysis may easily prove to be in singularly bad taste. Queen Victoria's womanly and royal virtues are written in golden letters upon the face of the vast Empire over which she reigned. Her faults may well lie buried, for some time yet, in her grave under the shadow of Windsor.

In the muniment-room of the Castle are preserved the private records of her life-work. Over a thousand bound volumes of letters, from and to the Queen upon all subjects, public and domestic, are there ; and over a hundred volumes of her Journals written in her own hand.

It is a unique record. The private papers of George III. have disappeared. Of those of George IV. and William IV., only a few are in existence. Selections from the correspondence of the Queen up to 1861 were published by permission of King Edward. These selections from her early Journals have been made by the gracious leave of King George. It may be many years before it would be wise or prudent to make public any more of the private history of Queen Victoria's reign. Those who, by good fortune, have had access to these records can, however, safely predict that whatever hereafter leaps to light, the Queen never can be shamed.

INTRODUCTORY NOTE TO CHAPTER I

WHEN the Queen's Journal opens she was thirteen years and two months old. When she was four years younger Sir Walter Scott was presented to the little Princess Victoria and noted that she was " educating with much care." At that time she was supposed not to know that she was the " heir of England," but Scott thought that if the little heart could be dissected it would be found that some little bird had carried the matter. According to Baroness Lehzen, the truth was not revealed until a year before the Princess commenced to write her first Journal. There was a picture painted of her about this time, and it corroborates Lord Albemarle's description of the little girl of extreme fairness whom he watched watering, at Kensington, a child's garden, wearing a large straw hat and a suit of white cotton, her only ornament being a coloured fichu round the neck.

The Princess was guarded with extreme care. Leigh Hunt noticed that she was invariably followed, when walking, by a footman in gorgeous raiment. She told her daughters many years later that she was so carefully tended until the day of her accession, that she had never been permitted to walk downstairs without someone holding her hand.

The Princess's journey commenced August 1, 1832, although the first part of what her Uncle, King William, called her Royal Progresses was not her first trip into the country. With her mother she paid several visits to Ramsgate and Broadstairs. She had stayed with Lord Winchelsea at Eastwell, near Ashford, and she had visited George IV. at the Royal Lodge in Windsor Park. She had spent an autumn at Norris Castle, Isle of Wight, and had been to Bath and Malvern.

Sir Walter Scott expressed a hope that she would not retain the name of Victoria, and when upon the accession of William IV. extra provision was demanded of Parliament for the little Princess Alexandrina Victoria of Kent, who then became heir-presumptive to the Crown, Sir Matthew White Ridley and Sir Robert Inglis desired to make the Parliamentary grant contingent upon the Princess, as Queen, assuming the style of Elizabeth II., on the ground that the name Victoria did not accord with the feelings of the people. The name Victoria, however, was destined to acquire lustre not inferior to that of Elizabeth.

The Princess's first Progress is minutely described in the first volume of her Journal. Before it ended, Robert Lowe, afterwards her Chancellor of the Exchequer, caught a glimpse of the child as she passed from the Bodleian to lunch with the Vice-Chancellor at Oxford. Her foot was on the threshold of public life.

CHAPTER I

1832

Wednesday, August 1st. We left K.P.[1] at 6 minutes past 7 and went through the Lower-field gate to the right. We went on, & turned to the left by the new road to Regent's Park. The road & scenery is beautiful. 20 minutes to 9. We have just changed horses at Barnet, a very pretty little town. 5 minutes past ½ past 9. We have just changed horses at St. Albans. The situation is very pretty & there is a beautiful old abbey there. 5 minutes past 10. The country is beautiful here: they have began to cut the corn; it is so golden & fine that I think they will have a very good harvest, at least here. There are also pretty hills & trees. 20 minutes past ten. We have just passed a most beautiful old house in a fine park with splendid trees. A ¼ to 11. We have just changed horses at Dunstable; there was a fair there; the booths filled with fruit, ribbons, &c. looked very pretty. The town seems old & there is a fine abbey before it. The country is very bleak & chalky. 12 minutes to 12. We have just changed horses at Brickhill. The country is very beautiful about here. 19 minutes to 1. We have just changed horses at Stony Stratford. The country is very pretty. About ½ past 1 o'clock we arrived at Towcester & lunched there.

[1] Kensington Palace.

43

At 14 minutes past two we left it. A ¼ past 3. We have just changed horses at Daventry. The road continues to be very dusty. 1 minute past ½ past 3. We have just[1] passed through Braunston where there is a curious spire. The Oxford canal is close to the town. 1 minute to 4. We have just changed horses at Dunchurch & it is raining.

For some time past already, and now, our road is entirely up an avenue of trees going on and on, it is quite delightful but it still rains. Just now we go at a *tremendous* rate. 4 minutes to 5. We have just changed horses at Coventry, a large town where there is a very old church (in appearance at least). At ½ past 5 we arrived at Meridon ; and we are now going to dress for dinner. ½ past 8. I am undressing to go to bed. Mamma is not well and is lying on the sofa in the next room. I was asleep in a minute in my own little bed which travels always with me.

Thursday, 2d August.—I got up after a very good night at 5 o'clock this morning. Mamma is much better I am happy to say, and I am now dressing to go to breakfast. 6 minutes to ½ past 7. We have just left Meridon, a very clean inn. It is a very bad day. 10 minutes to 9. We have just changed horses at Birmingham where I was two years ago and we visited the manufactories which are very curious. It rains very hard. We just passed through a town where all coal mines are and you see the fire glimmer at a distance in the engines in many places. The men, women, children, country and houses are all black. But I can not by any description give an idea of its strange and extraordinary appearance. The country is very desolate every where ; there are coals about, and the grass

---

[1] The Journal was written in pencil and inked over afterwards.

is quite blasted and black. I just now see an extraordinary building flaming with fire. The country continues black, engines flaming, coals, in abundance, every where, smoking and burning coal heaps, intermingled with wretched huts and carts and little ragged children. . . .

I received from the mayor an oaken box with a silver top and filled with the famous Shrewsbury cakes. We lunched there. We left it at a $\frac{1}{4}$ to 3. As we passed along the streets a poor unhappy hen, frightened by the noise flew on the carriage but she was taken off. We had our horses watered half way. When we arrived at the outskirts of Welshpool we were met by a troop of Yeomanry who escorted us for a long time and the little town was ornamented with arches, flowers, branches, flags, ribbons, &c., &c. The guns fired as we came up the park and the band played before Powis Castle; Lord Powis [1] and Mr. Clive met us at the door of his beautiful old Castle and Lady Lucy and Lady Harriet Clive were in the gallery. The Castle is very old and beautiful; the little old windows jutting in and out and a fine gallery with a dry-rubbed floor and some beautiful busts. I am now dressing for dinner. . . .

Thursday, 9th August.—I awoke at $\frac{1}{2}$ past 6 and got up at 7. I am now dressing. A little after 8 I went out in the garden, and at about $\frac{1}{4}$ to 9 we took breakfast. I began to write a letter after breakfast, and then dressed. At $\frac{1}{2}$ past 10 Mamma

[1] Edward, first Earl of Powis (1754–1839), was the eldest son of the great Lord Clive ; his eldest son, afterwards second Earl, married Lucy, daughter of the third Duke of Montrose ; his second son, Robert Clive, M.P., married Harriet, younger daughter of the fifth Earl of Plymouth : these are the ladies referred to in the text. The barony of Windsor, which had fallen into abeyance, was afterwards terminated in favour of Lady Harriet Clive.

received an address from the Mayor and Corporation of Beaumaris, and another from the gentlemen
inhabitants, and visitors of the town. At ½ past
11 we got into our carriages with my Cousins on
the box of ours. In passing the Menai-bridge, we
received a salute, and on entering the town of Car-
narvon, we were met, not only by an immense crowd,
who were extremely kind, and pleased, but by the
Corporation also, who walked before the carriage,
while a salute was firing. We then arrived at the
inn, where Mamma received an address. The
address being over we took luncheon, and after
that was over, we went to see the ruins of the Castle,
which are beautiful, while a salute was fired, from
the rampart. We then got into the *Emerald,* where
we were several times saluted, at the last being nearly
becalmed, we were towed by a steam packet, called
Paul Pry, which saluted us 4 times in the day. We
arrived at home at ¼ to 7, and dined at ½ past 7.
We drank Uncle Leopold's health in honour of his
marriage that day. I stayed up till ½ past 9. I
went to bed soon after, and was soon asleep. . . .

Wednesday, 29th August.—I awoke at ½ past 6
and got up at 7. It is now 6 minutes past 8 & I
am quite ready dressed. I then played. We breakfasted at ½ past 8 but without Lady Catherine [1]
who is very unwell. I then did my lessons & then
played. At ½ past 12 I went out walking. We
lunched at 1. At ½ past 3 went to Baron Hill
Sir R. Bulkeley's [2] place. We arrived there at a

[1] Lady Catherine Jenkinson, elder daughter of the third Earl of
Liverpool, was married later to Colonel Francis Vernon Harcourt,
son of the Archbishop of York and Equerry to the Duchess of Kent.

[2] Sir Richard Bulkeley, tenth Baronet, M.P. for Anglesey, afterwards Lord Lieutenant of Carnarvonshire. He had just married Maria
Frances, daughter of Sir Thomas Stanley-Massy-Stanley.

little after 4. We were received at the door by
Sir Richard & farther on by Lady Bulkeley whose
dress I shall describe. It was a white satin trimmed
with blonde, short sleeves & a necklace, ear-rings and
sévigné of perridos & diamonds with a wreath of
orange-flowers in her hair. We then went upon
the terrace & the band of the Anglesea Militia played
"God save the King." We then presented all the
bards & poets with medals. We then [went]
into the drawing-room and remained there till
dinner. In the drawing-room there were a great
many other people. At 5 we went to dinner, which
was in a temporary building which was lined in
the inside with pink and white linen. The dinner
was splendidly served & the china was rich and
beautiful. The fruit was magnificent. After dessert
was over Sir Richard made a speech and brought
out a toast in honor of Mamma & me. We then
left the room & went into the drawing-room. We
went upstairs into Lady Bulkeley's pretty little
dressing-room. Her toilet table was pink with white
muslin over it trimmed with beautiful lace & her
things on the toilet table were gold. We then went
downstairs and took coffee and the famous dog of
Lady Williams,[1] Cabriolle, played tricks. At about
7 we left Baron Hill & proceeded homewards.
Poor Lady Catherine who was not able to go was
in the evening much better. We arrived at home
at about a ¼ past 8. I then went downstairs &
stayed up till near 9. I was soon in bed and
asleep. . . .

Monday, 17th September.—I awoke at about 8,
& got up at near ½ past 8. We breakfasted at 9

---

[1] Lady Williams, wife of Sir John Williams of Bodelwyddan,
first Baronet.

downstairs. I then played and did other things. At 1 we lunched. I then played on the piano, & at a little before 3 played at billiards downstairs, with Victoire,[1] & then went out walking. When I came home I first worked & then we blew soap-bubbles.

Sunday, 14th October.—I awoke at 7 and got up at ½ past 7. At ½ past 8 we breakfasted. I then wrote my Journal and some music and at 11 we went to chapel for the last time and the sailors likewise for the last time. The service was performed as usual by Mr. W. Jones. It was over at ¼ past 12. I then walked out with Lehzen[2] and Victoire. At 1 we lunched. At 3 we went out riding, and as we passed through the Park gate the old woman at the lodge came out as usual, to open the gate and she thanked Mamma for what she had given her. We galloped over a green field which we had already done several times. Rosa went an enormous rate; she literally *flew.* We then went on towards the Menai bridge but turned back under the hill. We cantered a great deal and Rosa went the whole time beautifully. It was a delightful ride. When we came home Mamma got on Rosa and I got on Thomas and cantered him. We came in at ½ past 4. Alas! it was our last ride at *dear* Plas Newydd. I then walked on the terrace for a short time. At 7 we dined and I stayed up till ½ past 8. I was soon in bed and asleep.

Monday, 15th October.—I awoke at ½ past 5 and got up at 6. At 7 we breakfasted with all the family;

[1] Daughter of Sir John Conroy, Comptroller to the Duchess of Kent.
[2] Louise Lehzen became Governess to Princess Victoria in 1824. In 1827 George IV. created her a Hanoverian Baroness. When in 1830 the Duchess of Northumberland was made the Princess' Governess, her "faithful Lehzen" remained on as Lady in Waiting. She stayed at Court till 1842, when she returned to Germany.

VICTOIRE CONROY.

From a sketch by Princess Victoria

and a most beautiful falcon which Sir John Williams[1]
sent me was brought in that I might see it. The
sailors were so busy and so useful for I saw Kew
and Sparks going to and fro. At a ¼ to 8 we got
into our carriages and drove out amidst the shouts
of the sailors of the *Emerald,* who were standing
on the rigging two by two on the rope-ladders, till
the last man was at the very top of all. I looked
out of the carriage window that I might get a last
look of the *dear Emerald* and her *excellent crew.* As
we passed along the road we saw Mr. Griffith and
Mr. W. Jones and his family. . . .

10 minutes to 4.—We have just passed through
Northop. At about ½ past 4 we went through the
Park of Mr. Granville up to his castle. Lord
Grosvenor met us there at the head of his Cavalry.
And Lord Westminster[2] sent his own fine horses,
which were put to our carriage. At about ½ past
5 we arrived at Eaton Hall. We were received at
the door by Lord and Lady Westminster, Lady
Grosvenor and Lady Wilton. The house is magnificent. You drive up to the door under a lofty
vaulted portico with a flight of steps under it, and
it takes you to the hall, which is beautiful. The
floor is inlaid with various marbles, and arches
spring from the sides. Then you enter a beautiful
drawing-room ; the ceiling joins in a round gilt,

---

[1] Sir John Williams, afterwards Sir John Williams-Hay, second
Baronet, of Bodelwyddan.

[2] Robert, Earl Grosvenor (1767–1845), had in 1831 been created
Marquess of Westminster ; he had married Eleanor, only daughter of
Thomas, first Earl of Wilton. Richard, Lord Grosvenor, their eldest
son, married Elizabeth Mary, daughter of the first Duke of Sutherland ;
Thomas, the second son, inherited, under a special remainder, his grand-
father's Earldom of Wilton, and married Mary Margaret, daughter of
Edward, twelfth Earl of Derby.

with great taste and richness, while the sides arch towards the top. An organ on the right as you enter the room and a large fireplace on the left with stained glass windows. Then Lady Westminster after we had been downstairs a little, showed us our apartments, which are indeed beautiful. I was in bed at ½ past 8.

Tuesday, 16th October.—I awoke at 6 and got up at 7. I then dressed and took some tea. At ½ past 9 we breakfasted. The breakfast-room is magnificent. There are 4 fireplaces; and the windows are of stained glass very beautifully done. A massive lustre of gold with an eagle likewise in gold hangs from the ceiling in the middle of the room. Pillars arching to the top and gilt in parts rise from the sides. Several tables of oak and elm stand in the windows, and the breakfast was served in handsome silver tea and coffee pots; a crown of gold with precious stones contained the bread. Besides Lady Grosvenor and Lady Wilton, there were also Lady Egerton,[1] Mrs. Lane and Miss Bagot. After breakfast Lady Grosvenor brought her 4 children. We then went into our own rooms and I wrote my journal. At 12 Mamma went into the great saloon where all the ladies were and an address from the mayor and corporation of Chester arrived and then another from the gentlemen and inhabitants of Chester, presented by Lord Robert.[2] After this we looked about the room which is indeed beautiful. The ceiling is done in the same splendid manner and a magnificent lustre of gold and glass with a

[1] Wife of Sir Philip Grey Egerton, and daughter of George John Legh, of High Legh, Cheshire.

[2] Robert, third son of Lord Westminster, at this time M.P. for Chester and afterwards for Middlesex, was created in 1857 Lord Ebury.

coronet of velvet and pearls hung from the ceiling in the room. Two windows of stained glass, very handsomely done, are on different sides. A superb chimney-place with beautiful furniture and rich carpets, complete the room. 4 beautiful pictures painted by different artists are likewise in the room. We then walked out with most of the people; I walking in front with the eldest and third little girl, the second not being well. We walked about the garden and looked at an aloe which flowers only once in 100 years. We came in at ½ past 1, and lunched at 2. At ½ past 2 we went out driving; Lady Westminster and little Elinor,[1] the eldest child, were in our carriage; she is a delightful child. Lady Catherine and Lehzen followed in another carriage. We drove about the park which is beautiful. When we came home we walked in the kitchen gardens which are indeed very pretty. At ½ past 4 we came home and I worked. At 7 we dined. The dining-room is a fine room beautifully worked at the ceiling. Four large statues of Maltese stone occupy 4 corners, very beautifully executed; one with a helmet is Sir Gilbert le Grosvenor,[2] and the lady[3] next by him is the heiress of Eaton; on the opposite side the man is Sir Robert le Grosvenor, distinguished in the battle of Cressy; the lady near him is a Miss Davis who by intermarrying brought the possessions in town, as Grosvenor Square, Belgrave Square, etc., etc.[4] The window is stained

---

[1] Elinor, afterwards Duchess of Northumberland.

[2] Gilbert le Grosvenator, nephew of Hugh Lupus, Earl of Chester.

[3] Joan (temp. Henry VI.), only daughter and heiress of John Eton of Eton (now Eaton), married Raufe le Grosvenor, Lord of Hulme.

[4] Sir Thomas Grosvenor, third Baronet, M.P. for Chester, married Mary, only daughter and heiress of Alexander Davis, of Ebury, Middlesex. She died in 1730.

glass with the figure of Hugh Lupus on it. The dinner was served on plate, and the plateau was very handsome with gilt cups on it. The side table was covered with gold plate. After dinner we played at a game of letters and then I sang and Mamma and Lady Catherine sang and afterwards Lady Westminster played on the organ. I stayed up till 10. . . .

Thursday, 18*th October.*—When we went out after luncheon we went in the garden first and saw a Roman altar which had been dug up near Chester. At 7 we dined. The breakfast-room had been arranged for this purpose. A temporary floor had been arranged at the top of the room, for our table (for all the company who had come to the bow-meeting dined here), and the other four were lower. After the dinner (we being still at table) was over some glee-singers from Chester came and sang the grace in Latin. Then Lord Westminster gave out some toasts ; amongst others, " The King," " The Queen," Mamma and me ; which were received extremely well. After dinner was over, I gave the children, who had come when dinner was over, a little remembrance. I then took leave of the whole family and went to bed. I stayed up till 10.

Friday, 19*th October.*— . . . ½ past 4. We have just changed horses at Buxton, which is a pretty place. The houses are well built and form a crescent. The country about here is very pretty, high rocks covered with trees. There are all about here little rivulets and fountains, rippling over stones. At ½ past 6 we arrived at Chatsworth, which is a beautiful house. It was quite dark. It is built in the shape of a square joined by an arch under which one must drive. We were met at the door by the Duke of Devonshire [1] who conducted us up the staircase, which is made of wood, to our apartments which are indeed beautiful. In the corridor there are some beautiful statues. I dined by myself in my own room with Lehzen. I stayed up till ½ past 8. I was soon in bed and asleep.

Saturday, 20th October.—I awoke at ½ past 7 and got up at 8. At a little past 9 we breakfasted, us 5 by ourselves in a lovely room giving on the park and garden where one could see a cascade which ran all the way down. The room is small; the ceiling is painted and represents some mythology, with books round the room and a splendid carpet. At about 11 we went over the house with the company, which consisted of Lord and Lady Cavendish,[2] Lord and Lady Newburgh,[3] Mr. and Lady Caroline Lascelles,[4] Count Karoly, Mrs. Arkwright, Lady

---

[1] William Spencer, sixth Duke of Devonshire. His mother was Georgiana, famous for her beauty and its influence over George IV. and Lord Grey. The sixth Duke inherited from his mother his Whig proclivities. He was a patron of arts and letters. Devonshire House under his bachelor rule was a centre of hospitality. That the Duke never married, notwithstanding his admiration of the fair sex, gave rise to much speculation and gossip.

[2] William, Lord Cavendish, grandson of George Augustus Henry, first Earl of Burlington, and great-grandson of the fourth Duke of Devonshire. In 1858 he became the seventh Duke, and died in 1891. He married in 1829 Blanche Georgiana, daughter of the sixth Earl of Carlisle. He was beloved and respected by all who were privileged to know him. In the spheres of education and science his quiet activities were not unremarked. He was an admirable landlord and a most efficient man of affairs. For his careful education of his eldest son, the Marquess of Hartington, the nation owes him a large debt of gratitude.

[3] Thomas, seventh Earl of Newburgh, married 1817 Margaret, daughter of the Marquess of Ailsa. Died 1833.

[4] Rt. Hon. William S. S. Lascelles, M.P., third son of the second Earl of Harewood, married Caroline Georgiana, eldest daughter of the sixth Earl of Carlisle.

Clifford, Lord and Lady Wharncliffe,[1] Mrs. Talbot, Lord Morpeth,[2] Mr. Cooper, Mr. Henry Greville, and Miss Fanny Cavendish.[3] It would take me days, were I to describe minutely the whole. We went all over the house, and the carving of the frame-work of some looking-glasses was quite beautiful ; they are carved in the shape of birds, the plumage being so exquisite that if it was not of the colour of wood one might take them for feathers. It not only surrounds the mirrors but the ceilings of some of the rooms. We saw Lady Cavendish's little boy who is 10 months old, a beautiful child. We likewise saw the kitchen which is superb for its size and cleanliness ; and the confectionary which is as pretty and neat. The Duke's own apartments contain some superb statues of Canova and others ; likewise a beautiful collection of minerals. We saw the library and dining-room which are all beautiful. The library's ceiling is painted in figures ; and the carpet is beautiful. The conservatory which leads from the dining-room is very pretty. We then walked out in the garden, I went into another conservatory which contains a rockery with water falling from it. There are some curious plants there, amongst others two which are worthy of remark ; the one is called the pitcher-plant because at the end of each leaf hangs a little bag or pitcher which fills with the dew and supplies

[1] James Archibald (1776–1845), first Lord Wharncliffe, and his wife Elizabeth, daughter of John, first Earl of Erne.

[2] George William, Lord Morpeth, afterwards seventh Earl of Carlisle, a prominent but comparatively undistinguished member of every Whig Administration from 1835 to 1864.

[3] Sister of Lord Cavendish (afterwards seventh Duke of Devonshire) referred to above. She became the wife of *F. J.* Howard, M.P. for Youghal.

the plant when it wants water ; the other is called the
fly-catcher plant, because whenever a fly touches it,
it closes.   From the conservatory we went and looked
at a monkey which is in the garden, chained.   We
then went to the cascade and saw some other fountains very curious and pretty.   When we had come
on the terrace the Duke wished us to plant two trees
down under the terrace.   So we did, I planted an
oak and Mamma a Spanish chesnut.   After that
we went upon the terrace again and went up a plat-
form which had been arranged with carpets, to view
the cricket-match below ; the Buxton band playing
" God save the King " and the people hurraying
and others under tents looked very pretty.   From
there we went to the stables where we saw some
pretty ponies and a Russian coachman in his full
dress, and the only Russian horse which remained
reared at his command ; there were 3 other horses,
English ones, but trained like the other.   At about
½ past 1 we came home and lunched with the whole
party.   At ½ past 2 we went in a carriage and 6
with the Duke and Mrs. Cavendish, to Haddon Hall,
a very old and singular place.   The old tapestry
still remaining and iron hooks to keep it back.   We
then went to the Rookery, a small cottage belonging
to the Duke on the banks of the river Wye, very
pretty and cool.   From there we walked to the
Marble Mills and saw how they sawed and polished
the marble.   There was a little cottage where they
sold Derbyshire spar in different little shapes and
forms, and some pieces of marble too.   We then
drove home after having bought a good many things.
We came in at 5.   At 7 we dined and after dinner
at about ½ past 9 we looked at the cascade illuminated,
which looked very pretty, and the fountains, blue

lights, red lights, rockets, etc. At about 10 the charade began in 3 syllables and 4 scenes. The first act was a scene out of *Bluebeard*; Lady Caroline Lascelles and Miss F. Cavendish acting the ladies, and Count Karoly as Bluebeard, with Lord Newburgh and Mr. Lascelles as their friends. The next act was a scene of carrying offerings to Father Nile; Mrs. Talbot, Lady Cavendish, Lady Clifford, Miss Cavendish, and the two Miss Smiths as the vestals; and Lord Morpeth, Lord Newburgh, Count Karoly, Mr. Greville, Sir A. Clifford,[1] Mr Cooper, and Mr. Lascelles as the men. Mr. Beaumont was Father Nile. The third act was a scene of *Tom Thumb*; Lord Morpeth as Tom Thumb, and Lord Newburgh as the nurse. The fourth act was a scene out of *Kenilworth* (which was the word); Mrs. Talbot as Queen Elizabeth, Lady Cavendish as Amy, Lady Caroline and Miss Cavendish (who danced the menuet with Count Karoly) as her attendants; little Georgina Lascelles [2] as page to bear the Queen's train, Lord Morpeth as Lord Leicester, Lord Newburgh as an attendant, Count Karoly as Lord Shrewsbury, Mr. Cooper as Sir Walter Raleigh, and Lord Waterpark [3] and Mr. Greville as two more men of the Queen's, not to omit Lady Clifford as the Queen's lady, and Sir Augustus as a gentleman of the Queen. They were all in regular costumes. When it was over, which was at ¼ to 12, I went to bed. . . .

Wednesday, 24th October.— . . . At 1 we arrived at Alton Towers, the seat of Lord Shrewsbury.[4]

---

[1] Sir Augustus Clifford, formerly Usher of the Black Rod, married Elizabeth *F*rances, sister of the fourth Marquess Townshend.

[2] Afterwards wife of Charles William Grenfell, M.P.

[3] Henry Manners, third Lord Waterpark.

[4] John, sixteenth Earl of Shrewsbury (1791–1852).

This is an extraordinary house. On arriving one goes into a sort of gallery filled with armour, guns, swords, pistols, models, flags, etc., etc., then into a gallery filled with beautiful pictures and then into a conservatory with birds. We lunched there and the luncheon was served on splendid gold plate. We then walked in the gardens. At ½ past 2 we left it. . . .

Wednesday, 31st October.—I awoke at 7 and got up at ½ past 7. At ½ past 9 we breakfasted in the drawing-room, for the gentlemen who were going to hunt breakfasted in the other room, all the ladies and Sir John breakfasting with us. After breakfast at about ½ past 10 we went into the room where they were, and they gave us a toast with many cheers. After that we walked out to see the hunt. We saw them set off. It was an immense field of horsemen, who in their red jackets and black hats looked lively and gave an animating appearance to the whole. They had a large pack of hounds and three huntsmen or Whippers-in. They drew a covert near here in hopes of finding a fox, but as they did not they returned and we got into the carriage with Lady Selina [1] and Lehzen while all the huntsmen and the hounds followed. When we came to a field, they drew another covert and succeeded ; we saw the fox dash past and all the people and hounds after him, the hounds in full cry. The hounds killed him in a wood quite close by. The huntsman then brought him out and cutting off the brush Sir Edward Smith (to whom the hounds belong) brought it to me. Then the huntsmen cut off for themselves the ears and 4 paws, and lastly

---

[1] Lord Liverpool's second daughter, married, first, to Lord Milton, secondly to George Savile Foljambe, of Osberton, Notts.

they threw it to the dogs, who tore it from side to side till there was nothing left. We then went home. At 1 we lunched, and at 2, I, Lady Selina, Lady Louisa[1] and dear Lehzen went out walking, towards a farm of Lord Liverpool's, and when we had passed the farm and were going to return by the village, we heard the blast of a horn and we looked and saw the hounds and hunters going full gallop along a field which was below the field in which we were walking. They came and crossed the field in which we were and we saw all the riders leap over a ditch. We went back the same way that we might see them. When we came near home we saw them go home by the house. At ½ past 3 we came home. At ½ past 6 we dined, and I received my brush which had been fixed on a stick by the huntsman ; it is a beautiful one. Amongst the people who were here, those who remain are **Mr., Mrs., and Miss Corbett, Mr., Mrs., and Miss Child.** After dinner the young ladies played some pretty things from the *Pirata* and from *Fra Diavolo.* I stayed up till near 10. . . .

Wednesday, 7th November.— . . . ¼ to 4· We have just changed horses at Woodstock, and another detachment of Yeomanry commanded by Lord Churchill[2] ride with us now. We passed through Oxford on our way. At about a little past 5 we arrived at Wytham Abbey, the seat of Lord Abingdon.[3] We were received at the door by Lord and Lady Abingdon, Lady Charlotte Bertie and Lady

[1] Louisa, third daughter of Lord Liverpool, married John Cotes of Woodcote, Salop.

[2] *F*rancis, first Lord Churchill, third son of George, fourth Duke of Marlborough.

[3] Montagu, fifth Earl of Abingdon, married Emily, sister of the third Viscount Gage.

Emily Bathurst, their daughters. The house is very comfortable; in the drawing-room there is a lovely picture by Angelica Kauffman, Penelope. After staying a few minutes downstairs we went upstairs to our rooms which are very pretty and comfortable. At a little past 7 we dined with several other people. I stayed up till a little past 9.

Thursday, 8th November.—I awoke at a little to 8 and got up at 8. At a little past 9 we breakfasted with the whole party. At 10 o'clock we set out for Oxford in a close carriage and 4 with Lord Abingdon and Lady Charlotte Bertie; the other ladies going in carriages before us. We got out first at the Divinity College, and walked from thence to the theatre, which was built by Sir Christopher Wren. The ceiling is painted with allegorical figures. The galleries are ornamented with carving enriched with gold. It was filled to excess. We were most WARMLY and ENTHUSIASTICALLY received. They hurrayed and applauded us immensely for there were all the students there; all in their gowns and caps. Mamma received an address which was presented by the Vice-Chancellor, Dr. Rowly, and Mamma answered it as usual. Then Sir John[1] was made a Doctor of Civil Law. After that was over, we returned through Divinity College and proceeded in our carriages to the Council Chamber where Mamma received an address there, from the corporation of Oxford, and Sir John the freedom of the City of Oxford. We then went to Christ Church, which is very fine, viewed the hall and chapel and library. Dr. Gaisford[2] is the Dean of Christ Church and is at the head of that college. From there we went to

[1] Sir John Conroy.
[2] Thomas Gaisford, Dean of Christ Church, 1831–1855.

the Bodleian library which is immense. Amongst
other curiosities there is Queen Elizabeth's Latin
exercise book when she was of my age (13). We
went through Mr. Sneed's house to our carriages.
From there to All Souls' College where Mr. Sneed is
the warden. It is not a college for education, but
after they have taken their degree. We saw the
library and chapel which is very beautiful. We
then went to University College of which the Vice-
chancellor is the head. We lunched there and saw
the chapel which is very fine. From there we went
to New College of which Dr. Shuttleworth [1] is the
head. We saw the chapel and hall. From there to
the Clarendon printing-press which is very amusing
but would take up too much space and time to
describe. We then went home. We arrived at
home at $\frac{1}{2}$ past 3. At 7 we dined with some other
people who were Lord Cantelupe,[2] Lord Folkestone,[3]
Lord Loftus,[4] Mr. Gage,[5] Mr. Canning,[6] Lord Thomas
Clinton,[7] Mr. L. Gower,[8] Lord Boscawen,[9] etc. etc.

[1] Philip Nicholas Shuttleworth, afterwards (1840–1842) Bishop of
Chichester.

[2] George, Viscount Cantelupe (1814–1850), died in the lifetime of
his father, the fifth Earl de la Warr.

[3] Jacob, afterwards fourth Earl of Radnor (1815–1889).

[4] John Henry, afterwards third Marquess of Ely (1814–1857). His
wife was in after-years Lady of the Bedchamber to Queen Victoria,
and perhaps the most widely known of her ladies.

[5] Probably Henry Edward Hall Gage (1814–1875), eldest son
of the fourth Viscount Gage, in whose lifetime he died.

[6] Charles Canning (1812–1862), afterwards Viscount Canning and
Governor-General of India.

[7] Lord Thomas Clinton (1813–1882), third son of Henry, fourth
Duke of Newcastle, K.G.

[8] Mr. Granville Leveson-Gower, afterwards second Earl Granville
(1815–1891), well known as Secretary of State for Foreign Affairs in
Mr. Gladstone's Administration.

[9] George Henry, afterwards second Earl of Falmouth (1811–1852).

After dinner the young ladies sang to the guitar which one of them played. We then sang and Lord Abingdon. I stayed up till 10.

Friday, 9th November.— . . . At about ½ past 5 we arrived at Kensington Palace. We resumed our old rooms. At 7 we dined with Jane and Victoire Conroy, Lord Liverpool and Sir John. My aunt Sophia [1] came after dinner. I stayed up till a ¼ to 9.

Monday, 24th December.—I awoke at 7 and got up at 8. At 9 we breakfasted. At ½ past 9 came the Dean,[2] and I gave him Mamma's and my Christmas box. He stayed till ½ past 11. In the course of the morning I gave Mrs. Brock a Christmas box and all our people. At ½ past 1 we lunched. At ½ past 2 came Mr. Westall[3] till ½ past 3. At 4 came Mr. Sale[4] till 5. At a ¼ to 7 we dined with the whole Conroy family and Mr. Hore downstairs, as our Christmas tables were arranged in our dining-room. After dinner we went upstairs. I then saw Flora, the dog which Sir John was going to give Mamma. Aunt Sophia came also. We then went into the drawing-room near the dining-room. After Mamma had rung a bell three times we went in. There were two large round tables on which were placed two trees hung with lights and sugar ornaments. All the presents being placed round the tree. I had one table for myself and the Conroy family had

[1] Princess Sophia (1777-1848) was a daughter of George III., and younger sister of Princess Augusta Sophia (1768-1840). See p. 200.

[2] The Very Rev. George Davys, the Princess's instructor, at this time Dean of Chester, subsequently Bishop of Peterborough.

[3] Richard Westall (1765–1836), an R.A. since 1794 and painter of many historical pictures.

[4] John Bernard Sale (1779–1856), organist of St. Margaret's, Westminster, and afterwards of the Chapel Royal.

the other together. Lehzen had likewise a little table. Mamma gave me a little lovely pink bag which she had worked with a little sachet likewise done by her ; a beautiful little opal brooch and earrings, books, some lovely prints, a pink satin dress and a cloak lined with fur. Aunt Sophia gave me a dress which she worked herself, and Aunt Mary [1] a pair of amethyst earrings. Lehzen a lovely music-book. Victoire a *very* pretty white bag worked by herself, and Sir John a silver brush. I gave Lehzen some little things and Mamma gave her a writing table. We then went to my room where I had arranged Mamma's table. I gave Mamma a white bag which I had worked, a collar and a steel chain for Flora, and an Annual ; Aunt Sophia a pair of turquoise earrings ; Lehzen a little white and gold pincushion and a pin with two little gold hearts hanging to it ; Sir John, Flora, a book-holder and an Annual. Mamma then took me up into my bedroom with all the ladies. There was my new toilet table with a white muslin cover over pink, and all my silver things standing on it with a fine new looking-glass. I stayed up till ½ past 9. The dog went away again to the doctor for her leg. I saw good Louis [2] for an instant and she gave me a lovely little wooden box with bottles.

[1] The Duchess of Gloucester. See p. 65.

[2] An attached attendant, to whose memory, after her death, the Queen erected a tablet in St. Martin's-in-the-Fields. She was dresser to Princess Charlotte.

the other together.   Lehzen had likewise a little table.
Mamma gave me a little lovely pink bag which she
had worked with a little sachet likewise done by her ;
a beautiful little opal brooch and earrings, books,
some lovely prints, a pink satin dress and a cloak
lined with fur.   Aunt Sophia gave me a dress which
she worked herself, and Aunt Mary [1] a pair of amethyst
earrings.   Lehzen a lovely music-book.   Victoire a
very pretty white bag worked by herself, and Sir
John a silver brush.   I gave Lehzen some little
things and Mamma gave her a writing table.   We
then went to my room where I had arranged Mamma's
table.   I gave Mamma a white bag which I had
worked, a collar and a steel chain for Flora, and an
Annual ;   Aunt Sophia a pair of turquoise earrings ;
Lehzen a little white and gold pincushion and a pin
with two little gold hearts hanging to it ; Sir John,
Flora, a book-holder and an Annual.   Mamma then
took me up into my bedroom with all the ladies.
There was my new toilet table with a white muslin
cover over pink, and all my silver things standing
on it with a fine new looking-glass.   I stayed up
till ½ past 9.   The dog went away again to the
doctor for her leg.   I saw good Louis [2] for an instant
and she gave me a lovely little wooden box with
bottles.

[1] The Duchess of Gloucester   See p. 65

[2] An attached attendant, to whose memory, after her death, the
Queen erected a tablet in St. Martin's-in-the-Fields.   She was dresser
to Princess Charlotte.

H.R H. PRINCESS SOPHIA.

From a portrait by Sir W Ross

INTRODUCTORY NOTE TO CHAPTER II

WHEN the Princess was fourteen years old she obtained her first sight of Osborne, that future home in the Isle of Wight where she was destined to spend so many happy years, and which was associated with the closing scenes of her life. Osborne Lodge was the residence of Sir John Conroy. It occupied the site of Osborne Cottage, now the residence of the Queen's youngest daughter, Princess Henry of Battenberg. In spite of the changes made in the appearance of Osborne by the erection of Osborne House and the laying-out of the grounds round it, that portion of the estate where Osborne Cottage stands, and Whippingham Church, with its manifold associations, have much the same aspect as they had when first explored by Princess Victoria in 1833.

On her birthday, King William gave a children's party at St. James's in his niece's honour, and the ball was opened by the little Princess and her cousin Prince George of Cambridge, then a boy of fourteen, who was afterwards to be the Commander-in-Chief of her armies. The Princess speaks of the ball-room. It is difficult to be sure which room is meant by this. The eastern end of St. James's Palace had been destroyed by fire in 1809, and had only recently been rebuilt. The Palace was occupied by William IV. and Queen Adelaide, the Queen's rooms being in that portion which is now called Clarence House, and the King's apartments occupying the western end of what is now St. James's Palace proper. It was probably the room hung with yellow silk, next but one to the Throne-room, so familiar to those who attend the King's Levées, that the little Princess opened her first ball.

This was not her first introduction into Society. Three years before she had been seen at Court, and in 1831 she had attended a Drawing-room.

The Princess now acquired a habit (which she practised for many years) of making sketches from memory of the artists and scenes that struck her imagination during her visits to the theatre. There are many volumes at Windsor Castle full of the Princess's recollections of the theatre, drawn in pencil or in water-colour. Although the technique may be faulty, these sketches are full of movement and quaintly descriptive. They indicate an absorbed attention on her part, and a vivid memory. They suggest a power of concentration upon the thing she was about, which became in after-life a marked characteristic. From her journals and her sketches as a child of fourteen, an inference might be drawn that little escaped the acute observation of the little Princess. There are many who remember how in later life very little escaped the observation of the Queen.

CHAPTER II

1833

Tuesday, 15th January.—I awoke at 7 and got up at 8. At 10 minutes to 9 we breakfasted. At ½ past 9 came the Dean till ½ past 11. Just before we went out, Mamma's little dog, a beautiful spaniel of King Charles's breed, called Dash, and which Sir John gave her yesterday, came and will now remain here. At a ¼ past 12 Lehzen and I went out walking in the park. We met Mrs. Talbot. When we came home I fed dear Rosy who was *so* greedy. At ½ past 1 we lunched. At 3 came Mr. Steward [1] till 4. At 4 came Mons. Grandineau [2] till 5. Little Dash is *perfection*, he is already much attached to Mamma and lies always at her feet. At 7 we dined. Aunt Sophia came at 8. Sir John dined here. I stayed up till ½ past 8. . . .

Thursday, 31st January.—At 1 we lunched. At 2 I sat to Mr. Hayter [3] till 10 minutes to 4. At 5 we dined. Sir John dined here. At ½ past 6 we went with Lady Conroy, Jane and Victoire to the play to Drury Lane. It was the opera of *The Barber of*

[1] Thomas Steward, teacher of writing and arithmetic.

[2] M. Grandineau, teacher of French.

[3] Mr. (afterwards Sir) George Hayter (1792–1871), a ceremonial painter of some merit. He was the official limner of two Royal heiresses —*i.e.* Princess Charlotte and Princess Victoria. He was designated, somewhat equivocally, Painter in Ordinary to the Queen.

Seville. It is so well known that I need not describe it. The principal characters were Count Almaviva, Mr. Wood, who looked, sang, and acted *extremely* well ; Rosina, Mrs. Wood ; Figaro, Mr. Philipps, who sung very well ; Dr. Bartolo, Mr. Seguin, who acted very well. It was in 3 acts and I was very *much amused.* The after piece called *The Nervous Man* is only amusing in parts, for Mr. Farren[1] and Mr. Power, two excellent comic actors. We did not see the end of it. We came home at 12. . . .

Saturday, 9th February.—I awoke at 7 and got up at ½ past 7. At ½ past 8 we breakfasted. At ½ past 9 came the Dean till 11. At ½ past 12 we lunched. At 1 we paid a visit to my aunt the Duchess of Gloucester.[2] When we came home I fed dear little Rosa, and little Isabell. At ½ past 2 came Mr. Westall[3] till ½ past 3. At a ¼ past 5 we dined. Sir John dined here. At ½ past 6 we went to the play with Lady Conroy, Victoire and Lehzen as usual. It was the ballet of *Kenilworth.* The subject is taken from the novel by Sir Walter Scott, which being so well known I shall not describe. The principal characters were, Lord Leicester, Mons. Theodore Guerinot, who danced beautifully ; Amy Robsart, Mdlle. Pauline Leroux, who danced and acted *beautifully* and looked *quite* lovely ; Jenny, Madame Proche Giubilei, who acted very well and looked very pretty ; Queen Elizabeth, Mrs. Vining ; Varney, Mr. W. H. Payne ; Earl of Sussex, Signor Rossi ; Lord Shrews-

---

[1] William Farren (1786–1861), an actor of distinction himself, and a member of a histrionic family of unusual merit.

[2] Mary, fourth daughter of George III., who married her cousin William Frederick, Duke of Gloucester. She died in 1857. The Queen looked upon her " as a sort of grandmother," and described her as full of kindness, amiability, and unselfishness.

[3] See *post,* p. 104.

I—6

bury, Mr. Bertram. Besides these, Mdlle. Adele and Mdlle. Chavigny danced a pas de trois with Mons. Theodore Guerinot. They danced very well. At 20 minutes past 9 we came home. I then took tea. . . .

Friday, 5th April.—To-day is Good Friday. At 10 we went to prayers. Jane and Victoire also. The service was performed by the Dean, who gave us likewise a very good sermon. It was taken from the 8th chapter of the Acts of the Apostles, 30th verse. At a ¼ past 12 we went out walking. When we came home I fed sweet Rosy. At ½ past 1 we lunched. At 3 came Victoire till 5. At 7 we dined. At 8 came Aunt Sophia. I stayed up till ½ past 8. . . .

Saturday, 13th April.—I awoke at 7 and got up at 8. At a ¼ to 9 we breakfasted. At ½ past 9 came the Dean till ½ past 11. The Duchess of Northumberland[1] was present. At 12 we went out riding in the park with Victoire, Lehzen and Sir John. It was a *delightful* ride. We cantered a good deal. SWEET LITTLE ROSY went BEAUTIFULLY ! ! We came home at a ¼ past 1. At ½ past 1 we lunched. Neither of my masters came. At 6 we dined. The Duchess of Northumberland, Lady Charlotte St. Maur,[2] and Sir John dined here. At 20 minutes to 7 we went out with them to the Opera. We were very much *disappointed* for Taglioni did not make her début, nor Rubini. We had only one scene of *Il Barbière di Siviglia,* in which Signor Tambourini, who is a

---

[1] Charlotte Florentia, daughter of Edward, first Earl of Powis, and wife of Hugh, third Duke of Northumberland, K.G., Governess to the Princess.

[2] Daughter of the eleventh Duke of Somerset, afterwards wife of William Blount, of Orleton, Herefordshire.

beautiful singer and actor, appeared, and Donizelli.
After waiting for half an hour Laporte (the manager)
was called out, and he said that Mlle. Taglioni was
very unwell in bed, and Mad. Méric was likewise
ill, so that *Il Pirato* could not be performed, but
that Rubini would be there directly. After one
act of *Fidelio*, which was *shockingly* performed,
Rubini came on and sang a song out of *Anna Boulena*
quite beautifully. After that there was the ballet of
La Somnambula. The principal characters were
Mdlle. Pauline Leroux, who looked QUITE LOVELY
and acted prettily ; Mdlle. Adele ; Madame Proche
Giubelei who looked *very pretty* ; Messrs. Albert and
Coulon. We only saw part of it. We came home
at ½ past 11. . . .

Tuesday, 23rd April.—I awoke at 7 and got up at
½ past 7. At 9 we breakfasted. At ½ past 9 came
the Dean till ½ past 11. The Duchess of Northumberland was present. At a ¼ past 12 we went out
riding with Lady Conroy, Victoire, Lehzen, and Sir
John. We rode a little way in the park, but the fog
was so thick that we turned round and rode down by
Gloucester Road, and turned up by Phillimore Place,
where it was very fine and not at all foggy. *Dear*
Rosa went *beautifully.* We came home at ½ past 1.
At ½ past 1 we lunched. At 3 came Mr. Steward
till 4. At 4 came Mons. Grandineau till 5. At a
¼ to 7 we dined. Sir John dined here, and I dressed
DEAR SWEET LITTLE DASH for the second time after
dinner in a scarlet jacket and blue trousers. At
20 minutes past 8 Mamma went with Jane and Sir
John to the Opera. I stayed up till ½ past 8.

Wednesday, 24th April.—I awoke at 7 and got up
at 8. At 9 we breakfasted. At ½ past 9 came the
Dean till ½ past 11. At ½ past 1 we lunched. At 3

came Mons. Grandineau till 4. Madame Bourdin [1] did not come. At ½ past 6 Lehzen and I dined. At 7 I and Lehzen went into the large saloon, for Mamma gave a dinner to the King. There dined here, the King (the Queen being too unwell to come), the Duke of Cumberland, the Duke of Gloucester, the Archbishop of Canterbury, [2] the Lord Chancellor, [3] the Duke of Devonshire, [4] the Duke of Norfolk, [5] the Duke of Somerset, [6] the Duke and Duchess of Gordon, [7] the Duke of Rutland, [8] the Duchess of Northumberland, the Duchess of Sutherland, [9] the Duke of Cleveland, [10]

---

[1] The Princess's dancing-mistress.

[2] William Howley (1766–1848), Bishop of London 1813–28, Primate 1828–48. In the opinion of Lord Grey and the Whigs "a poor, miserable creature," but in reality a worthy, conscientious prelate.

[3] Lord Brougham.

[4] See *ante*, p. 53.

[5] Bernard Edward, twelfth Duke of Norfolk (1765–1842). He was given the Garter in 1834—the only K.G. of the Roman faith. He subsequently became a Protestant.

[6] Edward Adolphus, eleventh Duke of Somerset (1775–1855). A personage of no importance.

[7] George, fifth and last Duke of Gordon. A soldier. He fought in Ireland (1798) and at Walcheren (1809). A friend of the Prince Regent and a hard liver, but a high-minded, honourable man. Three of his sisters married the Dukes of Richmond, Manchester, and Bedford. The fourth married the Marquis Cornwallis. These achievements were due to the talents of the old Duchess of Gordon, a Scottish lady of strong character and accent.

[8] John Henry, fifth Duke of Rutland, K.G. (1778–1857), chiefly remarkable as the father of "Henry Sidney," one of Disraeli's well-known sketches of contemporary potentates.

[9] Elizabeth, Countess of Sutherland in her own right (1765–1839), married George Granville, Viscount Trentham, afterwards second Marquess of Stafford. He was created Duke of Sutherland in January 1833. She was habitually called the "Duchess-Countess" in the family, and is still so called.

[10] William Harry, third Earl of Darlington and first Duke of Cleveland, K.G. See *post*, p. 98.

the Marchioness of Westminster,[1] the Earl of Liverpool, the Earl and Countess Grey,[2] Lord Hill,[3] Lady Dover,[4] the Earl of Uxbridge,[5] the Earl of Albemarle,[6] Lord Amherst,[7] Lady Charlotte St. Maur, Lady Catherine Jenkinson, Lady Cust,[8] Lady Conroy, Sir George Anson,[9] Sir Frederick Wetherall,[10] and Sir John. At about 8 I went to my room with Lehzen. At 20 minutes past 9 I went into the saloon with her to meet the company. The Grenadier Guards' band played after dinner. I saw all the company go. I stayed up till 11. . . .

Saturday, 27th April.—I awoke at 7 and got up at a ¼ to 8. At a ¼ to 9 we breakfasted. At ½ past 9 came the Dean till 11. The Duchess of Northumberland was present. At 12 we went out walking. When we came home I fed dear little Rosa. At a ¼ past 1 we lunched. At ½ past 2 came Mr. Westall

[1] See *ante,* p. 49.

[2] Charles, second Earl Grey, Prime Minister. Lady Grey was Mary Elizabeth, daughter of the first Lord Ponsonby of Imskilly.

[3] Rowland, first Viscount Hill, Commander-in-Chief from 1828 to 1842—an office upon which he left no mark.

[4] Georgiana, second daughter of George, sixth Earl of Carlisle, wife of the Rt. Hon. George James Welbore, first Lord Dover.

[5] Henry, Earl of Uxbridge, afterwards second Marquess of Anglesey, a cavalier of spirit, and possessed of all the dashing qualities of the Paget family.

[6] William Charles, fourth Earl of Albemarle, Master of the Horse. A few days after her accession the Queen sent for him and said, "My Lord, you will immediately provide for me six chargers to review my troops."

[7] William Pitt, first Earl Amherst, quite inconspicuous as Ambassador to China 1816–17, and Governor-General of India 1823–28.

[8] Mary Anne, wife of Sir Edward Cust, afterwards Master of the Ceremonies to Queen Victoria.

[9] General Sir George Anson, G.C.B., Equerry to the Duchess of Kent, afterwards Groom of the Bedchamber to Prince Albert.

[10] General Sir Frederick Wetherall served on the staff of the Duke of Kent, and was subsequently his equerry and one of the executors of his will.

I—6*

till ½ past 3.   At 20 minutes to 3 I sat to Mr. Wyon [1]
to have my profile taken for a medal, till 10 minutes
to 5.   At 6 we dined.   Sir John dined here.   At a
¼ past 7 we went with Lady Conroy and Lehzen,
as usual, to the Opera.   It was the opera of *Cenerentola* by Rossini.   The principal characters were the
Prince, by Signor Donizelli ;   the Prince's servant,
Signor Tambourini who sung QUITE BEAUTIFULLY ;
the father of Cenerentola, Signor Zuchelli, who acted
uncommonly   well ;   Cenerentola,   Madame   Cinti
Damoreau ;   she sang QUITE BEAUTIFULLY, so round,
so softly, and so correctly.   It was her first appearance this season and she was called out.   The sisters
were two FRIGHTFUL creatures.   The ballet which
followed was *Flore et Zephir.*   Mdlle. Taglioni [2] made
her first appearance this season.   She is grown very
thin, but danced *beautifully,* so lightly and *gracefully,*
and each step so finished !   She took the part of
Flore, and was very prettily dressed in a plain gauze
dress, trimmed with flowers across her skirt ;   a wreath
of flowers round her head, and her hair quite flat.
Pearls round her neck and arms.   She looked *lovely,*
for she is all-ways smiling.   We went away soon.
We came home at 12. . . .

Friday, 3rd May.—At 12 we went with the
Duchess of Northumberland, Lady Charlotte St.
Maur, Lady Catherine Jenkinson, Lady Cust, Lady
Conroy, Lehzen, Sir George Anson, and Sir John, to
the Exhibition at Somerset House.   We were met
there by Sir Martin Shee [3] (the President), Mr. Westall,

---

[1] William Wyon, chief engraver at the Mint, afterwards R.A.

[2] Marie Taglioni (1809–84).   Until the invasion of Europe by
Russian ballet, Taglioni's name was the most famous in the annals
of classical operatic dancing.

[3] He was President from 1830 to 1850.   By his contemporaries

Mr. Howard [1] (the Treasurer), Mr. Daniel, and Sir William Beechy.[2] It was a very good exhibition. There were several very fine pictures by Sir Martin Shee. Seven by Mr. Westall. They were 4 landscapes, a drawing of Christ in the arms of Simeon in the temple; a sleeping Cupid, and the death of James 2nd. All very fine. There were 5 of G. Hayter's but I only saw 3, which were my picture, Lady Lichfield, and Mad. de Delmar's. There were 3 of Wilkie's, a portrait of the King, a very beautiful portrait of the Duke of Sussex, and Spanish monks, a scene witnessed in a capuchin convent at Toledo. There were several very fine ones of Howard, Daniel, Eastlake,[4] Landseer,[5] Calcott,[6] Pickersgill,[7] Hilton,[8] etc., etc. We came home at $\frac{1}{2}$ past 2. At $\frac{1}{2}$ past 4 we went out driving in the barouche, but we also walked. We came home at 5. . . .

Wednesday, 8th May.—At $\frac{1}{2}$ past 2 came Mons.

he was as much esteemed as Lawrence. America, however, has not yet discovered him.

[1] Henry Howard, appointed Professor of Painting to the Academy in 1833.

[2] Sir William Beechey, R.A. Formerly Portrait Painter to Queen Charlotte, and finely represented at Windsor by a series of charming portraits of Royal children.

[3] Now in the " Corridor " at Windsor Castle.

[4] Sir Charles Eastlake (P.R.A., 1850–65). He was appointed by Sir R. Peel secretary to the Fine Arts Commission, and later still Director of the National Gallery. A typical and meritorious P.R.A.

[5] Sir Edwin Landseer (1802–73). The most popular of British painters.

[6] Sir Augustus Wall Callcott (1779–1844). A chorister of Westminster Abbey; subsequently a painter. Elected R.A. 1810, and knighted 1837.

[7] Henry William Pickersgill, R.A. (1782–75), a fashionable portrait painter, patronised by famous men and women; he exhibited at the Academy for over sixty years. He is now quite forgotten.

[8] William Hilton, R.A., (1786–1839). His work was refined, but, owing to the pigment he used, has practically vanished.

Grandineau till ½ past 3.   At a ¼ past 4 we walked
through the gardens, and then drove in the barouche
in the park.   We came home at 5.   At ½ past 6
Lehzen and I dined.   At a little past 7 Lehzen and I
went into the saloon, for Mamma gave a dinner.
There dined here, H.R.H. the Duke of Orleans,[1]
who I was very glad to see, for I had not seen him
since nearly 4 years ; he brought Mamma a letter
from his Mother, the Queen of the French, with a
beautiful *déjeuner* of Sévres china ; a letter from
Aunt Louisa[2] (his sister), and a beautiful bracelet
with her hair in it ; for me a letter from Aunt Louisa
and a beautiful bracelet with her picture.   Prince
Talleyrand,[3] the Duchess de Dino,[4] the Duc de
Valençay (her son), the Marquess and Marchioness
of Lansdowne,[5] the Marquess and Marchioness of
Stafford,[6] the Earl and Countess of Tankerville,[7]

[1] The Duke, who was the eldest son of King Louis Philippe, was
born at Palermo in 1810, and in July 1842 was thrown from his
phaeton near the Porte Maillot in Paris, and died on the spot.   His
youth and popularity, his love of art and literature, and his professional
efficiency as a soldier might, had he lived, have served to give the events
of 1848 a different turn.   He was, however, a Bourbon.

[2] Wife of Leopold, King of the Belgians.

[3] The veteran Prince Talleyrand (1754–1838), once Bishop of Autun,
Republican, Bonapartist, Legitimist, and cynic ; everything by turns
and everything remarkably *long*.   See p. 331, and Vol. II. p. 61.

[4] The Duchesse de Dino (Princesse de Sagan), niece of Prince
Talleyrand.   Her own memoirs have preserved her memory.

[5] Henry, third Marquess of Lansdowne (1780–1863).   A typical and
most eminent Whig.   He twice refused to be Prime Minister, but held
office in every Whig Administration from 1830 to 1858.   He was
Chancellor of the Exchequer in the Ministry of "All the Talents."
He was a fine judge of art.   No statesman of his time was more
universally trusted.

[6] George Granville succeeded his father, the first Duke of Sutherland
(see *ante*, p. 68, n.), in July 1833.   His wife, Harriet Elizabeth
Georgiana, third daughter of the sixth Earl of Carlisle, was the first
Mistress of the Robes selected by Queen Victoria.

[7] Charles Augustus (1776–1859), fifth Earl of Tankerville, married

the Earl and Countess of Sefton,[1] the Earl and Countess Grosvenor,[2] the Earl of Lichfield,[3] the Earl and Countess Granville,[4] Lord Palmerston,[5] Lord Morpeth,[6] Lord Duncannon,[7] Lord Ebrington,[8] Mr. Van de Weyer,[9] Mr. and Mrs. Stanley,[10] Mr. Ellice,[11]

Corisande, daughter of Antoine, Duc de Gramont: she possessed great charm of manner and a fine turn of wit. She had many attached friends of both sexes. See Vol. II. p. 221.

[1] William Philip (1772–1838), second Earl of Sefton, married Maria Margaret, daughter of William, sixth Lord Craven.

[2] See *ante*, p. 49.

[3] Thomas William (1795–1854), second Viscount Anson, had been created in 1831 Earl of Lichfield. He married Louisa Catherine, daughter of Nathaniel Philips, of Slebech Hall, co. Pembroke.

[4] First Earl Granville, youngest son of first Marquess of Stafford (1773–1846), Ambassador to St. Petersburg 1804, and afterwards for many years at Paris. He married the daughter of the fifth Duke of Devonshire.

[5] Lord Palmerston, born 1781, died Prime Minister 1865. Lord Palmerston was now fifty-two years old. In years to come, this child of thirteen was destined to overthrow him, when at the height of his popularity, to receive him again as her Prime Minister, and to turn to him in the great crisis of her life twenty-eight years after their first meeting.

[6] See *ante*, p. 54.

[7] John William, Lord Duncannon. A Whig placeman. As Earl of Bessborough (1846) he became Lord Lieutenant of Ireland, and died in office in 1847.

[8] Hugh, Lord Ebrington, afterwards second Earl Fortescue. Lord Lieutenant of Ireland, 1839–41.

[9] Sylvain Van de Weyer (1802–74), Belgian Minister at the Court of St. James's, a trusted friend of King Leopold and of Queen Victoria. He had been a prominent leader of the Revolution in Belgium, 1830, and a protagonist of the separation of Belgium and Holland. His wit and charming personality gave him a prominent place in London society. He married the daughter of Joshua Bates, senior partner in Barings.

[10] Edward Geoffrey Stanley (1799–1869), the Rupert of debate, at this time Secretary for the Colonies, afterwards (as Earl of Derby) three times Prime Minister. Mrs. Stanley was Emma Caroline, daughter of Edward, first Lord Skelmersdale.

[11] Mr. Ellice (1781–1863), born at Montreal, M.P. for Coventry and

Mr. Abercromby,[1] the Aide-de-Camp in Waiting on H.R.H. the Duke of Orleans, Mr. Taylor, Lady Charlotte St. Maur, Lady Conroy, Sir George Anson, and Sir John. At about 8 I went with Lehzen away. The band of the Coldstream Guards played at dinner as well as after dinner, as it had the preceding night. At 20 minutes after 9 Lehzen and I went into the saloon. We met Aunt Sophia there. . . .

Saturday, 11th May.—At a ¼ to 7 we dined. Sir John dined here. At a little after 8 we went to the Opera with Victoire, Lehzen, and Charles. We came in at the end of the first act of *Medea.* Madame Pasta sang, and acted beautifully, as did also Rubini and Donizelli. The ballet was excessively pretty. It is called *Nathalie.* The principal dancers were Mdlle. Taglioni, who danced and acted QUITE BEAUTIFULLY ! ! She looked *very* pretty. Her dress was very pretty. It was a sort of Swiss dress ; she first appeared in a petticoat of brown and yellow, with a blue and white apron, a body of black velvet ornamented with silver, pointed upwards and downwards, over a light tucker drawn to her neck, with a black ribbon round it, a pair of small white sleeves, a little Swiss straw hat, with long plaits of her hair hanging down, completed her first dress. Her second dress was a petticoat of scarlet and yellow silk, with a white apron, the same body and sleeves, with a wreath of flowers on her head. Mdlles. Thérèse and

Secretary at War. He had been a very successful Government Whip ; nick-named " Bear " Ellice from his connection with the Hudson Bay Company. He married a sister of Earl Grey.

[1] James Abercromby (1776–1858), son of the gallant Sir Ralph Abercromby, who died in the moment of victory at Alexandria in 1801. At this time M.P. for Edinburgh. Became Speaker of the House of Commons in 1835, and was created Lord Dunfermline four years later.

Fanny Elsler; they are good dancers, but have neither grace nor lightness. Messrs. Albert, Coulon, and Daumont. In the middle of the ballet the Duke of Orleans came into our box for a little while. We saw most of the ballet. I was *very much* amused. . . .

Friday, 24th May.—To-day is my birthday. I am to-day fourteen years old! How *very old*!! I awoke at ½ *past* 5 and got up at ½ past 7. I received from Mamma a lovely hyacinth brooch and a china pen tray. From Uncle Leopold a very kind letter, also one from Aunt Louisa and sister Feodora. I gave Mamma a little ring. From Lehzen I got a pretty little china figure, and a lovely little china basket. I gave her a golden chain and Mamma gave her a pair of earrings to match. From my maids, Frances and Caroline, I also got little trifles of their own work. At ½ past 8 we breakfasted. After breakfast we went into the room where my table was arranged. Mamma gave me a lovely bag of her own work, a beautiful bracelet, two lovely féronières, one of pink topaz, the other turquoises; two dresses, some prints, some books, some handkerchiefs, and an apron. From Lehzen, a beautiful print of the Russell Trial. From Späth,[1] a glass and plate of Bohemian glass. From Sir Robert Gardiner,[2] a china plate with fruit. From Victoria and Emily Gardiner, two screens and a drawing done by them. From the Dean, some books. My brother Charles's present was not ready. At about ½ past 10 came Sir John and his three sons. From Sir John I received

---

[1] The Baroness Späth, Lady-in-Waiting to the Duchess of Kent.

[2] General Sir Robert Gardiner was Principal Equerry to Prince Leopold of Saxe-Coburg at his marriage with Princess Charlotte. In later life he was Governor and Commander-in-Chief at Gibraltar.

a very pretty picture of Dash, very like, the size of
life. From Jane, Victoire, Edward, Stephen, and
Henry, a very pretty enamel watch-chain. From
Lady Conroy a sandalwood pincushion and needle-
case. From Victoire alone, a pair of enamel earrings. The Duchess of Gordon sent me a lovely
little crown of precious stones, which plays " God
save the King," and a china basket. At 12 came
the Duchess of Northumberland (who gave me an
ivory basket filled with the work of her nieces), Lady
Charlotte St. Maur a beautiful album with a painting
on it ; Lady Catherine Jenkinson a pretty night-
lamp. Lady Cust, a tray of Staffordshire china.
Sir Frederick Wetherall, two china vases from Paris.
Doctor Maton,[1] a small cedar basket. Lady Conroy,
Jane, Victoire, Sir George Anson, Sir John, and the
Dean came also. Lady Conroy brought Bijou (her
little dog) with her, and she gave me a little sweet
smelling box. They stayed till ½ past 12. Victoire
remained with us. I gave her a portrait of Isabel,
her horse. At 1 we lunched. Victoire stayed till
½ past 2. At ½ past 2 came the Royal Family. The
Queen gave me a pair of diamond earrings from the
King. She gave me herself a brooch of turquoises
and gold in the form of a bow. Aunt Augusta gave
me a box of sandal-wood. From Aunt Gloucester,
Aunt Sophia, and Uncle Sussex, a féronière of pearls.
From Aunt Sophia alone, a bag worked by herself.
From the Duke of Gloucester, a gold inkstand. From
the Duke and Duchess of Cumberland, a bracelet of
turquoise ; and the Duchess brought me a turquoise
pin from my cousin George Cumberland. From
Princess Sophia Mathilda, a blue topaz watch-hook.

[1] William George Maton, M.D., Physician Extraordinary to the
Duchess of Kent and Princess Victoria.

From George Cambridge,[1] a brooch in the shape of a lily of the valley. Lady Mayo,[2] who was in waiting on the Queen, gave me a glass bottle. They stayed till ½ past 3 and then went away. I had seen in the course of the day, Sarah, my former maid, and Mrs. Brock. Ladies Emma and Georgiana Herbert[3] sent me a sachet for handkerchiefs worked by themselves. Ladies Sarah and Clementina Villiers[4] sent me some flowers as combs and a brooch. Mr. Collen sent me a little painting for my album. At a ¼ to 6 we dined. At ½ past 7 we went with Charles, the Duchess of Northumberland, Lady Catherine Jenkinson, Lehzen, Sir George Anson, and Sir John, to a Juvenile Ball that was given in honour of my birthday at St. James's by the King and Queen. We went into the Closet. Soon after, the doors were opened, and the King leading me went into the ball-room. Madame Bourdin was there as dancing-mistress. Victoire was also there, as well as *many* other children whom I knew. Dancing began soon after. I danced first with my cousin George Cambridge, then with Prince George Lieven,[5] then with Lord Brook,[6] then

---

[1] George (1819–1904), afterwards Duke of Cambridge and Commander-in-Chief. He was two months older than the Princess, so that he was now fourteen years old.

[2] Arabella, wife of the fourth Earl, a Lady-in-waiting to Queen Adelaide. She was a Miss Mackworth Praed.

[3] Daughters of the eleventh Earl of Pembroke. Lady Emma afterwards married the third Viscount de Vesei, and Lady Georgiana the fourth Marquess of Lansdowne.

[4] Daughters of the fifth Earl of Jersey. Lady Sarah afterwards married Prince Nicholas Esterhazy (see p. 190), eldest son of the famous diplomatist. Lady Clementina died unmarried in 1858.

[5] Younger son of Prince and Princess de Lieven. The Prince had been for over twenty years Russian Minister or Ambassador in London ; the Princess was the inveterate correspondent of Earl Grey.

[6] George Guy, afterwards fourth Earl of Warwick, and an A.D.C. to Queen Victoria. Died 1893. At this time he was fifteen years of age.

Lord March,[1] then with Lord Athlone,[2] then with
Lord Fitzroy Lennox,[3] then with Lord Emlyn.[4]
We then went to supper. It was $\frac{1}{2}$ past 11 ; the
King leading me again. I sat between the King and
Queen. We left supper soon. My health was drunk.
I then danced one more quadrille with Lord Paget.
I danced in all *8* quadrilles. We came home at
$\frac{1}{2}$ past 12. I was VERY much amused. . . ..

Sunday, 16th June.—I awoke at 7 and got up at
$\frac{1}{2}$ past 7. At a $\frac{1}{4}$ to 9 we breakfasted. At 10 we
went to prayers. At 10 came Victoire and went to
prayers with us. The service was performed by
Mr. Pittman, as the poor Dean had the misfortune
to lose his little girl Charlotte, of the scarlet fever,
which I was very sorry for. Mr. Pittman gave us a
beautiful sermon. It was taken from the 11th
chapter of the Gospel of St. Luke, 1st verse. At
1 we lunched. Victoire stayed till $\frac{1}{2}$ past 2. At
3 arrived my two cousins, Princes Alexander and
Ernst Würtemberg, sons of Mamma's sister, my
Aunt Antoinette.[5] They are both *extremely tall.*
Alexander is *very handsome* and Ernst has a *very
kind expression.* They are both EXTREMELY *amiable.*

[1] Charles Henry, Earl of March, afterwards sixth Duke of Richmond
and first Duke of Gordon of a new creation. He held several high offices
in Conservative Administrations, being Lord President of the Council
1874–80, and Secretary for Scotland 1885–6. He, like Lord Brooke, was
about fifteen at this time ; and was at Westminster School. In after-
years the Queen relied much upon his excellent political judgment.

[2] George, eighth Earl of Athlone (1820–43). The first Earl was
Godert de Ginkell, the well-known General of William III.

[3] A younger brother of Lord March ; drowned in the *President*
steamer in 1841. He was at this time thirteen years old.

[4] John Frederick, afterwards M.P. for Pembrokeshire and second
Earl Cawdor.

[5] Their father was Alexander, Duke of Würtemberg Prince
Alexander afterwards married Princess Marie, daughter of King Louis
Philippe ; she died in 1839, less than two years after their marriage.

At 4 we went out driving in the open carriage. We paid a visit to Aunt Gloucester, and then drove home through the park. We came home at a ¼ to 6. At a ¼ past 7 we dined. Besides Alexander, Ernst and Charles, Prince Reuss [1] and Sir John dined here. . . .

Thursday, 27th June.—At ½ past 9 we went to the Exhibition of the water-colours, with Alexander and Lehzen in our carriage, and Sir John in another. We met the Duchess of Northumberland there. It is a VERY FINE exhibition. From there we went to the British Gallery, where the works of Sir Joshua Reynolds, West, and Sir Thomas Lawrence are exhibiting. We came home at ½ past 11. At 1 we lunched. At 2 came Lady Stafford with her two little girls, Elizabeth [2] and Evelyn,[3] and Lady Caroline [4] with her little Georgiana. All beautiful children. At ½ past 4 we drove out in the park, and walked home through the gardens. We came home at ½ past 5. At 7 we all dined. Sir John dined here. At a little after 9 we went, with Alexander and Lehzen in our carriage, and Ernst, Charles and Sir John in another carriage following, to the Opera. We came in at the beginning of the 2nd act of *Norma,* in which Madame Pasta sung BEAUTIFULLY. After that Signor Paganini played by himself some variations, most WONDERFULLY ; he is himself a *curiosity.* After that was given the last act of *Otello* ; Desdemona, Madame Malibran,[5] who sang and acted

---

[1] A cousin of the Princess Victoria and of Princes Alexander and Ernst, the mother of the Duchess of Kent, having been a Princess of Reuss-Ebersdorff.

[2] Afterwards Duchess of Argyll.

[3] Afterwards Lady Blantyre.

[4] Lady Caroline Lascelles, and her daughter, afterwards Mrs. Grenfell.

[5] Madame Malibran was now about twenty-five years of age. See *post,* p. 168.

BEAUTIFULLY. After that was performed *La Sylphide* ; Taglioni danced BEAUTIFULLY and looked LOVELY. Fanny Elsler danced also *very well.* We saw the whole of the 1st act and half of the second. It was Laporte's benefit. I was VERY MUCH AMUSED. We came home at ½ past 1. I was soon in bed and asleep. . . .

Monday, 1st July.—I awoke at ½ past 4 and got up at a ¼ past 5. At a ¼ past 6 we all breakfasted. At 7 o'clock we left Kensington Palace, Sir John going in a post-chaise before us, then our post-chaise, then Lehzen's landau, then my Cousins' carriage, then Charles's, then Lady Conroy's, and then our maids'. It is a lovely morning. 5 minutes past 8 —we have just changed horses at Esher. Lynedoch Gardiner [1] brought us a basket full of beautiful flowers. 10 o'clock ; we have just changed horses at Guildford. POOR DEAR LITTLE Dashy could not go with us as he was not quite well, so he is gone with Mason with the horses. 4 minutes past 1 ; we have just left Liphook where we took our luncheon. 5 minutes to 2, we have just changed horses at Petersfield. 5 minutes to 3, we have just changed horses at Horndean. At 4 we arrived at Portsmouth. The streets were lined with soldiers, and Sir Colin Campbell [2] rode by the carriage. Sir Thomas Williams, [3] the Admiral, took us in his barge, on board the *dear Emerald.* The

---

[1] Henry Lynedoch Gardiner, son of General Sir Robert Gardiner. He was afterwards Equerry in Ordinary to Queen Victoria.

[2] Sir Colin Campbell (1792–1863), afterwards F.-M. Lord Clyde, Commander-in-Chief in India. He saw more active service than any British Field-Marshal before or since. No soldier was ever braver, more merciful, and more modest.

[3] Admiral Williams had rendered valuable services in conjunction with the army in the Low Counties, 1794–5 ; he was knighted in 1796, and became G.C.B. in 1831.

Admiral presented some of the officers to us. We stayed about ½ an hour waiting for the baggage to be put on board the steamer, which was to tow us. We then set off and arrived at Cowes at about 7. We were most civilly received. Cowes Castle, the yacht-club, yachts, &c., &c., saluting us. We saw Lord Durham [1] who is staying at Cowes. We drove up in a fly to Norris Castle, where we lodged two years ago, and where we are again living. My cousins and my brother were *delighted* with it. At about ½ past 7 we all dined. Lady Conroy and her family went to their cottage after dinner. . . .

Monday, 8th July.—At about 10 we went on board the *Emerald* with Alexander, Ernst, Lady Charlotte, Lady Conroy, Jane, Victoire, Sir John and Henry. We were towed up to Southampton by the *Medina* steam-packet. It rained several times very hard, and we were obliged to go down into the cabin very often. When we arrived at Southampton, Mamma received an address on board from the Corporation. We then got into the barge and rowed up to the new pier. The crowd was tremendous. We went into a tent erected on the pier, and I was very much fright-ened for fear my cousins and the rest of our party should get knocked about ; however they at last got in. We then got into our barge and went on board the *Emerald* where we took our luncheon. We

---

[1] John George Lambton (1792–1840), the first Baron (and afterwards first Earl of) Durham, son-in-law of Lord Grey, had been Ambassador to St. Petersburg, and was now Lord Privy Seal. Lord Melbourne sent him subsequently to Canada at a critical juncture in the history of British North America. The Ministry afterwards recalled him, but the report which he presented on Canadian affairs is regarded as having laid the foundations of all colonial self-government. He was a statesman of noble, unstained character ; but his high-strung temperament made life difficult both for him and his colleagues.

stayed a little while to see the regatta, which was going on, and then sailed home. It was a very wet afternoon. We came home at ½ past 5. At 7 we dined. Lady Conroy, Jane, Victoire, Sir John, and Henry dined here. . . .

Friday, 12th July.—I awoke at 6 and got up at ½ past 6. At 7 we breakfasted. It was a *sad* breakfast, for us indeed, as my dear cousins were going so soon. At about a ¼ to 8 we walked down our pier with them and there took leave of them, which made us both VERY UNHAPPY. We saw them get into the barge, and watched them sailing away for some time on the beach. They were so amiable and so pleasant to have in the house ; they were *always satisfied, always good humoured* ; Alexander took such care of me in getting out of the boat, and rode next to me ; so did Ernst. They talked about *such interesting things*, about their Turkish Campaign, about Russia, &c., &c. We shall miss them at *breakfast*, at *luncheon*, at *dinner, riding, sailing, driving, walking*, in *fact everywhere*.

About two hours after my cousins had gone, Mamma received the distressing news that my cousins' father, the Duke Alexander of Würtemberg,[1] who had been ill for some time, was dead. I was extremely sorry for them. Mamma immediately dispatched an estafette after them to Dover with the news. At 1 we lunched. It was a dull luncheon. At 4 we went out riding with Lady Charlotte, Lady Conroy, Jane, Victoire, Sir John and Henry. Victoire rode Alice, and Lehzen Isabel. The ride would have appeared to me much pleasanter had Alexander and Ernst been there. We came home at 6. We heard from a servant of ours, who had

---

[1] He was sixty-two years of age. See *ante*, p. 78.

crossed over with them to Portsmouth, that they had had a very quick and good passage and that they had not been at all sick. At 7 we dined. Lady Conroy, Jane, Victoire, Sir John, Edward, and Henry dined here. Here again they were missing. . . .

Thursday, 18*th July.*—At a ¼ to 10 we went on board the *Emerald* with Lady Charlotte, Lady Conroy, Jane, Victoire, Lehzen, and Sir John, and were towed by the *Messenger* steam-packet up to Portsmouth. We then got into the Admiral's barge, and landed in the docks. We then saw from an elevation, the launch of the *Racer,* a sloop of war. We then re-entered the Admiral's barge and went to the *Victory,* his flag-ship. We there received the salute on board. We saw the spot where Nelson fell, and which is covered up with a brazen plate and his motto is inscribed on it, " Every Englishman is expected to do his duty." We went down as low as the tanks, and there tasted the water which had been in there for two years, and which was excellent. We also saw the place where Nelson died. The whole ship is remarkable for its neatness and order. We tasted some of the men's beef and potatoes, which were excellent, and likewise some grog. The company consisted of Lady Williams, the Admiral's lady, Sir Graham and Lady Moore,[1] Mr. and Mrs. Ricardo, Sir Frederick and Lady Maitland,[2] etc., etc. We then partook of a luncheon at the Admiral's House and then returned on board the *Emerald.* We got home by 5. We both wished so much that *dear*

[1] Vice-Admiral Sir Graham Moore (1764–1843), G.C.M.G., afterwards Commander-in-Chief at Plymouth. He had been ordered in 1807–8 to escort the Royal Family of Portugal to Brazil ; he married Dora, daughter of Thomas Eden.

[2] Rear-Admiral Sir Frederick Lewis Maitland (1776–1839). He commanded the *Bellerophon* when Napoleon surrendered after Waterloo.

Alexander and *dear* Ernest had been there, I think it would have amused them. . . .

Friday, 2nd August.—I awoke at about a ¼ to 6 and got up at ½ past 7. At ½ past 8 we all breakfasted. We then saw several ladies and gentlemen. At about ½ past 9 we went on board the *dear little Emerald.* We were to be towed up to Plymouth. Mamma and Lehzen were very sick, and I was sick for about ½ an hour. At 1 I had a hot mutton chop on deck. We passed Dartmouth. At about 4 we approached Plymouth Harbour. It is a magnificent place and the breakwater is wonderful indeed. You pass Mount Edgecumbe, the seat of Lord Mount Edgecumbe.[1] It is beautifully situated. The Admiral, Sir William Hargood,[2] Captain Falkland his flag-captain, and Mr. Yorke[3] came on board. Captain Brown, who is on board the *Caledonia,* and Captain Macay, on board the *Revenge,* also came on board. As we entered the harbour, our dear little *Emerald* ran foul of a hulk, her mast broke and we were in the *greatest danger.* Thank God! the mast did not fall and no one was hurt. But I was *dreadfully* frightened for *Mamma* and for *all.* The poor dear *Emerald* is very much hurt I fear. Saunders was not at all in fault; he saved us by pulling the rope which fixed us to the steamer. We arrived at Plymouth at 5. It is a beautiful town and we were very well received. *Sweet Dash* was under Saunders's arm the whole time, but he never let him drop in all the danger. At 7 we dined. The hotel is very fine indeed. After dinner Sir John saw Saunders, who said that the

[1] Richard (1764–1839), second Earl, Lord Lieutenant of Cornwall.

[2] Sir William Hargood had commanded the *Belleisle* under Nelson at Trafalgar, becoming an Admiral and G.C.B. in 1831.

[3] Captain Charles Philip Yorke, R.N., then M.P. for Cambs., afterwards fourth Earl of Hardwicke.

mast of the *Emerald* was broken in two places, and that we had had the *narrowest escape possible* ; but that she would be repaired and ready for us to go back in her on Tuesday.

Saturday, 3rd August.—At 10 came Sir John Cameron,[1] the Governor, and his officers. At ½ past 10 came Sir William Hargood and his officers and captains. Soon after came Lord Hill, who is over here to inspect the troops, and Sir John Macdonald,[2] Sir Richard Jackson, and Captain Hill. At ½ past 11 Mamma received an address from the Mayor and Corporation of Plymouth, downstairs in a large room full of people. At 12 we went with all our own party to a review of the 89th, the 22nd, and the 84th regiments. Mamma made a speech, and I then gave the colours to the 89th regiment. The names of the two Ensigns to whom I gave the colours are Miles and Egerton. We then saw them march by in line. We then went to the Admiral's house where we had our luncheon, and then proceeded to the docks. We went in the Admiral's barge on board the Admiral's flag-ship, the *St. Joseph*, taken by Lord Nelson from the Spanish, in the battle of St. Vincent. We received a salute on board. She is a magnificent vessel of 120 guns. We saw her lower decks and cabins, which are extremely light, airy, roomy and clean. We then returned in the Admiral's barge, rowed round the *Caledonia* 120 guns, and the *Revenge* 76 guns. We landed at the Dockyard and went home. At 7 we dined. . . .

End of my third Journal-book. Norris Castle, August 11th, 1833. . . .

---

[1] Sir John Cameron had had a distinguished record in the Peninsula. From 1823 to 1833 he commanded the Western District.

[2] Adjutant-General, 1830–50.

Monday, 16*th September.*—At 10 we went on board
the *Emerald* with Lady Catherine, Lady Conroy,
Jane, Lehzen, Victoire, and Sir John, and sailed to
Portsmouth, where we were going to pay a visit to
their Majesties the Queen of Portugal [1] and the
Duchess of Braganza (her step-mother). We got
there at ½ past 11. We entered the Admiral's barge
with Lady Catherine, Lady Conroy, Lehzen, and Sir
John, and were rowed ashore. We landed at the
stairs in the dockyard. Mamma and I got into a
close carriage, and our ladies followed in an open
carriage. The whole way from the dock-yard to
the Admiral's house, where their Majesties reside, was
lined with troops and various bands were placed at
different distances. We were received at the door
by the gentlemen and ladies of the court. Inside the
hall we were met by the Queen and the Duchess.
The Queen led Mamma, and the Duchess followed
leading me into the room. The Queen was in England 4 years ago ; she is only a month older than I
am and is very kind to me. She was then already
very tall for her age, but had a very beautiful figure ;
she is grown very tall but also very stout. She has
a beautiful complexion, and is very sweet and friendly.
She wore her hair in two large curls in front and a
thick fine plait turned up behind. The Empress (or

[1] Donna Maria da Gloria, then aged about fourteen. She was the
daughter of Dom Pedro, who had been proclaimed Emperor of Brazil
in the lifetime of his father, John VI., and abdicated the throne of
Portugal in favour of Donna Maria. Dom Miguel, a younger brother of
Pedro, claimed the throne. Pedro had designed a marriage between
Donna Maria and Miguel, who in 1827 had been appointed Regent,
but, having been himself driven from Brazil by a revolution, Pedro
endeavoured to gain the throne decisively for his daughter. His second
wife, now known as Duchess of Braganza, was sister to Augustus, Duke
of Leuchtenberg, who at the age of twenty-five had married Donna
Maria, then barely sixteen, and died two months later. See p. 110.

Duchess as she is now called) was never before in England. She is only 21 and is very pleasing. She has beautiful blue eyes, and has a fine tall figure. She has black hair and wore ringlets in front and a plait behind. She was simply dressed in a grey watered moire trimmed with blonde. Their Majesties arrived at Portsmouth from Havre on the morning of the 8th of September; and proceeded to Windsor on the 10th, on a visit to the King and Queen, from whence they returned last Saturday, and they intend leaving Portsmouth to-day at 2 o'clock for Lisbon. The Queen and Duchess having desired us to sit down, talked some time with us. The Duchess then went and fetched her little girl, a child of 21 months old. We soon after went, the Queen leading Mamma and the Duchess me in the same manner as before. We returned in the same way. We lunched on board the *Emerald* and then were towed by the *Messenger* home. We came home at 3. . . .

Monday, 14th October.— . . . Ferdinand the 7th of Spain [1] died on the 29th of September, and his young and lovely Queen Christina instantly became Regent for the infant Queen Isabella the 2nd, her daughter, and who is only 3 years old. The Queen has a powerful enemy in Don Carlos and his wife, but she is very courageous and very clever. It is a singular coincidence that there should be a young Queen in Spain as well as in Portugal. At 7 we 4 dined. I stayed up till 9. . . .

[1] The death of Ferdinand without male issue caused a disputed succession in Spain. His brother Don Carlos relied on the Salic Law as established by the Pragmatic Sanction of 1711, which Ferdinand had revoked. Don Carlos and Dom Miguel subsequently entered into an alliance, while the young Queens Maria and Isabella mutually recognised each other, and were supported by England and France.

Monday, 9th December.—At 5 we dined. Sir John dined here. At ½ past 6 we went to the play to Drury Lane with Lady Conroy, Lehzen, and Sir John. It was Shakespear's tragedy of *King John*. The principal characters were : King John, Mr. Macready,[1] who acted *beautifully* ; Prince Arthur, Miss Poole, who acted delightfully ; Hubert, Mr. Bennett who acted well ; Faulconbridge, Mr. Cooper, who also acted well ; Philip King of France, Mr. Diddear ; Louis the Dauphin, Mr. Brendal ; Archduke of Austria, Mr. Thompson ; Queen Elinor, Mrs. Faucit [2] ; the Lady Constance, Mrs. Sloman ; Blanche of Castile, Miss Murray. The second piece was the melo-drama of *The Innkeeper's Daughter*, which is very horrible but *extremely interesting*, but it would take me too much time to relate the story of it. The characters were : Richard, Mr. Cooper, who acted *very well* ; Frankland, Mr. Ayliffe ; Monkton, Mr. Thompson ; Langley, Mr. Tayleure ; Harrop, Mr. Webster,[3] who looked *horrid* but acted well ; he was one of the leading characters in the play ; Edward Harrop, Mr. Richardson ; Wentworth, Mr. Baker; Hans Ketzler, Mr. T. P. Cooke, who acted very well ; Tricksey, Mr. Hughes ; William, Mr. Howell ; White, Mr. East ; Smith, Mr. Henry ; Allsop, Mr. S. Jones ; Mary, Miss Kelly,[4] who acted *quite beautifully* ; she is quite mature. Marian, Mrs. Broad. We came to the very beginning and stayed

[1] William Charles Macready (1793–1851), afterwards successively manager of Covent Garden and Drury Lane Theatres.

[2] An actress, and mother of Helen Faucit.

[3] Benjamin Webster, an excellent and humorous comedian from about 1819 to 1874.

[4] Frances Maria Kelly (1790–1882), for many years a popular favourite at Drury Lane, and a friend of Charles and Mary Lamb.

to the very end. We came home at 10 minutes past 12. I was VERY MUCH AMUSED. . . .

Thursday, 26th December.—I awoke at 7 and got up at 8. At 9 we breakfasted. At 1 we lunched. At ½ past 2 came Captain Burnes who has lately travelled over Northern East India. He gave us some very interesting accounts. He likewise brought with him to show us, his servant, a native of Cabul, dressed in his native dress. He is called Gulam Hussein ; is of a dark olive complexion and had a dress of real Cashmere made in the beautiful valley of Cashmere.

Friday, 27th December.—At ½ past 2 came Mr. T. Griffiths to lecture on Physics. The plan of the lecture was : Introductory—Objects of Alchymy, viz. Transmutation of Metals, the Elixir of Life, and the Universal Solvent ;—Objects of Chemistry, viz. the investigation of every substance in nature— Chemistry a science of experiment—Results of chemical action—Arts and Manufactures dependent on chemistry—Importance of Heat as a chemical agent—Its action on various substances—Conductors and Non-conductors of Heat—Nature of Flame. All these different subjects were illustrated by very curious and interesting experiments. It was over at ½ past 3. Lehzen, Lady Conroy, Victoire, the Dean, and Sir John were likewise present. I was *very much amused.* . . .

Monday, 30th December.—I awoke at 7 and got up at 8. At 9 we breakfasted. At 1 we lunched. At ½ past 2 came Mr. Walker to lecture. The plan of the lecture was : Properties of Matter—Particles infinitely small, divisible, and hard—Cohesion—Capillary attraction, Magnetic attraction, &c., &c.—Repulsion exhibited in various ways, as counteracting the preceding influences — Recapitulation — Mechanics : Gravity considered, its effects on descending and projected bodies—National weights and measures— Vis inertia, momentum, what—Mechanical Powers, explained by various machines, applications, &c. &c.—Draft of horses—Defect of wheel carriages, road, &c. pointed out—Some improvements suggested—Removal of Great Stone of St. Petersburg. The lecture lasted till a $\frac{1}{4}$ to 4. Lehzen, Lady Conroy, the Dean, and Sir John were present besides ourselves. At a $\frac{1}{4}$ to 7 we dined. Sir John dined here. At a $\frac{1}{4}$ past 8 we went with Lehzen, Lady Conroy, and Sir John to the play to Covent Garden. We came in for the last scene of *Gustavus*, the Masqued Ball, and stayed the whole of the pantomime, which is called *Old Mother Hubbard and her Dog ; or Harlequin and Tales of the Nursery.'"* The scenery was very pretty and the principal characters were : Venus, Miss Lee ; Cupid, Miss Poole who appeared in three other dresses : as a peasant boy, as a drummer, and as Mother Hubbard, and she looked *very* pretty and acted very well indeed. Old Mother Hubbard, Mr. Wieland ; Schock (her dog), Master W. Mitchinson. The Duchess Griffinwinkle Blowsabella (afterwards Pantaloon), Mr. Barnes. King Rundytundy O (afterwards Dandy Lover), Mr. W. H. Payne. The Princess Graciosa (afterwards Columbine), a very pretty person, Miss Foster. Prince Percineth (afterwards Harlequin) Mr. Ellar. Head Cook (afterwards Clown) Mr. T. Mathews. The panorama at the end was also pretty.

INTRODUCTORY NOTE TO CHAPTER III

THE year 1834 was spent very quietly by Princess Victoria. Her education progressed in simple and placid grooves, but her visits to the opera and the theatre became more frequent. She became devoted to Italian opera, and formed an attachment to music of the Italian school from which even Prince Albert, steeped as he was in German music, never contrived to wean her. She accepted then, and ever afterwards, Giulia Grisi as the supreme singer and artist. From the month of June, when she was present at a Festival in Westminster Abbey, to the end of the autumn, she devoted herself, at St. Leonards and at Tunbridge Wells, to the study of music and singing and to practising upon the harp.

This year the Whig Ministry of Lord Grey tottered and fell. In July King William, much to the surprise of politicians on both sides, entrusted Lord Melbourne with the formation of a Government. The King wanted a coalition and made a tentative effort to achieve it, but he did not succeed in obtaining the co-operation of either Party. It was not anticipated that Lord Melbourne's Government could last. In the month of November Lord Spencer died, and Lord Althorp, his son, who was Chancellor of the Exchequer, seized with unrestrained delight the opportunity to retire from public life. Lord Melbourne thereupon resigned, and Sir Robert Peel, returning hurriedly from Rome, formed an administration likewise destined to be short-lived.

If King William had some difficulty in finding a stable Ministry, his brother-monarch across the Channel was in no better plight. The Parliamentary difficulties in France reached a stage of such complexity, that it looked for a moment as if the French monarchy itself might succumb to the vehemence of political and partisan strife. The Citizen-King found it necessary to employ 100,000 troops to keep in awe the three cities of Paris, Marseilles, and Lyons. At this moment died Lafayette, one of the last links between the opening and concluding discords of the French Revolution. It was during this year that two foreigners of eminence, long resident in England, finally disappeared from London society. Princess Lieven left the Russian, and Talleyrand the French Embassy.

This year, too, saw the destruction, by fire, of the old Houses of Parliament, associated with so many historic memories. None of these events, however, caused a ripple upon the surface of the little Princess's secluded life at Kensington.

CHAPTER III

1834

Thursday, 16th January.—About a fortnight **or** three weeks ago I received the Order of Maria Louisa, accompanied by a very flattering letter from Her Majesty the Queen Regent of Spain, in the name of her daughter Queen Isabel the 2nd. Having some time ago asked for the handwriting of Her Majesty for my collection, the Queen hearing of it, sent me the Order accompanied by a very gracious letter. The Order is a violet and white ribbon, to which is suspended (en négligé) an enamel sort of star, and in high dress one superbly studded with diamonds.[1]

Sunday, 13th April.—At 10 we went to prayers with Lady Theresa[2] and Lehzen. The service was performed by the Dean, who gave us likewise a very good sermon. It was taken from the 3rd chapter of Acts, 23rd verse : " For Moses truly said unto the fathers, a Prophet shall the Lord your God raise up unto you of your brethren, like unto me ; him shall ye hear in all things whatsoever he shall say unto you. And it shall come to pass, that every soul, which will not hear that prophet, shall be destroyed

[1] This was the first of many Foreign Orders received by Queen Victoria. They have been carefully collected and arranged by King George and Queen Mary, and are displayed in Queen Mary's audience room in Windsor Castle.

[2] Lady Theresa Fox-Strangways, elder daughter of the third Earl of Ilchester, afterwards wife of the ninth Lord Digby.

from among the people." At 1 we lunched. At 7
we 3 and Lady Theresa also dined. After dinner came
Aunt Sophia. I stayed up till a ¼ to 9.

Monday, 14th April.—I awoke at 7 and got up
at ½ past 7. At ½ past 8 we all breakfasted. As I
am now about to return to my usual studies, I must
not omit to mention how very anxious my dear
Mamma was throughout my indisposition, and how
unceasing *dear* Lehzen was in her attentions and
care to me. . . .

Saturday, 19th April.—I awoke at 7 and got up
at 8. At 9 we breakfasted. At ½ past 9 came the
Dean till ½ past 10. At 12 we went out walking.
At 1 we lunched. At ½ past 2 came the Duchess of
Northumberland. At 3 came Lady Robert Grosvenor [1] with her little girl Victoria. She is a dear
little child, so clever and intelligent. At 4 came
Mrs. Anderson till 5. At 6 we dined. At a ¼ past
7 we went with Lady Conroy, Lehzen and Sir John
to the Opera. We came in just at the beginning
of the Opera of *Anna Boulena*. The characters
were : Anna Boulena, Mdlle. Guiletta Grisi.[2] She
is a most beautiful singer and actress and is likewise
very young and pretty. She sang *beautifully* throughout but particularly in the last scene when she is
mad, which she *acted* likewise *beautifully*. Giovanna
Seymour, Mrs. E. Seguin, who sings very well. Enrico,
Signor Tambourini, who sang beautifully. Ricardo
Percy, M. Ivanhoff, who sings very well. He has a
very pleasing though not a very strong voice. Between the acts there was a divertissement, in which

---

[1] Afterwards Lady Ebury. Sister of the first Earl Cowley. See p. 50.
[2] Giulia Grisi (1815–69) made her début at Florence, aged fourteen.
Théophile Gautier said of her that under her spell what was only an
opera became a tragedy and a poem. She first appeared in London
in 1834. She was afterwards married to the Count of Candia (Mario).

Mdlle. Theresa Elsler danced a pas de deux with
Mons. T. Guerinot, and Mdlle. Fanny Elsler with
M. Perrot. Mdlle. Fanny danced beautifully ; she
ran up the stage on the tips of her toes in a most
extraordinary manner. She likewise made many
other pretty little steps. M. Perrot (whom I had
never seen before) danced likewise quite beautifully.
We went away as soon as the 2nd act of the opera
was over. We came home at 12. I was VERY
MUCH AMUSED INDEED ! . . .

Saturday, 26th April.—I awoke at 7 and got up
at a ¼ to 8. At 9 we breakfasted. At ½ past 9
came the Dean till 11. The Duchess of Northumber-
land was present. At 12 we went to pay a visit to
Aunt Gloucester. At 1 we lunched. At 3 came
Mr. Steward till 4. At 4 came Mrs. Anderson till 5.
At 6 we dined. Sir John dined here. At a ¼ past 7
we went with Lehzen and Sir John to the Opera.
We came in just at the beginning of the opera of
Otello. The characters were : Otello, Signor Rubini
who sang quite beautifully and acted very well.
Iago, Signor Tambourini who sung likewise *beautifully.* Rodrigo, M. Ivanhoff who sung *very well.*
—— Signor Zuchello. Desdemona, Signora Giuletta
Grisi. She *sang* and *acted* quite beautifully ! and
looked lovely. She acted and sang *most sweetly
and beautifully* in the last scene ; and also in the
two trios in the 1st and 2nd acts. When the opera
was over she was called for, and she came on, led
by Rubini. At that moment a wreath of roses with
a small roll of paper inside was thrown on the stage ;
Rubini picked it up and placed it on her head.
They were very much applauded. We came away
directly after the opera. Lord Ilchester[1] and Lady

[1] Henry Stephen, third Earl (1787–1812).

Theresa joined us there. We came home at a ¼ to 12. I was VERY MUCH AMUSED INDEED ! ! ! . . .

Monday, 28th April.—I awoke at 7 and got up at a ¼ to 8. At a ¼ to 9 we breakfasted. At ½ past 9 came the Dean till a ¼ past 11. The Duchess of Northumberland was present. At 12 Lehzen and I drove out. At 1 we lunched. At 3 came Mr. Steward till 4. I then went to the painting room. At 7 we dined. After dinner while we were playing on the piano, arrived Uncle Ferdinand [1] and Charles.[2] Uncle Ferdinand is Mamma's second brother and she had not seen him for *16 years!* I have now seen all my uncles, except Uncle Mensdorff [3] (Aunt Sophie's husband), for Mamma's eldest brother, Uncle Ernest,[4] was here 3 years ago, the same year Uncle Leopold went to Belgium. Charles is looking very well and is grown much fatter. Uncle Ferdinand is not at all like my other Uncles. He is fair. It is a great pleasure for me to see both Uncle Ferdinand and Charles. I stayed up till 9. . . .

Thursday, 5th June.—At 11 arrived my DEAREST sister Feodora whom I had not seen for *6 years.* She is accompanied by Ernest, her husband, and her two eldest children Charles and Eliza. Dear Feodora looks very well but is grown much stouter since I

[1] Prince Ferdinand of Saxe-Coburg (1786–1851), uncle of the Prince Consort.

[2] Charles Emich, Prince Leiningen, son of the Duchess of Kent by her first husband, and half-brother of Princess Victoria.

[3] Emmanuel, Count Mensdorff-Pouilly (1777–1862), husband of Princess Sophia, eldest sister of the Prince Consort's father and of the Duchess of Kent. An emigrant from France in 1793, he attained high rank in the Austrian service. His sons were intimate companions of the Prince Consort.

[4] Ernest, Duke of Saxe-Coburg (1784–1844), father of the Prince Consort.

saw her.   She was married on the **18th of** February
1828 and went away to Germany a week after and
she never came here again since.   Hohenlohe looks
also very well.   As for the children they are the
DEAREST little loves I ever saw.   Charles is 4 years
and a half old.   He is very tall and is a sweet good-
tempered little fellow.   He is not handsome but
he is a very nice-looking boy.   He has light blue
eyes and fair hair.   Eliza is 3 years and a half old ;
she is also very tall and is a *perfect* little beauty.
She has immense dark brown eyes and a very small
mouth and light brown hair.   She is very clever
and amusing.   We then showed her their rooms,
and afterwards, at ½ past 12, we went to see the
dear children take their dinner.   They took it with
Mr. Rol, Charles's tutor.   At 1 we all lunched, that
is to say, Mamma, dear Feodore, Ernst Hohenlohe,
Charly, Lehzen, and I.   After luncheon, Feodore
and the others went upstairs.   At 2 Charles and
Eliza came down and stayed with us alone.   They
are *dear sweet* children ;   not at all shy and *so* good ;
they never hurt or spoil anything.   At a little after
2 came Lady Westminster.[1]   The *dear* children
behaved *so* well.   They are so very sensible.   They
staid till after 3.   Eliza speaks German and French
very nicely.   She has a French Swiss bonne called
Louise who speaks French with her.   At ½ past 4
we went out driving with *dear* Feodore and Lehzen.
We came home at 6.   At 7 we dined.   Besides
dearest Feodore, Ernest, Charles and Lehzen, Sir
J. Conroy dined here.   When the 2nd course was
put on, Charles and Eliza came in, and staid there.
They were very funny and amusing and talked
immensely.   They staid up till ½ past 8.   At ½ past 9

[1] See *ante*, p. 49.

saw her. She was married on the 18th of February 1828 and went away to Germany a week after and she never came here again since. Hohenlohe looks also very well. As for the children they are the DEAREST little loves I ever saw. Charles is 4 years and a half old. He is very tall and is a sweet good-tempered little fellow. He is not handsome but he is a very nice-looking boy. He has light blue eyes and fair hair. Eliza is 3 years and a half old ; she is also very tall and is a *perfect* little beauty. She has immense dark brown eyes and a very small mouth and light brown hair. She is very clever and amusing. We then showed her their rooms, and afterwards, at ½ past 12, we went to see the dear children take their dinner. They took it with Mr. Rol, Charles's tutor. At 1 we all lunched, that is to say, Mamma, dear Feodore, Ernst Hohenlohe, Charly, Lehzen, and I. After luncheon, Feodore and the others went upstairs. At 2 Charles and Eliza came down and stayed with us alone. They are *dear sweet* children ; not at all shy and *so* good ; they never hurt or spoil anything. At a little after 2 came Lady Westminster.[1] The *dear* children behaved *so* well. They are so very sensible. They staid till after 3. Eliza speaks German and French very nicely. She has a French Swiss bonne called Louise who speaks French to her. At ½ past 4 we went out driving with dear Feodore and Lehzen. We came home at 6. At 7 we dined. Besides dearest Feodore, Ernest, Charles and Lehzen, Sir J. Conroy dined here. When the 2nd course was put on, Charles and Eliza came in, and staid there. They were very funny and amusing and talked immensely. They staid up till ½ past 8. At ½ past 9

---

[1] See *ante.* p. 49.

H. S. H. Princess Adelaide
of Hohenlohe - Langenburg
from a portrait by Gutekunst

we went to the Opera with Ernst Hohenlohe, Charles,
Lehzen, and Sir John Conroy, poor *dear* Feodora
being too tired to go. We came in at about the
middle of the 2nd act of Rossini's Opera of *L'Assiedo
di Corrinto*. It is in 3 acts. The principal characters are: Mahomet (Emperor of the Turks),
Signor Tamburini, who sang beautifully and looked
very well. Cleomene (Governor of Corrinto), Mons.
Ivanoff who likewise sang very well. Nioclene, Signor
Rubini who also sang quite beautifully. Pamira,
Mdlle. Giuletta Grisi, who sang quite beautifully and
acted and looked *extremely well*. It was Laporte's
benefit, and the first time this opera was ever performed in this country. Then followed the 2nd
act of *La Sylphide* in which Taglioni made her first
appearance since an absence of some months. She
danced quite beautifully, quite as if she flew in the
air, so gracefully and lightly. She looked also very
well. There was also a Pas de Trois danced by
Mdlles. Theresa and Fanny Elsler and Mons. Theodore. Mdlle. Fanny danced *beautifully*. We came
home at 10 minutes to 1. There is only one thing
wanting to my happiness in being with my dear
sister and her children, that is that I cannot share
that happiness with one whom I love so very dearly
but who is far far away—that is my *most dear*
Uncle Ferdinand. . . .

Wednesday, 11th June.—*Dear* little Eliza and
Charles came down to breakfast. Eliza came into
my room and staid with me for some time. She
is a dear good little girl. At 1 we lunched. Eliza
came again into my room and staid with me for
nearly an hour. At 3 we went with Lady Flora
Hastings [1] and Lehzen to Windsor on a visit to

---

[1] Eldest daughter of Francis, first Marquess of Hastings, Lady of

their Majesties. We were very sorry to leave the
dear children. At a ¼ past 5 we arrived at Windsor.
The Queen, *dear* Feodore, Ernest and several ladies
and gentlemen of the court, received us at the door
and conducted us upstairs to the Queen's room, where
the King was. I was very happy to see my *dear*
sister again. Some time afterwards the Queen conducted us to our rooms which are very handsome.
At 7 we dined. Besides the King and Queen,
Feodore and Ernest, Mamma and I, Lady Flora and
Lehzen, there dined there : George Cambridge, the
Duke and Duchess of Richmond,[1] the Duchess of
Northumberland, the Duke of Grafton,[2] the Duke
of Dorset,[3] the Duke of Cleveland,[4] the Marquis
and Marchioness of Conyngham,[5] Lady Clinton
(Lady of the Bedchamber in Waiting), Lord and

the Bedchamber to the Duchess of Kent. This unfortunate lady
died in 1839.
  [1] Charles, fifth Duke (1791–1860). As Lord March he is often mentioned in the Duke of Wellington's correspondence. He was one of
the very few male human beings ever alluded to by the Iron Duke
in terms of affection. The Duchess was Caroline, daughter of the
Marquess of Anglesey.
  [2] George Henry (1760–1844), fourth Duke. An obscure Whig po-
tentate.
  [3] Charles, fifth Duke, but fourteenth Earl of Dorset, K.G. Master of
the Horse in various Tory Administrations. On his death, unmarried, in
1843, his honours (including the Earldom of Middlesex) became extinct.
A favourite of George IV. One of the first gentlemen jockeys. He
and his brother Germaine were famous at Newmarket as race riders.
He established Bibury races. He was of tiny physique, but smart,
and a great favourite with ladies.
  [4] William Harry, first Duke of Cleveland, of a new creation, a great-
grandson in the male line of a daughter of Barbara Palmer, Duchess of
Cleveland. He died in 1842, and his income was computed at £110,000
per annum. See *ante*, p. 68.
  [5] Francis, second Marquess (1797–1876), who, three years later,
brought to the Princess at Kensington the news of her accession.
Lady Conyngham was a daughter of Lord Anglesey.

Lady Frederick Fitzclarence,[1] Lord Denbigh,[2] Lady
Sophia Sidney,[3] Miss Eden,[4] Miss Hope Johnston,
Miss Wilson, Lord Albemarle,[5] Sir Frederick Watson,
Colonel Lygon,[6] Mr. Wood,[7] &c., &c. The Queen
went first with Ernest, then came the King who
led Mamma and I in, and then came Feodore with
the Duke of Richmond. The rest I do not recollect.
I sat between the King and the Duke of Dorset. I
stayed up till ½ past 9.

Thursday, 12th June.—I awoke at 7 and got up
at a ¼ to 8. At ½ past 9 we breakfasted, with the
King, the Queen, Feodore, Ernest, George Cambridge,
the Duchess of Northumberland, and Lady Clinton.
All the other ladies breakfasted together. We then
went into the Queen's room. At a ¼ past 12 we
went to Ascot Races with the whole company in
9 carriages. In the first went the King, the Queen,
Mamma and I. In the second Feodore, the Duchess
of Richmond, the Duchess of Northumberland and
Lady Clinton. In the third Lady Flora, Lady
Sophia Sydney, the Duke of Richmond, and the

[1] Second son of William IV. and Mrs. Jordan. The eldest son was
created Earl of Munster, 1831 ; the younger children (except those who
had attained higher rank by marriage) were granted the style of younger
children of a marquess. Lady Frederick was a daughter of the Earl
of Glasgow.

[2] William Basil Percy (1796–1865), seventh Earl of Denbigh,
Chamberlain to Queen Adelaide.

[3] Lady Sophia Fitzclarence, daughter of William IV. She married
Sir Philip Sidney, afterwards created Lord De l'Isle and Dudley of
Penshurst.

[4] Emily, sister of the second Lord Auckland.

[5] See *ante*, p. 69.

[6] Edward, fourth son of the first Earl Beauchamp.

[7] Afterwards Sir Charles Wood (1800–85) and first Viscount Halifax.
Married the daughter of Charles, Earl Grey. He served in many
administrations ; finally as Secretary of State for India and Lord Privy
Seal. A typical Whig statesman of high probity and wisdom.

Duke of Cleveland. In the fourth Lehzen, Miss Hope Johnston, the Duke of Grafton, and the Duke of Dorset. How all the others went I do not know. At about 1 we arrived on the race course and entered the King's stand with all our party. The races were very good and there was an immense concourse of people there of all ranks. At about ½ past 2 we had luncheon. At a little after 6 we left the stand and returned to the castle in the same way as we came except that, as it rained very hard, we came home in shut carriages. At 7 we arrived at the castle. At ½ past 7 we dined. The company at dinner were the same as yesterday with the exception of Lord and Lady Conyngham not dining here, and a few other gentlemen having dined here. We went in in the same way. I sat between the King and the Duke of Cleveland. I stayed up till a ¼ to 11. I was very much amused indeed at the races. . . .

Sunday, 27th July.—At 9 we breakfasted. How sad I felt at breakfast not to see the door open and DEAR Feodore come in smiling and leading her dear little girl; and not to get the accustomed morning kiss from her. At 11 we went to the chapel with Lehzen, Lady Conroy, and Victoire. The Bishop of London preached a very fine sermon. Victoire Conroy stayed till ½ past 2. At 1 we lunched. I missed dear Feodore here again terribly. I miss her so much to-day. She used to be with me so much on Sunday always. We used to talk together so pleasantly. Last Sunday afternoon she painted in my room. At ½ past 3 we went with Lehzen to visit Aunt Gloucester, and then drove home through the park. How dull that drive appeared to me without dear Feodore. We came home at ½ past 5.

At 7 we dined. After dinner came Aunt Sophia. We passed a sad dull evening. I stayed up till a ¼ to 9. . . .

Sunday, 5th October.—. . . The news were received a few days ago that Dom Pedro, Regent of Portugal,[1] was dead. He expired on the 24th instant, at the age of 35. His daughter, Donna Maria, the young Queen, though only 15, is declared of age and able to govern by herself. The lovely young Empress is left a widow at the age of 22 only. It is a sad situation both for the young Queen and the poor Empress, in whom both I take the greatest interest as I know them personally. I saw Dom Pedro when he was in England about 3 years ago. At 11 we went to church. At 1 we lunched. At ½ past 3 we went out driving with Lady Flora and Lehzen, in the pony-carriage. We came home in the large carriage at 6. At 7 we dined. Lady Conroy, Jane, Victoire, Sir J., Messrs. E., S., and H. C. dined here. I stayed up till ½ past 9. . . .

ST. LEONARDS, *Wednesday, 4th November.*—I said in my last journal book that I would describe in this book all what passed yesterday. We reached Battle Abbey at about a ¼ to 1. We were received at the door by Lady Webster.[2] Battle Abbey was built by King William the Conqueror and stands on the site where the famous battle of Hastings was fought. The place is still preserved where Harold fell. She showed us first into a large hall supposed to be the highest in England. There are portraits of King

---

[1] See *ante,* p. 86.

[2] Charlotte, daughter of Robert Adamson of Westmeath and wife of Sir Godfrey Vassal Webster, of Battle Abbey, formerly M.P. for Sussex. Sir Godfrey's mother, Elizabeth Vassal, eloped from her husband with Lord Holland, and was the famous " Old Madagascar " of Holland House coteries.

I—8*

Charles the 2nd, King William the 3rd, and Queen Anne in it, &c. &c. There is also a very large picture of the battle of Hastings. Some old suits of armour are also in the hall. We saw also what were the cloisters now turned into a room. We saw the Beggars' Hall, a curious walk of the monks, and the garden. We lastly partook of some refreshment in a very pretty room in which there was a picture of the Emperor Napoleon, not full length, only to the waist; which is said to be very like. The outside of the abbey is very fine too. We left it again at ½ past 1. The tenants again accompanied us till Broadeslowe. There some gentlemen from Hastings met us and accompanied us to St. Leonards. We passed under an arch formed of laurels and decorated with flowers and inscriptions. As soon as we passed the 2nd arch the Mayor got out of his carriage and came to our door asking leave to precede us in his carriage. An immense concourse of people walking with the carriage. The mayor and aldermen preceding us in carriages as also a band of music. Throughout Hastings the houses were decorated with flowers, ribands and inscriptions, and arches of flowers and laurels. Ladies and children waving handkerchiefs and laurels on the balconies and at the windows. Cries of " Welcome, welcome, Royal visitors," were constantly heard. We reached Hastings at ½ past 2, and it was 4 o'clock before we arrived at our house at St. Leonards. It was indeed a most splendid reception. We stepped out on the balcony and were loudly cheered. One sight was extremely pretty. Six fishermen in rough blue jackets, red caps and coarse white aprons, preceded by a band, bore a basket ornamented with flowers, full of fish as a present for us. We found *dear*

Dashy in perfect health. Our house is very comfortable. At 6 we dined. Lady Conroy, Jane, Victoire, Messrs. E., S., H., and Sir J. C. dined here. After 8 the fireworks began and lasted till 9. They were very fine. I stayed up till 9.

Thursday, 5th November.—I awoke this morning at 7 and got up at ½ past 7. At 9 we breakfasted. At 12 Mamma received an address from the Mayor, Corporation, and Inhabitants of Hastings and St. Leonards. After 1 we lunched. At 7 we dined. Lady Conroy, Jane, Victoire, Messrs. E., S., and Sir J. C. dined here.

Tuesday, 11th November.— . . . At ½ past 11 we went out driving in the barouche with Lady Flora and Lehzen. We got out and walked and sent the barouche home. We afterwards got into the close landau with a postilion and horse in hand. As we came to the commencement of the town where a seminary is to be built, the hand-horse kicked up and getting entangled in the traces fell down, pulling the other with it; the horse with the postilion however instantly recovered itself but the other remained on the ground kicking and struggling most violently. Two gentlemen very civilly came and held the horse's head down while we all got out as fast as possible. I called for poor dear little Dashy who was in the rumble; Wood (our footman) took him down and I ran on with him in my arms calling Mamma to follow, Lehzen and Lady Flora followed us also. They then cut the traces, the horse still struggling violently. The other horse which had been quite quiet, being frightened by the other's kicking, backed and fell over into a foundation pit, while Wood held him, and he (Wood) with difficulty prevented himself from falling; the horse recovering

himself ran after us and we instantly ran behind a
low stone wall ; but the horse went along the road,
and a workman took him and gave him to Wood.
The other horse had ceased kicking and got up.
We ought to be *most grateful* to Almighty God for
His merciful providence in thus preserving us, for
it was a *very narrow escape.* Both Wood and Bacle-
berry behaved very well indeed. The names of the
two gentlemen who held the horse's head are Rev.
Mr. Gould and Mr. Peckham Micklethwaite.[1] The
latter I am sorry to say was hurt, but not very
materially. The poor horse is cut from head to
foot ; but the other is not at all hurt only very much
frightened. We walked home. . . .

Sunday, 30th November.— . . . We went to church
with Lady Flora and Lehzen. Mr. Randolph preached
a most beautiful sermon. It was taken from the
6th chapter of St. Paul's 2nd Epistle to the Corinthians, 1st and 2nd verses. " We then, as workers
together with Him, beseech you also that ye receive
not the grace of God in vain. For He saith, I have
heard thee in a time accepted, and in the day of
salvation have I succoured thee : behold, now is
the accepted time ; behold, now is the day of salvation." At 1 we lunched. At 3 came Victoire
Conroy till a ¼ past 6. At 7 we dined. Jane,
Victoire, Messrs. E., H., and Sir J. C. dined here.

Tuesday, 2nd December.—I awoke at 7 and got
up at ½ past 7. We received this morning the news
that my poor Uncle, the Duke of Gloucester,[2] was

---

[1] He was made a baronet in 1838 for this act. See *post*, p. 355.

[2] William Frederick (1776–1834), second Duke, was the son of William
Henry, first Duke, by Maria, Countess-Dowager Waldegrave, illegiti-
mate daughter of Edward Walpole, a younger son of the great Minister.
The Duke was an inoffensive man of quiet and mild disposition,

dead. He expired on Sunday evening, the 30th of
November, 1834, at 20 minutes to 7. I am very
sorry that we have lost him as he was always a
most affectionate and *kind* Uncle to me. Aunt
Mary, I hear, bears her loss wonderfully. Poor
Aunt Sophia Matilda, his only sister and who was
excessively fond of him, is dreadfully distressed at
losing her only brother. But her piety will enable
her to bear this great loss. He was so kind to
think of us the morning before he died. Aunt S.
Matilda told him that we had asked how he was,
upon which he answered, " Tell them that I say,
God bless them, and that I love them." This kind
message proved the quiet state of mind he was in.
He showed such piety, such peace and resignation,
that that proved a great comfort to his poor sister.
He was in his 59th year. . . .

Tuesday, 23rd December.— . . . I received from
dear Uncle Leopold this morning some most interesting autographs which are : Louis Seize's, Marie
Antoinette's, Henri IV.'s, the Duke of Marlborough's,
the Empress Maria Theresa's and her husband's,
and Lafayette's. . . .

Sunday, 28th December.—I awoke at 7 and got
up at 20 minutes to 8. At 9 we breakfasted. At
11 we went to church with Lady Flora and Lehzen.
Mr. Randolph preached a very fine sermon. It
was taken from the 1st chapter of St. Matthew,
21st verse : "And she shall bring forth a Son, and
thou shalt call His name Jesus : for He shall save
His people from their sins." At ½ past 1 we lunched.
I forgot to mention that I received this morning a

familiarly known as " Silly Billy." He married his cousin, Princess
Mary, daughter of George III. He was proud of his rank, but of
little else. See *ante*, p. 65.

very kind letter from dear Uncle Leopold, accompanied by a beautiful shawl and the autographs of Louis XV., his Queen, Marie Leczinska, and the Dauphin, father to Louis XVI. At $\frac{1}{2}$ past 2 we went out with Lady Flora and Lehzen and came home after 3. . . .

INTRODUCTORY NOTE TO CHAPTER IV

THE Princess attached importance to this year of her life. It appeared to her that she benefited more fully by her lessons, and began to realise their importance. About a month after her birthday she was confirmed at the Chapel Royal, St. James's, by the Archbishop of Canterbury. She was impressed by the solemnity of the occasion and frightened by the austerity of Archbishop Howley. This year marked an epoch in ways other than spiritual. She was allowed more freely to mix with her mother's guests. Personages of distinction were asked to meet her, and she had an opportunity of seeing some of the more eminent of those who were to be her future subjects, although she had scant opportunity of getting to know them well.

She went to Ascot this year in the Royal Procession, and then, in the autumn, her mother arranged for her a Progress on the lines of that which is recorded in her Journals of 1832. There is nothing, however, to show that she was alive to the trend of public events. The existence of Lord Melbourne's second Ministry was precarious. It was said that Lord Melbourne had against him the King, the Church, the Bar, the Agricultural and Monied interest, and a large minority in the House of Commons ; whereas he only had in his favour a small majority in the House of Commons, the manu-facturing towns, and a portion of the rabble. This was the Tory analysis of the political situation in 1835. " Threatened men and threatened Ministries enjoy a long life," and Lord Melbourne's was no exception.

The Princess was in frequent communication by letter with her Uncle, King Leopold. He sent her many interesting auto-graphs for the collection she at that time was forming. They corresponded about books. It was he who recommended her Sully's *Memoirs*, which, as her Journals show, she assiduously read, and he now and then referred in admonitory terms to her future regal responsibilities and duties.

On one occasion he sent her an extract from a French Memoir containing a severe criticism on the political character of Queen Anne, to which she replied that as he had endeavoured to point out to her what a Queen " ought not to be," she hoped he would give her some idea of what a Queen " ought to be." Those who are familiar with the character and disposition of King Leopold can imagine that he responded willingly to the invitation. It was upon this note that the year 1835 came to an end.

CHAPTER IV

1835

Monday, 5th January.—I quite forgot to mention that on the morning of the 20th of November a ship laden with either coal or chalk sank, but all the crew came off safe. Lieutenant Gilley and five men put off in a boat from the 3rd Martello Tower, in hopes of being able to save some of the goods of the sunken ship. The sea was very high, the boat slight and over-loaded, and they had scarcely left the shore when the boat was upset and they were *all six drowned*! The poor sister of the Lieutenant is residing here. Three of the poor men were married and left their poor widows (all young) plunged in the greatest grief. The body of Weeks, one of the married men and who had 3 children, was found two days after, at Pevensey. The poor Lieutenant's body was only found last Sunday, the 28th December, quite near here; and one of the other married men, called Conely, who had 4 children, was found the next morning near Hastings; and Andrews, the last married man, who had only been married a very short time, was found on Wednesday night, the 31st December, in the same place. It was a great gratification to the poor widows that their husbands' bodies have been found. We saw two of them at a distance the other day. They are all very decent-looking, tidy and nice

people. At a ¼ to 12 we went out walking with
Lehzen till 1. As we walked along by the towers
we met Mrs. Weeks, one of the widows, with her
little girl. She had a widow-cap and bonnet on,
and a Scotch cloak. She looks as pale as death but
has a mild sweet expression. . . .

Saturday, 24th January.—I awoke at 7 and got
up at a ¼ past 8. At ½ past 9 we breakfasted. At
10 came the Dean till 20 minutes to 11. It was
yesterday *15 years* that it pleased God to take my
most beloved Papa from us. Alas! *I* was but 6
months when this affliction came upon us ; and I
therefore never had the happiness to know him. . . .

Tuesday, 27th January.—I awoke at ½ past 7,
got up at a ¼ past 8. At ½ past 9 we breakfasted.
At 1 we lunched. I ought to have mentioned that
besides my lessons with the Dean (and also when
my other masters come) I have many occupations
with Lehzen. And now, though we are all in the
bustle of packing, I am constantly employed by
myself in various ways ; and I read French History
to Lehzen, and one of Racine's tragedies with her
in the afternoons which I delight in. I *love* to be
employed ; I *hate* to be *idle*. . . .

Thursday, 29th January.—I awoke at ½ past 5
and got up at 7. At 8 we all breakfasted. At a
¼ to 9 we left St. Leonards. Dear Lehzen, Lady
Flora, Lady Conroy &c. following in another carriage.
All our acquaintances were out to see us go (except
Mr. and Lady Mary Dundas). . . . For some reasons
I am sorry we have left St. Leonards, which are, the
nice walks, the absence of fogs, and looking out of
my window and seeing the people walk on the
esplanade, and seeing the sun rise and set, which
was quite beautiful. The rising began by the sky

being quite pink and blending softly into a bright blue, and the sun rose by degrees from a little red streak to a ball of red copper. The setting began by the whole horizon being orange, crimson and blue, and the sun sunk down a ball of fiery gold dyeing the sands crimson. But then again my reasons for *not* being sorry to go are, my not sleeping well there, my not having been well, and the roaring of the sea. We changed horses first at Battle, then at Stony Crouch, then at Woodgate, which was quite near *dear* Tunbridge, then at Sevenoaks, and lastly at Bromley. We reached Kensington Palace at 5. My room is very prettily newly papered, newly furnished, and has a new carpet, and looks very pretty indeed. Our bedroom also newly papered and furnished and looks very nice and clean. Pedro and my dear little wax-bills came quite safe. Dear Dashy was in our carriage and behaved like a darling. . . .

Monday, 6th April.—The melancholy news were received yesterday of the death of the Prince Augustus, Duke of Leuchtenberg,[1] which happened on the 28th of March. It is a *most lamentable* and dreadful event. His Royal Highness was in his 25th year, and in the flower of his age. Young, amiable, good and well-meaning; for since his arrival at Lisbon he had won the hearts of many by his affability and good-nature. He caught a cold, which he neglected and it ended in the quinsy. It is really quite dreadful for the poor young Queen, who is now left a widow at the early age of 16 ! Her Majesty completed her 16th year on the 4th of this month. It is likewise dreadful for his amiable and accomplished sister the young Empress-widow, who

[1] Brother of the Duchess of Braganza. See *ante,* p. 86.

is still in mourning for her husband, Dom Pedro; and also dreadful for his mother, the Duchess of Leuchtenberg. Not two months ago he was seen leading his young bride from the altar, and now all that prospect of happiness is cut off ! . . .

Saturday, 2nd May.—. . . At 6 we dined. Lady Flora dined here. At a ¼ past 7 we went to the opera with dear Lehzen and Lady Flora. It was Rossini's opera seria of *Otello* in 3 acts. The characters were : Desdemona, Mdlle. Grisi, who looked BEAUTIFUL and sung MOST EXQUISITELY and acted BEAUTIFULLY. She personates the meek and ill-treated Desdemona in a most *perfect* and *touching* manner. Elmiro (a Venetian patrician and father to Desdemona), Signor Lablache who sang and acted beautifully. . . . The finest parts are : the song which Otello sings in the 1st scene of the 1st act, and which Rubini sang beautifully. The duet between Iago and Roderigo in the 1st act which Tamburini and Ivanoff sang beautifully together. The song which Desdemona sings when she first comes on in the first act, which begins " Stanca di più combattere," and which Grisi sung *most exquisitely* ! (It is not by Rossini ; it is composed expressly for Grisi by Marliani.) The Finale to the 1st act which commences with that beautiful trio, " Ti parli l'amore," between Elmiro, Roderigo, and Desdemona, which Lablache, Ivanoff and Grisi sang most beautifully. It was enchored. And when Otello comes on and declares her to be his wife and Elmiro in his rage exclaims : " Empia ! ti maledico ! " and which Lablache did in a manner *most splendid* while Desdemona falls at his feet. The Duet between Iago and Otello in the 2nd act which Tamburini and Rubini sang most beautifully. The duet between

Roderigo and Otello which follows it and which was likewise beautifully sung. When Desdemona enquires from the people if Otello (who had fought with Roderigo) still lives, and when she exclaims in delight : " Altro non chiede il cor," and which Grisi did in a most splendid manner ; and when at the end of the 3rd act she kneels before her father and says, " L'error d'un infelice pietoso in me perdona : Se il padre m'abbandona, da chi sperar pieta ? " which she did in a most touching manner. The song in the 3rd act with the harp which Grisi sung most *beautifully*, as also the prayer ; and when Otello comes on to stab her and she reproaches him exclaiming : " Uccidimi se vuoi, perfido, ingrato " ; which Grisi did in such a mild and pathetic manner. He then stabs her and immediately afterwards himself. Grisi and Rubini were called out and were loudly applauded. We came in before the overture was begun and came away directly after the opera was over. It is a beautiful opera and I like it much better than *Anna Boulena*. . . .

Wednesday, 6th May.—I awoke at 7 and got up at 8. At a ¼ past 9 we breakfasted. At 11 we set off with Lady Flora and Lehzen for Windsor Castle, where we arrived at ½ past 1. At 2 we all lunched ; that is to say, besides the Queen, the Landgravine,[1] and us two,—the Duchess of Northumberland, Lady Brownlow,[2] Lady Sophia Cust, Lady De Lisle,[3] Lady

---

[1] Princess Elizabeth (1770–1840), daughter of George III., widow of Frederick, Landgrave of Hesse-Homburg. This Princess settled down into an atmosphere of venerated old age at Homburg. A statue was recently erected there and unveiled by the German Emperor to commemorate her virtues.

[2] Emma Sophia, daughter of the second Earl of Mount Edgcumbe, second wife of John, first Earl Brownlow.

[3] Daughter of William IV. Her husband had been raised to the Peerage in Jan. 1835. See *ante*, p. 99.

Falkland,[1] Lady Flora, Lehzen, the Baroness de Stein, Miss Mitchel, Miss Hudson, Lord Howe,[2] and Lord Denbigh.[3] At ½ past 2 we went out walking with the Queen, the Duchess of Northumberland, Lady Flora, Lady Sophia Cust, Lehzen, Miss Mitchel and Miss Hudson, Lord Howe, Lord Denbigh, Lord Brownlow, and Sir Andrew Bernard. We walked to Adelaide Cottage[4] and all got into carriages except the gentlemen who rode. The Queen, Mamma, the Duchess and I were in one carriage, and all the rest followed in others. We came home at 6. At ½ past 7 we dined. . . .

Thursday, 7th May.— . . . At 12 we went all over the Castle with the King, the Queen, the Landgravine, the Duchess, Lady Brownlow, Lady Flora, Lehzen, Miss Mitchel, Lord Howe, Lord Denbigh, Lord Brownlow, and Sir Andrew Bernard. . . .

Friday, 8th May.—I awoke at 7 and got up at 8. At ½ past 8 we breakfasted. The Queen came and sat with us at breakfast. At ½ past 9 we left Windsor with Lady Flora and Lehzen. I was very much pleased there, as both my Uncle and Aunt are *so very kind* to me. . . .

Monday, 18th May.— . . . At 7 we 3 dined. ½ past 9 we went into the first large room (as in the preceding parties) and received the company (the

[1] Another daughter of William IV., wife of Lucius, tenth Viscount Falkland.

[2] Richard William Penn (1796–1870), first Earl Howe, Chamberlain to Queen Adelaide. He was believed to have encouraged her in inciting the King against the Ministry of Lord Grey.

[3] William Basil Percy, seventh Earl of Denbigh. See *ante*, p. 99.

[4] Adelaide Cottage, built for Queen Adelaide, but never occupied by her except as a tea-house. It has been used ever since by successive Sovereigns for a similar purpose. The Cottage stands surrounded by charming gardens in the eastern corner of the private grounds of Windsor Castle.

list of which is adjoined). The singers which were Grisi, Rubini, Ivanoff, Tamburini, Lablache,[1] and Costa [2] for the piano, had just arrived. Our people were the same as the other day. When all the company had arrived which was at $\frac{1}{2}$ past 10, we all went into the other room which was arranged with chairs all across the room for the people to sit on. We were in the first row with Aunt Sophia and the Duchess of Cambridge and quite close to the piano. Grisi is *quite beautiful* off the stage. She is not tall, and rather pale ; and she has such a lovely mild expression in her face. Her face and neck has such a beautiful soft shape. She has such beautiful dark eyes with fine long eyelashes, a fine nose, and very sweet mouth. She was dressed in a white flowered silk, with blonde trimmings about the body and sleeves which reached to the elbows. Her beautiful dark hair was as usual quite flat in front with an amethyst bandeau round it, and a fine plait at the very back of her head. She is very quiet, ladylike and unaffected in her manners. I spoke to her, and she answered in a very pleasing manner. She has a very pretty expression when she speaks. Rubini is short and not good-looking. Ivanoff is also very short and has a very singular Calmuck face. Tamburini is short but very good-looking and gentlemanlike. Lablache does not look so tall off the stage

---

[1] Luigi Lablache (1794–1858), a first-rate comedian and the finest bass singer of his time. He made his début in London in 1830, in Cimarosa's opera *Il Matrimonio Segreto*. He taught Princess Victoria singing, and of all her teachers he was the favourite.

[2] Michael (afterwards Sir Michael) Costa, for many years the conductor of the orchestra at Covent Garden. His musical taste was considerable, but he was famous for his dominating personality, the hauteur of his demeanour, and above all for the perfect fit of his spotless white gloves.

as he does on it, and is likewise very gentlemanlike. The concert began with a trio from *L'Assiedo di Corrinto*, " Destin terribile " ; Grisi, Rubini and Ivanoff sang beautifully. Then Tamburini sang " Sorgete " from *L'Assiedo* beautifully. After this Lablache sang " Dove vai ? " from *Guillaume Tell* beautifully. Then Grisi sang " Tanti affetti," an aria from the *Donna del Lago*, most beautifully. Her *lovely* voice sounds beautiful in a room. Lablache and Tamburini then sang " Il rival salvar tu dei " most beautifully. It is from *I Puritani*. They sing beautifully together. Their two fine voices go so well together. Lablache's voice is immensely powerful but not too much so (for my taste), *even* in a room. Tamburini's too is most splendid. He is even a more skilful and finished singer than Lablache. Then came a trio " Allor che Scorre " from *Guillaume Tell*, between Rubini, Tamburini and Lablache, which they sang likewise extremely well. This ended the 1st act. Near the end of the 1st act Mme. Malibran arrived. She was dressed in white satin with a scarlet hat and feathers. She is shorter than Grisi and *not near so pretty*. We went into the refreshment room between the acts. We then sat down again and the 2nd act began with a *most lovely* polonaise, " Son Vergin vezzosa " from *I Puritani*, which Grisi sang most exquisitely, accompanied by all the singers except Malibran. Then Grisi and Tamburini sang " Che veggo oh Ciel," from *L'Assiedo* most beautifully together. Malibran then sang a song by Persiani very well. Her low notes are *beautiful*, but her high notes are thick and not clear. *I* like *Grisi by far better* than her. Then Grisi and Rubini sang a beautiful duet " Artuor dove sai " from *I Puritani* by Bellini, *beautifully.* His voice is delightful in a room. It is so sweet and so full of expression. Malibran and Lablache then sang a buffa duet " Con pazienza supportiamo," by Fioravente, beautifully. Lablache is *so* funny and *so* amusing. Lablache then sang a Neapolitan air (a buffa song) of his own composition and accompanying himself, *delightfully.* Then came a quartet " A te oh caro ! " from the *Puritani*, which Grisi, Rubini, Tamburini, and Lablache sung beautifully. This ended the *most delightful concert I ever heard.* Aunt Sophia, who had *never* heard any of these singers before, was delighted ; but no one could be *more enchanted* than *I* was. I shall never forget it. It was Mamma's birthday present for me ! Costa accompanied on the piano beautifully. I stayed up till 20 minutes past 1. I was MOST EXCEEDINGLY delighted. . . .

Sunday, 24th May.—Today is my 16TH birthday ! How very old that sounds ; but I feel that the two years to come till I attain my 18th are the most important of any almost. I now only begin to appreciate my lessons, and hope from this time on, to make great progress. I awoke at ½ past 6. Mamma got up soon after and gave me a lovely brooch made of her own hair, a letter from herself, one from dearest Feodore with a nosegay, and a drawing and a pair of slippers done by her. I gave her a drawing I had done. Dear Lehzen gave me a lovely little leather box with knives, pencils &c. in it, two small dictionaries and a very pretty print of Mdlle. Taglioni. Mamma gave her a pair of amethyst earrings and I gave her a penholder and a drawing done by myself. My maids Frances and Caroline gave me a pincushion done by Frances and a portefolio done by Caroline. Anne Mason (Lehzen's maid)

gave a small flower vase with flowers. *Dashy* gave
an ivory basket with barley-sugar and chocolate.
At 9 we breakfasted. I then received my table.
From my DEAR Mamma I received a lovely enamel
bracelet with her hair, a pair of fine china vases, a
lovely shawl and some English and Italian books.
From dearest Feodore a lovely enamel bracelet with
hers and the children's hair; from Charles some
pretty prints; from Späth a very pretty case for
handkerchiefs embroidered in silver; from Sir Robert
and Lady Gardiner a very pretty sort of china vase;
from Sir J. Conroy a writing-case; from the whole
Conroy family some prints; and from Mr. George
Hayter a beautiful drawing done by him. I quite forgot to say that I received a beautiful pair of sapphire
and diamond earrings from the King and a beautiful
prayer-book and very kind letter from the Queen.
I also received a prayer-book from a bookseller of
the name of Hatchard. At 10 we went down to
prayers with Lehzen and Charles. The service was
performed by the Dean who gave us likewise a *very*
good sermon. It was taken from the 24th chapter
of Joshua, 15th verse: " And if it seem evil unto you
to serve the Lord, choose ye this day whom ye will
serve; but as for me and my house we will serve
the Lord." After church, I received a Bible from Sir
F. Trench [1] with a picture of Norris Castle painted
on the margin; and also two small oil pictures from
an old Mrs. Pakenham, done by a Mr. King. I also
saw Mrs. Brock, Sarah (my former maid), and Mrs.

---

[1] General Sir Frederick Trench had served in Sicily and in the
Walcheren expedition, and was afterwards Aide-de-Camp to George IV.
He was M.P. for Scarborough at this time. A man of discernment
and taste. He advocated a scheme for making an embankment
along the Thames from Charing Cross to Blackfriars. He was
half a century ahead of his contemporaries!

Fletcher (our former housekeeper). At a ¼ to 1 came
Aunt Sophia who gave me with Aunt Gloucester
a very pretty diamond brooch. At 1 we lunched.
At ½ past 2 came the Duchess of Northumberland,
who gave me a very fine fillagree ornament in
the shape of a flower, and another little fillagree
ornament from Miss Wynn. Lady Flora, who
gave me a pretty paper-knife and penholder of
jasper from Arthur's Seat, the rock which overhangs
Edinburgh. Lady Theresa, who gave me a small
pocket-book of her own work. Lady Catherine,
who gave me a very fine velvet Music-book. Lady
Cust, who gave me a very fine japanned box. Sir
G. Anson who gave me a print; Sir Frederick
Wetherall, who gave me a little china scent-bottle.
Lady Conroy, Jane, and Victoire. At 3 came the
Duke of Sussex, who gave me a gold bracelet with
turquoises; and soon after Lady Charlotte St. Maur
who gave me a purse of her own work. At a ¼ past
3 came the Landgravine who gave me a head-orna-
ment of emeralds, and Aunt Augusta, who gave me
a chrisoprase bracelet. At 4 came the Duchess of
Cambridge,[1] who brought me a lovely turquoise
bracelet from Uncle Cambridge, and gave me a box
with sandal-wood instruments in it; Augusta who
gave me a small turquoise ring; and George who

---

[1] Augusta, youngest daughter of the Landgrave Frederick of Hesse.
She was married to H.R.H. the Duke of Cambridge in 1818. "I am
the happiest of men," wrote the Duke to Lady Harcourt from Cassel,
soon after his engagement, and he added, "The Princess is really everything both as to heart, mind and person that I could wish." There
never was a happier marriage. This Princess was the mother of
George, Duke of Cambridge, Commander-in-Chief of the British Armies,
of the Dowager Grand Duchess of Mecklenburg-Strelitz, and of Princess
Mary, Duchess of Teck. She was the grandmother of Queen Mary,
and died, regretted by all, in 1889.

gave me an album with a drawing of his in it.   At
20 minutes to 5 we drove out with Lehzen and
Charles.   At 7 we dined, Lady Flora, Lady Conroy,
Jane, Victoire, Messrs E. and H., and Sir J. Conroy
dined here.   After dinner came Aunt Sophia.   Mdlle.
David (sister to Mme. Dulcken) played on the piano.
I stayed up till ½ past 9.   My *dear* Mamma's great
present was that delicious concert which I shall
never forget. . . .

   Tuesday, 9th June.—I awoke at ½ past 8 and got
up soon after.   At ½ past 9 we breakfasted with the
King, the Queen, Charles, the Duchess of Northumber-
land, Lady Brownlow, Lady Catherine, and Lehzen.
At ½ past 10 we went with the whole party to Eton
College to see Eton Montem.   In the first carriage
were the King, the Duke of Cumberland, the Duke of
Cambridge, and George, who had all 3 just arrived;
in the 2nd, the Queen, Mamma, I, and Charles;
in the 3rd, the Duke and Duchess of Northumberland
and Lady Brownlow;   in the 4th Lord and Lady
Denbigh;   in the 5th Lady Sophia Cust, Lady De
Lisle, Miss Eden, and Mr. Schiffner;   in the 6th
Lord and Lady Frederick Fitzclarence and their
daughter;   in the 7th Lehzen, Miss Hudson, and
Miss Wilson.   All the other gentlemen rode.   This
is as near as I can remember.   We were received
by the Provost[1] and Dr. Hawtrey.[2]   We then went

   [1] Joseph Goodall (1760–1840), Provost of Eton for thirty-one years.
An excellent but obscure scholar.   It was his misfortune to be the
nominal superior of Dr. Keate.   He had the temerity on one occasion
at Windsor, in the presence of William IV., to tell Sir Henry Halford,
who was vain of his scholarship and fond of quoting Latin, that he
ought to be whipped for having made a false quantity.
   [2] Dr. Hawtrey (1789–1862), Headmaster of Eton for 18 years, he
then presided over the college as Provost for another 10.   A pro-
found and elegant scholar, a man of lofty ideals, intrepid soul and

into the yard under a sort of veranda and saw all
the boys pass by which was a very pretty sight.
Some of the costumes were very pretty. Some were
dressed like Greeks, some like archers, others like
Scotchmen, &c. We then went into the Provost's
house, and from thence saw the boy wave the standard.
We also saw the Library which is very curious and
old. Eton College was founded by King Henry the
Sixth. We then re-entered our carriages and drove
to Salt Hill where we again saw the standard waved
by the boy. We then drove home. The heat the
whole time was TREMENDOUS. We came home at
½ past 1. At 2 we lunched with the King, the Queen,
the Dukes of Cumberland and Cambridge, George,
the Duke and Duchess of Northumberland, Lord
and Lady Brownlow, Lady Denbigh, Lady De Lisle,
Lady Sophia Cust, Lady Frederick Fitzclarence,
Lord Howe, Lady Catherine, and Lehzen. At 4 we
went out driving. The Queen, Mamma, I and Charles
were in the first carriage ; the Duke and Duchess
of Northumberland and Lord and Lady Brownlow
in the 2nd ; Lord Denbigh and Miss Eden in the
3rd ; and Lady Catherine and Lehzen in the 4th.
We drove to the Virginia Waters. We went on the
water there, and at a ¼ to 6 re-entered the carriages
and reached home at 7. We went on the steps before
the Castle and saw all the boys and many other
people walking on the terrace. They cheered the
King and Queen *very loudly,* and me also. At 8 we
dined. We went in to dinner in the same way as
yesterday and the dinner-party was the same, only
that Lord and Lady Frederick were not there. The

warm heart, he raised the tone of masters and boys by sheer force of
his delightful personality. He doubled the numbers of the school as
well as its efficiency and influence.

Dukes of Cumberland and Cambridge and George
had left the Castle after luncheon. I stayed up till
a ¼ past 10. . . .

Tuesday, 14th July.—At 11 came the Dean till
12. At 12 came Mr. Westall till 1. At 1 we lunched.
The Duchess of Northumberland was present at the
first lesson. At ½ past 2 I sat to Mr. Collen till
½ past 3. At a ¼ to 4 came the Dean till a ¼ past 4.
At 5 we went out with Lehzen and came home at 6.
At a ¼ to 7 we dined. Lady Theresa dined here. At
8 we went to the opera with Lady Theresa and Lehzen.
It was the *dear Puritani*. Grisi was in perfect voice
and sang and acted beautifully; but I must say that
she shows her many fatigues in her face, and she is
certainly much thinner than when she arrived. It
is a great pity too that she now wears her front hair
so much lower than she did. It is no improvement
to her appearance, though (do what she may) *spoil*
her face she *never* can, it is too lovely for that. And
besides, she forgot to change her dress when she
came on to sing the Polacca. In general she comes
on to sing that as a bride, attired in a white satin
dress with a wreath of white roses round her head ;
instead of which she remained in her first dress
(likewise very pretty) of blue satin with a little sort
of handkerchief at the back of her head. Lablache,
Tamburini and Rubini were also all 3 in high good
voice. The exquisite quartet " A te o cara " and
the lovely Polacca " Son vergin vezzosa " were both
encored as was also the *splendid* duet " Il rival."
After the opera was over, Grisi, Rubini, Lablache,
and Tamburini came out and were loudly applauded.
The two last always make a separate bow to our box,
which is very amusing to see. We came away
immediately after the opera was over, for the ballet

is not worth seeing since La Déesse de la Danse has flown back to Paris again. She appeared for the last time on Saturday the 4th of this month. We came home at 10 minutes to 12. I was *highly amused* and *pleased*! We came in while Tamburini was singing his song, which is just before the lovely duet between Grisi and Lablache. . . .

Monday, 20th July.—I awoke at 7. Mamma told me this morning that she had received the melancholy news last night of the death of my dear Aunt Sophie, Countess Mensdorff,[1] who was here now nearly two years ago. It is so sudden and unexpected that we were *very much shocked, surprised* and *distressed* at the *sad* news. My poor dear Aunt had been for many years in very bad health, and when she visited us she was unable to walk alone almost; but as we had not heard that she was unwell even, it startled and shocked us very much. She went from Prague, already very unwell, in spite of Uncle Mensdorff's efforts to prevent her, to visit her youngest son Arthur who was in his garrison in a wretched little village in Bohemia, and it was there, far from her relations (except Uncle Mensdorff and Arthur), without any of the comforts which she was accustomed to, in a poor sort of cottage, that she breathed her last! My poor dear Aunt, I feel this loss *very* deeply. The more so for having seen her here! At ½ past 9 we breakfasted. At 10 we walked out with Lehzen till ½ past 10. The melancholy event happened on the 8th of this month! I feel the loss of my dear Aunt *very deeply*! Though I should be equally sad at losing her, had I *not* known her, because all Mamma's relations are *dear* to me; but having

---

[1] Countess Mensdorff was the sister of the Duchess of Kent, a Princess of Saxe-Coburg. See *ante*, p. 95.

H.S.H. Prince

is not worth seeing since La Déesse de la Danse has flown back to Paris again. She appeared for the last time on Saturday the 4th of this month. We came home at 10 minutes to 12. I was *highly amused* and *pleased*! We came in while Tamburini was singing his song, which is just before the lovely duet between Grisi and Lablache. . . .

Monday, 20th July.—I awoke at 7. Mamma told me this morning that she had received the melancholy news last night of the death of my dear Aunt Sophie, Countess Mensdorff,[1] who was here now nearly two years ago. It is so sudden and unexpected that we were *very much shocked, surprised* and *distressed* at the *sad* news. My poor dear Aunt had been for many years in very bad health, and when she visited us she was unable to walk alone almost; but as we had not heard that she was unwell even, it startled and shocked us very much. She went from Prague, already very unwell, in spite of Uncle Mensdorff's efforts to prevent her, to visit her youngest son Arthur who was in his garrison in a wretched little village in Bohemia, and it was there, far from her relations (except Uncle Mensdorff and Arthur), without any of the comforts which she was accustomed to, in a poor sort of cottage, that she breathed her last! My poor dear Aunt, I feel this loss *very* deeply. The more so for having seen her here! At ½ past 9 we breakfasted. At 10 we walked out with Lehzen till ½ past 10. The melancholy event happened on the 8th of this month! I feel the loss of my dear Aunt *very deeply*! Though I should be equally sad at losing her, had I *not known* her, because all Mamma's relations are *dear* to me; but having

---

[1] Countess Mensdorff was the sister of the Duchess of Kent, a Princess of Saxe-Coburg. See *ante*, p. 95.

H.S.H. Princess Sophia of Saxe-Coburg
Countess Mensdorff Pouilly
from a portrait by Dickinson

seen her, having lived with her in the same house for more than a week, having been in her room and seen her at her occupations, and having experienced her great kindness to me personally, makes it more striking still, and makes me feel the weight of the loss we have experienced more. At 1 we lunched. At 5 we drove out in the country with Lehzen till 7. At ½ past 7 we dined. I stayed up till a ¼ past 9. We passed a very sad evening. . . .

Thursday, 23rd July.— . . . Mamma received this afternoon a letter from Uncle Ernest enclosing the copy of one written by dear Uncle Mensdorff, giving all the sad details about my poor *dear* Aunt. I fear her sufferings must have been very severe at first and during her illness ; but at the last she seems to have had no suffering, no struggle. Her last moment was so quiet that Uncle Mensdorff thought she slept, and when he rose at 4 o'clock in the morning, he was pleased to see her sleep so quietly and said to his servant that he hoped the danger was over. Alas ! how different was it really ! My Aunt's maid went into the room and perceiving she did not breathe, called my Uncle in, who then saw the dreadful truth ! She slept truly, but she slept never more to wake ! What dear Uncle's feelings were at that moment, and what they still are, may be well imagined ! She has been placed temporarily in the vault of the convent of the Elisabetherin Nuns, at Kaden in Bohemia. The funeral was splendid. Thousands came from far and near and all her former friends followed her to her last abode, where she will suffer no more grief or pain ! Two regiments with their bands playing the funereal music followed and all the Nuns with burning tapers. They strewed the coffin with flowers when it entered the convent, and ornamented the vault in the same manner. It is a happiness to know that she was so much beloved. My poor dear Aunt, I loved her *dearly* and feel the loss deeply. Time may weaken, but it can never never efface the recollection of this loss. I shall always try to do what I can to please, and to contribute to the happiness of *dear* Uncle Mensdorff and my four cousins. They say that a smile was imprinted on her countenance when she died, and that she looked more friendly after her death than she had done some time previous to it. . . .

Thursday, 30th July.—I awoke at 7 and got up at 8. I gave Mamma a little pin and drawing done by me in recollection of today. I gave Lehzen a ring, also in recollection of today. I forgot to say that Mamma gave me 3 little books yesterday, two of which I have quite read through and the third in part. They are *A Method of Preparation for Confirmation*, by William Hale Hale; *An Address to the Candidates for Confirmation*, by Dr. John Kaye, Bishop of Lincoln; and *An Address to the Students of Eton College who are about to present themselves for Confirmation in 1833*. They are all 3 very nice books. At a $\frac{1}{4}$ past 9 we breakfasted. I forgot to say that dear Lehzen gave me 4 very pretty prints of religious subjects. At $\frac{1}{2}$ past 11 we went with Lady Flora, Lehzen, the Dean &c. to St. James's where I was to be confirmed. I felt that my confirmation was one of the most solemn and important events and acts in my life; and that I trusted that it might have a salutary effect on my mind. I felt deeply repentant for all what I had done which was wrong and trusted in God Almighty to strengthen my heart and mind; and to forsake all that is bad and follow all that is virtuous and right. I went with the firm

determination to become a true Christian, to try
and comfort my dear Mamma in all her griefs, trials
and anxieties, and to become a dutiful and affectionate daughter to her. Also to be obedient to *dear*
Lehzen who has done so much for me. I was dressed
in a white lace dress, with a white crape bonnet with
a wreath of white roses round it. I went in the
chariot with my dear Mamma and the others followed
in another carriage. We went into the King's
Closet with Lady Flora and Lehzen, where we were
received by the King and Queen. The Duke and
Duchess of Cambridge, Aunt Sophia, the Duke of
Cumberland, the Duchess of Weimar,[1] the Duchess
of Northumberland, the Marquis of Conyngham,
Earl Denbigh, Mr. Ashley, the Duke of Northumberland &c., were also there. We then went with all
into the Royal Pew in the Chapel. The usual morning service was performed ; after which we all went
down into the lower part of the Chapel. The King
went first leading me, the Queen followed leading
Mamma, and all the others followed after. I stood
without the rail before the Altar, between the King
and my dear Mamma. The Queen and all the rest
went into pews on each side of the Altar. The
Archbishop of Canterbury and Bishop of London[2]
stood on either side of the Altar. I took off my
bonnet. When the usual address had been read, I
(as is usual for all to do) replied " I do," and then

[1] Grand Duchess Marie, daughter of the Emperor Paul I. of Russia,
married Charles Frederick, Grand Duke of Saxe-Weimar-Eisenach, in
1804.

[2] Dr. Charles James Blomfield (1786–1857), a fine scholar, and a
Bishop of unusual administrative capacity. His influence in the
Church of England, both as Bishop of Chester and Bishop of London,
was second to none, until the day of his retirement in 1856. He died
at Fulham Palace in August 1857.

knelt down and received the benediction from the Archbishop. The whole was performed by the Archbishop who read also a very fine address to me, composed by him expressly for the occasion. He did the whole very well, and I felt the whole *very deeply*. My dear Mamma was very much affected by the whole. We went away from the Altar in the same way as we came and then went into the Closet again ; where the King gave me a very handsome set of emeralds, and the Queen a head-piece of the same kind. We then drove home. We came home at a $\frac{1}{4}$ to 2. I was very much affected indeed when we came home. My dear Mamma gave me a very lovely bracelet with her hair in it, and a very pretty set of turquoises. She gave dear Lehzen a very pretty bracelet. We received the joyful news this afternoon that my dearest sister Feodore had been safely confined on the 20th instant with a daughter [1] which is to be called Adelaide, Victoria, Mary, Louisa, Amelia, Constance. I hope to God that both Mother and Child will continue as well as they have hitherto been. At 6 we dined. At 7 we drove out with Lehzen till $\frac{1}{2}$ past 8. The heat continues intense ! I stayed up till $\frac{1}{2}$ past 9. . . .

Sunday, 2nd August.—I awoke after 7 and got up at $\frac{1}{2}$ past 8. At $\frac{1}{2}$ past 9 Lehzen and I breakfasted. At 11 we went to the Chapel with Lady Flora and Lehzen. The Dean performed the service ; and the Archbishop of Canterbury preached a very fine sermon. The text was taken from the 5th chapter of the 2nd epistle of St. Paul to the Corinthians, 10th verse : " For we must all appear before the judgement seat of Christ ; that every one may receive

---

[1] She married in 1856 Duke Frederick of Schleswig-Holstein, and was the mother of the present German Empress.

the things done in his body, according to that he hath done, whether it be good or bad." After the sermon was over we took the holy sacrament with Lady Flora, dear Lehzen, and Sir J. C. The Archbishop and the Dean administered it to us. It was the first time of taking it. It is a very solemn and impressive ceremony and when one recollects and thinks that we take it in remembrance of the death of our blessed Saviour, one *ought*, nay *must* feel deeply impressed with holy and pious feelings ! . . .

TUNBRIDGE WELLS, *Wednesday, 19th August.*— Today is my *poor dear* Aunt Sophie's birthday. . . . I read to Lehzen out of Sully's Memoirs. It is wonderful when one considers how many years ago they have been written. Upwards of 300 years, and how modern and pure the style is ! His account of the horrible massacre of St. Bartholomew is highly interesting as coming from the pen of an eye-witness ! I then played on the piano with Mamma and by myself. At $\frac{1}{2}$ past 12 we lunched. At 1 we went to the races with Lady Flora, Lehzen, and Sir G. Anson. It was very amusing. The day was beautiful and we sat under a sort of covering of cloth decorated with flowers, in our carriage. The Manor Stakes were won by a chesnut mare called Tirara belonging to a Mr. James Bacon. The Give-and-Take plate as it was entitled, was won by Mr. John Bacon's chesnut mare Malibran, and the Kent and Sussex stakes was won by Mr. Pegg's horse Little-thought-of. Amongst the numbers of beggars, itinerary musicians, actors etc. of all sorts and kinds, was a boy of 14 years old who called himself the son of an actor Williamson, very poorly dressed, who declaimed by heart a part of Marmion and of Campbell's poems with great feeling and talent. We came home at 5. At a $\frac{1}{4}$ past 7 we dined. When we came home I played on the piano and wrote my journal. Lady, the Misses, and M. S. Conroy, and Mr. Palmer dined here. After dinner came Mme. Dulcken. I stayed up till a $\frac{1}{4}$ past 9. . . .

Sunday, 23rd August.—I awoke at 7 and got up at 8. At a $\frac{1}{4}$ past 9 we breakfasted. After breakfast I wrote my journal and some extracts from the Peerage. At 11 we went with Lady Flora and Lehzen to church. Mr. Pope officiated and preached a sermon. The text was from the 6th chapter of St. Matthew, 10th verse : " Thy kingdom come." It was not one of his best sermons and it was not according to my liking. He can and has preached some very fine sermons. At 1 we lunched. After luncheon I wrote extracts again. Lehzen then read to me out of the Sketch-book while I worked. At $\frac{1}{2}$ past 4 we drove out with Lady Flora and Lehzen and came home at 6. I then wrote my journal. At a $\frac{1}{4}$ past 7 we dined. Sir George, Mr. and Miss Anson, Lady and the Misses and Mr. S. Conroy dined here. After dinner I took up Mrs. Butler's Journal[1] and read a little in it. It certainly is very pertly and oddly written. One would imagine by the style that the authoress must be very pert, and not well bred ; for there are so many vulgar expressions in it. It is a great pity that a person endowed with so much talent as Mrs. Butler really is, should turn it to so little account and publish a book which is so full of trash and nonsense which can

[1] Fanny Kemble, daughter of Charles Kemble, the actor, after attaining considerable success on the stage in England, went to America, and in 1834 married Pierce Butler. In 1835 she published an indiscreet journal which had considerable success.

only do her harm. I stayed up till 20 minutes past 9. . . .

Tuesday, 25th August.— . . . At ½ past 2 sat to M. Collen for my picture till ½ past 3, while Lehzen read to me in Mme. de Sévigné's Letters. How truly elegant and natural her style is ! It is so full of naïveté, cleverness and grace. Then I played on the piano. At 4 we walked out with Lady Flora and Lehzen and came home at 5 minutes to 5. In our walk we met a man with beautiful parrots. Amongst them was one dear little paroquet of a green colour with a pale brown head and so very tame that Mamma took it on her finger and it would hardly leave her. It talks also, the man says. It is not so remarkable for its fine plumage than for its great tameness. Mamma bought the dear little thing. It is now in Mamma's room. . . .

Friday, 28th August.—At ½ past 11 came the Dean till 1. I read first in the Old Testament, then in Clarendon, and finished with the *Spectator*. At 1 we lunched. I read after luncheon in the Bishop of Chester's *Exposition of the Gospel of St. Matthew.* It is a very fine book indeed. Just the sort of one I like ; which is just plain and comprehensible and full of truth and good feeling. It is not one of those learned books in which you have to cavil at almost every paragraph. Lehzen gave it me on the Sunday that I took the Sacrament. I have given up reading Smith's *Theology.* It is more a book to refer to than to read all through. . . .

Tuesday, 1st September.—I awoke at 7 and got up at ½ past 7. At ½ past 8 we breakfasted. At ½ past 9 we left *dear* Tunbridge Wells with Lady Flora and Lehzen. I am *very* sorry to leave the dear place. I am so very fond of it. I liked Boyne

House better a good deal than old Mount Pleasant. . . .
We changed horses first at Tunbridge Town, then at
Sevenoaks, and lastly at Bromley. We reached
Kensington Palace at 2. At a ¼ past 2 we lunched.
Lady Flora went home after luncheon to her own
family. At 3 we went over to Aunt Sophia's (all
our carpets being taken up), to receive the Duc de
Nemours. Aunt Sophia of course was *not* present.
The Duc de Nemours is nearly 21. That is to say
His Royal Highness will complete his 21st year on
the 25th of October. He is Aunt Louisa's 2nd
brother. He is tall, has a very fine slender figure,
and is extremely fair. He is good-looking but not so
much so as his brother the Duke of Orleans. The
Duc de Nemours is extremely pleasing but rather
timid. He brought Mamma a letter from his Mother,
the Queen of the French, and a beautiful set of instruments made of French pebbles for me, from her.
I wrote my journal then. We then saw Lady
Catherine Jenkinson, and afterwards my Uncle
Sussex. I then wrote my journal and did various
other things. At a ¼ past 7 we dined. Lord Liverpool and Lady Catherine dined here. After dinner
came Princess Sophia. I stayed up till ½ past 9. . . .

Friday, 4th September.—I awoke at 7 and got up
at ½ past 7. At ½ past 8 we all breakfasted. At
½ past 9 we left Wansford. It is a very nice clean
Inn. We passed through Stamford, a large and
populous town, after having changed horses at
Witham Common. We changed horses 2ndly at
Grantham, also a large town. These 3 are in Lincolnshire. 3rdly at Newark, also a large town, and
lastly at Scarthing Moor. The country from Wansford to Scarthing Moor was like yesterday, extremely
flat and ugly. From Scarthing Moor to Barnby

Moor, where we arrived at 5 o'clock, the country is rich and wooded, but very flat. This Inn (Barnby Moor) is extremely clean and pretty. Newark, Scarthing Moor and Barnby Moor are all in Nottinghamshire. I am struck by the number of small villages in the counties which we passed through today, each with their church. And what is likewise peculiar is, that the churches have all steeples of a spiral shape. I read in the *Alhambra* again in the carriage. Finished the 1st vol. and began the 2nd. We all walked in the little garden behind the house for a short time. When we came in I wrote my journal. At a ¼ to 7 we all dined. After dinner Lady Catherine played on the piano, for there was one in the Inn. She played a variation of Herz's, one of Hünten's, and the Polacca ; and she accompanied us while we sang " Il rival." I stayed up till 9.

Saturday, 5th September.—I awoke at ½ past 6 and got up at 7. Read in the *Exposition of St. Matt.'s Gospel* while my hair was doing, and also in the Venetian History. Last night I also read in the Gospel and in Mme. de Sévigné. At a ¼ to 8 we all breakfasted. At a ¼ to 9 we left Barnby Moor. It is a remarkably nice and clean Inn. We changed horses 1st at Doncaster, a very pretty town, 2ndly at Ferry bridge where there is a fine bridge, and lastly at Tadcaster. All these towns are in Yorkshire. We reached Bishopthorpe (the Archbishop of York's Palace) at 2. It is 2 miles and a half from York. It is a very large house and part of it is very old. Besides the Archbishop [1] and Miss

---

[1] Edward Vernon-Harcourt (1757–1847), Archbishop of York, was the third son of the first Lord Vernon. He assumed his mother's name of Harcourt on succeeding to the family estates of Stanton Harcourt and Nuneham Courtenay. He married Anne, third daughter of first

Harcourt (his daughter), the Duchess of Northumberland, Lady Norreys,[1] Sir John and Lady
Johnstone[2] (Lady Johnstone is the Archbishop's
daughter), Mr. and Mrs. and Miss Granville Harcourt,[3]
Colonel Francis Harcourt,[4] Mr. Vernon, are staying
in the house. After half an hour we lunched in a large
dining-room. We then went to our rooms which are
very nice. I finished the *Alhambra*. It is a most
entertaining book and has amused me very much. I
wrote my journal when I came into my room. Wrote
a letter to Feodore and read in the Venetian History.
The country through which we travelled today is
very flat and ugly, but extremely rich. I find the
air in Yorkshire cooler than in Kent and the South
of England. I read in Mrs. Butler's journal which
amuses me. There are some very fine feelings in it.
At a $\frac{1}{4}$ to 7 we dined. Besides the people whom I
mentioned, Mr. Charles Harcourt,[4] Mr. William Harcourt, the Lord Mayor and Lady Mayoress, Colonel
York, Colonel[5] and Mrs. Wildman, &c. After dinner
Lady Norreys and her cousin Miss Vernon sang a
duet from *La Gazza Ladra* beautifully, and also
" Suoni la tromba." They are both extremely pretty.

Marquess of Stafford. A most sumptuous prelate. He was the grandfather of Sir William Vernon Harcourt, M.P.

[1] Daughter of Mr. and Mrs. Granville Harcourt, and wife of Montagu,
Lord Norreys, M.P. for Oxfordshire, afterwards sixth Earl of Abingdon.

[2] Sir John, second Baronet (1799–1869), father of Lord Derwent.
His wife was Louise, second daughter of Archbishop Harcourt.

[3] George Granville Harcourt, M.P. for Oxfordshire and eldest son
of the Archbishop. His first wife was Elizabeth, daughter of the
second Earl of Lucan. She died in 1838, and in 1847 Mr. Harcourt
married Lady Waldegrave, the well-known and much-liked chatelaine
of Strawberry Hill. The last of the great Ladies (she was the daughter
of John Braham, the singer) who knew how to combine hospitality
with fine political and social discernment.

[4] See p. 135.

[5] Owner of Newstead Abbey, bought from Lord Byron in 1818.

They are pupils of Tamburini. We sang something then. I like Miss Vernon's voice the best of the two. We then went to prayers. After that I sang the Barcarola from *Faliero*, frightened to death. I stayed up till a ¼ to 11. . . .

BISHOPTHORPE, *Wednesday, 9th September.*—. . . At a ¼ past 11 we went to the York Minster with the same party as yesterday with the exception of Lord and Lady Norreys and Mrs. Vernon, who remained at home. The Minster was fuller than on the preceding day. It was Handel's Oratorio of *The Messiah*. It is considered very fine, but I must say that, with the exception of a few Choruses and one or two songs, it is very heavy and tiresome. It is in 3 parts. In the 1st part Grisi sang " Rejoice greatly " *most beautifully.* She pronounces the English so *very well*, and sang the whole in such excellent style. . . . The Hallelujah Chorus at the end of the 2nd part and another at the end of the 3rd act are the finest things besides " Rejoice greatly." But I am not at all fond of Handel's music, I like the present Italian school such as Rossini, Bellini, Donizetti &c., *much better.* . . .

Friday, 11th September.— . . . Lablache and Rubini sang only once each. Alas ! it will be a long time before I shall hear their two fine voices again. But time passes away quickly and April and the dear Opera will soon return. I am to learn to sing next year. Mamma promised I should ; and I hope to learn of Lablache. What a delightful master he would be to learn of ! Grisi sang " Laudate Dominum," by Mozart, accompanied by Dr. Camidge [1]

---

[1] Matthew Camidge, organist at York Minster 1799–1842. For five generations the family of Camidge supplied organists in the county of York.

on the organ. She executed the delicate passages
in it *beautifully*. Between the two parts we lunched
at the Deanery with our party and many others.
Grisi came in with her uncle while we were at luncheon.
She is extremely handsome, near-by, by day-light.
Her features are not small, but extremely fine, and
her eyes are beautiful as are also her teeth. She
has such a sweet amiable expression when she smiles,
and has pleasing quiet manners. She had an ugly dingy
foulard dress on, with a large coloured handkerchief
under a large muslin collar. And she had a frightful
little pink bonnet on, but in spite of all her ugly
attire she looked very handsome. She is a most
fascinating little creature. . . . Grisi sang the last
air " Sing ye to the Lord." Never did I hear anything so beautiful. It was a complete triumph !
and was quite electrifying ! Though a very little
bit and with very little accompaniment, the manner,
the power with which she sang it, and the emphasis
which she put into it, was truly splendid. I shall
just write down the lines :

> Sing ye to the Lord, for He hath triumphed gloriously :
> The horse and his rider hath He thrown into the sea.

She pronounced it beautifully. When she had sung
" The horse and his rider hath He thrown " she paused
a moment, and then came out most emphatically
with " *into the sea !* " . . .

Saturday, 12th September.— . . . At 11 we left
Bishopthorpe, but not without regret. They are a
very amiable family. Miss Harcourt is a very nice
person. She ought by rights to be called Miss
Georgiana Harcourt, the Archbishop's eldest daughter
being unmarried, but as she never goes out and does
not make the *honneurs* in the house, Miss Georgiana

is always called Miss Harcourt.[1]   The Archbishop
has *10* sons, 5 of whom were at Bishopthorpe ; 3
staying in the house, Mr. Granville Harcourt, Colonel
Harcourt,[2] and Mr. Egerton Harcourt, and two out
of the house, Mr. William Harcourt[3] and Mr. Charles
Harcourt,[4] staying at the residence.   Mrs. William
Harcourt is a very nice person.   We passed a
pleasant time at Bishopthorpe in spite of fatigues
which were *not slight* and which I begin to *feel*. . . .

CANTERBURY, *Thursday*, 29*th September*.—I awoke
at 6 and got up at ½ past 7.   At ½ past 8 we all
breakfasted.   At ½ past 9 Mamma received an
address from the Mayor and Corporation here.   We
then saw some officers.   After this we left Canterbury.   It is a very clean nice Inn.   It was a fine
day.   We reached Ramsgate at ½ past 12.   The
people received us in a most friendly and kind way.
The whole was very well conducted, and the people
were very orderly.   The streets were ornamented
with arches of flowers and flags.   The open, free,
boundless (to the eye) ocean looked very refreshing.
There is nothing between us and France but the sea,
here.   We have got a small but very nice house,
overlooking the sea.   At a ¼ past 2 we walked down
to the Albion Hotel to see the preparations made
for dear Uncle Leopold and dear Aunt Louisa.   At a
little past 4 we went down to the Hotel with Lady
Flora, Lehzen and Lady Conroy, as the steamer

---

[1] She afterwards married Major-General George A. Malcolm, C.B.

[2] At Nuneham there is a snuff-box, inset with diamonds, given by
Queen Victoria to Col. Francis Harcourt, and engraved " for services
rendered to her while still at Kensington."

[3] Rev. William Harcourt (1789–1871), Canon of York.   He inherited
the Harcourt estates and was the father of Sir William Vernon Harcourt, M.P.   His wife was Matilda Mary, daughter of Col. W. Gooch.

[4] Rev. Charles Harcourt, Canon of Carlisle.

was in sight. With beating hearts and longing eyes we sat at the window, anxiously watching the steamer's progress. There was an immense con-course of people on the pier to see them arrive. After about half an hour's time, the steamer entered the Harbour, amidst loud cheering and the salute of guns from the pier, with the Belgian flag on its mast. My *dearest* Uncle Leopold, King of the Belgians, and *dearest* Aunt Louisa were very warmly received. It was but the people's duty to do so, as dear Uncle has lived for so long in England and was so much beloved. After another ¼ of an hour of anxious suspense, the waiter told us that " Their Majesties were coming." We hastened downstairs to receive them. There was an immense crowd before the door. At length Uncle appeared, having Aunt Louisa at his arm. What a happiness was it for me to throw myself in the arms of that *dearest* of Uncles, who has always been to me like a father, and whom I love so *very dearly* ! I had not seen him for 4 years and 2 months. I was also delighted to make the acquaintance of that dear Aunt who is such a perfection and who has been always so kind to me, without knowing me. We hastened upstairs, where Uncle Leopold and Aunt Louisa showed them-selves at the window and were loudly cheered ; as they ought to be. I do not find dear Uncle at all changed. On the contrary I think he looks better than he did when I last saw him. Aunt Louisa is not quite so tall as Mamma, and has a very pretty slight figure. Her hair is of a lovely fair colour ; her nose is aquiline, her eyes are quite lovely ; they are light blue and have such a charming expression. She has such a sweet mouth and smile too. She is delightful, and was so affectionate to me directly.

She pronounces English extremely well and speaks
it very fluently. She almost always speaks it with
Uncle. She was very simply dressed in a light brown
silk dress, with a sky-blue silk bonnet and white
veil. Uncle and Aunt are accompanied by Comtesse
Henri de Mérode (Dame d'Honneur to Aunt Louisa),
and General Goblet.[1] M. Van de Weyer is also here.
We then left them and Lehzen and I drove home and
Mamma and the rest walked home. At a little
after 7 we dined. Dear Uncle Leopold, dear Aunt
Louisa, the Duc de Nemours (who had only arrived
half an hour ago), Comtesse H. de Mérode, General
Goblet, General Baudrand,[2] M. Van de Weyer, Dr.
Clark,[3] Mr. and Miss V. Conroy, dined here. I sat
between Uncle Leopold and the Duc de Nemours;
two *delightful* neighbours. When I say *next* to a
person, as for instance I said the other day, and many
days, " I sat next to the Duc de Nemours," " I sat
next to the Duke of Norfolk," &c., &c., I mean, as I
did today, that I sat *between* or *next* to them at *dinner.*
The Duc de Nemours, now that I see him and Aunt

[1] Albert Joseph Goblet, Count d'Alviella, a Belgian officer of
distinction much esteemed by King Leopold. He was often a guest
of M. Van de Weyer, and was well known in London Society. When
sent as Belgian Minister to Berlin, the King of Prussia refused to
receive him on the ground that he had deserted the King of Holland.

[2] General Comte Baudrand (1774–1848). Originally intended for
the Bar, he became, by choice, a soldier, and served with distinction
in Italy under the Republic, and under Napoleon at Waterloo he was
Chief of Staff of the Army of the North. After the Restoration he
was appointed Governor of the Prince Royal, with whom he paid
many visits to England.

[3] Afterwards Sir James Clark (1788–1870). He was physician to
Princess Charlotte and Prince Leopold of Saxe-Coburg, and afterwards
to the Duchess of Kent and Princess Victoria. He was not only the
Queen's most trusted physician, but an adviser and friend. He recom-
mended Balmoral to the Queen and the Prince as their Highland home.
He attended the Prince during his last hours.

Louisa together, is not like her. He has such a
good kind expression in his face ; and Aunt Louisa
has the most *delightful sweet* expression I ever saw.
She is quite delightful and charming. She is so
gay and merry too. She had a white moiré dress
on, and her fine hair was so well done, in a plait behind
and curls in front with a row of pearls and three
black velvet bows in it. After dinner came two
other gentlemen of the Duc de Nemours, Colonel
Boyer and Monsieur Larnac. We passed a *most
delightful* evening. . . .

Thursday, 5th November.—I awoke at 7 and got
up at 8. Dressed, walked over to my room and
breakfasted at 9. Read in the Exposition of St.
Matt.'s Gospel, and in the Venetian History while my
hair was doing. *Dear good* Lehzen takes such care
of me, and is so unceasing in her attentions to me, that
I shall never be able to repay her sufficiently for
it but by my love and gratitude. I never can sufficiently repay her for all she has *borne* and done for
me. She is the *most affectionate, devoted, attached,*
and *disinterested* friend I have, and I love her
most *dearly*. . . .

Wednesday, 2nd December.— . . . We walked on
the Pier which was very amusing. There are a
number of foreign ships in the harbour ; Portuguese,
Finland, and a number of French fishing-boats.
The dress of the French fishermen is very picturesque.
There were some Spanish sailors playing on the pier,
who looked very singular. Amongst others there
was a little French fisher-boy playing with another
boy with a pulley. He had a funny round rosy face,
and was dressed in a loose blue woven whoolen
jacket, with huge boots which reached to his knees,
and a red cap. Mamma asked him what he was

doing, upon which he answered with naïveté, "Nous sommes à jouer un peu." She asked him where he came from; "De Dunkirk," was his reply. He said this all, and some other things, in such a funny naif way, and with such a sly arch smile, that it was quite amusing. He asked for a " sou," and we gave him 6 pence, which pleased him very much. . . .

INTRODUCTORY NOTE TO CHAPTER V

WHEN the Princess was seventeen the shadow of coming events was cast over her placid life. Her Journals contain evidence of this. She became aware that her Uncle, King Leopold, had begun to think with grave anticipation of the high position she might before long have to occupy, and of the project of uniting her in marriage to some Prince worthy to share with her the anxieties and responsibilities of a Throne. She knew that he had fixed upon her cousin, Prince Albert of Saxe-Coburg.

In May of this year she saw the Prince for the first time. William IV. did not favour the views of King Leopold. His candidate was a younger son of the Prince of Orange. Both Princes were invited to London, and both were present at a ball given by the Duchess of Kent in honour of her daughter attaining the age of seventeen.

The young Princess was not attracted by the Prince of Orange. It would be an exaggeration to say that she felt more than a sisterly affection for Prince Albert. She thought him good-looking and charming, and they sketched and sang together. He found her very amiable and astonishingly self-possessed. There is not a trace on either side of deeper sentiment. When the Prince left England, she wrote to her Uncle Leopold expressing anxiety to fall in with his wishes in respect of her future marriage as in everything else, but there is no indication that her heart was touched. The seed, however, was sown which was to ripen later, and ultimately to bear fruit, the sweetest she was destined to taste in her long life.

The plans of King Leopold were an open secret, and roused considerable interest in all classes. On his return home Prince Albert was entertained in Paris at an official dinner given by Lord Granville, which was taken to mean that good progress had been made with the scheme of the projected marriage.

In the course of this year the Princess resided at Claremont, then the property of King Leopold. Her life there was one of great simplicity. There were lately living a few old people in the village of Esher who remembered the little Princess attending the ancient church, now disused, dressed in spotted muslin with a large poke bonnet.

Perhaps owing to the consciousness that his candidate had failed to create a favourable impression, King William during this year displayed more than usual hostility to his sister-in-law, the Duchess of Kent. The King's behaviour to her mother undoubtedly saddened the life of the little Princess, more especially as it was in somewhat strong contrast to the kindness with which she herself was treated by King William and Queen Adelaide.

Meanwhile the stream of public events rolled smoothly along.

CHAPTER V

1836

Monday, 11*th January.*— . . . . We went out walking at a ¼ to 2 with Lady Flora and Lehzen; it had cleared up and was quite mild and bright. We walked on the pier and got into a boat. There was a good deal of swell in the Harbour, and at the mouth of it our boat pitched and rolled a good deal; Mamma began to look queerish, but I thought it very pleasant. There were numbers of people on the pier. The 3 Portuguese vessels hoisted their Portuguese standards, as did also the two Spaniards. We landed at the same stairs where we embarked. The whole of Ramsgate seemed to be out on the pier. We walked to the head of the pier and back again and got into the carriage. We drove to the cliff where the stairs called "Jacob's ladder" are. We got out there and went down the stairs, and walked on the other side of the pier. We took a parting look at the end of the pier, of all the ships, the pier &c., for we go tomorrow. There were, I think, 7 French boats in the Harbour; and there were numbers of little French boys on the pier; we gave them something, but they (for the first time) proved dissatisfied and rebellious. They quite attacked Lehzen, who always gives the money, coming round her on all sides, stretching out their hands, saying " Donnez-moi ʃun sou," " Je n'ai pas un," " Madame, Madame,

141

donnez-moi un sou," &c. Some little urchins were
rusés enough to say " C'est pour nos matelots, nous
allons à bord dans l'instant." Lehzen threw them
a shilling, whereupon they all fell on the ground in
one heap, scrambling after it. They were quiet for
a little while, but a few little determined fellows
came again and followed us for sometime. They at
length got something, and went away. Cela était
fort amusant et très ridicule à voir. . . .

Wednesday, 13th January.—I awoke at a little
past 6 and got up at 7. Dressed and had my hair
done. We breakfasted at 8. We left Sittingbourne
at 9. It was a bitterly cold day, though bright and
clear. We changed horses at Rochester, 2ndly at
Gravesend, and 3rdly at Blackheath. We reached
Kensington Palace at a little before 2. We instantly
went upstairs, that is to say, up *two* staircases, to
our new sleeping and sitting apartments which are
very lofty and handsome. To describe them minutely
and accurately would be impossible. Our bedroom [1]
is very large and lofty, and is very nicely furnished,
then comes a little room for the maid, and a dressing-
room for Mamma ; then comes the old gallery which is
partitioned into 3 large, lofty, fine and cheerful
rooms.[2] One only of these (the one near Mamma's
dressing-room) is ready furnished ; it is my sitting-
room and is *very* prettily furnished indeed. My
pictures are not yet in it. The next is my study,
and the last is an anteroom ; this last has no fire-

---

[1] This room was in later years the room of Princess May, now
H.M. the Queen. It forms part of the Palace temporarily appropriated
to the London Museum, and is dedicated to the relics of Queen
Victoria's childhood. In this room Queen Mary was born.

[2] The partitions were taken down after the accession of King
Edward, and the great gallery restored to the condition in which it
was left by William III.

place, but the two others have, and my sitting-room
is very warm and comfortable. There is another
room, belonging to me, on another side of the bed-
room (Lehzen's former bed-room) which is not
freshly furnished, but is a passage &c. Lehzen is
now in our former bed-room. When I went down
into my poor former sitting-room,[1] I could not help
looking at it with affection, and pleasant recollections,
having passed so many days of my life and many
very pleasant ones there ; but our new rooms are
much more airy and roomy. . . .

Thursday, 14th January.— . . . Read out of
Mme. de Sévigné while my hair was doing to Lehzen.
We all breakfasted at a ¼ past 9. Carried things
from my old room, upstairs to my new room, and
put them into the new presses. Wrote my journal.
My pictures are being hung up and my room is in a
great confusion ; the workmen in my study are
making a great noise, so that I am *un peu confuse.*
Walked about. We lunched at 1. Arranged things.
Saw Dr. Clark at 2. Received a most kind and long
letter from dearest Aunt Louise in which she tells
me that Uncle Leopold and my little cousin are well,
as also Uncle Ferdinand, who is with them ; and
that the Duke of Orleans[2] (whom she calls *Chartres,*
as the whole family generally do) is better but not
quite well yet. She further adds, that the dear
Queen of the French who had a very bad cold, is
better. . . .

Wednesday, 3rd February.—I awoke at 7 and got up
at a ¼ to 8. Read in the Irish History while my

---

[1] Now occupied as a sitting-room by Princess Henry of Battenberg.

[2] When King Louis Philippe was Duc d'Orléans his eldest son was
Duc de Chartres, and the earlier name survived. In later years the
Comte de Paris' younger brother became Duc de Chartres. See p. 72.

hair was doing. At 9 we breakfasted. Pasted my name in some of my books. At 10 came the Dean till 11. Read with him first in the Old Testament and then in Hume. Pasted my name in some of my books. I have got all the same pictures I had in my former room, hung up in my present room, with the exception of some old prints and of the two ugly oil pictures of my Father and Mother, and with the addition of Hayter's drawing of Mamma and I. My fine casts of the *dear* French family are also hung up in my sitting-room ; they only came home today as the frame had to be mended. I am so fond of them. Various prints are also being hung up in my study. Wrote my journal. Drew. . . .

Saturday, 6th February.— . . . I have quite forgotten to mention that the young Queen of Portugal was married by proxy on the 1st of January to—*my Cousin Ferdinand,* Uncle Ferdinand's eldest son, and who completed his 19th year on the 29th of last October.[1] The negotiations to this purpose have been going on since last September, and have only just now come to an end. Count Lavradio, whom we saw just before we went to Ramsgate, went to Cobourg to meet Uncle Ferdinand and my dear Cousins Ferdinand and Augustus, there. Dear Uncle Leopold has managed a *great* deal of the business ; he is ever ready and ever *most able* to assist his family. Uncle Ferdinand has not long left Brussels, where he came to settle and arrange about the marriage. Dear Uncle Ferdinand is, of course, full of anxiety for the welfare and happiness of

---

[1] Prince Ferdinand was nephew of the Duchess of Kent (the son of her brother Ferdinand), and was married to Maria da Gloria, Queen of Portugal. Their sons Pedro V. and Luis both succeeded to the Throne. Count Lavradio had been sent to Coburg to negotiate the alliance.

his son. Ferdinand will soon come to Brussels with Augustus on his way to Lisbon and they will also come here. I cannot say how happy I am to become thus related to the Queen of Portugal, who has always been so kind to me and for whom I have always had a great affection. She is warm-hearted, honest and affectionate, and when she talks, is very pleasing. We have known each other since our 8th year (for there is only a month's difference of age between us). She is far from plain too ; she has an exquisite complexion, a good nose and fine hair. I hear that Ferdinand is full of good and excellent qualities, has a pure and unsophisticated mind, and is very good-looking. . . .

Saturday, 20th February.— . . . At ½ past 3 came the Dean till 4. Read with him in Milton's *Paradise Lost.* Practised on the piano for Mrs. Anderson.[1] Drew while Lehzen read to me out of that Rapport about Fieschi.[2] Practised again on the piano. At ½ past 7 we dined. Aunt Gloucester, the Prince of Hesse-Philippsthal-Barchfeldt,[3] the Archbishop of York and Miss Harcourt, the Duke of Wellington, Count[4] and Countess Charles Pozzo di Borgo, the Earl and Countess of Lincoln,[5] Viscount

[1] Mrs. Anderson was Princess Victoria's music-mistress. She was a pupil of Felix Mendelssohn's, and a most beautiful musician. She taught music to all the Queen's children and died between 1870 and 1880. Her husband was for many years " Master of the Queen's Musick," *i.e.* Private Band.

[2] Fieschi had attempted to assassinate King Louis Philippe.

[3] Ernest (born 1789), brother of the reigning Landgrave.

[4] Son of Count Pozzo di Borgo, Russian Ambassador. This diplomatist was born in Corsica in 1768, and he began life as a Corsican Deputy to the National Assembly. Agent of the Holy Alliance in Europe, he was the most ardent advocate of the Legitimist cause in France. His talents were remarkable, and his causerie was much appreciated in London society.

[5] Henry, Earl of Lincoln (1811–64), afterwards fifth Duke of New-

I—11

and Viscountess Beresford,[1] Lord Hill, Lady Caroline
Legge,[2] Lady Theresa Strangways, Sir Robert and
Lady Peel, General Upton and Sir Samuel Higgins
dined here. I sat between the Duke of Wellington
and Count C. Pozzo di Borgo. The Count is a very
agreeable man. His wife, the dear little Countess,
looked lovely ; she is such a charming person ; she
is the 3rd daughter of the Duc de Crillon and is called
Valentina. Lady Lincoln is also a very charming
young person ; she was so pretty but she is very
much changed as she was very ill all last summer
and is still very far from well. I sat a good deal
with her and the little Countess Pozzo, and found
them very amiable and cheerful. . . .

Saturday, 27th February.— . . . It was Miss
Joanna Baillie's[3] Tragedy of *The Separation* in
5 acts, performed for the 2nd time. The principal
characters are : Garcio (an Italian Count), Mr.
Charles Kemble,[4] who acted finely in parts but is
dreadfully changed ; Rovani (his friend), G. Bennett

castle, a Peelite and Secretary for War during the campaign in the
Crimea. He was a holder of other high posts in the Government.
An able man, but no one except Mr. Gladstone ever thought him
capable of holding the highest. His father returned Mr. Gladstone
for his close borough of Newark. Lady Lincoln was a daughter of
the tenth Duke of Hamilton, and was divorced in 1850.

[1] William Carr Beresford (1770–1854), better known as Marshal
Beresford, so called from his supreme command of Portuguese troops in
the Peninsula, the hero of Albuera, the bloodiest battle of the war.
Created Baron Beresford of Albuera and Dungarvan 1814, and Viscount
in 1823. He married Louisa, widow of Thomas Hope of Deepdene.

[2] Daughter of third Earl of Dartmouth.

[3] Miss Joanna Baillie (1762–1851), a writer of many plays, now
forgotten. She is remembered as a lady to whom Sir Walter Scott
wrote freely. She resided at Hampstead, and was visited by many
distinguished men of letters. Sir Walter edited, and Kemble acted,
one of her plays.

[4] Charles Kemble (1775–1854), the youngest of the family whose
chief ornament was Mrs. Siddons. A meritorious comedian.

who acted disagreeably and affectedly; the Marquis of Tortona, Mr. Pritchard, a poor odd-looking creature; Margaret (wife to Garcio), Miss Helen Faucit,[1] who acted well in the pathetic quiet parts. I had not seen Charles Kemble since 5 years, and I did not quite recollect his countenance; those however who had seen him in his good days, when he was an excellent actor and a very handsome man, found the change *very great*. *I*, for *my* part, like Macready by far better. Kemble whines so much and drawls the words in such a slow peculiar manner; his actions too (to me) are overdone and affected, and his voice is not pleasant to me; he makes terrible faces also which spoils his countenance and he looks old and does not carry himself well. He was very fine, however, at the end of the 3rd act when he snatches the picture out of his wife's hand, and when he discovers it to be that of her brother Ulrico whom he murdered,—the way in which he throws the picture on the ground and sinks trembling and gasping against the bed, while his countenance pourtrays the violent feelings of remorse, horror and conscience this Kemble did *very finely*, and also when he takes leave of Margaret. He *was* undoubtedly a very fine actor, nay, still *is*, but he is not natural enough for my taste. I *do* think Macready is so feeling and natural, particularly now; he was perhaps formerly rather affected and violent at times. His voice too I like so much and he does not drawl the words; I like him best after Young, who

[1] Helen Faucit was now nineteen, and had just made her debut as Julia in *The Hunchback*. The "Margaret" of the present occasion was her first original part. She married Mr. (afterwards Sir) Theodore Martin in 1851, and was as much esteemed by Queen Victoria for her womanly qualities as by the public for her impersonation of Rosalind. She died in 1898.

was the *most beautiful* actor I ever saw, or who perhaps ever existed in this country, except Garrick and John Kemble (Charles K.'s elder brother). I only saw Young twice but I shall never forget it. I saw him 1st in *Macbeth* and then I saw him take his final leave of the stage in *Hamlet.* I must say a few words about G. Bennett [1] and Miss Helen Faucit. Bennett, whom I have seen act really extremely well in *The Miller and His Men*, in *Pizarro*, in *King John* as Hubert, &c., &c., was extremely disagreeable yesterday as Rovani; he twisted his arms, hands, legs, back and even eyes in all directions, and drawled his words in speaking most disagreeably. Miss Faucit is plain and thin, and her voice is much against her, but when she is gentle and pathetic she is far from disagreeable; she rants and screams [2] too much also, but as she is very young, they say she may *become* a good actress. The Tragedy though well written is rather unnatural and very heavy in parts; I must say *I* greatly prefer *The Provost of Bruges* and think it by far more natural. Kemble and Miss Faucit were called out and were much applauded. . . .

Monday, 29th February.— . . . At ½ past 7 we went to the play to Mme. Vestris's [3] Olympic, with Lehzen and Sir J. C. I had never been there before; it is a very small but pretty, clean little theatre.

---

[1] George John Bennett, an actor never in the front rank. He was associated with Phelps throughout his long management of Sadler's Wells, and played respectable parts.

[2] When, as Lady Martin, forty years later, she appeared as Rosalind on a special occasion, in the interests of charity, these characteristics were found to be unimpaired.

[3] Madame Vestris (1797–1856), daughter of Bartolozzi the engraver. She married at sixteen Armand Vestris, and secondly Charles Mathews. Her histrionic powers were not remarkable, but her reputation as a singer and producer of extravaganza stood high.

P.V. del: J.L.P.
April 1837.

Mr Charles Mathews
as Dapperwit in The Rape
of the Lock.

CHARLES MATHEWS.

From a sketch by Princess Victoria.

It was the burletta of *One Hour* or *The Carnival Ball* in one act. The principal characters are : Mr. Charles Swiftly, Mr. Charles Mathews,[1] a most *delightful* and *charming* actor ; he is son to the celebrated old Mathews who died last year. He is quite a young man, I should say not more than five or six and twenty.[2] His face is not good-looking, but very clever and pleasing ; he has a very slight, pretty figure, with very small feet and is very graceful and immensely active ; he skips and runs about the stage in a most agile manner. He is *so* natural and amusing, and never vulgar but always very gentlemanlike. He is a most charming actor. . . .

Charles Mathews is the most delightful and amusing actor possible. He is the only child of his parents and was intended for an architect and studied in Greece and Italy for that purpose ; but having a penchant for the stage, he abandoned his profession and had become an actor ; we see how it has succeeded —*most perfectly !* . . .

Wednesday, 2nd March.— . . . Lady Burghersh [3] told me that she knew Charles Mathews very well when she was in Florence, where he was come for the purpose of studying architecture ; she said she had often acted with him in their private theatricals and that he always showed a great talent for acting, and that he then performed as a gentleman ; he *now*

---

[1] Charles Mathews (1803–78), one of the most delightful comedians of all time. Destined for the Church, educated as an architect, he did not make his debut on the stage until he was thirty-two years old. He married Madame Vestris, and his Autobiography and Letters were edited by Charles Dickens.

[2] He was thirty-three years old.

[3] Priscilla, daughter of William, first Lord Maryborough and afterwards third Earl of Mornington, was the Duke of Wellington's niece. Her husband, Lord Burghersh, was afterwards eleventh Earl of Westmorland.

acts quite like a gentleman, and looks so too; he is a charming performer I think. Lady Burghersh also said that he looks younger than he is, for that he must be 3 or 4 and thirty. He told her when at Florence that he had a great passion for the stage, but, as his father was greatly averse to his son becoming an actor, he refrained from doing it during his father's lifetime. . . .

Thursday, 17th March.— . . . We reached Windsor Castle at 6. We went to the Queen's room where Ferdinand and Augustus were presented to the King. We then went to our rooms. At ½ past 7 we dined in St. George's Hall with an immense number of people. Ferdinand looked very well. He wore the 3 Portuguese Orders in one ribbon, which he has the right of doing as husband to the Queen of Portugal. Ferdinand led the Queen in to dinner and the King led Mamma and I. I sat between the King and George Cambridge and opposite dear Ferdinand. After dinner we went into a beautiful new drawing-room[1] where we remained till the gentlemen came from dinner. We then all went into the Waterloo Gallery where the ball was. The King went in first, then the Queen and Mamma, and then dear Ferdinand with me at his arm. I danced 3 quadrilles; 1st with dear Ferdinand, then with George Cambridge, and lastly with dear Augustus. During the evening dear Ferdinand came and sat near me and talked so dearly and so sensibly. I do *so* love him. Dear Augustus also sat near me and talked with me and he is also a dear good young man, and is very handsome. He is extremely quiet and silent, but there is a great deal in him. I am so fond too of my Uncle Ferdinand. I stayed

[1] This room is now known as " the State Drawing-room."

up till 1. I was much amused and pleased. Uncle
Ferdinand brought me two kind notes from Uncle
Leopold and Aunt Louise. Ferdinand is so fond of
Aunt Louise. He told me : " Oh, je l'aime tant ! "
Both he and Augustus speak French extremely well.
This dinner and ball were in honour of dear Ferdinand.

Friday, 18*th March.*— . . . At ½ past 9 we
breakfasted with the King, the Queen, dear Ferdinand
(who came nearly at the end of the breakfast, having
slept a long while), dear Uncle Ferdinand, Augustus,
Charles, Prince Ernst of Hesse P.B.,[1] the Duchess
of Northumberland, George Cambridge, Lady Ely,[2]
Lady Flora, and Lehzen. After breakfast Mamma
and I went into the Queen's room and looked at some
of her many pretty things. Wrote my journal. At
½ past 11 we drove out with the Queen and dear
Ferdinand in our carriage, Ferdinand and I sitting
on the back seat and the Queen and Mamma on the
front seat. Uncle Ferdinand, Augustus, Charles and
Prince Ernest of Hesse P.B. followed in another, and
all the rest in other carriages. We went to see a
hunt and saw a stag let out of a cart and all the
horsemen followed in great numbers. It was a very
pretty sight, and a beautiful warm day. We were all
in open carriages. I talked a good deal with Ferdinand, and like him *more* and *more*; he is so sensible,
so natural, so unaffected, and unsophisticated and so
truly good. His tutor, who has been with him 13
years, M. Dietz, and whom he told me he is very
fond of, will go with him to Lisbon as his " secrétaire
intime," he told me. He (M. Dietz)[3] came with

---

[1] Prince Ernest of Hesse-Philippsthal-Barchfeldt. See p. 145.

[2] Anna Maria, wife of second Marquess of Ely. She was the
daughter of Sir H. W. Dashwood, Bart. She died in 1857.

[3] See *post,* p. 297.

several other gentlemen to Kensington yesterday. Ferdinand is so fond of Augustus; the separation will be dreadful for the two brothers; and he is very fond of his sister Victoire. We came home at ½ past 1. Wrote the *brouillon* of a French letter to Aunt Louise. At 2 we lunched with the whole party. I sat between the King and Uncle Ferdinand. Wrote my letter to Aunt Louise. Wrote my journal. Walked about. At about ½ past 5 dear Ferdinand, Uncle Ferdinand, and dear Augustus came into our room for a little while. At ½ past 7 we dined; again in St. George's Hall and with the same large company as the day before. Ferdinand went first (as he did also yesterday) with the Queen; then came the King with us two. I sat between the King and George Cambridge, and opposite dear Fernando. After dinner Uncle Ferdinand and my Cousins came and sat near us every now and then. Dear Ferdinand has elicited universal admiration from all parties; the King is very much pleased with him, and the Queen is quite taken with him. He is so very unaffected, and has such a distinguished appearance and carriage. They are both very dear and charming young men; Augustus is very amiable too, and when known, shows much good sense; he is very quiet and gentle. There is such an innocence and simplicity in them, and such a childish gaiety, and again they are very grown-up and nice in their manners, which are very unaffected and pleasing. Stayed up till ½ past 11. . . .

Friday, 1st April.—Today is Good Friday. At ½ past 9 we breakfasted with dear Uncle Ferdinand, dear Augustus, Charles, Lady Flora and Lehzen. I sat between dear Augustus and Charles. I stayed downstairs till a ¼ past 10. Received the Order

of Ste. Isabelle from my Cousin Donna Maria. The
ribbon is very pale pink and white. Went up stairs,
and wrote part of the *brouillon* of a French letter to
Aunt Louise. Dear good Augustus came up at $\frac{1}{2}$ past
10 and stayed till 11. These visits please me very
much ; he is *so* quiet, and goes about looking at the
things in the room, sits down and reads the newspapers, and never is in the way He is a dear boy, and
is so extremely good, kind and gentle ; he has such a
sweet expression and kind smile. I think Ferdinand
handsomer than Augustus, his eyes are so beautiful,
and he has such a lively, clever expression ; *both*
have such a sweet expression ; Ferdinand has something *quite beautiful* in his expression when he speaks
and smiles and he is *so* good. They are both very
handsome and *very dear* ! Ferdinand is superior to
Augustus in various ways, and is by far more forward
for his age in his mind than the latter. They have
both learnt, and know, a great deal, and are both
very orderly and tidy. At 11 we went down to
prayers with Charles, Lehzen, Lady Flora &c. &c.
The service was performed by the poor Dean who
gave us likewise a sermon. We saw him for an instant after the service was over. He is very calm
and resigned. We remained with Uncle a little while
downstairs. Finished my *brouillon* of my French
letter. Began to copy it. Went downstairs to see
some paintings done by a Mr. Cowen. They are very
well done indeed. Augustus came in also and looked
at them for a moment. Came up to my room and
went on writing my letter to dear Aunt Louise.
Dearest Uncle Ferdinand came up to me for a few
minutes and then went down again. Augustus came
up and stayed a little while, while I was writing my

¹ A landscape painter.

letter and then went down.   I gave him this morning
a seal and some prints which pleased him very much.
Finished my letter to Aunt Louise and wrote my
journal.   At 25 minutes to 4 *dear* good Augustus came
up and sat in my room looking at annuals till 4.   He
assisted me in sealing my letters, and we both made
a mess, and he burnt a cover in sealing it, dear boy,
for me, which made us both laugh.   He went down
for 5 minutes, came up again, and Uncle, after staying
a few minutes, fetched him away to pay visits to the
Duke of Sussex and Princess Sophia.   Played and
sung.   At 10 minutes to 6 came Mrs. Wellesley [1]
who is going tomorrow and will reach Stuttgardt
on Friday.   Augustus came in and we stayed with
Uncle and him a few minutes downstairs.   Oh !
could I but have some more such days, with that
dear Uncle and dear Augustus, whom I love so much !
I shall feel very lonely and unhappy when they leave
us. . . .

   Sunday, 10th April.— . . . Read to Lehzen part
of *The Directions and Advices* which dearest Uncle
Leopold has written down for Ferdinand, most
cleverly and beautifully done.   They are written in
French and are divided into 3 parts.   The part I
have read is *Affaires Politiques,* which is divided
into headings of all the departments of the Government.   Dear Uncle has studied [2] the Portuguese Constitution, Government, People, Country, &c., &c.,
so completely since the intended marriage of Ferdi-

   [1] Olivia Cecilia, daughter of Charlotte, Baroness de Ros. She
married (1833) Henry Richard Wellesley, afterwards first Earl Cowley
and British Ambassador at Paris. She died in 1885.
   [2] King Leopold used Stockmar for the purpose of educating Prince
Ferdinand very much as he used him to train Prince Albert and
Princess Victoria in the duties of a Sovereign. King Leopold believed
that he had reduced the rules of Sovereignty to a science. See p. 196.

nand with the Queen of Portugal, that he is as familiar
with the whole as though he were in the country.
Dear Uncle Leopold is so clever and so prudent and
so kind ; he has taken so much pains and trouble
about Ferdinand and I must say he is repaid for his
trouble by the affection and gratitude Ferdinand has
for him ; and certainly he has *not* thrown away his
time in so doing, for Ferdinand is not only *very good*,
but *clever*, and therefore with Uncle's advice he will
succeed, I am sure. Van de Weyer is a most trusty,
clever person, and as he has also copies of these
papers, will be of the greatest use to Ferdinand. I
see by the part I have read, which contains most
valuable, important and sage advice, one thing which
I am very glad of, which is, that the Queen will
associate Ferdinand with her in the Council, &c.,
that he is always to be present at all her Councils.
Uncle advises him to listen and not to give his opinion
until he has become acquainted with the characters
of the persons in the Council, and then, after having
well weighed what he means to say, to give his
opinion. There is so much of all the advice which
I wish I could insert here, but which I have no time
to do.[1] . . .

Monday, 11th April.—Lehzen read to me while
I was dressing and I read to her while my hair was
doing, one of the parts of the Directions for Ferdinand,
called *Observations Générales*, and began the last
one called *Note communiquée au Comte de Lavradio.*
Dear Uncle Leopold is so clever and governs Belgium so beautifully, that he is a model for every

---

[1] In later years Queen Victoria used similar language about the
Prince Consort. In her case it was not an altogether accurate description of the facts. Her dominant character occasionally asserted
itself.

Sovereign and will contribute to the happiness and re-organisation of Portugal, as he has done to Belgium ; for *that* country owes *all* its prosperity, happiness, everything, to dearest Uncle Leopold ; it was in a sad state when Uncle arrived, and by his great prudence, sagacity, and extreme cleverness, Belgium is now one of the most flourishing Kingdoms in Europe. . . .

Tuesday, 3rd May.— . . . At 10 minutes past 11 came *Lablache* till 10 minutes past 12. He complained much of the cold weather, and said " qu'ils étaient tous enrhumés " and that they had all been very hoarse last night at a concert, except Rubini. I like Lablache very much, he is such a nice, good-natured, good-humoured man, and a very patient and excellent master ; he is so merry too.[1] *En profile* he has a very fine countenance, I think, an aquiline nose, dark arched eye-brows, and fine long eyelashes, and a very clever expression. He has a profusion of hair, which is very grey, and strangely mixed with some few black locks here and there. I sung first the recitative of " Notte d'orrore," from *Marino Faliero*, several times over. Then Mamma and I sung " Mira oh ! Norma " and " Si fine al ore," both twice over and " Qual cor tradesti " twice over. Then I sang twice with Lablache " Io son ricco e tu sei bella," a very pretty little duo from *L'Elisire d'Amore* by Donizetti. He sang this delightfully, he has such a fine voice and pronounces so distinctly and so well. *En conclusion* I sang " Vivi tu." I liked my lesson extremely ; I only wish I had one every *day* instead of one every *week*. . . .

Friday, 13th May.— . . . Mme. Malibran de

---

[1] His portrait by Winterhalter hangs among Queen Victoria's "friends " in the ante-room to the Corridor at Windsor. See p. 114.

Bériot[1] (as she now calls herself since her marriage with the eminent violinist de Bériot) was in very fine voice and sang extremely well indeed, twice. She sang first the prayer which Anna sings in her sleep in the 2nd act of *La Sonnambula*, and " Ah ! non giunge unam pensiero ! " I prefer Grisi's singing of these very much to Malibran's ; there is a sweetness, mildness and softness, accompanied with such beautifully clear execution, in the *former*, which the *latter* does *not* possess in the high notes. Malibran's deep tones are beautiful, touching and feeling, but her high notes are harsh, sharp and *voilée*. The 2nd thing she sang was pretty and well adapted to her voice. . . .

Wednesday, 18*th May.*— . . . At a ¼ to 2 we went down into the Hall, to receive my Uncle Ernest, Duke of Saxe-Coburg-Gotha, and my Cousins, Ernest and Albert, his sons. My Uncle was here, now 5 years ago, and is looking extremely well. Ernest is as tall as Ferdinand and Augustus ; he has dark hair, and fine dark eyes and eyebrows, but the nose and mouth are not good ; he has a most kind, honest and intelligent expression in his countenance, and has a very good figure. Albert, who is just as tall as Ernest but stouter, is extremely handsome ; his hair is about the same colour as mine ; his eyes are large and blue, and he has a beautiful nose and a very sweet mouth with fine teeth ; but the charm of his countenance is his expression, which is most delightful ; *c'est à la fois* full of goodness and sweetness, and very clever and intelligent. We went upstairs with them, and after staying a few minutes with them, I went up to my room. Played and sang. Drew. At a little after 4 Uncle Ernest and my Cousins came up to us and stayed in my room till

[1] Madame Malibran. See *post*, p. 168.

10 minutes past 5. Both my Cousins are so kind and
good; they are much more *formés* and men of the
world than Augustus; they speak English very well,
and I speak it with them. Ernest will be 18 years
old on the 21st of June and Albert 17 on the 26th
of August. Dear Uncle Ernest made me the present
of a most delightful *Lory*, which is so tame that it
remains on your hand, and you may put your finger
into its beak, or do anything with it, without its
ever attempting to bite. It is larger than Mamma's
grey Parrot, and has a most beautiful plumage; it
is scarlet, blue, brown, yellow, and purple. At 6 we
went with Lehzen, Lady Flora &c., to dine at
the Archbishop of York's, and I was very sorry
to leave my dear Uncle and Cousins behind us at
home. . . .

Thursday, 19th *May*.—Read in the *Exposition*
while my hair was doing. At 9 we breakfasted with
Uncle Ernest, Ernest, Albert, Lehzen and Charles.
I sat between my dear Cousins. At ½ past 10 Lehzen
and I walked in the gardens and came home at ½
past 11. At a ¼ to 12 came the Dean till ½ past 12.
Read with him in the New Testament and in Clarendon. At ½ past 12 came Mr. Steward till ½ past 1.
Played and sung. At a ¼ past 2 came the Dean till 3.
Read with him in Paley. At 3 came Mrs. Anderson
till 4. At a ¼ to 5 we walked in the gardens with
Lehzen till ½ past 5. Wrote my journal. At 7
we dined. Besides us 3 and Uncle, my Cousins and
Charles,—Count Kolowrat (one of Uncle Ernest's
gentlemen), Lady Flora and the Miss Conroys &c.,
dined here. I sat between dear Ernest and dear
Albert. After dinner came Aunt Sophia. Received
a very kind letter from dear Aunt Louise and some
ribbons. Stayed up till ½ past 10. I like my

10 minutes past 5. Both my Cousins are so kind and good; they are much more *formés* and men of the world than Augustus; they speak English very well, and I speak it with them. Ernest will be 18 years old on the 21st of June and Albert 17 on the 26th of August. Dear Uncle Ernest made me the present of a most delightful *Lory*, which is so tame that it remains on your hand, and you may put your finger into its beak, or do anything with it, without its ever attempting to bite. It is larger than Mamma's grey Parrot, and has a most beautiful plumage; it is scarlet, blue, brown, yellow, and purple. At 6 we went with Lehzen, Lady Flora &c., to dine at the Archbishop of York's, and I was very sorry to leave my dear Uncle and Cousins behind us at home. . . .

Thursday, 19th May.—Read in the *Exposition* while my hair was doing. At 9 we breakfasted with Uncle Ernest, Ernest, Albert, Lehzen and Charles. I sat between my dear Cousins. At ½ past 10 Lehzen and I walked in the gardens and came home at ½ past 11. At a ¼ to 12 came the Dean till ½ past 12. Read with him in the New Testament and in Clarendon. At ½ past 12 came Mr. Steward till ½ past 1. Played and sung. At a ¼ past 2 came the Dean till 3. Read with him in Paley. At 3 came Mrs. Anderson till 4. At a ¼ to 5 we walked in the gardens with Lehzen till ½ past 5. Wrote my journal. At 7 we dined. Besides us 3 and Uncle, my Cousins and Charles,—Count Kolowrat (one of Uncle Ernest's gentlemen), Lady Flora and the Miss Conroys &c., dined here. I sat between dear Ernest and dear Albert. After dinner came Aunt Sophia. Received a very kind letter from dear Aunt Louise and so ribbons. Stayed up till ¼ past 10. I Kl.

H. S. H. Prince Albert of Saxe Coburg

aged nine

from a portrait by Schneider, Dec. Colburg

Cousins extremely, they are so kind, so good, and so merry. . . .

Saturday, 21st May.— . . . At ½ past 7 we dined with Uncle Ernest, Ernest, Albert, Charles, Lady Flora, Count Kolowrat, Baron Alvensleben, &c. I sat between my dear Cousins. After dinner came Princess Sophia. Baron de Hoggier, who had arrived from Lisbon the day before, came after dinner, and took leave, on his way home. I sat between my dear Cousins on the sofa and we looked at drawings. They both draw very well, particularly Albert, and are both exceedingly fond of music ; they play very nicely on the piano. The more I see them the more I am delighted with them, and the more I love them. They are so natural, so kind, so *very* good and so well instructed and informed ; they are so well bred, so truly merry and quite like children and yet very grown up in their manners and conversation. It is delightful to be with them ; they are so fond of being occupied too ; they are quite an example for any young person. . . .

*Sunday, 22nd May.—*I awoke at 7 and got up at 8. Read in *Cornwallis on the Sacrament* while my hair was doing. At a ¼ past 9 we all breakfasted. I sat between *i miei carissimi cugini.* At a ¼ past 10 dear Lehzen and I walked out in the gardens and came home at a ¼ to 11. Received the news of the death of my poor old Nurse, Mrs. Brock, which took place the day before yesterday. She was not a pleasant person, and undoubtedly had, as everybody has, her faults, but she was extremely attached to and fond of me, having been with me from my birth till my fifth year, therefore it is impossible, and it would be very wrong, if I did not feel her death. My chief regret is, that she did not live till I was my own mistress, and could make her quite comfortable.[1] . . .

Tuesday, 24th May.—I awoke at 7. Today I complete my 17th year; a very old person I am indeed! I am most thankful that I was brought through this year safely, and I beseech my heavenly Father to extend His benediction and blessing over me for this year and for many others. . . .

Friday, 10th June.—At 9 we all breakfasted for the *last* time together! It was our last HAPPY HAPPY breakfast, with this dear Uncle and those *dearest*, beloved Cousins, whom I *do* love so VERY VERY dearly; *much more dearly* than any other Cousins in the *world*. Dearly as I love Ferdinand, and also good Augustus, I love Ernest and Albert *more* than them, oh yes, MUCH *more*. Augustus was like a good, affectionate child, quite unacquainted with the world, phlegmatic, and talking but very little; but dearest Ernest and dearest Albert are so grown-up in their manners, so gentle, so kind, so amiable, so agreeable, so very sensible and reasonable, and so *really* and truly good and kind-hearted. They have both learnt a good deal, and are very clever, naturally clever, particularly Albert, who is the most reflecting of the two, and they like very much talking about serious and instructive things and yet are so *very very* merry and gay and happy, like young people ought to be; Albert used always to have some fun and some clever witty answer at

[1] This is the first indication in the Journals that Princess Victoria realised her future position. It is known that for many years knowledge of her possible accession to the Throne was withheld from her. When it was determined that she should be enlightened, a Family Tree was inserted by her governess between the pages of an English history. The child examined it minutely for some time, and turning to Baroness Lehzen said, " Then I shall be Queen."

breakfast and everywhere; he used to play and
fondle Dash so funnily too. Both he and Ernest are
extremely attentive to *whatever* they hear and see,
and take interest in everything they see. They were
much interested with the sight of St. Paul's yesterday.
We remained down with them till 10. I then went
up to my room and came down again at a little after
10. We remained with them again, Uncle Ernest
going in and out of the room. I am so very fond
of *him* too; now that I know him much better and
have talked with him, I love him as much as dear
Uncle Ferdinand. He is so mild, so kind and so good.
Dearest Albert was playing on the piano when I
came down. At 11 dear Uncle, my *dearest beloved*
Cousins, and Charles, left us, accompanied by Count
Kolowrat. I embraced both my dearest Cousins
most warmly, as also my dear Uncle. I cried bitterly,
very bitterly. . . .

Sunday, 31st July.—Read in *The Young Divine*
and began to read in *Ikon Basilike* in one vol.,
a book which came out a few days after poor
Charles I. had been beheaded; while my hair was
doing. It is said to have been written by him during
his captivity, and contains meditations and prayers;
but the Dean, who gave it me a few days ago, told
me that great disputes have arisen as to whether it
was really written by Charles, or whether some friend
of his had collected sayings and meditations he might
have heard the King make, and put them together
and that this point has not been settled yet. Whatever it may be, and by whomever it may have been
written or compiled, one thing is certain, that it is
a very good and pious book and is authentic as to
its contents. . . .

Wednesday, 3rd August.—Read in the *Exposition*

ı—12

and in *The Conquest of Granada* while my hair was doing. At 9 we breakfasted. At a ¼ to 10 we went to the British Gallery with Lehzen to see the Exhibition by the ancient Masters (all private property). Never did I see anything more beautiful than this collection of the *immortal Masters'* paintings, for so I must call them as their names will never pass away. There were such numbers of beautiful paintings, that I really know not which to name in preference. Upon the whole, I think the finest were those by Murillo and Guido. The finest by Murillo are " The Angels coming to Abraham," " The return of the Prodigal Son," splendid both, belonging to the Duke of Sutherland. " St. Joseph leading the infant Saviour who carries a basket of carpenter's tools," quite in another style but beautiful; " Santa Rosa, espousing the infant Saviour," exquisite; and " Portrait of Don Andres de Antrade and his favourite dog," very fine. The finest by Guido are, " The Assumption of the Virgin," the expression of the Virgin's face is beautiful; two different heads of St. Peter, both very fine. " The Magdalen," beautiful. The finest by Vandyke are " The Virgin and Infant Saviour," very lovely. . . . At a ¼ to 4 we went with Lehzen and Lady Flora to Chiswick, to the Victoria Asylum or Children's Friend Society. It is a most interesting and delightful establishment, and has been founded almost entirely by Lady George [1] and Miss Murray. It is for poor vagrant girls, who are received under the age of 15; and Miss Murray says that they have never had a girl 6 months who did not become a perfectly good child. I forget how young they

[1] Daughter of Lieut.-General Francis Grant and widow of Lord George Murray, Bishop of St. David's and second son of the second Duke of Atholl.

receive children, but there are — [unintelligible] girls
in all, and they are divided, a few being in an infant
school upstairs. When they have become quite
good and can read, write and do work of all kinds
necessary for a house, they are sent abroad, mostly
to the Cape of Good Hope, where they are apprenticed
and become excellent servants. Miss Murray told
us many curious stories of the depraved and wretched
state in which many arrive, and how soon they become
reformed and good. There is one little girl in particular, a very pretty black-eyed girl, 11 years old,
called Ellen Ford, who was received two months ago
from *Newgate,* and who boasted she could steal and
tell lies better than anybody. She had been but two
or three days in the school, and she got over 3 high
walls, and stole a sheet ; she was caught and brought
back again. Miss Murray spoke to her, and found
that the poor girl had no idea whatever of a *God,* and
had a drunken father, a low Irishman ; this man
had lost his 1st wife and married again, and this
step-mother taught the girl nothing but stealing
and lying. Miss Murray told her of God, and spoke
to her very seriously ; the girl was put in solitary
confinement for that night and was taken out the
next morning ; and ever since she has been a perfectly
good girl. There are many cases of the same sort
which Miss Murray said she could relate. Before
I finish this chapter I must mention the Matron, a
most respectable excellent person, called Mrs. Bower-
hill ; she is assisted by her two daughters, and by an
old woman for work ; but besides this old woman,
the children do all the work themselves. We came
home at ½ p. 6. I was very much pleased indeed
with all I saw. Miss Murray gave me a book into
which she had copied several of the letters of the

children from abroad, and very nice well-written letters they are. Miss Murray's exertions are immense and most praiseworthy for the Children's Friend Society. There is a Committee of Ladies who meet every other Tuesday I believe; but Lady George and Miss Murray go down 3 times a week and oftener. At a ¼ p. 7 we dined. After dinner came Princess Sophia. Stayed up till 10 minutes to 10. . . .

Monday, 8th August.—I awoke at 7 and got up at 8. At a ¼ past 9 we breakfasted. At a ¼ to 10 Lehzen and I walked out till ½ past 10. Arranged things for packing. At 11 came my good Lablache and stayed till 20 minutes past 12. I sang 1st " Come per me sereno," from *La Sonnambula.* Then he sang with me " Claudio, Claudio, ritorna fra le braccia paterne," twice over; then he sang with me " Se un istante all' offerta d'un soglio," also from *Elisa e Claudio.* The former of these two was the one that I sang so very ill on Saturday, but which Lablache did not mind at all. *He* thought it went better today; but he is too indulgent. *He* was in delightful voice, and sang *beautifully.* After this he sang " Non temer il mio bel cadetto " from *Il Posto abbandonato,* by Mercadante, with me. His volubility of tongue is wonderful; he can sing such quantities of words and at such a rate. There are plenty in this Duo, and still more in " Quand amore," and in " Voglio dire," both from *L'Elisire d'Amore.* Then he sang my favourite " O amato zio " from my dear *Puritani,* with me. After this he sang " O nume benefico " with us; then " Ridiamo, cantiamo," and then, *alas! per finire,* " Dopo due lustri ahi! misero," from *Donna Caritea,* by Mercadante. Lablache told me that he likes *Guillaume*

Tell the best of *all* Rossini's operas, *Otello* the best
of his Operas Seria, and *Il Barbiere* the best of his
buffa operas. *Ha ragione.* His son (Lablache's) is
gone, he told me; he went yesterday, as did also
Rubini. I asked him if any other of his 8 children
sang, or were musical. He replied, "Non, ils sont
trop jeunes; l'ainé n'a que douze ans." And the
youngest of all, he says, is only *2* years old. There
is an opera tomorrow, but the boxes &c., &c.
are let, shocking to say, at the play-house prices,
and "C'est un pasticcio," he said. It is not in the
regular number of nights. He said that I have
improved greatly in my singing since he has sung
with me. After the last trio, I took leave of *il mio
buon e caro Maestro* with *great* regret. I must repeat
again that he is not only a most delightful, patient,
and agreeable master, but a most good-humoured,
pleasing, agreeable and honest man; his manners
are very gentlemanly and quiet, and he has something very frank, open and honest in his countenance;
everybody who knows him agrees in his being such
a good man. I have had *26* lessons of Lablache and
shall think back with great delight on them; and
shall look forward with equal delight to next April,
when I hope Lablache will be here, so that I can
resume them again. It was such a pleasure to hear
his fine voice and to sing with him. Everything
that is pleasant, alas! passes so quickly in this " wide
world of troubles." How often I have experienced
that, in greater pleasures, when my dear relations
have left me! But then there are the pleasant *recollections* of all that is past, and one must be happy
one has had them. I was exceedingly delighted with
this my *last* lesson; the time seemed to fly even faster
than usual, for it always appeared to me that these

i—12*

pleasant lessons were over in an instant. Lablache accompanied really very fairly, and when he came to any difficult parts, he put in " des accords," which did just as well. I have already mentioned how very obliging he is; he was always ready to sing anything I like and to stay as long as I liked. He is extremely active for his size, which really is very considerable. It amused me always to see him come in and go out of my room; he walked so erect and made such a fine dignified bow. So now all, all is over for this season, not only the Opera but my favourite singing-lessons too. . . .

Wednesday, 10th August.— . . . A propos, I shall never forget when, in my first singing-lesson, I was so frightened to sing before **Lablache**, he said in his good-natured way, " Personne n'a jamais eu peur de moi," which I am sure nobody can ever be who knows him. . . ..

CLAREMONT, *Friday, 16th September.*—At ½ past 9 we breakfasted, that is to say, dearest Uncle, we two, Lehzen &c., Lady Catherine not being well enough, and Uncle's two gentlemen being gone to town. Went up to my room and copied out music. At about a ¼ to 12 dearest Uncle came and sat with me till ½ p. 12. He talked over many important things. He is *so* clever, *so* mild, and *so* prudent; *he* alone can give me good advice on *every* thing. His advice is perfect. He is indeed " il mio secondo padre " or rather " *solo* padre " ! for he is indeed like my real father, as I have none, and he is so kind and so good to me, he has ever been so to me. He has been and always is of such use to me and does *so* much good. . . .

Sunday, 18th September.—Baron Moncorvo brought yesterday the distressing news that the same unfortunate revolution which took place in Spain, has likewise taken place in Portugal, and that the Queen was forced to proclaim the constitution of 1820 similar to the one of 1812.[1] It happened between Friday the 9th and Saturday the 10th, in the night. I do so feel for poor dear Ferdinand in this trying moment, as also for the poor good Queen. The difference between this and the one in Spain was : that in *Portugal* they behaved respectfully towards dear Ferdinand and Donna Maria, and in Spain they almost insulted the Queen Regent. In Portugal, thank God ! no blood has been shed. As soon as the Empress heard what had happened, or rather what would happen, she hastened to the Palace de Necessidades, where Ferdinand and the Queen were, arrived there at 3 o'clock in the night, and remained there till all was over. The Princess Isabella, the Queen's Aunt (and the former Regent), also came and remained with them. Uncle Leopold was much shocked and distressed when he heard it, as were we also, I am sure. . . . Dear Uncle came up for a minute and brought us 3 letters which Van de Weyer had written to him, giving a detailed account of these horrid transactions at Lisbon. Van de Weyer's conduct throughout this dreadful business, when everybody else seems to have lost their heads and senses, was most courageous, prudent and judicious ; and if his and Ferdinand's advice had been followed, the Queen would *not* have been obliged to sign the Promulgation of the *Constituçion* of 1820. Van de Weyer says that *all* was given up " avec la plus

---

[1] The mutiny and riots in Portugal were, it was contended, the outcome of the appointment of Prince Ferdinand as Commander-in-Chief. This appointment had been made on the advice of the Duc de Terceira, the Prime Minister. See *ante*, p. 144.

affreuse lâcheté ! " without a struggle or attempt, when *all might yet have been saved.* . . .

Wednesday, 21st September.— . . . Dear Uncle came up and fetched us down to breakfast, as he has done already once before, and twice for dinner. He always accompanied us upstairs when we went to bed. It was our last breakfast with him ; I sat, as usual, near him and General Goblet.[1] To hear dear Uncle speak on any subject is like reading a highly instructive book ; his conversation is so enlightened, so clear. He is universally admitted to be one of the first politicians now extant. He speaks so mildly, yet firmly and impartially, about Politics. Uncle tells me that Belgium is quite a pattern for its organisation, industry and prosperity ; the finances are in the greatest perfection. Uncle is so beloved and revered by his Belgian subjects, that it must be a great compensation for all his extreme trouble. He is so mild, gentle and kind, and so clever and firm. . . .

Monday, 26th September.— . . . Read in the Morning Post of today the melancholy and almost incredible news of the *death* of—*Malibran* ![2] which took place at Manchester on Friday night at 12 o'clock, at the early age of 28. She had gone there for the festival which took place the week before last, and only sang on Tuesday the 13th instant, and tried to do so on the Wednesday but was unable, after which she was taken so alarmingly ill that all singing was over. On Saturday the account in the papers was that she was out of danger, but the

---

[1] See *ante*, p. 137.

[2] Madame Malibran (1808–36), daughter of Manuel Garcia. She was a distinguished singer and a woman of considerable talent. Her first husband was a French merchant, M. Malibran. At the time of her death she was married to M. de Bériot.

MADAME MALIBRAN.

From a sketch by Princess Victoria

improvement was only transient and on Friday night this wonderful singer and extraordinary person was no more.   She will be, and is, a very *great* loss indeed ; for, though I liked and admired Grisi by far more than Malibran, I admired many parts of the latter's singing very much, in particular those touching and splendid low notes which gave one quite a thrill. In point of cleverness and genius there is not a doubt that Malibran far surpassed Grisi ; for she was not proficient alone in singing and acting, she knew Spanish (her own language), Italian, French, English, and German perfectly, as also various Italian *patois.* She composed very prettily, drew well, rode well on horseback, danced beautifully, and enfin *climbed* well, as General Alava told us, who knew her very well ; he said you could speak with her on any subject and she was equally *à son aise.*   She was born in 1808 at Paris, and is the daughter of a famous Spanish singer called *Garcia* ; she married first an old French merchant called *Malibran*, from whom she was divorced ; and secondly this spring the incomparable violinist De Bériot.   Mamma saw her make her debut as *Maria Garcia*, only 16 years old, in *Il Crociato*, at the Italian Opera in London, as " un giovinetto Cavalier."   There is something peculiarly awful and striking in the death of this great Cantatrice, undoubtedly the *second in the world*, (Grisi being the *first* in *my opinion*).   To be thus cut off in the bloom of her youth and the height of her career, suddenly, is dreadful ! . . .

Wednesday, 28th September.— . . . The news from Lisbon are far from good, I am *sorry to say.* Mamma received a letter from Van de Weyer this morning, dated 11th Sept., in which he said that there had been another *émeute* the afternoon before,

which however had been dissipated, and that both
dearest Ferdinand and Donna Maria showed great
calmness and dignity.   It is a great trial for poor
dear Ferdinand and for the good Queen.   Van de
Weyer says they are all in a very uncomfortable
situation. . . .

Friday, 30*th September.*— . . . Read in *The
Times* last night a distressing account of the details
of poor Malibran's illness and death.   Poor young
creature ! she seems to have been neglected at a
time when her life might perhaps still have been
saved ; for she complained of head-ache and shivering
the same afternoon she arrived (Sunday 11th Sept.).
On the Wednesday night after singing that fine but
now painful Duo " Vanne se alberghi in petto," she
was taken so very very ill.   Notwithstanding all
this she got up on Thursday morning and was dressed
with the assistance of Mrs. Richardson, landlady of
the Mosely Arms Hotel at Manchester, for she had
no female attendant, a man-servant of De Bériot's
being (as is said in the newspapers, for all what I
have hitherto related about her illness and death
is taken from the newspapers) their only servant.
In spite of every effort to prevent her, the poor dying
Malibran insisted upon going to the Oratorio that
morning, and was accordingly carried to her carriage ;
but being seized with hysterics she was instantly
taken back.   She never left her room, and scarcely
her bed, from that time till her death.   Dr. Belluo-
mini, her own Physician, only arrived on Sunday
the 18th, though other physicians had attended her
(from Manchester) before.   She was perfectly in-
sensible when she died, as also two or 3 days before
her death.   De Bériot was distracted and over-
powered on learning of her death, in another room

whither they had compelled him to retire when it
was drawing to a close. He never saw her afterwards, and left the place 2 hours after all was over.
It is the most melancholy end that could be imagined !
To come to an inn in a foreign land with nobody to
nurse her, and *die* there ! What a sad and tragical
end to her bright career! I can still hardly believe
it possible that she, whom I can see before me as she
was at our own concert, dressed in white satin, so
merry and lively, and whose pathetic voice when
speaking I can hear, is now in the silent tomb ; for
the funeral was to take place at 10 o'clock this
morning with great splendour. And so today, all,
all is over with poor Malibran ! . . .

Sunday, 9th October.— . . . We went to the church
at Ramsgate with Lady Catherine and Lehzen. Mr.
Harvey preached. The text was from the 5th
chapter of the 2nd Epistle to Cor., 10th verse :
" For we must all appear before the judgment seat
of Christ ; that every man may receive the things
done in his body according to that he hath done,
whether it be good or bad." Came home at 20
minutes to 1. Wrote my journal. Copied out
music. At a ¼ to 3 we went to the chapel with Lady
Catherine and dear Lehzen, &c. The service was
read by Mr. Lewis, and Dr. Longley (late Master of
Harrow School) preached, and *most beautifully* ; so
mildly and emphatically ; his voice is very good, his
pronunciation very pure, his delivery calm and
impressive, his language beautiful yet simple, and
his appearance very pleasing. He must be between
30 and 40, I should say. The text was from the 3rd
chapter of Daniel, 16th, 17th, and 18th verses :
" Shadrach, Meshech, and Abed-nego answered and
said to the King, O Nebuchadnezzar, we are not

careful to answer thee in this matter. If it be so, our God whom we serve is able to deliver us from the burning fiery furnace, and He will deliver us out of thine hand, O King. But if not, be it known unto thee, O King, that we will not serve thy gods nor worship the golden image which thou hast set up." It was a most beautiful sermon in every way, and I was *very much* pleased and impressed with it. Dr. Longley is to be Bishop of Ripon.[1] . . .

Thursday, 27th October.— . . . Read in *The Conquest of Granada* while my hair was doing. At 9 we breakfasted. Wrote a letter to my brother. At 10 came the Dean till ½ p. 11. Read with him in the N.T., in *The Life of Colonel Hutchinson*, and in Paley. *The Life of Colonel Hutchinson* is written by his wife, who wrote it for her children after their father's death. Colonel Hutchinson lived in the time of Charles I., the Commonwealth, and even of Charles II. He was on the Puritanical side, and though a very good man, signed the King's death-warrant, being very *strong* on his side, which is to be seen by Mrs. Hutchinson's writings ; his and her feelings being totally opposite to Clarendon's, render it interesting, though it is more a private account of his life than any public History of the Times, but of course a good deal of history will be mixed up in it as Col. Hutchinson had a good deal to do in the wars. Mrs. Hutchinson's style is remarkably quaint and ancient, indeed in some parts so much so as to render it almost ridiculous, but there are again some very pretty feeling parts in it (indeed feeling and pious throughout it), one of which, in which she speaks of her husband and herself I shall quote ; before I

---

[1] He was translated to Durham in 1856. In 1860 he became Archbishop of York and in 1862 Primate of All England.

do so, however, I must say that the editor, a descendant of the family, has left the orthography just as she
wrote it, which is very antiquated and imperfect :
" The greatest excellence she (Mrs. Hutchinson) had
was the power of apprehending and the vertue of
loving his (Col. H.'s) soe as his shadow, she waited
on him every where, till he was taken into that region
of light, which admits of none, and then she vanisht
into nothing." There is likewise another passage
speaking of a son she lost : " . . . call'd by his owne
name John, who liv'd scarce six yeares, and was a very
hopefull child, full of his father's vigor and spiritt,
but death soone nipt that blossome." Lehzen of
course still continues reading to me while I dress, the
delightful letters of Mme. de Sévigné ; we are now
in the middle of the 10th vol., and I like them more
and more, they are so beautiful, so easy, they show
the character of the person who wrote them so
perfectly, you become acquainted with her and hers,
and there are such tender and beautiful feelings
expressed in them, towards that daughter who was
her all & all ; and the style is so elegant and so
beautiful. I shall quote a passage relating to a
vexation she had about not procuring the " députa-
tion " for her son M. de Sévigné : " Ne faut-il point
être juste et se mettre à la place des gens ? c'est ce
qu'on ne fait jamais." How true this is. Then how
pretty this is, in writing to Mme. de Grignan : " Vous
me louez trop de la douce retraite que je fais ici ; rien
n'y est pénible que votre absence." There is certainly nothing so beautiful of the kind, in any language as these letters. I shall just quote two passages
from the extracts in *The Edinburgh Review* of Sir
James Mackintosh's life, about Mme. de Sévigné :
" In the midst of all the rage felt at Paris against

King William, the admirable good-sense and natural moderation of Mme. de Sévigné catches a glimpse of his real character, through the mists of Rome and Versailles : ' Le prince n'a pas songé à faire périr son beau-père. Il est à Londres, à la place du Roi, sans en prendre le nom, ne voulant que rétablir une religion qu'il croit bonne, et maintenir les loix du pays sans qu'il en coûte une goutte de sang. . . . Pour le Roi d'Angleterre il y (St. Germains) parait content,—et c'est pour cela qu'il est là.' Observe the perfect good-sense of the last remark, and the ease and liveliness with which it is made. Tacitus and Machiavel could have said nothing better ; but a superficial reader will think no more of it than the writer herself seems to do."—Again, further on : " The style of Mme. de Sévigné is evidently copied not only by her worshipper Walpole, but even by Gray ; who notwithstanding the extraordinary merits of his matter, has the double stiffness of an imitator and of a college recluse." . . .

Friday, 28th October.—I awoke at 7 and got up at 20 minutes to 8. Read in the *Exposition* while my hair was doing. Received a most kind dear and pretty letter from dearest Aunt Louise, from which I will copy a passage : " I have today not much to say. It is my brother Nemours' birthday ; and in the same time, the anniversary of the death of my dear governess " (Mme. de Mallet, who died when Aunt Louise was at Paris last year) " of the best and truest friend I had for twenty years, to make me melancholy. In her was broken the first link of the chain of my strong and youthful affections. How many more shall I live perhaps to see destroyed ? " How pretty and feeling this is ; it comes straight from her dear good heart. I can well say of my *precious* Lehzen what she says of Mme. de Mallet, that she is my " best and truest friend " I have had for nearly 17 years and I trust I shall have for 30 or 40 and *many* more ! . . .

Tuesday, 1st November.— . . . Read in *The Conquest of Granada*, and wrote my journal. There are two lines in *Rokeby* (which is so full of beauty that I could copy the whole and not find one part which is not full of loveliness, sweetness, grace, elegance, and feeling, for the immortal bard who wrote these beautiful poems never *could* write an *ugly* line in *my* opinion) which struck me, as well as the Dean, who is, s'il est permis de le dire, poetry-mad, as most splendid. . . . Oh ! Walter Scott is my *beau idéal* of a Poet ; I do so admire him both in Poetry and Prose ! . . .

Thursday, 3rd November.— . . . After 7 we dined. The Duke of Wellington, the Countess of Ashburnham,[1] and Lady Elinor Ashburnham,[2] Lord and Lady Radstock,[3] Lord and Lady Barham,[4] Colonel Stopford,[5] Colonel Barnard, Mr. Sicklemore, and Mr. Mayhew dined here. I sat between the Duke of Wellington and Lord Radstock. The Duke looked remarkably well and was in very good spirits. Lady Barham looked very handsome ; she had a reddish brown velvet turban and a dark velvet dress. She

---

[1] Charlotte, daughter of the fifth Duke of Northumberland, widow of the third Earl of Ashburnham.

[2] Afterwards wife of the Rev. Algernon Wodehouse.

[3] Granville George (1786–1857), second Lord Radstock, Vice-Admiral of the Red.

[4] Charles Noel (1781–1866) had succeeded in his father's lifetime to his mother's barony of Barham. He was created Earl of Gainsborough in 1841. In 1833 he married his fourth wife, Frances, daughter of the third Earl of Roden, afterwards a Lady of the Bedchamber to Queen Victoria.

[5] Hon. Edward Stopford, second son of third Earl of Courtown.

is a likeness of the Duchess of Sutherland in dark, but the Duchess is handsomer, in figure and all together handsomer, having a finer nose and mouth than Lady Barham. Lady Barham has a beautiful brow and fine dark expressive eyes with a fine pale complexion, but the lower part of her face, particularly the mouth and chin, are not at all good. She looks 28 and is only 22. . . .

Sunday, 6th November.— . . . We walked home at 1. Read in *Astoria*. Added a few lines to my letter to Feodore. Wrote one to Aunt Sophia and my journal. At ½ p. 2 we went out with *dearest* Lehzen and came home at a little before 4. Received a most kind letter from dearest Uncle Leopold accompanied by a " supplément extraordinaire " to the *Moniteur Universel,* giving an account of the " échauffourée " which took place at Strasburg on the 30th October, headed by Louis Napoleon Buonaparte,[1] a young man of 28 years old, son of the Duchesse de St. Leu (Hortense), and who tried to make the Troops rise in his favour, but the latter proved faithful to their King (Louis Philippe) and country, as they ought ; and the Prince and Rebels have been put in prison. The Queen of the French sent Uncle the paper. . . .

Sunday, 20th November.— . . . Read a letter of Lord Palmerston's to Mamma relative to the late unfortunate affairs at Lisbon, which is very consolatory. Marshal Saldanha was charged to bring about the reaction, which was to spread first in the provinces and then to the capital and the Queen was *not* to give the first impulse.[2] Unfortunately poor Donna Maria

---

[1] Afterwards Napoleon III.

[2] The Queen had been led to believe that a counter-revolution would be popular, but the movement was a failure.

was hurried into this step by the jealousy of those about her. The friends of the Duke of Terceira, unwilling that Marshal Saldanha should have the credit of the reaction, snatched it out of his hands and brought on all this confusion. However, Lord Palmerston concludes with this : " The result of the whole is, that the Queen's position is *better* than it *was*, not so *bad* as it *might* have been after such a failure, but *much less good* than if she had waited patiently till the proper time for action had arrived. The Prince behaved throughout with spirit, courage and firmness and has acquired by his conduct the respect of both parties." That our beloved and precious Ferdinand has behaved in such a way is most *delightful* for me, who *love him* like the *dearest of Brothers*. It could not be otherwise, I was sure. . . .

Tuesday, 29th November.— . . . At 8 we left poor West Cliff House. . . . We reached Canterbury in safety in spite of the rain and some wind, but not very long after we left it, it began to blow so dreadfully, accompanied by floods of rain at intervals, that our carriage swung and the post-boys could scarcely keep on their horses. As we approached Sitting-bourne, the *hurricane*, for I cannot call it by any other name, became quite frightful and even alarming ; corn stacks were flying about, trees torn up by their roots, and chimneys blown to atoms. We got out, or rather were *blown* out, at Sitting-bourne. After staying there for a short while we got into the carriage where Lady Theresa and Lehzen were, with them, which being larger and heavier than our post-chaise, would not shake so much. For the first 4 or 5 miles all went on more smoothly and I began to hope our difficulties were at an end. Alas ! far from it. The wind blew worse than before and in going down the hill just before Chatham, **the** hurricane was so tremendous that the horses stopped **for** a minute, and I thought that we were undone, **but** by dint of whipping and very good management **of** the post-boys we reached Rochester in safety. Here we got out, and here it was determined that **we** must pass the night. Here we are therefore, and here we must remain, greatly to my annoyance, for I am totally unprepared, Lehzen's and my wardrobe maid are gone on to Claremont, and I hate sleeping at an **Inn.** I had been so glad at the thought of not doing so this time, mais " l'homme propose **et** Dieu dispose," and it would have been temerity **to** proceed, for a coach had been upset on the bridge just before we arrived, and the battlements of **the** bridge itself were totally blown in. . . .

Sunday, 18*th December.*— . . . I sat between Mr. Croker [1] and Col. Wemyss.[2] Der erste ist ein kluger, aber nach meiner Meinung, nicht angenehmer Mann ; er spricht zu viel. He has a very excellent memory and tells anecdotes cleverly but with a peculiar pronunciation of the *r.* He said that the Duke of Wellington had told him that the character of the 3 nations, the English, Scotch, and Irish, was very apparent in the army. He said (the Duke), " It may seem like a joke what I am going to say, but it is quite true ; the *Scotch* were pleased when the *money* arrived, the *Irish* when they got into a *wine country,*

[1] The Rt. Hon. John Wilson Croker (1780–1857), M.P. for Downpatrick and Secretary to the Admiralty. Immortalised in *Coningsby* as " Mr. Rigby," he has remained the type of malignant and meddling politician that Disraeli desired to expose. His title to respect is that he was one of the earliest contributors to *The Quarterly Review,* which was founded by John Murray in 1809.

[2] William Wemyss, afterwards Lieut.-General and Equerry to Queen Victoria.

and the *English* when the *roast beef* came up." He told many anecdotes and made many remarks upon the various nations, ein wenig sehr stark. Il aime trop à étaler, il n'a pas de tacte ; il prend trop le ton supérieur. . . .

CLAREMONT, *Saturday,* 24*th December* (*Xmas Eve*).— I awoke after 7 and got up at 8. After 9 we breakfasted. At a little after 10 we left Kensington with dearest Lehzen, Lady Conroy and—*Dashy* ! and reached Claremont at a ¼ to 12. Played and sang. At 2 dearest Lehzen, Victoire and I [? went out] and came home at 20 minutes p. 3. No one was stirring about the Gipsy encampment except George, which I was sorry for, as I was anxious to know how our poor friends were after this bitterly cold night. Played and sang. Received from dearest best Lehzen as a Christmas box : 2 lovely little Dresden china figures, 2 pair of lovely little chased gold buttons, a small lovely button with an angel's head which she used to wear herself, and a pretty music book ; from good Louis a beautiful piece of Persian stuff for an album ; and from Victoire and Emily Gardiner a small box worked by themselves. Wrote my journal. Went down to arrange Mamma's table for her. At 6 we dined. Mr. Edmund Byng [1] and Mr. Conroy dined here. Mr. Byng is going to stay here a night or two. Very soon after dinner Mamma sent for us into the Gallery, where all the things were arranged on different tables. From my dear Mamma I received a beautiful massive gold buckle in the shape of two serpents ; a lovely little delicate gold chain with a turquoise clasp ; a lovely coloured sketch of dearest Aunt Louise by Partridge, copied

---

[1] Second son of fifth Viscount Torrington, sometime a Commissioner in the Colonial Audit Office.

from the picture he brought, and so like her; 3 beautiful drawings by Munn, one lovely sea view by Purser, and one beautiful cattle piece by Cooper (all coloured), 3 prints, a book called *Finden's Tableaux, Heath's Picturesque Annual for* 1837, *Ireland*; both these are very pretty; *Friendship's Offering*, and *The English Annual for* 1837, *The Holy Land* illustrated beautifully, two handkerchiefs, a very pretty black satin apron trimmed with red velvet, and two almanacks. I am very thankful to my dear Mamma for all these very pretty things. From dear Uncle Leopold, a beautiful turquoise ring; from the Queen a fine piece of Indian gold tissue; and from Sir J. Conroy a print. I gave my dear Lehzen a green morocco jewel case, and the *Picturesque Annual*; Mamma gave her a shawl, a dress, a pair of turquoise earrings, an annual, and handkerchiefs. I then took Mamma to the Library where my humble table was arranged. I gave her a bracelet made of my hair, the clasp of which contains Charles', Feodore's and my hair; and the *Keepsake* and *Oriental Annual*. Lehzen gave her two pair of little buttons just like mine. I danced a little with Victoire. Stayed up till 11.

Sunday, 25th December (*Xmas day*).—At 9 we all breakfasted. Mamma, Lehzen and I read prayers. Arranged my new drawings. At a little before 2 dearest Lehzen, Victoire and I went out and came home at 3. As we were approaching *the camp*,[1] we met Rea coming from it, who had been sent there by Mamma to enquire into the story of these poor wanderers. He told us (what I was quite sure of before) that all was quite true, that the poor young woman and baby were doing very well, though very

[1] A gipsy encampment.

weak and miserable and that what they wanted chiefly was fuel and nourishment. Mamma has ordered broth and fuel to be sent tonight, as also 2 blankets; and several of our people have sent old flannel things for them. Mamma has ordered that the broth and fuel is to be sent each day till the woman is recovered. Lehzen sent them by our footmen a little worsted knit jacket for the poor baby, and when we drove by, Aunt Sarah,[1] the old woman and the Husband all looked out and bowed most gratefully. Rea gave them directly a sovereign. I cannot say how happy I am that these poor creatures are assisted, for they are such a nice set of Gipsies, so quiet, so affectionate to one another, so discreet, not at all forward or importunate, and *so* grateful; so unlike the gossiping, fortune-telling race-gipsies; and this is such a peculiar and touching case. Their being assisted makes me quite merry and happy today, for yesterday night when I was safe and happy at home in that cold night and today when it snowed so and everything looked white, I felt quite unhappy and grieved to think that our poor gipsy friends should perish and shiver for want; and now today I shall go to bed happy, knowing they are better off and more comfortable. . . .

Thursday, 29th December.— . . . At 12 we went out with dear Lehzen and came home at 2. Everything still looked very white and the ground rather slippery but not so much as yesterday. It snowed part of the time we were walking. I saw Aunt Sarah and the least pretty of the two sisters-in-law, who has returned, in a shop at Esher. How I *do* wish I could do something for their *spiritual* and *mental* benefit and for the education of their children and in

---

[1] One of the gipsies

particular for the poor little baby who I have known
since its birth, in the admirable manner Mr. Crabbe
in his *Gipsies' Advocate* so strongly urges ; he be-
seeches and urges those who have kind hearts and
Christian feelings to think of these poor wanderers,
who have many good qualities and who have many
good people amongst them. He says, and alas !
I *too well* know its truth, from experience, that whenever any poor Gipsies are encamped anywhere and
crimes and robberies &c. occur, it is invariably laid
to their account, which is shocking ; and if they are
always looked upon as vagabonds, how *can* they
become good people ? I trust in Heaven that the
day may come when *I* may do something for these
poor people, and for this particular family ! I am
sure that the little kindness which they have experienced from us will have a good and lasting effect on
them ! . . .

GYPSY WOMEN.

From a sketch by Princess Victoria

INTRODUCTORY NOTE TO CHAPTER VI

THIS was her *annus mirabilis*, her wonder-year. The earlier months passed much as usual. On 24th May she was eighteen years old. The entry in her Journal shows some presentiment of what was to come. In less than a month she had stepped from out of the precincts of that quiet, ill-furnished palace in Kensington Gardens into the full glare of the Throne. The 20th June was her most wonderful day, but although keenly alive to its significance and glory, she never lost her self-control. The hidden forces which even her Journals failed to reveal, appear so to have moulded her character that she was enabled to appreciate and yet resist the glamours of this supreme moment. There is not a trace of doubt or misgiving. She was conscious of a mysterious duty imposed upon her by Divine Providence, and although she obviously felt her inexperience, she never for a moment doubted her fitness for her task. King William died at Windsor soon after two in the morning, and three hours later the Archbishop and Lord Conyngham were at Kensington Palace. The Princess received them in a dressing-gown hastily thrown over her nightdress, her feet in slippers, and her fair hair loose about her head. Four hours later she received for the first time Lord Melbourne, the Prime Minister, who was destined until the day of her marriage to exercise a potent influence over her thoughts and actions. Her caution in the selection of confidantes, her wariness in granting her approval, and her care to safeguard the regal tradition, are clearly apparent from the day of her accession. Although she accepted advice, she never appeared to yield. There is nothing in these Journals that displays the inner thoughts of the Queen, in a light differing from that in which her conduct appeared both to her Ministers and to her courtiers. Then, as in after-years, she fulfilled the hope publicly expressed by Lord John Russell, that she would prove to be an Elizabeth without her tyranny and an Anne without her weakness.

It must be remembered that from the day of her accession the Crowns of Great Britain and Hanover were divided. Her uncle, Ernest, Duke of Cumberland, succeeded to the Throne of Hanover. The fear that he might succeed to the Throne of Great Britain had always haunted the minds of the people, and added to the feeling of gladness with which they welcomed the young Queen. On the second day of her reign the name Alexandrina was dropped for ever, and she was thenceforth known, as she desired to be, by the name of Victoria.

CHAPTER VI

1837

Sunday, 8th January.— . . . The service was performed by the Dean, who gave us likewise a sermon. The text was from the 1st Chapter of Isaiah, — verse : —" Wash you, make you clean." At 12 dear Lehzen and I went out and came home at 10 minutes p. 1. It is today a week that we took leave of our poor good friends the Gipsies, and I am quite sorry when I pass the spot so long enlivened by their little camp, and behold it empty and deserted, and with almost no trace to be seen of their ever having been there. They had been there more than a month, for they encamped there about 5 days after we arrived here and have been there ever since until last Wednesday or Thursday. To *my* feeling, the chief ornament of the Portsmouth Road is gone since their departure. But this is their life ; they are happy and grateful and we have done them some good. The place and spot may be forgotten, but the Gipsy family Cooper will *never* be obliterated from my memory ! . . .

Tuesday, 10th January.— . . . At a ¼ p. 3 came M. Van de Weyer, who arrived in London last night from Lisbon. He gave us most interesting and most valuable information about Portugal ; praised **our** *dearest* Ferdinand to the skies, said he showed cleverness, firmness, and character which no other young man of his age hardly ever showed; said the poor Queen was totally indifferent to whatever happened, but was extremely obedient to Ferdinand who had great power over her. He told us much to distress us, but said that the present ministers were ready to do anything that was right. He is a most clever, clear-sighted, sensible little man, Van de Weyer himself. He looks much careworn and fatigued, and *no* wonder at it. . . .

Tuesday, 7th February.—Read in *Bajazet*. Read to Lehzen out of *Polyeucte* and finished it; it is certainly *very* beautiful and full of most beautiful and highminded feelings, but the end is, to my feelings, rather unnatural. Lehzen dictated to me some passages from *Polyeucte*. . . .

Thursday, 9th February.— . . . Read to dear Lehzen out of the newspapers Lord John Russell's very able and judicious speech on bringing in the Irish Corporation bill; and out of the Irish History. . . . Read in *Bajazet* and wrote my journal. Lehzen dictated French to me. Played and sang. Read in Raumer's *Königinnen*. Read in Clive's life [1] while my hair was doing. At 6 we dined. Read in *Bajazet*. Sang, and Mamma also. Stayed up till 10. Read in School Shakespeare while my hair was undoing.

Saturday, 8th April.—At 10 came the Dean till 11. Read with him in the N.T. and in Boswell's *Life of Johnson*. At $\frac{1}{2}$ p. 11 I went down and sat to Mr. Lane [2] till a $\frac{1}{4}$ to 1. He showed me 4 very beautiful

---

[1] Sir John Malcolm's *Life of Clive*, a biography now unreadable, but made famous by Macaulay, who took it as a peg upon which to hang his Essay.

[2] Richard James Lane (1800–72) had in 1829 made a well-known

coloured drawings by Chalon, 3 portraits,—Mrs.
Ashley, very like ; Miss Fanny Wyndham as Contino
in *Scaramuccia*, ridiculously like ; and Bellini as
Figaro ; the 4th is a very beautiful head and hands
of Juliet asleep after she has taken the draught.
Mr. Lane likewise showed me a very beautiful minia-
ture of Lady Blessington [1] painted by Chalon about
15 years ago ; and a beautiful drawing of C. Kemble as
Falstaff, done by himself. He is a great friend of
Kemble's and admires him beyond everything. He
is also very intimate with Mr. Macready, and says
he is such an excellent father and husband. Charles
Mathews, he says, speaks Italian as well as he does
French. . . . At 20 minutes p. 7 we went with dear
Lehzen, Lady Theresa, Charles and Lord Ilchester
&c. to the Opera. It was my dear *I Puritani*, and
they were singing the opening Chorus when we came
in. Grisi, Rubini, Lablache, and Tamburini made
their first appearance this season, and were all
enthusiastically cheered on their appearance, in
particular my worthy Master and Rubini. There
is not a word of truth in what was said about Grisi, for

portrait of the Princess at ten years old. He was afterwards distinguished for his skill in lithography, reproducing many works of
well-known artists. The portrait he was painting at this time now
hangs in the Corridor at Windsor.

[1] Lady Blessington (1789–1849) was at the zenith of her career,
editing Books of Beauty, writing novels, and entertaining celebrities
at Gore House, Kensington. She was married when young and beautiful to Lord Blessington, an elderly and easy-going Peer, whose daughter
by his first wife was the wife of Count d'Orsay. This unfortunate
young woman was eclipsed in the affections of d'Orsay by her
stepmother. After Lord Blessington's death, d'Orsay and Lady Blessington presided over a brilliant salon at Kensington Gore, principally
attended by the male sex. Lady Blessington recorded in several
volumes her conversations with Byron. Disraeli, as a young man,
flaunted his most elaborate waistcoats at Gore House.

I never saw anything look more lovely that she did, and she sang deliciously, as did also Rubini whose voice seems to get if possible finer each year. It is useless to add that the singing of these 4 incomparable and unequalled *artistes* was, as always, perfection ! with the exception perhaps of Lablache's being a little hoarse at times ; he did not look well and was not in his usual spirits I thought. The Quartet " Ah ! te o cara," the Polacca, " Suoni la tromba," and " Ella è tremante " were all loudly encored. After the Opera was over the 4 cantanti were called out and loudly cheered. . . .

Tuesday, 11th April.—Heard that poor Lady De L'Isle,[1] the King's eldest daughter, had expired at 10 o'clock the night before. On the death of old Mrs. Strode last February, the King made Lady De L'Isle housekeeper of Kensington Palace ; and she arrived here about 2 or 3 days after we came from Claremont, was confined with a daughter about a month ago, and was going on very well, when she was taken so alarmingly ill, I think on Sunday. It is very awful and very dreadful for her 4 poor children.

After 9 we breakfasted. At a little before 10 came the Dean till 12 minutes to 11. Read with him in the N.T. and in Hume. At 11 came my good Lablache and stayed till 6 minutes to 12. He was as good-humoured, kind, ready, and gentlemanlike as ever ; there never is any difference in his manners or ways, may he be ill, well, tired or not tired, he is always in the same ready good-humour. He is perhaps a little greyer, *mais voilà tout.* He was in splendid voice and sang beautifully. It was quite a delight for me to hear his fine and unique voice

[1] See *ante*, p. 99.

again and to sing with him; it is such a support
to my voice and he accompanies so agreeably. I
sang first with him the favourite duo of mine:
" Voglio dire," from *L'Elisire d'Amore*; then " Una
furtiva lagrima," a pretty little Aria from the same
opera, which I repeated and which Catone used to
sing so nicely, as also " Quanto è bella quanto è cara "
from *L'Elisir*, which I also sung. After this Lablache
sang with Mamma and me " Se il fratel stringere "
from *Belisario*, which he *had never seen* or even *heard*
before ! . . .

Thursday, 20th April.—I got up at 8. Read in
the *Exposition* while my hair was doing. After 9
we breakfasted. Played and sang; practised for
Lablache. Drew. At 20 minutes to 2 we went to the
Drawing Room with dear Lehzen, Lady Mary Stopford,[1] Sir George Anson &c. The poor Queen not
being well, the King held the Drawing-room, and
(strange to say) Princess Augusta represented her.
There were several young ladies presented, amongst
whom were Lady Wilhelmina Stanhope (daughter
to the Earl and Countess Stanhope),[2] a beautiful
girl; Lady Fanny Cowper[3] (daughter to the Earl
and Countess Cowper), also pretty; Lady Mary

---

[1] Eldest daughter of third Earl of Courtown.

[2] Philip Henry, fourth Earl, and Lucy Catherine, daughter of Robert
Low Carrington. Lady Wilhelmina married in 1843 Lord Dalmeny,
by whom she had a son (the present Lord Rosebery) and three other
children. After Lord Dalmeny's death in 1851, she married in 1854
the fourth Duke of Cleveland. She was one of the Queen's train-
bearers at her Coronation. She died in May 1901.

[3] Daughter of the fifth Earl Cowper, and niece to Lord Melbourne.
She afterwards married Lord Jocelyn. She was a great favourite with
Queen Victoria. After the Queen's marriage and her own marriage
she became one of the Queen's Ladies of the Bedchamber, and held
that post till shortly before her (Lady Jocelyn's) death.

Grimston,[1] Miss Louisa Percy,[2] Miss Wynn (niece to the Duchess of Northumberland), Victoire Conroy, &c. The poor Duchess of Northumberland was unable to attend me, having a bad cold. We came home at 20 minutes p. 3. . . .

Friday, 19th May.—Got up at 8. Wrote the *brouillon* of a French letter to dearest Aunt Louise while my hair was doing. After 9 we breakfasted. The children played in the room. At 10 Mary,[3] Lehzen, I and the children went out walking and came home at 10 minutes to 11. Wrote my letter to dearest Aunt Louise. At $\frac{1}{2}$ p. 11 came M. Guazzaroni till 12. Received a letter from *the King* by Lord Conyngham. . . .

Read in W. Scott's Life. Received an address from the Mayor and City of Lincoln, which was presented by Colonel Sibthorp [4] and Mr. Edward Lytton Bulwer,[5] the two Members. I was attended by my dearest Lehzen, and Mamma by Lady Flora. Played and sung &c. Wrote my journal. Drew.

[1] Third daughter of the first Earl of Verulam, and afterwards wife of the fourth Earl of Radnor. The three young ladies mentioned here were afterwards trainbearers to Queen Victoria at her coronation.

[2] Daughter of Vice-Admiral Josceline Percy, and afterwards wife of Colonel Charles Bagot.

[3] Marie, Countess of Blebelsberg, born 1806, married Prince Charles of Leiningen (see p. 95). She died 1880.

[4] Colonel Sibthorp, the eccentric member for Lincoln, whose personal appearance was much satirised in *Punch*.

[5] Afterwards Sir Edward Bulwer Lytton and Lord Lytton of Knebworth. He was distinguished as a writer of novels that enjoyed a great vogue, and as a genuine man of letters. His abilities were of a far higher order than his writing. His ability was his own, but he wrote for the public. He earned a considerable fortune by his pen. For a time he chose to be a politician, and was Secretary for the Colonies in Lord Derby s Government. His marriage was famous for its failure. His son Robert was Viceroy of India, Ambassador in Paris, and a poet of more than average merit.

Felt very miserable and agitated. Did not go down to dinner, but dined in my own room at 8 o'clock. Stayed up till 10.

Saturday, 20th May.—Got up after 8. After 9 we breakfasted. The dear children were in the room and played very merrily. Wrote a letter to the King, which Mamma had previously written for me. At 3 minutes past 11 came my buon Maestro Lablache, looking pale and coughing, and complaining he was still unwell and feared he would remain so till the weather became warmer. . . .

Wednesday, 24th May.—Today is my 18th birthday ! How old ! and yet how far am I from being what I should be. I shall from this day take the *firm* resolution to study with renewed assiduity, to keep my attention always well fixed on whatever I am about, and to strive to become every day less trifling and more fit for what, if Heaven wills it, I'm some day to be ! . . . At ½ p. 3 we drove out with Mary and dear Lehzen and came home at 5. The demonstrations of loyalty and affection from all the people were highly gratifying. The parks and streets were thronged and everything looked like a *Gala* day. Numbers of people put down their names and amongst others good old Lablache inscribed his. . . . At ½ p. 10 we went to the ball at St. James's with the Duchess of Northumberland, dear Lehzen, Lady Flora and Lady Conroy &c. The King though much better was unable of course to be there, and the Queen neither, so that, strange to say, Princess Augusta made the *honneurs* ! I danced first with Lord Fitzalan,[1] 2ndly with Prince Nicholas Esterhazy,[2]

---

[1] Grandson of the twelfth Duke of Norfolk who died in 1842. He succeeded as fourteenth Duke and died in 1860.

[2] Son of Prince Paul Esterhazy, Austrian Ambassador. See p. 77.

LUIGI LABLACHE.

From a sketch by Princess Victoria.

who is a very amiable, agreeable, gentlemanly young man; 3rdly with the Marquis of Granby [1]; 4thly with the Marquis of Douro [2] who is very odd and amusing; and 5thly and lastly with the Earl of Sandwich [3] who is an agreeable young man. I wished to dance with Count Waldstein who is such an amiable man, but he replied that he could not dance quadrilles, and as in my station I unfortunately cannot valse and gallop, I could not dance with him. The beauties there were (in my opinion) the Duchess of Sutherland, Lady Frances (or Fanny) Cowper, who is very pleasing, natural and clever-looking. . . . The Courtyard and the streets were crammed when we went to the Ball, and the anxiety of the people to see poor stupid me was very great, and I must say I am quite touched by it, and feel proud which I always have done of my country and of the English Nation. I forgot to say that before we went to dinner we saw the dear children. I gave my beloved Lehzen a small brooch of my hair.

Friday, 26th May.— . . . Wrote a letter to dear Uncle Leopold, to dearest Albert from whom I received a most kind and affectionate letter for my birthday yesterday, and to Ernest Hohenlohe. Finished my *brouillon* of Aunt's letter and began to

---

[1] Charles (1815–88), afterwards sixth Duke of Rutland, K.G.; he died unmarried. A man of grim manners but not unkindly heart.

[2] Arthur Richard (1807–84), afterwards second Duke of Wellington, K.G. Almost better known by his courtesy title of Lord Douro. Had he not been the son of the Great Duke, his uncommon talents might have earned for him a career of distinction. In appearance he singularly resembled his august father, and late in life he was addicted to a style of costume which led people to say that he wore his father's old clothes. He, however, possessed a pretty wit.

[3] John William (1811–84), seventh Earl of Sandwich, afterwards Master of the Buckhounds.

write it. At 2 we went with dear Lehzen and I received two more Addresses, one from Kidderminster presented (not *read*) by Lord Foley [1] ; the other from the Borough of Louth by ——. First of all the Sheriffs of the City came and wished to know when we should be pleased to receive the Address from the Mayor and Corporation of London. . . .

Monday, 29th May.—At ½ p. 1 we went to the Drawing-Room with the Duchess of Northumberland, dear Lehzen, Lady Mary Stopford, Lady Catherine Jenkinson, Lady Flora Hastings, Lady Cust, Sir George Anson, &c. The King and Queen being both unwell, though better, the Drawing-room was held by the Princess Augusta !! It was an immensely full one—2000 people, and we did not get home till a ¼ p. 5. The handsomest people there were : the Duchess of Sutherland, Lady Fanny Cowper, the Marchioness of Abercorn,[2] Lady Seymour,[3] Mrs. Blackwood, &c., &c. Countess Emanuel Zichy (Miss Strachan that was) and who was also at our Concert, was presented. Count Zichy is very good-looking in uniform, but not in plain clothes.

---

[1] Thomas Henry, fourth Lord Foley (1808–69).

[2] Louisa, a daughter of the sixth Duke of Bedford, married James, second Marquess and first Duke of Abercorn. This Duke and his Duchess are generally thought to have been meant by the "Duke" and "Duchess" in Lord Beaconsfield's novel *Lothair*.

[3] The three remarkable Sheridan sisters (granddaughters of R. B. Sheridan, the dramatist) were Lady Seymour (afterwards Duchess of Somerset and Queen of Beauty at the Eglinton Tournament), Lady Dufferin (the Mrs. Blackwood mentioned above), and Mrs. Norton. They possessed in an uncommon degree the gift of beauty inherited from Miss Linley, their grandmother, and gifts of mind inherited from Sheridan. Not only Mrs. Norton, but also Lady Dufferin, wrote verse and prose with distinction. *Stuart of Dunleath*, a novel by Mrs. Norton, was much and justly admired. She inspired George Meredith with the conception of *Diana of the Crossways*.

Count Waldstein looks remarkably well in his pretty Hungarian uniform. . . .

Tuesday, 30th May.—At ½ p. 2 we went into the saloon with Mary and Princess Sophia, I being attended by the Duchess of Northumberland and dear Lehzen, and Mamma by all her ladies and gentlemen. The Lord Mayor, Aldermen and Commons of the City of London presented Mamma 1st with an Address to which she read an answer, and then me with a very kind one. I only answered the following words, from my own accord : " I am very thankful for your kindness and my Mother has expressed all my feelings." The Addresses were read by the Recorder of London (Mr. Law). There were all together 150 who came up with the Lord Mayor. . . .

Sunday, 4th June.—Read in the *Exposition* while my hair was doing. At ½ p. 9 we breakfasted. The children played in the room. Wrote a letter to dear Feodore. Drew. At 11 we went to Chapel with dear Lehzen. The whole service was performed by Mr. Jackson. Wrote my journal. Wrote. Drew. At a little after 3 came my good and honest friend, *Stockmar*,[1] and stayed with me till ½ p. 3. He had a very pleasant and useful conversation with me ; he is one of those few people who tell plain honest truth, don't flatter, give wholesome necessary advice, and strive to do good and smooth all dissensions. He is Uncle Leopold's greatest and most confidential attached and disinterested friend, and I hope he is the same to me, at least, I feel so towards him ; Lehzen being of course the *greatest* friend I have. . . .

Thursday, 15th June.—After 9 we breakfasted. The children played in the room. At 10 Mary, dear

[1] Baron Stockmar. See p. 196.

Lehzen and I drove out and came home at 10 minutes to 11. *Wrote*!! The news of the King are so very bad that all my lessons save the Dean's are put off, including Lablache's, Mrs. Anderson's, Guazzaroni's, &c., &c., and we see *nobody*. I regret rather my singing-lesson, though it is only for a short period, but duty and *proper feeling* go before *all pleasures.*—10 minutes to 1,—I just hear that the Doctors think my poor Uncle the King cannot last more than 48 hours! Poor man! he was always kind to me, and he *meant* it well I know; I am grateful for it, and shall ever remember his kindness with gratitude. He was odd, very odd and singular, but his intentions were often ill interpreted!—Wrote my journal. At about a ¼ p. 2 came Lord Liverpool and I had a highly important conversation with him—*alone.* . . .

Friday, 16*th June.*— . . . Began and read to Lehzen out of De Lolme *On the English Constitution.* I forgot to mention that Lehzen finished reading to me on the 16th of May the delightful letters of Mme. de Sévigné, and began on the following day *Les Mémoires de l'Impératrice Joséphine,* par Mdlle. Le Normand, en 2 tomes, which is written in a very affected and flourished style, but is amusing. The news of the poor King were a shade better. At a little after 5 we drove out with Mary and Lehzen and came home at a ¼ to 7. At ½ p. 7 we dined. Saw the children before dinner. Sang *un poco.* Stayed up till ½ p. 10.

Saturday, 17*th June.*—Read in the *Exposition* while my hair was doing. After 9 we breakfasted. The children played in the room. At 10 Mary, dear Lehzen, the dear children and I drove out and came home at 11. I like Mary very much; she is a very honest, warm-hearted, good soul, and very susceptible of kindness shown to her; she is extremely discreet and retiring too. The news of the King are worse again today. Wrote my journal &c. Arranged some prints &c. At a little after 2 came Baron Stockmar and stayed till near 3. The news of the poor King were *very* bad! Drew. At a ¼ to 5 we drove out with Mary, Lehzen and dear little Edward, who was very funny and amusing. We came home at 6. . . .

Sunday, 18*th June.*—Got up at 8. After 9 we breakfasted. The children played in the room. At 10 we went down to prayers with dear Lehzen. The Dean read and preached. The text was from the 2nd Chapter of St. John's epistle, 5th verse. Drew and painted. Mary came up with Edward and stayed some time. Edward also remained alone with me for a ¼ of an hour. Painted. Saw Stockmar, who brought me a letter from Uncle Leopold!!—Painted. The poor King, they say, can live but a few hours more! —Wrote my journal. . . .

Monday, 19*th June.*—Got up at a ¼ p. 8. Read in *Les Veillées du Château* while my hair was doing. After 9 we breakfasted. The children played in the room. At a ¼ p. 10 Mary, Lehzen, the children and I drove out and came home at a little after 11. Read in *Les Veillées du Château*. Wrote my journal. Saw Dr. Clark. Saw Ernest Hohenlohe who brought me the news from Windsor that the poor King was *so* ill that he could hardly live through the day. He likewise brought me a very kind message from the poor Queen, and also one from the poor old King. After 7 we dined. Saw the children before dinner for a minute. Stayed up till a ¼ p. 10. Read in W. Scott's life while my hair was undoing.

Tuesday, 20*th June.*—I was awoke at 6 o'clock

by Mamma, who told me that the Archbishop of Canterbury [1] and Lord Conyngham [2] were here, and wished to see me. I got out of bed and went into my sitting-room (only in my dressing-gown), and *alone,* and saw them. Lord Conyngham (the Lord Chamberlain) then acquainted me that my poor Uncle, the King, was no more, and had expired at 12 minutes p. 2 this morning, and consequently that I am *Queen.* Lord Conyngham knelt down and kissed my hand, at the same time delivering to me the official announcement of the poor King's demise. The Archbishop then told me that the Queen was desirous that he should come and tell me the details of the last moments of my poor, good Uncle ; he said that he had directed his mind to religion, and had died in a perfectly happy, quiet state of mind, and was quite prepared for his death. He added that the King's sufferings at the last were not very great but that there was a good deal of uneasiness. Lord Conyngham, whom I charged to express my feelings of condolence and sorrow to the poor Queen, returned directly to Windsor. I then went to my room and dressed.

Since it has pleased Providence to place me in this station, I shall do my utmost to fulfil my duty towards my country ; I am very young and perhaps in many, though not in all things, inexperienced, but I am sure, that very few have more real good will and more real desire to do what is fit and right than I have.

Breakfasted, during which time good faithful Stockmar [3] came and talked to me. Wrote a letter

[1] Dr. Howley. See *ante,* p. 68.
[2] Second Marquess. See *ante,* p. 98.
[3] Baron Christian Stockmar (1787–1863), physician to Prince

to dear Uncle Leopold and a few words to dear good
Feodore. Received a letter from Lord Melbourne [1]
in which he said he would wait upon me at a little
before 9. At 9 came Lord Melbourne, whom I saw
in my room, and of COURSE *quite* ALONE as I shall
always do all my Ministers. He kissed my hand and
I then acquainted him that it had long been my
intention to retain him and the rest of the present
Ministry at the head of affairs, and that it could not
be in better hands than his. He then again kissed
my hand. He then read to me the Declaration which
I was to read to the Council, which he wrote himself
and which is a very fine one. I then talked with
him some little longer time after which he left me.
He was in full dress. I like him very much and feel
confidence in him. He is a very straightforward,
honest, clever and good man. I then wrote a letter
to the Queen. At about 11 Lord Melbourne came
again to me and spoke to me upon various subjects.
At about $\frac{1}{2}$ p. 11 I went downstairs and held a
Council in the red saloon. I went in of course quite
alone, and remained seated the whole time. My
two Uncles, the Dukes of Cumberland [2] and Sussex,[3]

Leopold, and subsequently his confidential agent. He abandoned
medicine for statecraft, in which he became an expert. He was entrusted by King Leopold to superintend the education of Prince Albert
and guide Queen Victoria, both of which services he performed with
consummate tact and integrity. He was their devoted friend and
counsellor to the end of his life. See *ante*, p. 154.

[1] William Lamb, Viscount Melbourne (1779–1848), was at this time
Prime Minister and fifty-eight years old.

[2] Ernest Augustus (1771–1851), fifth son of George III. He was
considered unscrupulous, and was certainly most unpopular in this
country. He now succeeded William IV. as King of Hanover. Although of autocratic temperament, he granted his subjects a demo-
cratic constitution, much to their surprise.

[3] Augustus Frederick (1773–1843), sixth son of George III. His
marriage to Lady Augusta Murray was declared void under the Royal

and Lord Melbourne conducted me.   The declaration, the various forms, the swearing in of the Privy Councillors of which there were a great number present, and the reception of some of the Lords of Council, previous to the Council in an adjacent room (likewise alone) I subjoin here.   I was not at all nervous and had the satisfaction of hearing that people were satisfied with what I had done and how I had done it.   Receiving after this, Audiences of Lord Melbourne, Lord John Russell, Lord Albemarle (Master of the Horse), and the Archbishop of Canterbury, all in my room and alone.   Saw Stockmar. Saw Clark, whom I named my Physician.   Saw Mary.   Wrote to Uncle Ernest.   Saw Ernest Hohenlohe who brought me a kind and very feeling letter from the poor Queen.   I feel very much for her, and really feel that the poor good King was always so kind personally to me, that I should be ungrateful were I not to recollect it and feel grieved at his death.   The poor Queen is wonderfully composed now, I hear.   Wrote my journal.   Took my dinner upstairs alone.   Went downstairs.   Saw Stockmar. At about 20 minutes to 9 came Lord Melbourne and remained till near 10.   I had a very important and a very *comfortable* conversation with him.   Each time I see him I feel more confidence in him ; I find him very kind in his manner too.   Saw Stockmar.   Went down and said good-night to Mamma &c.   My *dear* Lehzen will ALWAYS remain with me as my friend but will take no situation about me, and I think she is right.

Wednesday, 21st June.—Got up at 8.   At 9 we

Marriages Act.   He had by her two children, Sir Augustus d'Este and Mlle. d'Este (afterwards wife of Lord Chancellor Truro).   He married, secondly, Lady Cecilia Buggin (*née* Gore, daughter of the Earl of Arran), and to her was granted the title of Duchess of Inverness.

all breakfasted. At $\frac{1}{2}$ p. 9 I went to St. James's in state. Mamma and Lady Mary Stopford were in my carriage, and Lord Albemarle, Col. Cavendish, Lady Flora Hastings, and Col. Harcourt in the others. . . . After the Proclamation Mamma and the ladies repaired to an adjoining room and left me in the Closet. I gave audiences to Lord Melbourne (a long one), the Earl Marshal (Duke of Norfolk), and Garter King at Arms (Sir John Woods), relative to the funeral of my poor Uncle the late King ; to Lord Albemarle, Lord Hill, Lord Melbourne (again for some time), and the Lord President (Lord Lansdowne). I then held a Privy Council in the Throne Room. It was not fully attended and was not the third part so full as it had been on the preceding day. The Marquis of Anglesey,[1] the Chancellor of the Exchequer (Mr. Spring Rice),[2] Lords Wharncliffe,[3] Ashburton,[4] and Wynford,[5] Sir Hussey Vivian,[6] and

---

[1] Henry William Paget, first Marquess of Anglesey (1768–1854). Commanded the Cavalry at Waterloo. When a round shot tore between him and the Duke of Wellington, he turned to the Duke and said, " By God ! I have lost my leg," and the Duke replied, " By God ! I believe you have." This conversation sums up the two men. Lord Anglesey was a Field-Marshal and Viceroy of Ireland, where he displayed a tendency to liberal ideas that were not considered in accordance with his profession or station. There was never a more gallant soldier, and he " had not a fold in his character."

[2] Chancellor of the Exchequer. An intelligent politician and responsible for the adoption of the penny post. He was anxious for the Speakership, but failed to win the fancy of the House of Commons. He passed to the House of Lords as Lord Monteagle in 1839 and died in 1866.

[3] James, first Lord Wharncliffe. A Yorkshire magnate and Member of Parliament. Created a Peer 1826. See *ante*, p. 54.

[4] Alexander Baring, first Lord Ashburton (1774–1848). President of the Board of Trade in Lord Grey's Administration.

[5] Sir William Draper Best (1767–1845), first Lord Wynford, formerly Chief Justice of the Common Pleas.

[6] A distinguished soldier, at this time Lieut.-General and Master of

some Judges were sworn in as Privy Councillors and kissed hands. After the Council I gave audiences to Lord Melbourne, the Archbishop of Canterbury, and all the Bishops except one or two, the Lord Chancellor and all the Judges ; Sir Hussey Vivian (Master General of the Ordnance), Lord John Russell, Lord Glenelg,[1] Mr. Poulett Thomson,[2] Lord Howick,[3] Lord Palmerston, and Lord Minto.[4] I then returned home at 1. I must say it was quite like a dream and a sad one, when I was seated in the Closet where but barely 5 weeks ago I beheld for the last time my poor Uncle. At 2 came Stockmar till after 3. Wrote to the Duchess of Gloucester and Princess Augusta.[5] Walked. Saw the Duke of Norfolk. Wrote my journal. At 7 we dined. At 10 minutes to 9 came Lord Melbourne and stayed with me till 10. I had an agreeable and important and satisfactory conversation with him. Stayed up till a ¼ p. 10. Lord Hill told me a curious

the Ordnance. M.P. for Windsor. Afterwards created Lord Vivian (1841).

[1] Charles Grant, first and only Lord Glenelg (1778–1866), at this time Secretary for the Colonies. Three years before he had been proposed as Governor-General of India, but his nomination was rejected by the Board of Directors.

[2] Afterwards Lord Sydenham (1799–1841). At this time President of the Board of Trade. In 1839 he was appointed Governor-General of Canada. He died there, aged forty-one, from a fall from his horse.

[3] Henry George, afterwards third Earl Grey (1802–94), at this time Secretary-at-War and Colonial Secretary. An honest and fearless statesman, but a difficult colleague.

[4] Gilbert, second Earl of Minto (1782–1859), First Lord of the Admiralty. In 1832 he had been sent on a special mission to Berlin "to mollify the King of Prussia." This type of mission has always been popular with the Whigs.

[5] Daughter of George III. She lived at Frogmore and at Clarence House. See *ante*, p. 61.

coincidence which is that the 21st of June, the day on which I was proclaimed, is likewise the anniversary of the Battle of Vittoria !

Thursday, 22nd June.—Got up after 8. After 9 we breakfasted. The children played in the room. At a ¼ p. 10 I walked out with Mary, Lehzen, Charles and Edward, and came home at 20 minutes to 11. Wrote to the Duchess of Gloucester. Wrote my journal. At 12 came the Judge Advocate General (Mr. Cutlar Ferguson) [1] to submit various sentences of Court Martial to me. He is a very clever intelligent man and explained all the cases very clearly to me. I, of *course*, saw him alone. . . .

Friday, 23rd June.—Got up at ½ p. 8. After 9 we breakfasted. The children played in the room. I do not mention the VERY *frequent* communications I have with Lord Melbourne, Lord John Russell,[2] &c., &c., &c., as also the other official letters I have to write and receive, for want of time and space. Saw good Stockmar, who remained in my room for some time. Saw the Marquis of Conyngham, then Lord Hill, who explained to me finally about the Court Martials, then Sir Henry Wheatley [3] and Col. Wood,

[1] Robert Cutlar Ferguson had been counsel for one of the defendants in the trial of Arthur O'Connor and others for treason at Maidstone in 1798. O'Connor was acquitted, but the presence in Court of Bow Street runners to arrest him on a second charge caused a scene of much confusion, one consequence being the prosecution of Cutlar Ferguson, Lord Thanet, and others for an attempted rescue. Ferguson was imprisoned for a year and fined £100. Upon his liberation he went to Calcutta, where he established himself in large and lucrative practice. He died in 1838.

[2] Lord John Russell (1792–1878) was at this time forty-five years old. Home Secretary and Leader of the House of Commons. He was at the height of his combative powers as a Parliamentarian, and his zeal for Whig doctrine at home and Liberal statesmanship abroad was undiminished.

[3] Private Secretary to William IV.

who as Executors of the late King, brought me his Will. At ½ p. 12 arrived Lady Catherine [1] who remained in one of my sitting-rooms till now and still remains (4 o'clock) answering letters, &c., &c. Saw the Duke of Argyll (Lord Steward) at ½ p. 2. I wrote a letter to the Marchioness of Tavistock [2] while Stockmar was here, asking her to become one of my Ladies of the Bedchamber. Lay down. Wrote to the Marchioness of Lansdowne, [3] asking her to become my first Lady of the Bedchamber. At ½ p. 5 I drove out with Mary and Lehzen, and came home at ½ p. 6. After 7 we all dined. I had a GREAT deal of business to do after dinner. Saw Stockmar. Received a very kind letter from Lady Lansdowne accepting the situation. After dinner came Princess Sophia. Stayed up till after 10.

Saturday, 24th June.—Got up after 8. At ½ p. 9 we all breakfasted. The children played in the room. Wrote a letter to the Duke of Sussex, and to good Spāth. At 11 came Lord Melbourne and stayed till 12. He is a very honest, good and kind-hearted, as well as very clever man. He told me that Lady Tavistock had accepted the situation. And he read to me the answer which I was to give to the address from the House of Lords. He told me that the Duke of Argyll would bring the Address but would not read it ; and consequently I was not to read mine. Wrote. At 12 came Lady Catherine Jenkinson and remained in my room till near 3. Saw Stockmar at a little after 12. Saw Sir Frederick Wetherall. [4] Saw Lord John Russell. *Wrote.*—I

---

[1] Lady C. Jenkinson, daughter of the Earl of Liverpool. See p. 46.
[2] Anna Maria, daughter of the third Earl of Harrington.
[3] Louisa Fox-Strangways, daughter of the second Earl of Ilchester.
[4] He had been executor to the Queen's father. One of her first

really have immensely to do; I receive so many communications from my Ministers but I like it very much. . . .

Sunday, 25th June.—Got up at 8. At ½ p. 9 we breakfasted. The children played in the room. At 10 I went down to prayers with Mamma, Mary, Lehzen, and Charles. The service was read by the Dean who was much affected when he read the prayers in which my name is now mentioned in the place of my poor Uncle, the late King. He preached a very good and appropriate sermon; the text of which was from the 3rd chapter of the Epistle General of St. Peter, 13th and 14th verses. . . . At a few minutes p. 12 came the Chancellor of the Exchequer (Mr. Spring Rice) and stayed some time. He is a very clever and good man. . . . At about 20 minutes p. 4 came Lord Melbourne till 20 minutes p. 5. He is a good, honest, kind-hearted and clever man, and I like to talk to him. . . .

Monday, 26th June.—Got up at 8. Before 9 we breakfasted. At ½ p. 9 went with Mamma to Windsor. I was attended by Lady Tavistock and Colonel Cavendish,[1] and Mamma by Lady Flora Hastings. We arrived at the Castle, which looked very mournful and melancholy with the flag half mast high, at about a ¼ p. 11. We went instantly to the poor Queen's apartments.[2] She received me *most kindly* but was at first much affected. She

acts was to discharge the debts contracted by the Duke of Kent, which the Duchess had never been able to pay off. See *ante*, p. 69.

[1] Colonel the Hon. H. F. C. Cavendish (1789–1873), son of Lord Burlington. Clerk-Marshal to the Queen. Married as his second wife Frances Susan, sister of Lord Durham.

[2] Queen Adelaide, the Queen Dowager, a Princess of the House of Saxe-Meiningen. Her attitude towards the young Queen was absolutely perfect, in its simple dignity and freedom from every taint of envy.

however soon regained her self-possession and was
wonderfully calm and composed. She gave us many
painfully interesting details of the illness and last
moments of my poor Uncle the late King. He bore
his dreadful sufferings with the most exemplary
patience and always thanked Heaven when these
sufferings were but slightly and momentarily alleviated. He was in the happiest state of mind
possible and his death was worthy his high station.
He felt so composed and seemed to find so much
consolation in Religion. The Queen is really a most
estimable and excellent person and she bears the
prospect of the great change she must soon go
through in leaving Windsor and changing her position in a most admirable, strong and high-minded
manner. I do not think her looking ill and the
widow's cap and weeds rather become her. I saw
Ernest Hohenlohe, Gustav and Prince Ernest of
Hesse P.B. We left Windsor at ½ p. 12. It gave
me a very painful feeling to think that the remains
of my poor Uncle were in the Castle. Altogether
the whole rather upset me. We came at ½ p. 2. I
forgot to say that Lord Melbourne told me that the
Duchess of Sutherland [1] has accepted the office of
Mistress of the Robes, and the Countess of Charlemont [2] of one of my ladies of the Bedchamber. At
½ p. 2 came the Duchess of Sutherland, whom I am
delighted to have as my Mistress of the Robes; she
was looking so handsome and nice. At about 10
minutes to 4 came Lord Melbourne and stayed till
½ p. 4. I talked with him as usual on Political
affairs, about my Household, and various other
Confidential affairs. . . .

[1] Georgina Howard, daughter of the sixth Earl of Carlisle.
[2] Anne, wife of Francis William, second Earl of Charlemont.

however soon regained her self-possession and was wonderfully calm and composed. She gave us many painfully interesting details of the illness and last moments of my poor Uncle the late King. He bore his dreadful sufferings with the most exemplary patience and always thanked Heaven when these sufferings were but slightly and momentarily alleviated. He was in the happiest state of mind possible and his death was worthy his high station. He felt so composed and seemed to find so much consolation in Religion. The Queen is really a most estimable and excellent person and she bears the prospect of the great change she must soon go through in leaving Windsor and changing her position in a most admirable, strong and high-minded manner. I do not think her looking ill and the widow's cap and weeds rather become her. I saw Ernest Hohenlohe, Gustav and Prince Ernest of Hesse P.B. We left Windsor at ½ p. 12. It gave me a very painful feeling to think that the remains of my poor Uncle were in the Castle. Altogether the whole rather upset me. We came at ½ p. 2. I forgot to say that Lord Melbourne told me that the Duchess of Sutherland [1] has accepted the office of Mistress of the Robes, and the Countess of Charlemont [2] of one of my ladies of the Bedchamber. At ½ p. 2 came the Duchess of Sutherland, whom I am delighted to have as my Mistress of the Robes; she was looking so handsome and nice. At about 10 minutes to 4 came Lord Melbourne and stayed till ½ p. 4. I talked with him as usual on Political affairs, about my Household, and various other *Confidential* affairs. . . .

[1] Georgina Howard, daughter of the sixth Earl of Carlisle.
[2] Anne, wife of Francis William, second Earl of Charlemont.

H. M. Queen Adelaide
from a portrait by Sir W. Ross

Tuesday, 27th June.—Got up at ½ p. 8. At a ¼ to 10 we breakfasted. The children played in the room. Wrote my journal. At about 20 minutes p. 11 came Lord Melbourne and stayed till ½ p. 12. At a little after ½ p. 12 came Lord Palmerston and stayed till a little p. 1. He is a clever and agreeable man. Saw Lord John Russell and Lord Melbourne for a minute. At a few minutes p. 2 I went down into the saloon with Lady Lansdowne ; Col. Cavendish, the Vice-Chamberlain (Lord Charles Fitzroy),[1] and the Comptroller of the Household (Mr. Byng)[2] were in waiting. Lord Melbourne then came in and announced that the Addresses from the House of Commons were ready to come in. They were read by Lord John Russell and I read an answer to both. Lord Melbourne stood on my left hand and Lady Lansdowne behind me. Most of the Privy Councillors of the House of Commons were present. After this Lord Palmerston brought in the Earl of Durham,[3] who is just returned from St. Petersburg. I conferred on him the Grand Cross of the Bath. I knighted him with the Sword of State which is so enormously heavy that Lord Melbourne was obliged to hold it for me, and I only inclined it. I then put the ribbon over his shoulder. After this the foreign Ambassadors and Ministers were severally introduced to me by Lord Palmerston. I then went upstairs and gave audiences to the Earl of Mulgrave [4] and to the

[1] Second son of the fourth Duke of Grafton.

[2] George Byng, afterwards second Earl of Strafford.

[3] Lord Durham, by his charming manners, had overcome certain prejudice which had been felt in St. Petersburg on his appointment He was exceedingly popular with the Emperor. He returned to England, it was said, " a greater aristocrat than ever " See *ante*, p 81.

[4] Lord Mulgrave was created Marquess of Normanby in 1838. A member of Lord Melbourne's Administration in 1834, he was sent

Earl of Durham. The latter gave a long account of Russia. Did various things. Saw Stockmar. As I did not feel well I did not come down to dinner, but dined upstairs. I went down after dinner. Stayed up till 10. I wore the blue Ribbon and Star of the Garter in the afternoon. . . .

Saturday, 1st July.—Got up after 8. At ½ p. 9 we breakfasted. Edward played in the room only, Ernest not being good. Wrote. I repeat what I said before that I have *so many* communications from the Ministers, and from me to them, and I get so many papers to sign *every* day, that I have always a *very great* deal to do ; but for want of time and space I do not write these things down. I *delight* in this work. Saw Lord Melbourne. At about ½ p. 11 or a ¼ to 12 came Mr. Spring Rice. Saw Lord John Russell. Wrote &c. At 2 came Sir Henry Wheatley to kiss hands upon being appointed my Privy Purse. At a little after 2 I saw Stockmar for a minute. At 10 minutes p. 2 came Lord Palmerston and stayed till 6 minutes p. 3. We talked about Russia and Turkey a good deal &c. He is very agreeable, and clear in what he says. Saw Stockmar for some time afterwards. Wrote my journal. I forgot to mention that I received a letter from dearest Aunt Louise in the morning. The children played in my room for a little while. At ½ past 5 I drove out with Mamma and dear Lehzen and came home at 20 minutes to 7. At ½ p. 7 we dined. Stayed up till a ¼ p. 10.

Sunday, 2nd July.—Got up at ½ p. 8. At ½ p. 9 we breakfasted. The children played in the room.

to Ireland as Viceroy, and then returned to the Cabinet as Secretary of State. While the Whigs were in office he was never without a place. He was subsequently Ambassador in Paris, and under Lord Palmerston supported Napoleon III. through the stormy days of the *coup d'état.*

At 10 I went to prayers with Mamma, Mary, and dear Lehzen. The service was performed by the Dean who gave us also a very good sermon. The text was from the 6th chapter of St. Matthew, 9th and 10th verses. Wrote, signed, &c. Wrote to dear Feodore. Received a kind long letter from dear Uncle Leopold. At 10 minutes to 2 came Lord Melbourne till a few minutes p. 3. Talked with him about many important things. He is indeed a most truly honest, straightforward and noble-minded man and I esteem myself *most* fortunate to have such a man at the head of the Government ; a man in whom I can safely place confidence. There are not *many* like him in this world of deceit ! Mary and the children came up for a few minutes. At a little before 4 came Stockmar and stayed till a little before 5. He is a most honest, excellent, disinterested and straightforward man, and most exceedingly attached and devoted to me ; he has been, and is, of the greatest use to me. . . .

Saturday, 8th July.—Got up at a little after 8. At ½ p. 9 we breakfasted. The children played in the room. Signed, &c. Sat to Mr. Lane for a few minutes. Wrote to the poor Queen from whom I received a *very* kind letter last night ; &c., &c. Saw good Stockmar for some time. Saw Lord John Russell. At a few minutes p. 12 came my good and honest friend Lord Melbourne and stayed till 20 minutes p. 1. Talked over many important things. Saw Mr. Spring Rice. . . . I forgot to say that Lord Melbourne wrote me word yesterday evening that Lady Mulgrave [1] was very desirous to become one of

---

[1] Lady Mulgrave was Maria Liddell, eldest daughter of the first Lord Ravensworth. She had married, in 1818, the second Earl of Mulgrave, who was created Marquess of Normanby in 1838. See p. 205.

my Ladies of the Bedchamber, and I told Lord Melbourne this morning that I would make her one of my ladies. Wrote to Lady Lyttelton [1] to ask her to become one of my ladies of the Bedchamber (in a *year*), for she is still in widow's weeds. .. . . . At a ¼ p. 7 I, Mamma, Mary and Lehzen dined, Charles having gone at 5 o'clock to Windsor to attend the funeral of my poor Uncle, the late King. It was very very sad to hear from ½ p. 8 till nearly 10 o'clock, those dreadful minute guns ! Alas ! my poor Uncle, he now reposes in quiet and peace ! As Lord Melbourne said to me, the first morning when I became Queen, that the poor King " had his faults as we all have, but that he possessed many valuable qualities." I have heard from all sides that he was really very fond of me, and I shall *ever* retain a grateful sense of his kindness to me and shall never forget him. Life is short and uncertain, and I am determined to employ my time well, so that when I am called away from this world my end may be a peaceful and a happy one ! . . .

Tuesday, 11*th July.*—Got up at 8. At ½ p. 9 we breakfasted. The children played in the room. At a little after 10, sat to Mr. Lane for a few minutes. Saw Col. Cavendish. Wrote, &c., &c. At ½ p. 11. came Stockmar who brought me the unwelcome news of poor Lord Melbourne's continued indisposition and total incapability of coming to see me to-day, which I regret for two reasons : first because I have many things to ask him, 2ndly because I like very much to talk to him, as he is so quiet in what he says. . . .

---

[1] Sarah, daughter of the second Earl Spencer and widow of the third Lord Lyttelton. Afterwards Lady Superintendent to the Princess Royal and the Prince of Wales and the other Princes and Princesses. A shrewd observer and a woman of fine judgment and high ideals.

Wednesday, 12th July.—Got up at 8. At ½ p. 9 we breakfasted. Did various things. At ½ p. 10 came Stockmar and stayed for some time. At ½ p. 11 came Lord Melbourne and stayed till ½ p. 12. He looked and said he was better, but not quite well. Dressed. At a little before 2 I went with Mamma and the Duchess of Sutherland (in my carriage), Charles and Mary and Lady Tavistock and Lord Albemarle (in the next carriage), and Lady Mary Stopford and Colonel Cavendish in another. I was in full dress and wore the Order of the Bath. I went in state with a large escort. I was received at the door by the Lord Chamberlain, the Lord Steward, &c., &c., and was by them conducted into the Closet, where some people kissed hands. I then went into the Throne Room, Lord Conyngham handing me in, and a Page of Honour (Master Ellice) bearing my train. I sat on the Throne. Mamma and Mary stood on the steps of the Throne on one side, and the Duchess of Sutherland and Lady Tavistock stood near me (behind). I then received the two Addresses (of which, as also of all the other things, I subjoin an account), and read Answers to both. I then returned to the Closet; and went into another room to put on the Mantle of the Bath [1] (of crimson satin lined with white silk); I then saw Lord Melbourne in the Closet for a few minutes. After this I went again into the Throne-room, and seated myself on the Throne. I then conferred the

---

[1] There is no record of any previous Sovereign wearing the robes of the Bath on such an occasion. Certainly they have never been worn since. A little later in her reign the Queen was always reluctant to exchange the red ribbon of the Bath for the blue ribbon of the Garter. By the advice of Lord Melbourne, however, she was in the habit of wearing the red ribbon when holding an investiture of the Order.

Order of the Bath (*not sitting* of course) upon Prince Esterhazy. After this I again went into the Closet. Mamma, Mary, Charles and Lady Mary Stopford then went home; it was 3 o'clock. I then took off my Mantle. Received two Deputations from the Sheriffs &c., to ask when I would receive two more Addresses from the City. My two Ladies attended me, but after this they went into another room, where they remained till I went. I then gave an Audience to Lord Lansdowne. After this I held a Privy Council. After the Council I gave audiences to the Earl of Yarborough [1] (who thanked me very much for having appointed his amiable daughter, Lady Charlotte Copley, one of my Bedchamber Women); to Lord Melbourne, Lord John Russell, Lord Mulgrave, and Lord Hill. I then left the Palace, the Duchess of Sutherland (who looked lovely, as she always does), and Lady Tavistock, going with me in my carriage, in the same way as I came, and got home at a ¼ to 5. . . .

Thursday, 13th July.—Got up at 8. At ½ p. 9 we breakfasted. It was the *last time* that I slept in this poor old Palace,[2] as I go into Buckingham Palace today. Though I rejoice to *go* into B.P. for many reasons, it is not without feelings of regret

[1] He had just been created Earl of Yarborough. Lady Charlotte was the wife of Sir Joseph Copley. He died in 1846.

[2] The Queen always retained a strong sentiment for Kensington Palace. Part of the old building had been condemned by the Office of Works to be pulled down, but the Queen refused her sanction. During the last year of her reign the Queen made an arrangement with Lord Salisbury and Sir M. Hicks-Beach that, in consideration of Her Majesty giving up the use of Bushey House and the Ranger's House at Greenwich, the Government should purchase and place at her disposal Schomberg House, and should restore Kensington Palace. Parliament voted £36,000 for this purpose, on the understanding that the State Rooms should be opened to the public.

that I shall bid adieu *for ever* (that is to say *for ever* as a DWELLING), to this my birth-place, where I have been born and bred, and to which I am really attached ! I have seen my dear sister married here, I have seen many of my dear relations here, I have had pleasant balls and *delicious* concerts here, my present rooms upstairs are really very pleasant, comfortable and pretty, and *enfin* I like this poor Palace. I have held my first Council here too ! I have gone through painful and disagreeable scenes here, 'tis true, but still I am fond of the poor old Palace. Lord Melbourne told me yesterday that the Hon. Miss Dillon [1] (to whom I had offered it), has accepted the situation of Maid of Honour. I always saw Lord Melbourne and also Stockmar in my Private Sitting-room (the first of the three), but all the other Ministers &c. &c. I saw in the further room (the farthest of the 3). Did various things. Saw Stockmar for some time. The poor rooms look so sad and deserted, everything being taken away. Wrote my journal. At a little after 2 I went with Mamma and Lady Lansdowne (in my carriage), Lehzen, and Col. Cavendish (in the next) to Buckingham Palace. I am much pleased with my rooms.[2] They are high, pleasant and cheerful. Arranged things. At a little after 4 Lady Lansdowne brought Miss Pitt [3] and Miss Spring Rice [4] (the two Maids of

[1] Louisa, daughter of the thirteenth Viscount Dillon, afterwards wife of Sir Spencer Ponsonby Fane.

[2] These are the rooms now occupied by Queen Mary. The " audience " room opened out of the sitting-room.

[3] Hon. Harriet Elizabeth Pitt, younger daughter of the third Lord Rivers. She married in 1841 Charles Dashwood Bruce, nephew of the Earl of Elgin.

[4] Mary Alicia Spring Rice, eldest daughter of the Chancellor of the Exchequer. She afterwards married James Garth Marshall of Headingley and Monk Coniston.

Honour in Waiting, and who lodge here) to kiss
hands. Miss Pitt is a *very* pretty, elegant, nice girl,
and Miss Spring Rice is a nice, clever-looking girl.
Saw Stockmar. Lady Lansdowne afterwards brought
Miss Davys to kiss hands, who is a very nice girl
(though not at all pretty). I then walked round the
garden (which is large and very pretty) with Mamma.
Dear *Dashy* was quite happy in it. . . .

Honour in Waiting, and who lodge here) to kiss
hands. Miss Pitt is a *very* pretty, elegant, nice **girl,**
and Miss Spring Rice is a nice, clever-looking **girl.**
Saw Stockmar. Lady Lansdowne afterwards brought
Miss Davys to kiss hands, who is a very nice girl
(though not at all pretty). I then walked round the
garden (which is large and very pretty) with Mamma.
Dear *Dashy* was quite happy in it. . . .

H. R. H. Princess Victoria

INTRODUCTORY NOTE TO CHAPTER VII

THE break between the life of Princess Victoria and that of the young Queen was now complete. Changes came innumerable and fast. Her Household was formed, and it reflected the complexion of Lord Melbourne's Ministry, which had been established in power after the General Election by a majority of thirty-eight. The Queen left the home of her childhood for ever. She was the first Sovereign to occupy Buckingham Palace. The building had been begun by George IV., and although finished by William IV., had never been prepared for occupation. It remained an inconvenient house until it was added to in after-years by Prince Albert. Although Baron Stockmar, the old medical attendant of King Leopold, who had been domiciled in England by command of his master, was reputed to be acting as the Queen's Private Secretary, that post was in reality occupied by Lord Melbourne himself. He was both Private Secretary and Tutor to the young Queen at this stage of her career. Her political education proceeded fast, and she learned with avidity. Her good sense and composure were indeed remarkable. It was noted by all that she was considerate and thoughtful to her elderly relatives, and to the friends and servants of her predecessor. Her girlish charm was attractive to those who were privileged to be about her, and its influence over her subjects was soon widespread. When within a month of her accession she appeared in the House of Lords to dissolve Parliament in accordance with the Law, she read her Speech, said Fanny Kemble, who was present, with splendid effect. This well-qualified judge observed that the Queen's voice was exquisite, that her enunciation was as perfect as the intonation was melodious, and that it was impossible to hear more excellent utterance than that of the Queen's English by the English Queen.

It is difficult always to remember that the writer of these Journals was at this epoch little more than a child, that she had been educated almost exclusively by women, and that she had lived on the whole a very solitary life, hampered by the unhappy conditions attached to a girl who possesses no brothers and sisters, and is in addition heir to a Throne. She was now suddenly thrown almost entirely among men, grave and old, all of whom were engaged in administering the complicated affairs of that Kingdom of which she was Queen. It is difficult to imagine a greater contrast. How rapidly the youthful Princess became a woman under the pressure of these extraordinary circumstances becomes clear from her Journals. They indicate a curious maturity, through which, however, there peeps occasionally the face and figure of a child.

CHAPTER VII

1837

Friday, 14*th July.*—Got up after 8. At ½ p. 9 I, Mamma, Lehzen, and Lady Flora breakfasted up-stairs. Wrote, signed, &c. Saw Sir F. Watson, Col. Cavendish, Sir H. Wheatley, Stockmar. At a little after 11 saw Sir John Hobhouse [1] for a little while. He is a very clever and agreeable man. I saw him (where I shall see all the Ministers &c.) in the small room [2] which opens into my sitting-room. Wrote my journal. Dressed. At a few minutes to 2 I went with Mamma and the Duchess of Sutherland (in my carriage), Lady Charlemont and Lord Albemarle (in the next carriage), and Charles, Mary, and Lady Flora (in the other) to St. James's. I was in full dress and wore the blue ribbon and star of the Garter, and the Garter round my arm. I was

---

[1] President of the Board of Control. He had enjoyed the friendship of Byron, travelled with him, and was one of his executors. He was created Lord Broughton in 1851. His *Recollections of a Long Life,* edited by his daughter, Lady Dorchester, throw much light on the political events of his time. He was so strong a partisan that his judgments of statesmen and political events have to be treated with reservations ; but he was a type of politician, cultivated, independent, conscientious, and high-minded, that is becoming rarer as constituencies become less fastidious.

[2] The Queen invariably saw her Ministers in an " audience " room and never in her private sitting-room. An exception was made in the case of Lord Melbourne, the Prime Minister.

received in the same way as before. I went into the Throne Room, sat on the Throne, and received three Addresses in the same way as on Friday. Two of the Addresses were *very fully* attended and the room became intensely hot. I then put on the Mantle and Collar of the Garter (of dark blue velvet lined with white silk). Gave a few minutes audience to Lord Melbourne. I then went into the Throne Room (did not sit on the Throne), held a Chapter of the Garter and conferred that Order on Charles. Mamma, Charles and Mary went away immediately after this, but I remained and gave a long audience to Lord Melbourne, who read to me the Speech which I am to deliver when I prorogue Parliament. He reads so well and with *so* much good feeling. I am sorry to see him still looking ill. I then saw the Duke of Devonshire.[1] Came home with my two Ladies at ½ p. 4.

Saturday, 15th July.—At a few minutes p. 2 I went into one of the large drawing-rooms and held a Cabinet Council, at which were present all the Ministers. The Council lasted but a very short while. I then went into my Closet and received Lord Melbourne there. He stayed with me till 20 minutes to 4. He seemed and said he was better. He has such an honest, frank, and yet gentle manner. He talks so quietly. I always feel peculiarly satisfied when I have talked with him. I have *great* confidence in him. Saw the Duke of Argyll[2] and Lord Albemarle. At 10 minutes to 4 came Lord Palmer-

---

[1] See *ante*, p. 53.

[2] George William, sixth Duke of Argyll, son of John fifth Duke, and his wife, one of the beautiful Gunning sisters, Elizabeth, widow of the sixth Duke of Hamilton. This lady was created Baroness Hamilton in her own right, and her husband was also accorded a barony of Great Britain, thus entitling him to a seat in Parliament.

ston and stayed about 20 minutes. He is a very clever and agreeable man. I then saw Lord Glenelg for a short while. Played and sang. Wrote my journal. At a ¼ to 8 I dined. Mamma being unwell did not come to dinner. Besides the people in the House which made with me 6,—Charles, Mary, the Duke of Sussex, Princess Sophia, the Duke of Norfolk, the Earl and Countess of Mulgrave, the Earl and Countess of Durham, the Earl of Liverpool and the Ladies Jenkinson, the Lord and the Equerry in Waiting, and Lord John Churchill [1] dined here. I sat between Uncle Sussex and the Duke of Norfolk. After dinner, at 10 o'clock came *Thalberg*,[2] the most famous pianist in the world! He played four things, all by heart. They were all Fantasias by him ; (1) on *The Preghiera of Mosé*, (2) on "God save the King" and "Rule Britannia," (3) on *Norma*, (4) on *Les Huguenots*. *Never, never* did I hear anything at all like him! He combines the most *exquisite, delicate* and touching feeling with the most wonderful and powerful execution! He is unique and I am quite in ecstasies and raptures with him. I sat quite near the piano and it is quite extraordinary to watch his hands, which are large, but fine and graceful. He draws tones and sounds from the piano which no one else can do. He is *unique*. He is quite young, about 25, small, delicate-looking, a very pleasing countenance, and extremely gentlemanlike.

---

[1] Fourth son of the fourth Duke of Marlborough ; a Captain, R.N. Died at Macao in 1840.

[2] Sigismund Thalberg (1812–71) was now in the full flood of success. He wrote many fantasias on operatic themes, *e.g.* on *Robert le Diable*, *Zampa*, etc. In 1845 he married a widow, the daughter of Lablache. As a composer he never succeeded in emulating his success as a pianist. Later in life he abandoned music, and became a professional vine-grower.

He is modest to a degree and very agreeable to talk to. J'étais en extase ! . . .

Monday, 17*th July*.—Got up at 8. At ½ p. 9 we breakfasted. Saw Sir F. Watson and Col. Cavendish. Saw Stockmar. At ½ p. 1 I went in state to the House of Lords, with the Duchess of Sutherland and the Master of the Horse in my carriage, and Lady Lansdowne and Lady Mulgrave in another. Had I time I would give a very minute account of the whole, but as I have *very* little, I will only say what I feel I wish particularly to name. I went first to the Robing-room, but as there were so many people there I went to a Dressing-room where I put on the Robe which is enormously heavy. After this I entered the House of Lords preceded by all the Officers of State and Lord Melbourne bearing the Sword of State walking just before me. He stood quite close to me on the left-hand of the Throne, and I feel always a satisfaction to have him near me on such occasions, as he is such an honest, good, kind-hearted man and is my *friend*, I know it. The Lord Chancellor stood on my left. The house was very full and I felt somewhat (but very little) nervous before I read my speech, but it did very well, and I was happy to hear people were satisfied. I then unrobed in the Library and came home as I went, at 20 minutes p. 3. . . .

Wednesday, 19*th July*.—Got up at ½ p. 8. At ½ p. 9 we breakfasted. Saw Sir F. Watson, Col. Cavendish, and Stockmar. At 20 minutes p. 11 came Lord Melbourne till a ¼ p. 12. Talked over many things. Dressed. At a ¼ p. 1 I went with the Duchess of Sutherland and Lady Portman in my carriage, to St. James's. I received two addresses on the Throne and read answers to them.

After that Col. Buckley [1] and Col. Wemyss kissed hands on being appointed Equerries, as also the Hon. William Cowper (nephew to Lord Melbourne) as Groom in Waiting. Also many others. I gave audiences to various foreign Ambassadors, amongst which were Count Orloff,[2] sent by the Emperor of Russia to compliment me. He presented me with a letter from the Empress of Russia accompanied by the Order of St. Catherine all set in diamonds. (I, of course, as I generally do every evening, wore the Garter.) The Levee began immediately after this and lasted till ½ p. 4 without one minute's interruption. I had my hand kissed nearly *3000* times! I then held a Council, at which were present almost all the Ministers. After this I saw Lord Melbourne for a little while, and then Lord Palmerston. . . .

Wednesday, 2nd August.— . . . After dinner I sat on the sofa with the pretty amiable little Countess C. Pozzo di Borgo and Lady Salisbury,[3] and Count Pozzo di Borgo and Prince Auersperg [4] sat near us. Prince Auersperg is a very nice, good-looking young man, very quiet, good-humoured and retiring. Lady Seymour is certainly *exceedingly* beautiful ; she has not the splendid eyes and fine expression of her sister Mrs. Norton, but altogether she is hand-

---

[1] Edward Pery Buckley, afterwards General and M.P. See p. 327.

[2] Alexis, Count Orloff, famous both as general and diplomatist. He had fought in the war of 1829 against Turkey, and signed the Treaty of Adrianople in 1829. He had been sent to enlist English sympathies for Holland as against Belgium in 1832. He also was a signatory of the important treaty of Unkiar Skelessi, and represented Russia in the Congress of Paris in 1856.

[3] Lady Salisbury was Frances Mary, daughter and heir of Bamber Gascoyne, grandson of Sir Crisp Gascoyne, Lord Mayor of London 1752. He was the first Lord Mayor who occupied the Mansion House.

[4] Afterwards an intimate counsellor of the Emperor of Austria, Hereditary Great Chamberlain, and President of the Council.

somest, and there is a sweetness and gentleness about her which neither Mrs. Norton nor Mrs. Blackwood have.[1]   Stayed up till ½ p. 10. . . .

Wednesday, 9th August.—Got up at a little after 8 and breakfasted at ½ p. 9.   Saw Sir Frederic Watson and Col. Buckley.   Began a letter to dear Uncle Leopold. Saw Stockmar. Finished my letter to Uncle Leopold and wrote my journal.   At 7 minutes to 12 came Lord Melbourne and stayed till a ¼ to 2. Talked over many serious subjects.   I'm somewhat anxious about the Elections but I trust in Heaven that we shall have a Majority for us, and that the present Government may remain firm for *long*. Lord Melbourne spoke so candidly, so disinterestedly, and so calmly about all this.   Wrote my journal. Drew.   At 3 came the Queen Adelaide's sister, Ida, Duchess of Saxe-Weimar,[2] with 3 of her children. Her 2nd son, Edward, 14 years old, who was born here [3] and consequently is my subject, and her little girls, Anna and Amalie, 9 and 7 years old.   Edward is a very nice boy.   I stayed some time with them and then went down and drew in my room while Mamma took them into the garden. . . .

Tuesday, 15th August.—Got up at ½ p. 8, and breakfasted in my own room at a ¼ to 10.   Put on my habit and went with dear Lehzen, Miss Cavendish,[4] Lord Albemarle, Col. Cavendish, Col. Buckley and Stockmar, to the Mews, which are in the garden. The Riding-house is very large.   Sir George Quentin and Mr. Fozard (who has a situation in my

[1] See *ante,* p. 192: note on the Sheridan sisters.
[2] Wife of Duke Bernard of Saxe-Weimar-Eisenach, younger brother of Grand Duke Charles Frederick.   See p. 125.
[3] At Marlborough House.
[4] Carolıne Fanny, daughter of Colonel Cavendish.   Maid-of-honour, and Extra Woman of the Bedchamber.

Stables) &c., were there. I had not ridden for 2 years ! I first rode a bay horse, a delightful one called Ottoman, and cantered about a good while. I then tried for a minute another horse which I did not like so well. I then remounted Ottoman. After him I mounted a beautiful and very powerful but delightful grey horse, a Hanoverian, called Fearon. Miss Cavendish rode also the whole time ; she rides very nicely. Came home at 20 minutes to 12. Mamma came into the School when I had been riding a little while. . . .

Wednesday, 16*th August.*—Got up at ½ p. 8, and breakfasted before 10 in my own room. At ½ p. 10 I went to the Riding House with Mamma, Miss Cocks,[1] Miss Cavendish, dearest Lehzen, Col. Cavendish, and Col. Buckley. I rode 1st a horse called Rosa (not my poor little Rosa), then Monarch, rather a nice horse, then Emma, not a bad horse, then Fearon, my favourite, and lastly Emperor, a *very* nice chestnut horse. Mamma and my Maids of Honour also rode. Came home at 12. At 7 minutes past 1 came Lord Melbourne and stayed till a ¼ to 3. . . .

WINDSOR CASTLE, *Tuesday,* 22*nd August.*—Got up at a ¼ to 9 and breakfasted at 10. Saw Col. Buckley. Wrote to the Grand Duchess of Oldenbourg.[2] Arranged various things. At 20 minutes to 12 came my kind, good friend Lord Melbourne and stayed till ½ p. 1. I am quite sorry to think I shall not see him till next Monday, when he comes down to me at Windsor,

---

[1] Caroline Margaret, Maid-of-honour, eldest daughter of John, afterwards second Earl Somers. She subsequently married Canon Courtenay, one of the Queen's chaplains.

[2] Princess Cecile of Sweden, third wife of Grand Duke Augustus of Oldenbourg.

for I am so fond of him, and his conversations do me much good ; he is such a thoroughly straightforward, disinterested, excellent and kindhearted man. He goes down to Brocket Hall tonight with his sister Lady Cowper, Lady Fanny, and Mr. Cowper (my Groom), and the younger brother, Spencer Cowper. I hope the country air and rest will do him good. Saw Sir H. Wheatley, and Stockmar. Wrote my journal. Saw Sir F. Wetherall,[1] and Prince Ernest of Hesse P.B.[2] At ½ p. 2 I went with Mamma, Lady Charlotte Copley, and Lady Flora in my carriage ; dear Lehzen, Miss Cocks, Miss Cavendish, and Col. Buckley going in the other, to Windsor Castle, where I arrived at ½ p. 5. I had escort of Lancers. All along the road the people were very loyal and civil, and my poor native place, Kensington, particularly so. When we reached the Long Walk at Windsor a larger escort of the 1st Life Guards met me ; the Walk was thronged with people, where a dinner was given to them in honour of my arrival. The people were remarkably friendly and civil. Unfortunately it began to rain before we reached the Long Walk. Windsor looked somewhat gloomy and I cannot help feeling as though *I* was not the Mistress of the House and as if I was to see the poor King and Queen. There is sadness about the whole which I must say I feel. Lady Tavistock, who is in waiting for 4 weeks, Lord Conyngham, and the Lord Steward received me at the door. I inhabit the Queen's rooms, though not in the same way as she did. At ½ p. 7 we dined. . . .

Saturday, 26th August.—Got up at a ¼ to 9 and at 10 we breakfasted with all the Ladies including Lady Charlemont and Lady Barham. To-day is my

---

[1] See *ante*, p. 69.   [2] See *ante*, p. 145.

dearest cousin Albert's 18th birthday, and I pray Heaven to pour its choicest blessings on his beloved head! Took leave of Lady Barham as both she and he go away. . . .

Sunday, 27th August.— . . . At ½ p. 2 we all went into the drawing-room and received the King of Würtemburg [1] who came to take leave. He was accompanied by Count Mandelsloh, Baron Spitzemberg, and General Fleischmann. He took luncheon with us and the whole party including Lord Glenelg, whom I asked to stay another night. By some mistake Lord Tavistock did not come to luncheon. I sat between the King and Count Mandelsloh. After luncheon I showed the King the State Rooms &c. and at 4 he took leave and went away. He leaves England on Tuesday and is much pleased with what he has seen. . . .

Monday, 28th August.— . . . I hope Lord Melbourne will stay here for some days. At 4 I rode out with Mamma, Lady Charlotte Copley, Lady Mary Stopford (who got into the carriage and drove), Miss Cavendish, Miss Cocks, Lord Melbourne, Lord Conyngham, Lord Torrington,[2] Col. Cavendish, Col. Buckley, and Mr. Rich. As Sir George Quentin and Mr. Fozard *always* ride out with us, I shall not mention them any more. Lady Tavistock and Lehzen followed in a pony carriage. I rode Duchess, a nice bay horse, but rather too quiet and not near so pleasant as Monarch. Mamma rode Barbara. Lord Melbourne rode his own horse, a very fine black mare which came down from London this day. It was a very pleasant ride and we came home at a ¼ p. 6. . . .

---

[1] King William I., who succeeded his father, Frederic, in 1816.
[2] George, seventh Viscount, a Lord-in-waiting.

Tuesday, 29th August.—Got up at ½ p. 8 and at ½ p. 9 we breakfasted with all the ladies. Wrote my journal. At ½ p. 11 or rather at a ¼ to 12 came Lord Melbourne and stayed till a ¼ to 2. At 3 I walked over the House with Mamma and most of the ladies, and Lord Conyngham, Col. Buckley, Col. Cavendish, &c. The offices are not good. We then walked a little while on the Terrace. Played on the piano or rather more sang with Mamma. At 7 o'clock arrived my *dearest most beloved* Uncle Leòpold and my *dearest most beloved* Aunt Louise. They *are both*, and *look both, very well*; dearest Aunt Louise is looking so well and is grown *quite* fat. I and Mamma as well as my whole court were all at the door to receive them. It is an inexpressible *happiness* and *joy* to me, to have these dearest beloved relations with me and in *my own* house. I took them to their rooms, and then hastened to dress for dinner. At 8 we dined. . . . Dearest Aunt Louise went in first with Lord Lansdowne, then I with dear Uncle, and Mamma with M. Van de Weyer. I sat between dear Uncle and my good Lord Melbourne ; two delightful neighbours. Dear Aunt Louise sat opposite. After dinner I sat on the sofa with dearest Aunt Louise, who is really *an angel,* and Lord Melbourne sat near me. Uncle talked with Lord Palmerston. It was a most delightful evening. . . .

Friday, 1st September.— . . . I rode Monarch who went delightfully, and Aunt Louise and Mamma the same horses as the preceding day. The weather looked lowering when we went out. When we were about the middle of Queen Anne's Walk, there came a most unexpected and violent flash of lightning which was followed instantaneously by a tremendous clap of thunder. My horse jumped a little, but very

little, but Aunt Louise's being very much alarmed by the thunder, *ran away, full gallop,* to our great horror, and poor dear Aunt lost her hat ; thank God ! the horse stopped after 100 yards at the foot of a hill and was led back. We had meanwhile got into a close carriage with the three ladies, and dear Aunt Louise who was not the *least* frightened but only " quite ashamed " as she said, also got in, and we drove home (all six) in a tremendous thunderstorm and deluge of rain. We reached home in perfect safety at 5 o'clock. . . .

Friday, 8th September.—Got up at a $\frac{1}{4}$ to 9 and at a little before 10 I breakfasted with dearest Uncle Leopold, dearest Aunt Louise, Mamma and the Duke of Sussex. Talked with Uncle Leopold for some time. How I wish I had time to take *minutes* of the very interesting and highly important conversations I have with my Uncle and with Lord Melbourne ; the sound observations they make, and the impartial advice they give me would make a most interesting book.) At 11 Lord Melbourne came to me and stayed with me till 20 minutes to 1. He is a most excellent, kindhearted, honest and upright man, and my beloved Uncle is delighted with him, which makes me very happy, as I am so fond of Lord Melbourne, and he *has been* and *is such* a *kind friend* to me. Uncle and he perfectly agree in Politics too, which are the *best* there *are*. Lord Melbourne goes to town, I'm sorry to say, today, but will be back here tomorrow. Saw dearest Uncle Leopold. Talked with him. Signed. Wrote my journal. . . .

Tuesday, 12th September.— . . . After dinner I sat part of the evening on the sofa with Lady Tavistock, dearest Uncle Leopold and Lord Melbourne sitting near me ; they talked very interestingly

together. The rest of the evening I sat on the sofa
with dearest Aunt Louise, who played a game at
chess with me, to *teach* me, and Lord Melbourne sat
near me. Lord Tavistock, Lord Palmerston, Mrs.
Cavendish, Sir J. Hobhouse and Mme. de Mérode,[1]
sat round the table. Lord Melbourne, Lord Palmerston, Sir J. Hobhouse, and later too Lord Conyngham, all gave me advice, and *all different* advice,
about my playing at chess, and *all* got so *eager* that
it was very amusing ; in particular Lord Palmerston
and Sir J. Hobhouse,[2] who differed totally and got
quite excited and serious about it. Between them
all, I got quite beat, and Aunt Louise triumphed
over my Council of Ministers ! . . .

Monday, 18th September.— . . . After dinner I
sat on the sofa part of the evening with Lady Tavistock, Lord Melbourne sitting near me, and the rest
with my *dearest* Aunt Louise, with whom I played
a game at chess, and *beat* her ; Lord Palmerston,
Lord Melbourne, and Lord Conyngham sat near
me advising me. At 11, our *last happy evening*
broke up, and Aunt Louise took leave in the kindest
way imaginable of the whole party except my
gentlemen ; and good Lord Melbourne was touched
to tears by this leave-taking. I cannot say *how*
I shall miss my dearest Aunt Louise ; she combines with *great* cleverness and learning, so much
merriment, and has all the liveliness and fun
of a girl of 16, with all the *sense* and *deep* thought
of one of 30 and much older even. And I think

[1] Wife of M. de Mérode, who was First Minister in Belgium and a
faithful friend to King Leopold.

[2] Lord Broughton (Sir John Hobhouse), in his Reminiscences, refers
to this game of chess, and to the slight confusion there was between
" the two Queens on the board and the two Queens at the table."

she is *so lovely*, so graceful, she has such an angelic
expression in her clear eyes ; and she dresses *so well*,
morning and evening.   And then my beloved Uncle
whom I look up to and *love* as a *father*, how I shall *miss*
his protection out *riding*, and his conversation ! . . .

Thursday, 28th September.—Got up at ½ p. 8 and
breakfasted with Mamma at a ¼ to 10.   Wrote to
the Duchess of Gloucester.   Saw Sir Jeffrey Wyatt-
ville.[1]   Wrote to the Queen and my journal. (At
12 Lord Melbourne came to me and stayed with me
till 10 m. p. 1.   Dressed, in a habit of dark blue with
red collar and cuffs (the Windsor Uniform which all
my gentlemen wear), a military cap, and my Order
of the Garter, as I was going to review the Troops.
At 2 I mounted Leopold, who was very handsomely
harnessed ; all the gentlemen were in uniform, that
is to say Lord Hill, Lord Alfred Paget [2] (who looked
remarkably handsome in his uniform of the Blues),
Prince Lichtenstein,[3] Baron Reisehach, &c., and my
other gentlemen wore the Windsor uniform with
cocked hats.   Mamma and Miss Cavendish rode, as
did also my pretty little page, George Cavendish,

[1] Sir Jeffrey Wyatt (1766–1840), the architect, whose most
important work was the transformation of Windsor Castle, including
the addition of thirty feet to the height of the Round Tower.   The
principal feature of this work is the solid and " fortress-like " appearance, which is conspicuous in the Castle.   His name had been originally Wyatt, but George IV., after laying the foundation-stone of the
new work, sanctioned the curious addition of " ville " to the surname.
Although he was an architect of considerable technical skill, his powers
of destructiveness were quite remarkable.   He hardly left a stone
of Windsor Castle unturned.

[2] Equerry to the Queen, son of the first Marquess of Anglesey by his
second marriage with Lady Charlotte Cadogan.   Sometime M.P. for
Lichfield and Clerk-Marshal of the Royal Household.   Lord Broughton
described him as " a handsome Calmuck-looking young fellow."

[3] Prince Aloysius Joseph de Lichtenstein succeeded his father,
Jean Joseph, in 1836.

who looked so pretty in his uniform, mounted on a little pony all harnessed like a large horse. Lord Palmerston also rode. All the other ladies and gentlemen, including Lord Melbourne, drove in carriages after us. The Lancers escorted us. When we came upon the ground, which is in the Home Park, I rode up with the whole party to where a Sergeant was stationed with the colours, and there stopped, and the regiments saluted me. I saluted them by putting my hand to my cap like the officers do, and was much admired for my manner of doing so. I then cantered up to the Lines with all the gentlemen and rode along them. Leopold behaved most beautifully, so quietly, the Bands really play-ing *in* his face. I then cantered back to my first position and there remained while the Troops marched by in slow and quick time, and when they manœuvred, which they did beautifully. The Troops consisted of the 1st Regiment of Life Guards who are beautiful, of the Grenadier Guards, and of some of the Lancers. They fired and skirmished a good deal, and near us, and Leopold never moved. The whole went off beautifully ; and I felt for the first time like a man, as if I could fight myself at the head of my Troops. We rode back to the Castle at ½ p. 4, and I mounted Barbara and rode out with Mamma, Prince Lichtenstein, Lord Melbourne, Lord Palmerston, Baron Reischach, Lord Torrington, Lord Alfred Paget, Miss Cavendish, Lady Mary, Mr. Murray and Miss Murray, and came home at 7 m. to 6. Lord Melbourne rode near me.

Friday, 29th September.—Got up at a ¼ to 9 and breakfasted at 10 with Mamma. Wrote to dear Ferdinand and to the good Queen of Portugal while my hair was doing before breakfast. Wrote to dearest Aunt Louise and my journal. At 12 Lord Melbourne came to me and stayed with me till ½ p. 1. He read to me a Paper about the Civil List, and explained it to me, and so *clearly* and *well* he explained it ; he reads very well too, so distinctly and with *so* much good emphasis. . . .

Saturday, 30th September.—Got up at a ¼ to 9 and breakfasted at 10 with Mamma. Saw Lord Albemarle. Wrote my journal. At a ¼ p. 11 Lord Melbourne came to me and stayed with me till a ¼ to 12. At a ¼ to 12 came the Queen with her sister the Duchess of Saxe-Weimar and stayed with me till 1 o'clock. The poor Queen was very much composed, though it must have been a very painful and severe trial for her, considering she had not been here since she left the Castle, the night after the poor King's funeral. I showed her all my rooms with which she was much pleased ; and she went by herself to see the room where the King died. I sang a little and Mamma also, while they were there. . . .

Tuesday, 3rd October.—Got up at a ¼ to 9 and at a ¼ p. 10 I breakfasted with Mamma. Wrote to dearest Uncle Leopold and my journal. Saw Sir H. Wheatley. At ½ p. 12 Lord Melbourne came to me and stayed with me till 5 m. to 2. He read to me some Despatches from Canada which are not very satisfactory. Saw Princess Augusta. At ½ p. 3 I rode out with Mamma, Lord Melbourne, Lord Palmerston, Lady Mary, Lord Torrington, Mr. Murray, Mr. Brand, Col., Mrs. and Miss Cavendish, and Miss Murray, and came home at 6. We rode all round Virginia Water, a beautiful ride, and cantered almost the whole way home. It was the hottest summer evening that can be imagined, not a breath of air, and hotter coming home than going out. Alas ! it was our last ride here! I am *very sorry* indeed to go! I passed such a very pleasant time here; the pleasantest summer I EVER passed in *my life,* and I shall never forget this first summer of my Reign. I have had the *great* happiness of having my beloved Uncle and Aunt here with me, I have had very pleasant people and kind friends staying with me, and I have had *delicious* rides which have done me a world of good. Lord Melbourne rode near me the whole time. The more I see of him and the more I know of him, the more I like and appreciate his fine and honest character. I have seen a great deal of him, every day, these last 5 weeks, and I have always found him in good humour, kind, good, and most agreeable; I have seen him in my Closet for Political Affairs, I have ridden out with him (every day), I have sat near him constantly at and after dinner, and talked about all sorts of things, and have always found him a kind and most excellent and very agreeable man. I am very fond of him. *]* Wrote my journal. . . .

BRIGHTON, *Wednesday, 4th October.—* . . . I constantly regret I cannot write down many of the pleasant and instructive conversations I have with clever people, such as Lord Melbourne, Lord Palmerston, Lord Holland, &c., &c. And many of the Foreign Despatches which I read, in particular some of the Private letters of the Ambassadors and Ministers to Lord Palmerston, are *so* interesting and well written that I wish I could note them down. I read one of Mr. Villiers'[1] from Madrid to-day, which is remarkably well written. . . .

---

[1] George Villiers (1800–70), British Plenipotentiary at Madrid. In 1838 he became fourth Earl of Clarendon, was Lord Lieutenant of Ireland in critical times, 1847–52, and afterwards, with great distinc-

Tuesday, 24th October.—Got up at 25 m. p. 8 and breakfasted at a ¼ to 10 with Mamma, having signed &c. before breakfast. Wrote my journal &c. At 3 m. to 11 Lord Melbourne came to me and stayed with me till ½ p. 12. Talked over many things and gave him a letter I had received this morning from Uncle Leopold, to read ; he took it with him. Sat to Sir David Wilkie. Before I left the painting room, I sent for Lord Melbourne to see the Picture, with which he was much pleased. It is to be my *First Council*,[1] and a great many Portraits will be introduced into the picture ; Lord Melbourne will be painted standing near me. Wrote my journal. . . .

Sunday, 29th October.— . . . At a little after 3 I *tried* to drive out with Lady Mulgrave, Lady Gardiner and Miss Paget [2] following, but we were obliged to come home again almost directly as it rained the whole time. It is really most provoking weather. Finished my letter to Feodore, and wrote one to my *Cousin Marie.*[3] Saw Stockmar for one instant. At 7 we dined. . . .

tion, Secretary of State for Foreign Affairs in 1853, again in 1865 and in 1868. He was not a statesman of very original mind, or of great initiative, but he was honest and prudent and highly regardful of his country's interests. His manners were delightful and his conversation varied with anecdotes and punctuated by wit. He was one of the principal attractions in London society during the first half of the nineteenth century.

[1] This picture hangs in the Corridor at Windsor Castle. The likenesses are excellent, but the artist has painted the Queen in a white dress, whereas she wore black. The actual dress worn by the Queen is now exhibited in the London Museum at Kensington.

[2] Matilda Susannah, daughter of Hon. Berkeley Paget, fifth son of the first Earl of Uxbridge. She was a Maid of Honour to the Queen, and died in 1871.

[3] Princess Marie of Orleans, daughter of King Louis Philippe. See *ante*, p. 78.

Wednesday, 1st November.—Got up at a ¼ to 9
and breakfasted at 10 with Mamma.   Received before
breakfast a letter from Ferdinand and one from Mary
with a very pretty little ring in it.   At ½ p. 10 my
excellent, kind friend Lord Melbourne came to me
and stayed with me till 12.   Talked over many
things ; and talked over some *disagreeable business*
about which Lord Melbourne is *very kind* (as he is
about *everything,* for he is the best-hearted, kindest
and most feeling man in the world) and very anxious.
Showed him dear Ferdinand's letter.   Poor Ferdinand's position and the unfortunate state of Portuguese affairs distress him much ; he takes everything so much to heart, which is generally not the
case with a Statesman.   I observed to Lord Melbourne that there were not many very good preachers
to be found ; he replied in the affirmative and
added, " But there are not *many very good anything,*"
which is *very true. . . .* I then took leave of him,
told him I was very sorry he went, to which he
replied he was also very sorry.   I shall see him again
however on Saturday when I go to town.   I am
very sorry to lose his agreeable company (as I always
like to have those who are kind to me, and *my*
friends, with me) these last days here.   And I am
very sorry to think that the summer and autumn
(the pleasantest *I* EVER passed) are over !   How
time flies when pleasantly spent ! !   Lord Melbourne
also was much better for this quiet life and liked
it too.   He is a great friend of Lehzen's which
makes me *more* fond of him still.   I always saw
Lord Melbourne in my little sitting-room ; I being
seated on a sofa, and he in an armchair near
or close opposite me ; the other ministers and
visitors I saw in another little room just the same

size as this one, where Lehzen always sits ; it is close to the other, one little room only being between the two. . . .

BUCKINGHAM PALACE, *Saturday, 4th November.* —Got up at ½ p. 7. Wrote my journal while my hair was doing. Received a few lines from Lord Melbourne. At 9 I breakfasted with Mama. Saw Stockmar. At 10 minutes to 10 I left Brighton with Mama and Lady Mulgrave ; Miss Dillon, Lady Mary Stopford, dearest Lehzen and Col. Cavendish following in another carriage. Lady Gardiner went in her own carriage. I took leave of Miss Paget before I went ; both her and Miss Dillon's waitings were out on Thursday, but I did not wish to give the other Maids of Honour the trouble of coming down only for two days and then going back again. Miss Paget is a very good, quiet, nice, unaffected girl. We changed horses first at Hickstead, 2ndly at Crawley, 3rdly at Redhill, and lastly at Croydon, and reached Buckingham Palace at 3. It is a journey of 52 miles. . . . I have changed my rooms, that is to say, I sit in my dressing-room, and make it both my sitting and dressing-room, which is much more comfortable and cheerful than the other rooms on the other side ; and I shall see all my Ministers &c. in the former breakfast room,[1] next my dressing-room, which is now very prettily furnished and looks very nice and cheerful. Lehzen's little sitting-room is next this room. At a few m. p. 4 came my good Lord Melbourne, whom I was happy to see well and in good spirits, though a little tired with the deal

---

[1] These rooms, partly remodelled and redecorated, are now occupied by Queen Mary. Up to the death of Queen Victoria no material change was made in them. In 1901 they were much altered, although the main features remain as before.

he has to do ; he stayed with me till 10 m. p. 5, and
we talked over various important things. I, of
course, saw him in the *new Ministerial Room. . . .*

Thursday, 9th November.—Got up at ½ p. 9 and
breakfasted by myself in my room at ½ p. 10.
Played on the piano and sang. Wrote my journal.
Dressed for the Lord Mayor's dinner, in *all my finery*.
At 2 I went in the state carriage and 8 horses with
the Duchess of Sutherland and Lord Albemarle ; all
my suite, the Royal Family, &c., went before me. I
reached the Guildhall at a little before 4. Throughout
my progress to the city, I met with the MOST gratifying, affectionate, hearty and brilliant reception from
the greatest concourse of people I ever witnessed ;
the streets being *immensely crowded* as were also the
windows, houses, churches, balconies, every where.
I was then conducted by the Lord Chamberlain, the
Lord Mayor and Lady Mayoress preceding me, and my
whole suite following me,—to a private drawing-room,
where I found Mamma, the Duchess of Gloucester,
the Duchess of Cambridge, and Augusta, and all
their Ladies. All my Ladies came in there. After
waiting some little time, I sent for Lord Melbourne
and Lord John Russell, to ask them some questions,
and they came in for a minute or two, and then went
away. After waiting a little longer, I was conducted
by Lord Conyngham in the same way as before, the
Royal Family and my Ladies &c. following, to the
Council Room, where were the Dukes of Sussex and
Cambridge and George,—all my Ministers, all the
Foreign Ambassadors and Ministers &c., &c., the
Lord Mayor, all the Aldermen, the Lady Mayoress
and all the Aldermen's wives. I was seated in
a large arm-chair, all the others standing. The
Recorder then read an Address, to which I read an

answer ; when the Lord Mayor was presented I said
to Lord John Russell (what I had previously been
told to do), " I desire you to take proper measures
for conferring the dignity of Baronet on the Lord
Mayor." I then knighted the Sheriffs, one of whom
was Mr. Montefiore, a Jew, an excellent man [1] ; and
I was very glad that I was the first to do what *I*
think quite right, as it should be. The Lady Mayoress
and all the Aldermen's wives were then presented.
After this we returned, as before, to the Private
Drawing room and remained there till a $\frac{1}{4}$ p. 5 when
we went to dinner. . . . I drank a glass of wine with
the Lord Mayor (John Cowan) and the late Lord
Mayor. The Lord Mayor is a quiet little old man of
70 (they say). When my health was given out,
there was great cheering and applause. I left dinner
in the same way I came in at about $\frac{1}{2}$ p. 7 ; and we
went as before into the Private Drawing room and
waited there till the carriages were ready. All the
Royal Family went away before me. I went at
$\frac{1}{2}$ p. 8 in a usual carriage (not a state carriage) with
the Duchess of Sutherland and Lord Albemarle as
before. We came back just in the same way as we
went, only that each carriage had only a pair of
horses, and there were no people on foot walking by
the carriage. The crowd was, if possible, greater
than it had been when I went in the day ; and they
cheered me excessively as I came along. The streets

[1] Sir Moses Montefiore (1784–1885), created a baronet in 1846. His
life, prolonged for over a hundred years, was one of flawless generosity
and personal kindness to the poor and afflicted of his own race,
especially in the eastern provinces of Russia and in Turkey. He
obtained consideration for poor Jews from the Russian and Turkish
Governments, and his seven pilgrimages to Jerusalem were all undertaken with a view to improving the questionable lot of the Chosen
People.

were beautifully illuminated on all sides, and looked very brilliant and gay. I got home by 20 m. to 10, and quite safely ; I trust there have been no accidents. I cannot say HOW gratified, and HOW *touched* I am by the very brilliant, affectionate, cordial, enthusiastic and *unanimous* reception I met with in this the *greatest* Metropolis in the *World* ; there was not a discontented look, not a sign of displeasure— all loyalty, affection and loud greeting from the immense multitude I passed through ; and no disorder whatever. I feel *deeply grateful* for this display of affection and unfeigned loyalty and *attachment* from my good people. It is much more than I deserve, and I shall do my utmost to render myself worthy of all this love and affection. I had a very bad headache in the morning, but it went off during all the ceremonies ; it was somewhat bad when I came home, but I went to bed immediately after I had signed a few papers. . . .

Sunday, 12th November.— . . . Saw Stockmar. Walked. Signed. Wrote my journal. Read Despatches. At a little after 7 we dined. Our whole party made only 12 in number, which were, us 10 (for Miss Davys and Col. Cavendish had gone home and Lady Mary was ill), Lord Melbourne and Mr. Cowper. Lord Melbourne led me in and I sat between him and Mr. Cowper. I was happy to see Lord Melbourne in very good spirits ; he was very amusing about Theatricals and has peculiar tastes of his own about actors. He has such an honest, blunt, and amusing manner of coming out with his remarks and observations. After dinner I sat on the sofa with Mamma, and Lord Melbourne sat near me the whole evening. Mr. Cowper (who, as usual, was very amusing), and Lady Mulgrave sat near the table.

Lord Melbourne does not, I think, look quite as well as he used to do when at Windsor and Brighton ; he looks paler and tired often ; and he says he feels the want of exercise. I fear since I have come to the throne he has still more to do than he had before ; but he is always ready to assist me in every way, and will not admit that I trouble him.' Stayed up till 11. It was a very pleasant evening.

Monday, 13th November.— . . . I do not mention when I get communications from Lord Melbourne and when I write to him, for that occurs *every* day and *generally* 2 or 3 times a day, so that it would take up too much time ; I also receive communications from all the other Ministers ; the one with whom I communicate *oftenest* after Lord Melbourne is Lord Palmerston. . . .

Thursday, 16th November.— . . . At a ¼ p. 2 Lord Melbourne came to me and stayed with me till 12 m. p. 3. He read me the Speech again, as it is settled to be now ; and became touched to tears in reading the concluding part which alludes to my youth and reliance on the Loyalty of my People— kind, excellent, good man. Talked over various things. . . .

Friday, 17th November.— . . . After dinner I went at ½ p. 6 with all the dinner party, except Lehzen (who again went with Mr. Rich to the play in a box opposite), Miss Davys (who did not go), and Lord Alfred Paget (who was on the escort and rode by the carriage), to the play to Covent Garden, the Duchess of Sutherland and Lord Albemarle going with me in the carriage. I met with the same brilliant reception, the house being *so* full that there was a great piece of work for want of room, and many people had to be *pulled* out of the Pit by their wrists and arms into the Dress Circle. I never saw such an exhibition; it was the oddest thing I ever saw. My Ladies took it by turns, (their standing behind me, I mean). Mamma sat near me, and Lady Mary stood behind her. The performances were the fine but dreadful tragedy of *Werner* by Lord Byron, and the 1st act of *Fra Diavolo*. . . .

Monday, 20th November.—Got up at a ¼ to 9 and breakfasted by myself at a ¼ p. 10. Played on the piano. Saw Mr. Spring Rice. Dressed for going to the House of Lords, exactly in the same costume as last July. When I was dressed I saw the Duchess of Gloucester, the Duchess of Cambridge, and Augusta[1] and little Mary.[2] At ½ p. 1 I went in the State Carriage with the Duchess of Sutherland and Lord Albemarle; Lady Lansdowne, Lady Barham, and all my gentlemen (except Lord Conyngham who went as a Peer and not in my suite), and 3 Pages, going in 6 other carriages, to the House of Lords to open Parliament. I arrived there at 2, and was conducted to the Library—all the Great Officers of State, the Lord Chancellor, the Lord President, the Lord Privy Seal, preceding me—Lord Melbourne walking quite close before me bearing the sword of state. I robed in the Library, all the above-mentioned people, my ladies and gentlemen, being there, and then proceeded into the House of Lords—the manner of going in being the same as before—and seated myself on the Throne; Lord Melbourne standing quite close to me on my left; I feel a satisfaction in having this excellent man near me on such important public occasions. I read the Declaration about Transubstantiation, or rather re-

---

[1] Princess Augusta of Cambridge. See Vol. II., p. 150.
[2] Princess Mary, afterwards Duchess of Teck.

peated it after the Chancellor—the Commons having been summoned to the Bar. After this I read the Speech (which I think an excellent one) and which people were pleased to say I read well. The House was very full. I then returned to the Library and unrobed. Good, kind Melbourne was quite touched to tears after I read the Speech. I could only say a very few words to him. I came home, as I went, at a $\frac{1}{4}$ p. 3. Lehzen was at the House, which I am very glad of, and *she* was pleased with my manner. . . . The Duke of Sussex was the mover of the Address in the House of Lords, and made a very able and judicious speech, Lord Melbourne wrote me word. I got Lord Melbourne's despatch while I was at dinner, and I left the table for a minute to read it. Lord Melbourne likewise informed me that " the Address was voted without a dissentient voice " ; and that the Duke of Wellington spoke fairly ; adhering to his declaration of last Session, and saying that the manner in which the Measures for Ireland were mentioned in the Speech would facilitate his intention to support Ministers in their measures. None of the Ministers spoke. I hail this bright and unanimous beginning as an auspicious augury of the coming Session and I trust that all will do well. . . .

Friday, 24th November.— . . . Saw Lord Conyngham and Edwin Landseer, who brought a beautiful little sketch which he has done this morning, of a picture he is to paint for me of Hector and Dash. He is an unassuming, pleasing and very young-looking man, with fair hair. At 1 Lord Melbourne came to me and stayed with me till a $\frac{1}{4}$ to 2. Talked over various things. . . .

Tuesday, 28th November.— . . . At 20 m. to 1

came Lord Melbourne and stayed with me till 2.   I
was glad to see him looking well and in high spirits.
He said it was " a very good debate " in the House
of Lords ; that the Duke of Wellington had been
somewhat eager but had been put down.   The House
sat till p. 11, and Lord Melbourne only got his
dinner then.   I showed him Lord John's account of
the Debate in the H. of Commons.   He said there
was a good deal in this *large* majority as the Opposition had made rather a point of it to carry it.   Lord
Melbourne was quite touched in saying this, as he
knows how anxious I am the Government should be
firm for the peace of the Country and for my own
peace and happiness ; as also when he spoke of the
readiness with which the Civil List would be voted.
He is *so* kind to me ; I have the GREATEST confidence
in him.   He is so truly excellent.   I cannot say
HOW happy I am at this *good* beginning !   Lord
Melbourne even said, everything went much better
than they expected.   I trust most fervently that all
will continue thus well. . . .

Wednesday, 29th November.— . . . At 20 m. p.
12 Lord Melbourne came to me and stayed with me
till 2.   He told me there had been a very short debate
upon the Duke of Newcastle's [1] bringing in a Bill
for the Repeal of the Catholic Emancipation Act (a
most absurd idea).   He (the Duke of Newcastle) was
only supported by Lord Lorton [2] and Lord Winchilsea.

[1] Henry, fourth Duke.   He had been so strenuous an opponent
of the Reform Bill, that, after its rejection, a mob set fire to
Nottingham Castle, his property.   Mr. Gladstone was M.P. for Newark
owing to the Duke's influence, which was withdrawn in 1845 when
Mr. Gladstone supported Peel on the Corn Laws.

[2] Robert Edward, second son of the second Earl of Kingston, born
1773.   He was a Lieut.-General and was created Viscount Lorton in the
Irish peerage in 1806.   He was a Representative Peer.

Lord Melbourne and Lord Brougham spoke. I read
the speech of the former (Lord Melbourne) in the
papers ; it is, as all his speeches and sayings are, remarkably judicious and clever. . . . At ½ p. 7 we
dined. . . . I sat between the Duke of Wellington
and the Marquis Conyngham. The former I thought
looking very old, and silent and out of spirits. I
think he does not feel à son aise dans sa position ;
he fears to displease his friends and does not wish
to oppose the Ministry violently. . . . I sat on the
sofa with Lady Mulgrave and Lady Barham ; Lady
Wilhelmina Stanhope[1] and Lady Caroline Strangways[2] sitting near me. Lady Wilhelmina is not so
handsome as she was ; she is not to be compared,
in my opinion, to Lady Fanny Cowper, whose great
charm, besides her lovely face, fine complexion and
beautiful figure is her great quietness, and unaffected
manners, and unconsciousness of her beauty. Lady
Wilhelmina is nevertheless an agreeable, clever
girl. . . .

Monday, 4th December.—Got up at ½ p. 9. . . .
At about 10 m. to 1 came Lord Melbourne and stayed
with me till 2. Talked about many things, and
amongst others about the Pensions which give so
much trouble. Lord Melbourne said he thought it
" quite an abomination to meddle with the pensions "
which people now had ; that upon the whole, hereafter, he was rather against giving pensions, for he
said, " if people know that you have the power to
grant them, they apply without end, and it is very
difficult to refuse " ; " it requires," he added,
" nerves of iron to refuse," and " if you have none

---

[1] See ante, p. 188.
[2] Second daughter of Lord Ilchester, afterwards wife of Sir Edward
Clarence Kerrison.

to give away, why there is an end of it." I think
this is all very true. . . .

Wednesday, 6th December.—At 1 came Lord Mel-
bonrne and stayed with me till a ¼ p. 2. He told
me that there was a good deal of speaking in the
House of Lords yesterday, upon the 2nd reading of
the Imprisonment for Debt Bill, and that they sat
till 10 o'clock. The bill, though opposed in detail,
by some, was read a 2nd time, and was referred to
a Commitee. In the House of Commons, the
Municipal Corporation Bill for Ireland was introduced
without opposition. There was some debate upon
an affair of the dismissal of a Col. Verner in Ireland
(which was done, as Lord Melbourne told me at
Windsor, against his (Lord M.'s) wish, and which he
still dislikes, but which cannot be helped now), on
account of a toast he gave at a public dinner. Lord
Morpeth quite put him (Col. Verner) down, by " a
triumphant speech,'" as Lord John wrote me word ;
I always shew these reports of Lord John to Lord
Melbourne. . . . Lord Melbourne led me in, and I
sat between him and Lord Canning, who is exceedingly
shy. Lord Melbourne was in good spirits and we
talked a good deal upon various subjects ; I made
him laugh very much by telling him what the
Duchess of Sutherland told me *he* had told *her* about
Lord Brougham's speech on education, which was :
" That it was tiresome to hear, tiresome to educate,
and tiresome to be educated." He said, " I think
it is very true." . . .

Thursday, 7th December.—Went into the Drawing room where Mr. Landseer showed me two *most*
beautiful pictures, done by himself, one large, the
other small, which he had brought for me to see ;
the figures and animals are all most beautifully

I—17

painted and grouped; and most exquisitely finished, so that I looked at them through a *magnifying glass*; I never saw anything so exquisite in every way. He also showed me a sketch in oils (small) of Lord Melbourne which is like, but too fat, and though flattered is not in my opinion half pleasing enough. It is very well done; he also showed me a sketch of Mrs. Lister done in *one* sitting, and exceedingly pretty. He had only had two sittings of Lord Melbourne. He certainly is the cleverest artist there is. Sat to Mr. Hayter for a long while. Showed him some of my drawings which he praised and told me where they were in fault. Drew. Tried to sketch little Mary Barrington while her mother amused her. . . .

Friday, 8th December.— . . . After dinner I sat on the sofa with Lady Ashley,[1] who was very agreeable and talked to me of her children &c. One of her charms is her being so natural. Lord Melbourne sat near me the whole evening. He talked to me about the play, about Joan of Arc, whom he admires, and said, " It is clearly proved that what she did is not to be attributed to any impropriety of conduct." Many historians have chosen to blemish the character of this poor, innocent maid, who was *so* great. He asked me if I had ever read Barante's *History of the Princes of the House of Burgundy,* in 8 vols., which gives a whole account of Joan ; which I have not. M. de Barente is French Ambassador at St. Petersburg. Lord Melbourne also spoke to me of Lord Ashley, who he says is a very good

[1] Lady Emily Cowper. She married Lord Ashley, afterwards Earl of Shaftesbury. She, her sister Lady Fanny, and her brothers Spencer Cowper and Wilham Cowper (afterwards Cowper-Temple), were children of the fifth Earl Cowper, whose wife, a sister of Lord Melbourne, married, secondly, Lord Palmerston in 1839. Spencer Cowper married the widow of Count d'Orsay, the step-daughter of Lady Blessington.

man ; and less eager in Politics than he was ; Lord Ashley is a high Tory. He " adores " Lady Ashley, Lord Melbourne says. Lord Melbourne also told me that when I first came to the Throne, Lord Ashley " wrote to Emily " (Lady Cowper) " and said, ' Why, it's shocking that Lord Melbourne has only put Whig ladies about the Queen '; upon which Lady Cowper said, ' Why, Lady Barham is not such a great Whig '; ' Oh ! ' said Ashley, ' *she* is quite terrible, *she* is the worst of all.' " This amused me much. There is no end to the amusing anecdotes and stories Lord Melbourne tells, and he tells them all in such an amusing funny way. Spoke to me about horses ; he told me his pretty black mare is rather crippled by his having travelled her about so much, and that she must get rest. Lady Ashley says that Lady Cowper dotes upon her grandchildren and would give them and let them do anything. Stayed up till 11. It was a *very* pleasant evening.

Saturday, 9th December.— . . . I forgot to say that Lord Melbourne got a letter after dinner from Mr. Cowper (which he showed me) from the House of Commons, in which he said, " The Debate is going in our favour." Lord Melbourne spoke to me about several of the speakers in the House of Commons ; spoke of Sir E. Sugden [1] whom he says is a very clever lawyer, and said, " His father was a hair-cutter ; he cut my hair very often." This is a singular thing. Told me of an affront which the " Demagogue Hunt " [2] offered William Peel one day,

[1] Edward Sugden (1781–1875). Afterwards Lord St. Leonards, and Lord Chancellor in the Derby Administration of 1852. A dry but efficient lawyer, an excellent interpreter of any man's Will but his own, which was disputed.

[2] Henry Hunt had been a great agitator, notably in the years 1816–20. He was elected for Preston in 1830.

in the House of Commons, on the latter's attacking him. William Peel said something derogatory about Hunt's extraction, upon which Hunt replied : " If *my* father was the *first gentleman* of his family, *your* father was the *last gentleman* of *his* family." . . .

Tuesday, 12th December.— . . . Lord Melbourne, though looking pale, I was happy to see in very good spirits. A few minutes after we had sat down, he turned to me and said, " We have had a great *set-to* in the House of Lords." (He added that Lord Brougham [1] had made an unexpected opposition against the Message which Lord Melbourne read in my name the day before, pressing my increase of income for my Mother. Lord Duncannon told me that Lord Brougham had lately taken to making cutting attacks against my Ministers, and that he had most unhandsomely attacked my excellent Lord Melbourne, called him " a Courtier," &c., &c., which, no wonder, roused Lord Melbourne's temper, and that he returned it Lord Brougham most admirably. He always speaks well, but particularly well this time, Lord Duncannon said. I turned to Lord Melbourne and said I had heard he had spoken so well, " as you always do," I added.) But he is so modest and backward about his own extraordinary merits. He said to me, there might be a like difficulty in the H. of Commons upon this Message. Spoke to me about many other things and about boys at school, and told me a very amusing anecdote about himself. He and Lady Mulgrave were saying how imprudent

[1] Lord Brougham, not having been included in the second Administration of Lord Melbourne, was unsparing in his criticisms of his old colleagues. As Lord Melbourne once pointed out in reply to one of Brougham's brilliant attacks, the reasons for excluding Lord Brougham from any Ministry must have been very grave, if measured by the obvious reasons for including him.

it was to tell children things which they might not repeat. So he said, " When I was a boy of ten, and came home, my Mother was asking me about the boys at school, and I mentioned who were there, and amongst others the present Lord Boston.[1] My Mother said ' Oh ! every Irby is a fool,' which is very true ; so, when I went back to school, I told this, and said, ' My Mother says every Irby is a fool.' This was repeated, and written back to Lord Boston,[2] and created most dreadful offence." We then spoke about Magnetism, which every body is mad about now ; and I said it was very disagreeable to be magnetised, as people got to say such odd things in this *magnetic* state. " Why," said Lord Melbourne, " people say odd enough things without being magnetised." . . . Spoke of Lord and Lady Ashley, their happiness and fondness for each other. I spoke to him of Lady C. Barrington's [3] gratitude to me, at which his eyes filled with tears. He is the kindest, best, and tenderest hearted man I know ; he is so truly excellent, and moral, and has such a strong feeling against immorality and wickedness ; and he is *so* truly kind to me. . . .

Friday, 22nd December.— . . . Lord Melbourne spoke to me a good deal about the Privy Purse, about its expenses, the Pensions on it, &c., &c. About the Household Expenditure ; about many other things concerning expenditure ; about the late Kings, George 4th and William 4th's fancies, &c., &c. His ideas about all these things are so reasonable and so excellent. . . . I sat between

---

[1] George, third Lord Boston (1777–1869).

[2] Frederick, second Lord Boston (1749–1825).

[3] Daughter of the second Earl of Chichester ; married in October 1837 to the Rev. and Hon. L. J. Barrington.

Lord Melbourne (who led me in) and Lord Palmerston. I was delighted to see Lord Melbourne in excellent spirits, and looking much better. He was very clever and funny about education, at dinner; his ideas are excellent about it, I think. He said that he thought almost every body's character was formed by their Mother, and that if the children did not turn out well, the mothers should be punished for it. I daresay *his* noble, fine and excellent character was formed by his mother,[1] for she was a remarkably clever and sensible woman. He told me that the Civil List Bill was read a third time that evening, without any opposition. The news are, I grieve to say, very bad from Canada[2]; that is to say rumours and reports by the Papers, though we have no Official Reports. But Lord

---

[1] Lady Melbourne was a daughter of Sir Ralph Milbanke, and William Lamb was her favourite son. When Peniston, her eldest son, died, she encouraged William to devote himself to politics and to abandon the Bar.

[2] The Canadian question was one of the most difficult of the early years of the Queen's reign. Upper and Lower Canada were totally dissimilar in race, tradition, and natural position. Lower Canada was peopled mainly by French Roman Catholics, Upper Canada by Scottish Protestants, and the mode of Government in both was as cumbrous and inappropriate as it could well be, and afforded unquestionable ground for grievance on the part of the inhabitants. In 1836 a rebellion broke out in the Lower Province headed by Papineau, who had been Speaker of the Assembly. This was followed by an insurrection in the Upper Province, which was quelled in a striking and almost quixotic manner by Sir Francis Head, the Governor, who, dismissing all his regular troops to the Lower Province, trusted to the people to put down the malcontents, and succeeded. Lord Durham was sent out in 1838 as High Commissioner and Governor-General. His report on the proper method of administering the Colony is historical, and ultimately formed the basis of settlement. His acts were not approved by the Whig Government and were annulled by them. He anticipated his recall by resigning and coming home before the end of 1838.

Melbourne hopes that it may not be so bad as it is rumoured. There certainly is open Rebellion. This makes it expedient that Parliament should meet again on the 16th January and not adjourn *till* the 1st Feb. as was at first intended. . . .

Tuesday, 26th December.— . . . At 3 I left Buckingham Palace (with regret, as I had passed a pleasant time there), with Mamma and Lady Mulgrave; Lady Mary, Miss Cocks, Mrs. Campbell, Col. Grey,[1] Lehzen, Miss Dillon, and Miss Davys following in 2 other carriages. We arrived at Windsor Castle at ½ p. 5. It was quite dark. The Castle looked very cheerful and comfortable, and I cannot say *how* much it put me in mind of last summer and of the VERY VERY HAPPY days I spent there. . . .

Wednesday, 27th December.— . . . Besides our party of yesterday, the Duke and Duchess of Sutherland and the Duke of Argyll (who all stay here till Monday, 1st Jan.) dined here. The Duchess was looking so well; neither she nor the Duke have ever been staying at Windsor before and are delighted with the Castle. I sat between the Duke of Sutherland and Mr. Cowper. I talked a great deal with the latter, and a great deal about Lord Melbourne. He says that all the people who have never seen Lord Melbourne and come to have interviews with him, and those Members of the H. of Commons

---

[1] Charles, second son of Lord Grey, the ex-Premier. He was Equerry to the Queen, and had a year or two earlier defeated Disraeli at the High Wycombe election. He became Private Secretary to Prince Albert and later to the Queen. He spent all the years of his life in the Queen's service, and was always helpful, wise, and unbiassed in the advice he tendered her. The present Earl Grey, Lady Victoria Dawnay, Lady Antrim, and Lady Minto are his surviving children. Many good judges considered his abilities of a higher order than those of his father.

who dine with him and have not seen or known him
before and expect to find the Prime Minister a very
proud, stiff person, are quite delighted with his very
kind, unaffected, merry and open, frank manner,
which I think everybody *must* and *ought* to be. He
told me some amusing anecdotes about him, &c.,
&c., and many other funny things. Lord Melbourne
is very absent when in company, often, and talks to
himself every now and then, loud enough to be
heard but never loud enough to be understood. I
am now, from habit, quite accustomed to it, but at
first I turned round sometimes, thinking he was talking to me. Mr. Cowper says he does not think his
uncle is aware of it ; he says he is much less absent
than he used to be. . . .

who dine with him and have not seen or known him
before and expect to find the Prime Minister a very
proud, stiff person, are quite delighted with his very
kind, unaffected, merry and open, frank manner,
which I think everybody *must* and *ought* to be. He
told me some amusing anecdotes about him, &c.,
&c., and many other funny things. Lord Melbourne
is very absent when in company, often, and talks to
himself every now and then, loud enough to be
heard but never loud enough to be understood. I
am now, from habit, quite accustomed to it, but at
first I turned round sometimes, thinking he was talking to me. Mr. Cowper says he does not think his
uncle is aware of it ; he says he is much less absent
than he used to be. . . .

H. S. H. Charles Prince of Leiningen
from a portrait by R. J. Lane

INTRODUCTORY NOTE TO CHAPTER VIII

THE impression produced by the Queen at this time is vividly described by Princess Lieven in a letter to Lord Aberdeen. "I have seen the Queen twice," she writes; "I have seen her alone, and I have seen her in Society with her Prime Minister. She possesses a composure, an air of command, and of dignity, which with her childlike face, her tiny figure, and her pretty smile, create one of the most extraordinary impressions that it is possible to imagine. She is extremely reserved in conversation. It is said that prudence is one of her highest qualities. Lord Melbourne adopts, when he is near her, an attitude of affection, of content, of self-consciousness mingled with a great deal of respect, which with his easy manners, the obvious habit of holding the first place amid her surroundings, his dreaminess at one moment, and his gaiety at another, make a picture you can easily realise. The Queen is full of amiability towards him."

That is a glimpse of the external setting in which these Journals were composed. Lord Melbourne never forgot, from the outset, that the girl to whom he was acting as guardian and tutor was the Sovereign of these Realms. His letters from the first are written in the conventional form of a Minister addressing the Sovereign. Although he obviously tried in conversation to amuse the Queen, and to impart to her youthful intelligence some knowledge of Society, and of the world of Affairs in which she was about to take part, he did not shrink from the graver topics of statecraft, and did not spare her the details of public matters that must have been difficult for her to grasp and comprehend.

There is a passage in one of his letters, written about this time, in which he is explaining to the Queen the powers and duties which it was intended to transfer from the Secretary of State, who combined at that time the administration of Colonial and Military affairs, to a new Secretary of State for War. Lord Melbourne adds these words: "Your Majesty will not suppose that Lord Melbourne by laying before you the whole case has an idea of throwing the weight of such a decision entirely upon Your Majesty. Lord Melbourne will deem it his duty to offer to Your Majesty a decided opinion upon the subject." This passage illuminates, if taken in conjunction with Princess Lieven's descriptive passage, the atmosphere in which Lord Melbourne and the Queen were living at this time. To this young Queen he was Roger Ascham and Burleigh in one and *in petto*.

CHAPTER VIII

1838

Monday, 1st January.— . . . The Duke of Suther-land told me the other night, that Lord Melbourne's mother (whom he knew) was a very agreeable, sensible, clever woman, and that Lord Melbourne was very like her as to features ; Lady Melbourne was very large latterly. Lord Melbourne's father, on the contrary, the Duke said, was very far from agreeable or clever ; he was a short fat man and not like any of his children. He died at the age of 80. The Duchess of Sutherland spoke to me last night about Lady Caroline Lamb,[1] Lord Melbourne's wife ; she was Lord Duncannon's only sister, and the strangest person that ever lived, really half crazy, and quite so when she died ; she was not good-looking, but very clever, and could be very amusing. She teazed that excellent Lord Melbourne in every way, dreadfully, and quite embittered his life, which it ought to have been her pride to study to render a happy one ; he was the kindest of hus-bands to her, and bore it most admirably ; any other man would have separated from such a wife.

[1] Lady Caroline Ponsonby, daughter of the third Earl of Bessborough, a lady of eccentric mind and habits. She was thrown off her mental and moral balance by her acquaintance with Lord Byron, not perhaps so surprising as the fact that she never recovered either even after Byron's death.

He has now the greatest horror of any woman who is in any way eccentric or extravagant, which shows how very much he must have suffered from such a wife. The Duchess told me the strangest stories about her. . . .

Tuesday, 2nd January.— . . . I rode a new horse, a most *delightful* creature, called Tartar; he is taller than Barbara, excessively pretty, and of a very dark brown colour; he has a very springy charming canter and action, is full of spirit, and yet as quiet as a lamb, never shies and is the best-tempered creature possible; to crown all these valuable qualities, Tartar is exceedingly sure-footed. It was a delightful ride and we cantered a great deal coming home; the roads were so dirty that my habit was quite heavy with mud. Changed my dress and walked out with Lady Mulgrave and Lehzen and came home at ½ p. 3. Read Despatches from Canada which are very interesting. . . .

Thursday, 4th January.— . . . At ½ p. 5 came my excellent, kind friend, Lord Melbourne, whom I was quite delighted to see again after such a long absence, the longest that has taken place since I came to the Throne. I thought him in very good spirits, and looking well, though pale, and as kind, amiable and mild as ever; never do I find any difference in this excellent man, may he be very tired, or not tired, he is always equally kind and gentle, though he may at times be low. I was agreeably surprised to find him in good spirits, for from his letters and all the troubles and difficulties he has had of late, I feared it might not be so. He spoke to me first a good deal about Canada; said they were all agreed as to what was to be done, namely to repeal a Statute (*which*, I cannot say), and *for* the present, govern as Canada had been governed before ; but that Lord Howick was of a different opinion and thought that these strong measures ought to be accompanied by conciliatory measures, which Lord Melbourne said would not answer the purpose and have a bad effect ; Lord Howick, he said, was excessively eager about this, for various reasons which Lord Melbourne explained to me ; " if Lord Howick was to resign," he added, " I do not think that would affect the Government ; it would be a bad thing for there is a good deal of strength in him." The other question, about the Army, he considered a more difficult one ; the five Ministers who signed the Report relative to the changes meditated in the office of the Secretary of War, are, Lord John Russell, Lord Howick, Lord Palmerston, Sir J. Hobhouse, and Mr. Spring Rice. Lord Howick and Lord John, he said, are the only two who are eager about it ; the others he believed signed it reluctantly, particularly Mr. Rice. We spoke a good deal about this difficult question ; there is, in my opinion, a good deal for and a good deal against it. It is, as Lord Melbourne says, creating a new Minister with new powers, by giving the Secretary at War great power over the Army. There have been, as Lord Melbourne says, great abuses which it would be desirable to remedy. Spoke about the Troops to be sent to Canada ; about Mr. Rice's wish to take the Chair ; about *his* reasons for doing so ; how to replace *him* ; about the present Speaker ; about the quarrel in Belgium relative to the cutting of timber in the Grünewald ; about the King of Hanover's foolish proceedings ; how they are viewed in Germany ; about some despatches from Sir Frederick

Lamb,[1] saying that Metternich was much displeased at the expulsion of the Archbishop of Cologne, at the manner of doing it, and at the impolicy of the act. Lord Melbourne said he had dined once or twice at Lord Holland's[2] since I had seen him. I was quite happy to talk to him again, as there were many subjects on which I wanted explanation and he explains *so* well and so clearly and agreeably.... My good Lord Melbourne led me in and I sat between him and Lord Torrington. He (Ld. M.) spoke to me about many things ; about riding and horses ; about *bad ears* for Music ; said that everybody would suppose from Scott's writings that he was very fond of and understood music very well ; whereas Lord Melbourne said, *he* said : " In music I don't know *high* from *low* ! " . . .

Tuesday, 9th January.— . . . At 22 m. to 12 came my excellent Lord Melbourne and stayed with me till 27 m. p. 12. He had informed me by a note in the morning, that he should be obliged to go to London which I am extremely sorry for ; Lord Glenelg wrote to him wishing to see him, and both he and Lord Glenelg were to see Lord Durham at *four* about this Canadian business. *I* shall say more of this hereafter. Lord Melbourne said : " It will

[1] Lord Melbourne's brother, afterwards Lord Beauvale, Ambassador Extraordinary at Vienna. As a diplomatist he was irreproachable, handsome, agreeable, and adroit. In private life he was not altogether *sans reproche*. Without his brother William's literary acquirements, and with less sarcasm and pungent wit, he yet had a vigorous understanding, much information, and no little capacity for affairs. At sixty years of age, and in broken health, he married a very young lady, the daughter of Count Maltzahn, the Prussian Minister at Vienna.

[2] Henry Richard, third Lord Holland of the 1762 creation, was Chancellor of the Duchy of Lancaster. Under the auspices of his wife, Holland House, Kensington, was for many years the Zoar of weary Whig politicians. See *ante*, p. 101, note.

be a long interview, I dare say ; probably last 2 hours, and there would be no time to be back,"— meaning for dinner tonight, so he will only come back at 4 tomorrow ; I am *very* sorry to lose him *even* for *one* night. Spoke a good while about this. Spoke about this army business, upon which Lord Melbourne will see Lord Howick. He said, " It would be madness to propose at this moment a complete change in the Administration of the Army, when we have got all these affairs of Canada." He spoke of this a good deal ; and seemed to hope Lord Howick would give it up ; he said the others would be ready to do so if he did. . . . Though I think Lord Duncannon agreeable and amusing, I cannot find in him or in any of the other Ministers, that kindness, mildness, and open frankness, and *agreeability* (to use a word of Lady Mary Stopford's) which I find in my kind friend Lord Melbourne ; *he alone* inspires me with that feeling of great confidence and I may say *security,* for I feel *so safe* when he speaks to me and is with me ; what he says is all so kind and good, and he never says anything which could alarm or hurt me. But I should not *wish* to be on the same confidential footing with any of my other Ministers as I am with this truly excellent friend. . . .

Wednesday, 10*th January.*— . . . Lord Melbourne said that he had seen Lord Durham who seemed very much inclined to accept the Proposition of going to Canada ; he (Ld. D.) was not quite satisfied with all the plans proposed by Government, and particularly with a Council of 17, which he said was too many ; that he could not manage more than 4 or 5. Lord Durham requires, Lord Melbourne added, a large outfit, as he would not spend any of his private fortune; and he would not go till the Navigation was open. Lord Melbourne then told me that he had seen Lord Howick who seemed " disposed to reconsider " the question of the army, and said he would not press parts of it, and would give way on some points. This is a great satisfaction and I think Lord Melbourne seemed quite happy about it. . . .

Wednesday, 17th January.— . . . My excellent Lord Melbourne led me in, and I sat between him and Lord Glenelg. Lord Melbourne *said* he was, and I was happy to see he *looked*, better. He said, as he led me in, that the Majority in the House of Commons of the night before was very favourable. He spoke to me about Greece; said he had heard from his brother that they were very uneasy at Vienna about the state of Greece; said that the only person who showed any sense or character there was the Queen of Greece,[1] but that she was very young and was placed in rather a rougher situation than suited her; that the Archduke John[2] had told Sir Frederic (on his return from Greece) " that she was like a Brazillian Paraquite in a wood of firs covered with snow," meaning that she was in a position not suited to her; I said to Lord Melbourne that I had heard in the Summer that there were hopes of there being an *heir* in some time; he said, " I am afraid not." He told me that the Archduke John had likewise told his brother that the Emperor of Russia[3] was beginning to sink under the immense weight and fatigue of governing such an empire as

[1] Amelia, daughter of the Grand Duke of Oldenbourg, married to Otho L, King of Greece.
[2] Uncle of the Emperor.
[3] Nicholas I., reigned 1826–55.

Russia ; we spoke about him some time ; and also
a good deal about the Austrian Royal Family ; Lord
Melbourne told me that the Emperor of Austria [1]
was worse, and hardly able to do anything ; but,
that as his *mental faculties decreased,* his *bodily
strength increased.* Spoke of Aunt Louise ; of the
Queen of Portugal ; of Clementine, Augustus, &c.,
of Feodore, her happiness, her not being rich ; he
spoke of the poverty of the younger branches in
high families in England, and of their being often
obliged to gain their livelihood in inferior situations ;
he said that he thought his nephew Lord Cowper
was cleverer and had " a sounder understanding "
than William Cowper. . . . Spoke about Shakespear's plays ; *Hamlet, Macbeth, Lear,* &c., &c. ; he
thinks the 2 first named the finest ; he said : " I
think the German critics understand Shakespear
better than we do here " ; mentioned Goethe's *Wil-
helm Meister,* and Schlegel's book upon Shakespear,
which he thinks very good ; he knew, or at least
saw, Schlegel here ; he knew Mme. de Staël ; spoke
of her, of her daughter, the Duchess de Broglie ;
spoke of actresses ; of their marrying out of their
sphere ; of its often not answering ; of Lady Harrington,[2] Lady Craven [3] (the Dowager), Lady Derby
(the late),[4] Mrs. Butler ; of marriages in *general,*
and most cleverly and sensibly ; of their often being
broken off—the reasons why. Lord Melbourne said,

[1] Ferdinand I., born in 1793, succeeded his father, Francis I., in
1835. He was brother to Napoleon's second wife, Marie Louise.

[2] Charles, fourth Earl of Harrington, married Maria, daughter of
Samuel Foote the actor.

[3] William, first Earl of Craven, married Louisa, an undistinguished
actress, daughter of John Brunton of Norwich.

[4] Edward, twelfth Earl of Derby, married Elizabeth Farren, a
Haymarket actress of considerable beauty and charm.

" Why, you see, a gentleman hardly knows a girl till he has proposed, and then when he has an unrestrained intercourse with her he sees something and says, ' This I don't quite like.' " . . .

Friday, 19th January.— . . . The cold increases, the snow is getting deep, and I hear the Thames is frozen over very nearly, which has not happened since 1814. At ½ p. 1 came my excellent friend Lord Melbourne and stayed with me till 3. He looked well, I was very happy to see, and said he was not at all tired. He said that they had got through this Canada business very well ; that Lord Brougham made a good though very violent speech ; that the Duke of Wellington's was very fair ; in fact very friendly ; that he (Lord Melbourne) thought the only difficult part to defend was the not having sent more troops ; " but," he added, " there the Duke of Wellington came to our assistance, and said there were not too few troops." Spoke about Canada for some time. . . . In speaking of the Duke of Wellington he said : " He has no oratorical powers ; he attempts no ornament, but speaks generally very much to the point ; he cannot always express what he feels and understands." He added that people sometimes who were great in action could not express well in words what they meant and conceived ; spoke of all the Duke's family, and said he thought the Duke was the cleverest ; asked me if I had ever read the Duke's Despatches, and said they were worth looking at, to see the way he did them. . . . Lord Melbourne told me, in speaking of the Duke of Wellington, " His people are very angry with him ; they think he is leaving them." How wrong of these people ! I told Lord Melbourne what my Uncle Leopold had written to me about him (Ld M.),

I—18

which seemed to please him. Talked of other things. Talked for some time with him and Lord Palmerston, about education, punishments, &c., Lord Melbourne was amazingly funny and amusing about this. I said I thought solitary confinement a good punishment : Lord Melbourne replied, " I think it's a very stupefying punishment." I mentioned the system of *silence* as a very good one and quoted myself as a proof of its having answered, which made them laugh very much. Lord Melbourne said, "It may do very well with a lively child ; but with one of a sulky, *grumpy* disposition it would not answer." . . . I said I thought it cruel to punish children by depriving them of their meals and saying they should go without their supper, &c. Lord Melbourne replied, " Why, when I was a child, they had contrived to annoy me so, and had made me cry so much, that I had lost all appetite."

Saturday, 20th January.— . . . At ½ p. 12 Lord Glenelg presented Lord Durham to me on his appointment ; Lord Glenelg then left the room and Lord Durham remained with me for about ½ an hour, I should say. He spoke entirely about Canada which subject he seems to understand thoroughly ; said he considered the task he was about to undertake, a most difficult one ; and he *might* not succeed ; but that he would do his utmost to restore tranquillity in Canada ; said he wished to have my authority, when the rebellion was quelled, to conciliate these deluded people and to hold out mercy to them. He spoke at much length about all this,— about what he intended to do,—the difficulty of the task, &c., &c. At ½ p. 1 came Lord Melbourne and stayed with me till 20 m. p. 2. He seemed well. He said, " I am sorry to say I received a letter from

Lord Howick this morning and that he makes a great demur about this Army affair." Lord Melbourne then added that as it was such a difficult question and as it could be done " as it were by one blow," and as the Army disliked it so much and altogether it was such a bad time for it, and he thought it such a difficult question, that he could not give way to him upon it, and could not advise me to do it ; he added he would not mind it near so much if it were brought before Parliament and there fairly discussed, for then if it passed, it would be done by the authority of Parliament ; but in this way, it was so entirely to be done by me, as it were, that he really could not agree to it ; moreover that if even it were a very good thing in itself (which he does not think it), this would not be the moment for doing it ; none of the other Ministers he thought were eager for it ; but if it were proposed in the Cabinet and carried by a majority against Lord Howick, he (Ld. H.) might resign (which Lord M. says would be a bad thing, but would not affect the Government), and Lord Melbourne did not know what Lord John Russell might *then* do, if Lord Howick held out on it ; which would then affect the Government. I told Lord·Melbourne that if it could be of any use, he might say that *I quite* agreed with him (Lord Melbourne) and that he might rely upon me ; which assurance pleased him, though I think he must long be aware of my firm resolution to support this kind and true friend of mine, as he truly and really is, in every way. . . . Got a few lines (when I went to my room) from Lord Melbourne (I generally *hear from* him and *write to him* every day, and very often *two* or *three* times a day), in which he said that great difference had prevailed and did prevail in the Cabinet respecting the Details about Canada. A Cabinet had been held immediately after he left me. I am *very* sorry to hear this.

Sunday, 21st January.— . . . After dinner before we sat down, I talked to Lord Melbourne about some important things; I asked him the cause of the differences in the Cabinet ; he said that he wished, and also most of the others, that the Legislative Council in Canada should be chosen from those which composed the present Legislative Assembly,— whereas Lord Howick and some others wished the Council should be chosen from the Country at large, and not from the Assembly ; Lord Melbourne was against this and for this reason ; we should probably lose by such an Election many of the *English* party, now in the Legislative Assembly, and get a good many of the *French* party who would be hostile to us ; and consequently diminish our influence ; none of the other Ministers were as obstinately for this as Lord Howick—but he at length gave way. . . . He was very funny about a word which Lady Mary gave me to find out ; she gave me the ivory letters and I was to find out the word ; she gave me " thermometer," and she spelt it with an " a " instead of an " e," and laughed very much at her bad spelling ; upon which Lord Melbourne said, " It is a very good way to spell it, but not *the* way," which made us laugh. I said to him I was reading the first novel I had ever read—*The Bride of Lammermoor* ; he said it was a very melancholy—a terrible story—but admires it ; he mentioned *Old Mortality, Quentin Durward, The Fair Maid of Perth,* and *Kenilworth,* as Scott's best novels ; he said there was " a great deal of good " and " a great deal of bad " in his novels ; said he admired his poems very much, though most people said his novels were greatly superior in their way to his poems; spoke of Richard Cœur de Lion whom we both rather admire; of Henry IV. and Sully; Lord Melbourne said that Sully was a clever and good man, and greatly superior to those Ministers who followed him; Richelieu and Mazarin; " They were shocking fellows," he added. . . .

Tuesday, 23rd January.— . . . He spoke of what had just taken place in Canada; said Sir John Colborne [1] was an excellent officer. " A good officer," he added, " can generally effect with a small force, what a bad officer with a large force would fail in." Spoke about this question of the Army. Said that Lord Francis Egerton [2] had said in the House, " That the troops had done remarkably well and that he hoped nothing would be done to tamper with the management of the Army," evidently alluding, Lord Melbourne observed, to the intended changes in the Army. I told Lord Melbourne that Lord Adolphus Fitzclarence, on being told that I would continue to him and his brothers and sisters the same annual allowance they enjoyed from the late King, burst

---

[1] Afterwards Field-Marshal and first Lord Seaton. He was one of Wellington's generals in the Peninsula and at Waterloo. He was Lieutenant-Governor of Upper Canada, and on Lord Durham's recall was nominated to succeed him.

[2] Lord Francis Egerton was the second son of George Granville, first Duke of Sutherland. The immense fortune of Francis, third and last Duke of Bridgewater (the father of English inland navigation and, in conjunction with Brindley, constructor of the canal which bears his name) was devised to the first Duke of Sutherland for life, and thereafter to Lord Francis, who on attaining possession assumed the surname of Egerton, in lieu of Leveson-Gower. A " condition subsequent " tending to divest the property in a certain event was decided to be opposed to " public policy." Lord Francis was created Earl of Ellesmere in 1846.

into tears, and said it was unexpected, for they did
not dare to hope for anything. . . .

Wednesday, 24th January.— . . . Lady Falkland,[1]
whom I had not yet seen, was of course presented to
me by Lady Portman.[2] I (as usual to all Peeresses
and Ladies by courtesy) wished to kiss her, but she
insisted on kissing my hand first and then only
received her kiss from me. . . . I observed to Lord
Melbourne that it must be a great trial for poor Lady
Falkland dining here. . . . Lady Falkland must have
felt very low, and it must have been a sad trial for
her to see me for the 1st time in the place of her
poor father, but she behaved uncommonly well;
she is a very nice person. She looked pale and thin,
but still very pretty. I sat on the sofa with her;
Lord Melbourne sitting near me the whole evening;
and all the other ladies sitting round the table.
Spoke with Lord Melbourne about Lady Falkland &c.
Asked him what he thought was the best History
of the last 60 or 70 years. He said there was no
History of that time *only*, but that it must be got
from different books; that the *Annual Register* was
as good a book as any, if I wanted to look for any
particular event in any one year. That the beginning was written by Burke, and followed up by Dr.
Laurence &c. Said that being written at the time,
it was tinctured with party spirit. He said Adolphus's
History of George III. was curious as he had got a
good deal of information, and that the anecdotes
told in it were true, though the *names* of the people

---

[1] Lady Falkland. Amelia Fitzclarence, daughter of William IV.
See *ante*, p. 113.

[2] Edward Berkeley Portman, representative of an old Dorsetshire
and Somersetshire family, was created Baron Portman in 1837. In
1827 he married Emma, third daughter of the Earl of Harewood, who
was at this time one of the Ladies of the Bedchamber to Queen Victoria.

were sometimes wrong. Said that Hume's *History of England* was undoubtedly the best, in spite of his party prejudices, and that he thought I would like it much better now than when I read it before. Spoke of Clarendon's *History of the Rebellion* (which I told him I had read), which he thought curious, but likes his (Clarendon's) *Memoirs* better. Spoke of Mrs. Hutchinson's book, said I had been reading it ; he thinks that " a nice book " and " very curious " ; he knew the Editor of it ; spoke of Charles the First, whom I thought much to blame. . . . Spoke of Sismondi, whom he thinks a dull writer ; he recommends Barante's *History of the House of Burgundy* ; and Daru's *History of Venice* ; spoke of Voltaire's Histories ; of O'Driscol's *Ireland* which he likes and whom he knew ; of Scott's *History of Scotland* which he has not read, &c. &c. . . .

Thursday, 25th January.— . . . At ½ p. 3 came my excellent Lord Melbourne and stayed with me till ½ p. 4. He said, " I think we have patched this up," meaning the affair about the bill relating to Canada. " We mean to stand by the bill," he added, " and take our chance of a division." Lord John, he said, was very much for leaving the Preamble out, and was not at all pleased at being obliged to stand by it ; and Lord Melbourne said it was a bad thing "to force a man to do what he dislikes when he has a principal part to act in it," which is very true. He added something more about Canada and what was meant to be done, if they were beat about this clause. He said that Lord Howick's great violence irritated the others on the other side (in the Cabinet) ; Mr. Thomson was very eager against Lord Howick's ideas about Canada. I asked him if Mr. Poulett Thomson was eager ; he replied that he was, but that he could control himself, which Lord Howick could not, and was excessively cross, and kept saying he would resign and would not be party to this and that, which offended the others. . . . Spoke of Sir Robert Peel, who I observed I thought was more eager than the Duke of Wellington. Lord Melbourne replied he was not acquainted with Sir Robert Peel's character, could not judge of his feelings, did " not know if he was desirous of office or not." Said he believed that his (the Duke's) party were very angry with him for what he had said in the House of Lords, and therefore that Sir Robert was obliged to be more violent in order to keep his party together. " This I believe to be the truth," Lord Melbourne observed. . . .

Friday, 26th January.— . . . He told me that they had settled the matter about Canada. " We have settled to leave out the Preamble ; Lord Howick has given way, and owned he was in the wrong." He added : " It will be a triumph to the other party, but I don't much mind that." I said that I was surprised Lord Howick had given way. Lord Melbourne replied : " He is not devoid of candour," but that his opinions were so very strong that he did not feel able to " surrender them." Said that Sir Robert Peel had justly observed that : " what was the necessity of asking Parliament about what they *were going* to do " ; " we don't mean to oppose you ; we won't fetter you." " Why therefore ask our approbation of what you are going to do ? " " Act like any other Ministers and then afterwards we will approve or disapprove what has been done."[1]

---

[1] This high Constitutional doctrine was certain to meet with the approval of a Whig like Lord Melbourne. It has been the secret of ministerial responsibility and of executive power in the Constitution

" Now," Lord Melbourne said, " this is almost un-answerable." He is the fairest person about his opponents I ever knew ; *so* frank, so noble ! so candid ! . . . . Spoke of the Combinations of the workmen in Scotland and Ireland and England, which he says are quite frightful. This led him to speak of servants, of their combinations with trades-people, their being bribed, &c. He observed how disagreeable it was to recommend tradespeople or servants ; he said that his coachmaker had come to him this morning and begged him to write a letter to the Bishop of Ely to recommend him to him. " Very well," said Lord Melbourne, " I will write a letter if you wish which I will show you." " So I wrote to the Bishop of Ely," continued Lord Mel-bourne ; " ' My dear Lord,—Mr. Robson has been my coachmaker for many years, and I believe him to be a very good one, but so he ought, for I must say he is a very dear one.' ' Now,' I said to the man, ' here is the letter, you may read it if you like.' " . . . At 7 I went to Drury Lane with the Duchess of Sutherland, Lady Portman, Miss Caven-dish, Lady Mary Stopford, Lord Conyngham, Lord Headfòrt, and Col. Buckley (who this day replaced Col. Grey). It was Shakespear's tragedy of *Ham-let,* and we came in at the beginning of it. Mr. Charles Kean (son of old Kean) acted the part of Hamlet and I must say beautifully. His conception of this very difficult and I may almost say incompre-hensible character, is admirable ; his delivery of all the fine long speeches quite beautiful ; he is exces-sively graceful and all his actions and attitudes are good, though not at all good-looking in face ; the

of this country, and its working has been admired by many foreign observers.

two finest scenes I thought were the *Play-scene*, which he acts, they say, quite differently to any other actor who has performed Hamlet; and the scene with his mother, the Queen; it was quite beautiful when he rushed out after having killed Polonius, exclaiming, " Is it the King ? " He fights uncommonly well too. All the other characters were very badly acted. I came away just as *Hamlet* was over. They would recognise me between the 2nd and 3rd acts,—I was compelled to come forward, curtsey, and hear " God save the Queen " sung. The house was amazingly crowded and they received me admirably. Came home at ½ p. 10.

Saturday, 27*th January.*— . . . Told Lord M. I had been much pleased with *Hamlet* last night; observed it was a very hard play to understand, which he agreed in; he said he thought the end of it " awkward " and horrid; said he thought Hamlet was supposed to be mad, of a philosophical mind, and urged to do something which he did not like to do. He added that Mr. Fox always said that *Hamlet* possessed more of Shakespear's faults than almost any other play of Shakespear, &c., &c.—Saw Lord Palmerston who introduced Baron Munchausen, Minister from the Court of Hanover. . . . I told Ld. M. of my last recollection of Baron Munchausen,[1] namely, my giving him a commission to send me some wax dolls from Berlin, which made Lord Melbourne laugh excessively. He spoke of children's love for dolls, and that they sometimes think they are alive. Spoke of my former great love for dolls.[2]

---

[1] Baron Alexander von Munchausen, a Hanoverian diplomatist, was then about twenty-five. He was *not* the hero of a celebrated romance.

[2] That the Queen always retained a sentiment for her dolls may

. . . After dinner, talked (before I sat down) with all the gentlemen, &c. Spoke about Kean with Lord Melbourne ; about Landseer and the sketches which Lord Melbourne saw and none of which he " thought *like*," he said, though very clever. . *.* . Lord Melbourne said that *Richard III.* by Shakespear was a very fine play ; I observed that Richard was a very bad man ; Lord Melbourne also thinks he was a horrid man ; he believes him to have been deformed (which some people deny), and thinks " there is no doubt that he murdered those two young Princes." I was delighted to hear Lord Melbourne say he thought Henry 7th a very bad man, and reckless of blood ; spoke of the inhuman *murder*, I may call it, of the young Earl of Warwick ; he said that Ferdinand of Spain would not give his daughter Catherine to *Arthur* unless this poor Warwick was got rid of ; that Catherine felt this all along and observed that it dwelt upon her and " that it did not go well with her in the world " for this reason. He spoke of Henry VIII. ; said he was not so bad at first and had begun with good intentions ; spoke of Catherine of Arragon, &c., &c. ; that when Henry VIII. took a liking to somebody else, he only sought to get rid of the other in the quickest way. Spoke of the wars in Flanders. . . . He fell asleep for a little while in the evening, which is always a proof that he is not quite well. . . .

Tuesday, 30th January.— . . . I asked Lord M. what Lord Palmerston's Politics were at the time when he stood against Lord Lansdowne and Lord Althorp. Lord Melbourne said that Lord Palmerston then

be realised from the care with which they were preserved. They are exhibited in the London Museum at Kensington, arranged and ticketed with the names given to them by Princess Victoria.

belonged to the *high Tory* Party! Spoke of the change of opinions &c., &c. Spoke of the salaries &c. of my people, and spoke of Names, Christian names, for a long while ; said that Lady Vivian's[1] little girl was called *Lalage,* from Horace ; he thought the name rather pretty on account of the lines which he repeated and which are, I *think,* " Dulce ridentem, Lalagen amabo, Dulce loquentem." Told him of the intention there once was of changing my name, which he was surprised at, and could not think how it could have been done.

Thursday, 1st February.—The curious old form of pricking the Sheriffs was gone through ; and I had to prick them all, with a huge pin. This was the first Council that I have yet held at which Lord Melbourne was not present, and I must say I felt sad not to see him in his place as I feel a peculiar satisfaction, nay I must own almost *security,* at seeing him present at these formal proceedings, as I know and feel that I have a *friend* near me, when I am as it were alone among so many strangers. This may sound almost childish, but it is not so. Saw Lord John Russell. . . .

Saturday, 3rd February.—Received a communication from Lord Melbourne which I shall transcribe : " Lord Melbourne presents his humble duty to Your Majesty and acquaints Y.M. that the Canada Government Bill was read a second time in the House of Lords, with the single dissentient voice of Lord Brougham. Lord Melbourne sends the returns of the attendance and the speeches. Lord Brougham made a long and able speech, not over-violent for

---

[1] Letitia, wife of Sir Hussey (afterwards Lord) Vivian. The child Lalage married, in 1857, Henry Hyde Nugent Bankes, son of the Right Hon. George Bankes.

him. The Duke of Wellington made a moderate speech and concluded with some very able views " (I think) " of the subject. Lord Aberdeen and Lord Wharncliffe also spoke, both strongly condemning the conduct of Government." This note was dated from last night. Heard also from Lord John Russell that they had proceeded in the House of Commons with the Irish Corporation Bill and the Pluralities Bill. . . . Lord M. said they sat till near 12 o'clock last night. Said " it was a very good Debate.'" " The Duke of Wellington," he added, " again made a very fair speech " ; and that the Duke's remarks were very good about Canada, for that there was a great deal to say about it ; and that the Duke observed, " that each Mail brought the account of some new and very important event." He (Ld. Melbourne) said that Lord Aberdeen and Lord Wharncliffe " were very severe." I asked him if Lord Aberdeen was not rather a dull and heavy speaker ; he replied in the affirmative ; and said (in reply to my question as to whether he were a good speaker) that Lord Wharncliffe was a good speaker and spoke " very clearly." I asked him about Lord Brougham's speech which he said " was more bitter than violent ; very bitter, but a fine speech." Lord Melbourne told me : " We have not yet settled this Army Question ; but I am more and more convinced it would be madness to propose it ; and after this affair of Canada too." He seemed, however, I thought, sanguine about its being ultimately settled.

Sunday, 4th February.—Lord Melbourne asked if I had seen *King Lear* (which I had half intended to do last week) ; I said I had not. He said (alluding to the manner in which it is being performed at Covent Garden), " It is *King Lear* as Shakespear wrote it ; and which has not been performed so, since the time of Queen Anne." As it is generally acted, Lord Melbourne told me, it is altered by Cibber, who " put in a deal of stuff " of his own ; that it was a much finer play as Shakespear wrote it, but " most dreadfully tragic." That Dr. Johnson had seen it performed in that way, and that " it made such an impression on him that he never forgot it." I observed to him that I feared that, and did not like all that madness on the stage. Lord Melbourne said, " I can't bear that, but still it is a very fine play, and many think Shakespear's best." Spoke of the play of *Richard III.*, which I said I was going to see. Lord Melbourne said it was " a fine striking play." He observed that that scene where Richard makes love to Anne, at the funeral of Henry VI., did not belong to the play, but was taken from *Henry VI.* ; he said, " That is a very foolish scene ; I always thought it a most ridiculous scene ; and there is not the slightest foundation in History for it ; he married her 8 years afterwards." He added that Shakespear constantly mixed up events, in his Historical plays, without minding when they happened, and how far asunder.

Monday, 5th February.—Lord M. showed me a letter he had got this morning, from Lord Ebrington,[1] saying that Lord Tavistock (who, Lord Melbourne tells me, has great influence over Lord John, and was sent for) had prevailed on Lord John to put off the Army Question till June or July ; so that Lord Melbourne says they will get over it this Session ; and when a thing is put off, he added, it is often forgotten or the moment not found suitable for it. " But," continned Lord Melbourne, " when one gets over one

[1] See *ante*, p. 73.

difficulty, there always comes another ; and there is now another question of great difficulty, which is the Ballot." He then explained to me, that not only several of their supporters but even some of the Government had pledged themselves to the Ballot, and consequently after Lord John made that very decided declaration against the Ballot, these people said they must go against this ; amongst others Sir Hussey Vivian who has pledged himself to it ; and Lord Melbourne says if they should vote for it after Lord John's declaration, either they or perhaps Lord John will resign, and this " would make such gaps in the Government as would make it very difficult to fill up ; and Sir Hussey Vivian has written to Lord John this morning, and he to me, saying I shall have to choose whether I will accept Sir Hussey's or his resignation." Lord Melbourne however said he would see if he could manage it, which I fervently hope and trust he will ; but he is sadly teazed and plagued. He said, " There is a succession of difficulties in a Government." . . . At 20 m. to 7 I went with Lady Portman, Lady Tavistock, Miss Cavendish, Miss Pitt, Lord Conyngham, Lord Headfort, and Col. Buckley to Drury Lane theatre. We came in before the performance had commenced. It was Shakespear's tragedy of *Richard III.*, and Charles Kean's first appearance (in London) as Richard. The house was crammed to the ceiling ; and the applause was tremendous when Kean came on ; he was unable to make himself heard for at least five minutes I should say. He was dressed exactly like his father, and all those who were with me, and who had seen his father, were struck with the great resemblance to his father both in appearance and voice. It would be impossible for me to attempt to describe the *admirable* manner in which Kean delineated the ferocious and fiend-like Richard.   It was quite a *triumph* and the latter part particularly so ;   he was applauded throughout in the most enthusiastic manner.   He acted with such spirit too !   One of the best scenes was the one when the Lord Mayor urges him to accept the regal Dignity, which Kean did uncommonly well.   As also the disagreeable and absurd scene with Lady Anne. The manner in which he gave :   " So much for Buckingham," was truly *splendid*, and called down thunders of applause, as also many other of the scenes where he gets very much excited ;   he fought and died beautifully.   He was uncommonly well disguised, and looked very deformed and wicked. All the other parts were very badly acted, and the three women were *quite detestable*.   It is a fine, heart-stirring play, and there are some beautiful passages in it.   I but just escaped being recognised, for as the curtain was dropping and I left the box, they called out " the Queen."

Tuesday, 6th February.—At 17 m. p. 2 came my kind friend Lord Melbourne who said he was better, and stayed with me till 20 m. p. 3.   He spoke to me about Mr. Roebuck's [1] speech of last night ;   said " it was a very bitter speech."   I told him what Lord John had written to me of what took place in the House of Commons last night.   He spoke to me about this Parliamentary Elections Bill ;   said it would he thought not pass the House of Lords.   Gave me an

---

[1] Mr. (afterwards Rt. Hon.) John Arthur Roebuck.   A Liberal " free lance," who earned the *sobriquet* of " Tear-'em."   Lord John Russell had brought in a Bill for suspending the Constitution of Canada, and Mr. Roebuck, who was not at the time in Parliament, claimed to be heard at the bar of both Houses as agent for the Lower Province. He made a very able but bitter speech.

explanation about it, and about people's being unable to vote unless they had paid the rates up to the very day; and that many people wanted to get rid of this; but the Lords did not like that as they thought it was "meddling with the Reform Bill." I asked him if he had done anything more about the Ballot. He replied that he had heard from Lord John this morning, who said they had best wait the decision; he added that Lord John thinks he must resign if any of the others vote for the Ballot, as after his very strong declaration against it, he would consider their voting for it as "passing a censure upon him"; Lord Melbourne said he did not quite think that, and that he thought Lord John took it rather too seriously; but he added: "Lord John does." Lord Melbourne said he thinks it better not to take much notice of who vote for or against it; and he added "we took no notice of it when Lord Charles Fitzroy voted for it (Ballot) last year; he is a very foolish man, I think." I said to him that I believed the *Cabinet* were all agreed upon this question; he replied they were; "that is to say either to vote against its being made an open question, or not to vote at all." He added that Sir John Hobhouse and Mr. Poulett Thomson did not vote at all, having he believed pledged themselves before they came into the Ministry. . . . Lord Melbourne told me he had dined at home the night before. Spoke to him about the play of *Richard III.*, and of Kean; spoke of Richard III. himself, who he (Ld. M.) believes to have been crooked and deformed, and to have murdered the two young Princes; though, he said, that great pains had been taken to trace it all in the *Historical Doubts* by Horace Walpole and to prove the contrary. He also mentioned the well-

I—19

known old story of the old Countess of Desmond,[1] who "said she had danced with him" (Richard) "the night of his Coronation and that he was a very handsome man." Spoke of the Duke of Wellington; he said "The Duke of Wellington is amazingly sensible to attention; nothing pleases him so much as if one asks him his opinion about anything." He added that many people were offended with the Duke's abrupt manner of speaking; I observed that I thought that was only a manner, and that he did not mean it so. "No more do I," replied Lord Melbourne. Spoke of Lord Ebrington, who Lord Melbourne has known a long while and says is a clever man and possesses a considerable influence over Lord John; Lord Tavistock also he added, has influence over his brother John; "but," said Lord Melbourne, "Lord Tavistock has also got some strange notions; he lives a great deal in the country; and people who live a great deal in the country pick up strange ideas." I asked him if he thought there would be much opposition to the Irish Poor Laws in the House of Lords. "I think there will be none," he said. "I don't think there will be any difficulty about any of the *Questions*—it's only this Ballot." I asked him if he had seen Lord John about it. He replied that others had, but that "I don't like to speak to him about it; I feel rather awkward about speaking to him about it, as last year he wanted me to make it an open question and I refused; and now

[1] Catherine, widow of the twelfth Earl of Desmond, died in 1604, having survived her husband seventy years. There seems much doubt about the principal dates of her life, *e.g.* those of her birth and marriage, but she is *said* to have attained the remarkable age of 140 years, and to have died by a fall from a cherry-tree. Sir Walter Raleigh records that he knew her and that she "was married in Edward IV.'s time."

that I want him to relax he would say, ' Why, what have you to say ? ' " He said Lord John was " very unbendable " about it. Lord Melbourne wanted him not to be so very particular about it, and let them vote for or against it (its being an open question) and not take much notice of it ; but Lord John said that after *his* declaration *that* would *affect him.* I asked who were the others who wanted to vote for it. " Why, Sir Hussey Vivian is the one of the greatest consequence, and Parnell," [1] he replied. " The fact is, Vivian should not have pledged himself ; he carried his election in a way he should not have done."

Wednesday, 7th February.—Lord Melbourne said he had just been to see Lord Durham " who wants more force." He (Ld. D.) said that the Duke of Wellington had told him he ought to have 75,000 men in Canada, to put it down. Lord Melbourne further told me that the Duke of Wellington had been to see Lord Durham on Friday, he thinks ; stayed with him for an hour and a half ; had gone with him through the whole thing, had told him how to manage the troops by sending them from one place to another, and told him all his ideas of doing the thing. Lord Melbourne seemed quite pleased about it.[2] I showed Lord Melbourne a letter I had got from Stockmar, about which Lord Melbourne said he would write to Stockmar. Spoke about my asking Sir Robert Peel &c. to dinner, which led us to speak about Lady Ashley,

---

[1] Henry Brooke Parnell had been member for Maryborough in the Irish House of Commons, and was now member for Dundee. He was made Paymaster-General on that office being constituted in 1838. Afterwards created Lord Congleton.

[2] The Duke never allowed political feeling to interfere with what he considered public duty. As a politician he was a Tory ; but as a soldier he had no politics.

who, Lord Melbourne says, is decided in her politics, though not violent ; she is a Tory ; Lord Melbourne says she does not talk about it much ; but he thinks she has at one time discussed it with her mother, who of course is a Whig ; I said I supposed Lady Fanny had no ideas of her own about Politics ; he replied, " Why I think she is a Tory." I was surprised ; said laughing I thought it very wrong, and very odd, as all her brothers were Whigs. Spoke to him at dinner about various things ; he told me Mr. Roebuck is a small man with " small finely cut features," and that he speaks well—" plainly, without ornament."

Thursday, 8th February.—He said he thought there would be some debate in the H. of Lords about the third reading of the Canada bill tonight ; he thinks Lord Ellenborough [1] will speak. I asked him if he (Ld. E.) was a clever man ; he replied, " He is a disagreeable, conceited man, but a clever man." . . . Lord Melbourne told me today that when he was as young as Lord Canning is now, he " was very shy " ; " I think I was about as shy as anybody could be," he said.

Friday, 9th February.—Got the following communication from Lord Melbourne. " The Canada Bill was read a third time yesterday evening without division, but after a Debate which lasted until ten

---

[1] Lord Ellenborough (1790–1871) was a son of the Chief Justice, and sat in several Conservative Cabinets. He was Governor-General of India in 1844, and recalled from his post by the directors of the East India Company in opposition to the wish of the Cabinet, who at once recommended him for an earldom. He was too imaginative and daring for the post of Governor-General at this period of Indian administrative history ; but his memory was often revived in the person of a more daring and more brilliant successor in that high office.

o'clock. Lord Ashburton [1] made a speech generally upon the subject of Colonies, Lord Mansfield [2] made an elaborate attack upon the Government and in some measure complained of the Duke of Wellington and Sir Robert Peel for not having taken more active measures in opposition, and Lord Brougham repeated the observations which he had before made, with no diminution of vehemence. The speakers were Lord Ellenborough, Lord Glenelg, Lord Ashburton, Lord Mansfield, Lord Lansdowne, Lord Brougham, Lord Melbourne, Lord Fitzwilliam,[3] who spoke with great kindness of the Government, but declared his disapprobation of the Bill." I asked Lord Melbourne the other day how many Peers could constitute a House of Lords and be considered able to sit; he said *three*; and in the House of Commons 40 Members must be present to make a House of Commons. I likewise asked him if there was any particular form when a Peer takes his seat; he said *on his creation* there was a great deal of form; but on taking it in a new Parliament or upon succeeding to the Title there was hardly any. "You go up to the table," he added, "take the oaths, pay the fees, and shake hands with the Chancellor." Lord Melbourne also told me that any Peer may bring in any bill and lay it upon the table, and it is generally read a first time; whereas "in the H. of Commons, they must always move for leave to bring in a bill." He said that Lord Ashburton had got that "fashionable theory" that it was better to give up the Colonies

---

[1] Alexander, first Lord Ashburton, had been President of the Board of Trade in the brief Peel Administration of 1834–5. He married Miss Bingham of Philadelphia. See *ante*, p. 199.

[2] David William, third Earl of Mansfield (1777–1840).

[3] Charles William, fifth Earl (1786–1857).

I—19*

at once when they became at all unquiet ; which
Lord Melbourne observed with great justice, would
be just the way to encourage them to revolt ; for
they would then say, " Why, we have nothing to do
but to revolt to get rid of our masters." And " a very
dangerous thing to declare," Lord Melbourne observed. Spoke a long time about all this ; then
about George IV., who he said was not at all unhappy
at Princess Charlotte's death, on the contrary, he
was rather glad ; spoke of her—of Uncle Leopold—
her happiness with him—her death—that she might
have been saved if she had not been so much
weakened. I was delighted to see Lord Melbourne
in very good spirits, and very talkative, and *so*
agreeable ! Spoke of many things ; of M. de Barante,
the French Ambassador at St. Petersburg who Lady
Durham said she knew, as also his daughter who
was separated from her husband and excited pity as
he was known or supposed to have beat her. Upon
this Lord Melbourne said : " Why, it is almost worth
while for a woman to be beat, considering the ex-
ceeding pity she excites," which made us laugh.
Spoke of the dinner next day at the Lord Mayor's,
which Lord Melbourne said was called a private
dinner of about 50 or 60 persons, and which was
generally very dull. He spoke of the Duke of Wellington, and, with tears in his eyes at the Duke's
friendliness to Lord Durham, about Canada. I
asked him if it would do well if I asked Lord and
Lady Francis Egerton [1] the same day as the Duke
of Wellington dined here ; he replied extremely well,
and that it would " be very agreeable to both." I
told him that I was very thankful to him when he

[1] See *ante*, p. 261. Lady Francis was Harriet, eldest daughter of
Charles Greville, the father of the diarist.

told me *who* I should invite; he said, "I am afraid
I don't attend enough to that; I am rather neglect-
ful about it," which I would not allow. Spoke about
the Emperor of Austria—the Duchess of Sutherland
—her family; Lord Melbourne said she was naturally very proud; spoke about her house[1]; the lease
of which she wishes to buy, but which as it is Crown
property Lord Melbourne said she could not do; he
dreaded the time when the Duchess should learn
she could not do so; that he was afraid of writing
to her before she received the formal answer from
the Treasury; I told him, however, it would be
better if he did so, upon which he said: "Then it
shall be done." Spoke of Lady Ashley—Lady Hardwicke[2]—Lady Fanny; I asked him how she came
to be a Tory—and who could have made her so. He
said, "Why, I think her Nurse; people generally
get their ideas in that way." He told me he went
to Eton when he was nine years old; he went there
at Xmas in the year 1788, and stayed there till Mid-
summer 1796. Lord Holland left Eton about 3 months
after Lord Melbourne went there. He spoke most
cleverly and sensibly about Public Schools; said " I
am not at all bigotted about a Public School "; said
he was very happy at Eton; spoke of the many dis-
advantages and dangers of a Public School; amongst
which he mentioned the great habit of telling false-
hoods which boys get to do with impunity in order
to save themselves from punishment; and the disagreeable, bad, blackguard boys you were obliged to

[1] Stafford House was built by the Duke of York. It is Crown
property vested in the Commission of Woods and Forests. The present
(1912) Duke of Sutherland obtained an extension of the Crown lease
a few years ago.

[2] Charles Philip, fourth Earl of Hardwicke, had married Susan,
daughter of the first Lord Ravensworth. See *ante*, p. 84, n.

meet at such schools; and if a boy is weak, the
liability of being led and governed by such boys;
Lady Durham likewise entered into the conversation,
and she and Lord Melbourne and I went on discussing the subject for some time; Lady Durham
observed that it was a constant *War* between boy
and master at school, which however Lord Melbourne
thought the same with a Tutor; we all agreed that
it was very bad that no French was taught at the
Public Schools, for that boys never learnt it afterwards. Lady Durham said that Lord Durham had
had a great mind that their boy should learn no
Latin at all, which however Lord Melbourne said he
thought was a bad thing, for that he thought a man
could not get on well in the world without Latin in
the present state of society.[1]   I told Lord Melbourne
that though Lehzen had often said that she had
never seen such a passionate and naughty child as I
was, still that I had never told a falsehood, though I
knew I would be punished; Lord Melbourne said:
"That is a fine character"; and I added that
Lehzen entrusted me with things which I knew she
would not like me to tell again, and that when I was
ever so naughty, I never threatened to tell, or ever
did tell them. Lord Melbourne observed: "That
is a fine trait." I felt quite ashamed, on hearing this
praise, that I had said so much about myself. I
asked him if his sister's children had not been passionate when little. "Minny and Fanny were dreadfully passionate," he said, "and now they have both
very sweet tempers and are very calm." I observed
to him that I was sure *he* had never been so; he
answered, "dreadfully passionate, and so I am now,"
which I *would not* and *cannot* believe. . . .

[1] *Tempora mutantur.*

Tuesday, 13*th February.*—Lord M. spoke of the apparent cruelty, when a person is dying and is suffering dreadfully, and anything to hasten the end would be mercy and relief, that *that* is not allowed, and is considered unjustifiable by law. I mentioned to Lord Melbourne a case in which it had been done ; he told me an anecdote of Napoleon respecting this ; when his great favourite and friend Duroc was so frightfully wounded, the lower part of his body being carried away—Napoleon came to him, and Duroc implored him to give him laudanum to alleviate his sufferings and hasten his end, but Napoleon would not do it, and said he could not sanction such a thing. Lord Melbourne observed, " If they get the habit of doing such a thing " (hastening the end) " when a person is in a hopeless state, why, they *may* do it when a person is *not* in a hopeless state." Spoke of Lord Leveson [1] who is such a very odd-looking young man ; Lord Melbourne said that Lady Granville " was always very ugly," and that " she is *now* better looking than she used to be." Spoke of large dogs, which Lord Melbourne thinks dangerous pets, as you are always so completely at their mercy if they choose to do you harm. Spoke of Lady Lilford,[2] Lord and Lady Holland ; the latter, Lord Melbourne says, always thinks *first* of herself and then of Lord Holland, who quite obeys her. I asked Lord Melbourne if Lord Glenelg was at all obstinate ; he

---

[1] At the opening of the Queen's first Parliament in 1837 Lord Leveson [afterwards Lord Granville and Foreign Secretary] had moved in the House of Commons the address in reply to her speech, looking, wrote Disraeli, himself also a new member, " like a child." Lord Leveson was twenty-two years old, and the Queen had met him a few years earlier at Christ Church. See *ante*, p. 60. His mother, Lady Granville, was Henrietta, daughter of the fifth Duke of Devonshire.

[2] Lady Lilford was a daughter of Lord and Lady Holland.

said not now, but that he had been, and had given great trouble in '30 or '31, when he alone opposed in the Cabinet £25,000 being proposed as an outfit for the Queen Dowager; and that Lord Grey had been obliged to go and tell the King that he could not propose it, as Lord Glenelg was so much against it; Lord Melbourne said that neither the King or Queen ever forgave this and that the King could not *bear* Lord Glenelg; he could neither bear Lord John Russell, who, Lord Melbourne said, he always called " that young man "; he also disliked Sir John Hobhouse, and Mr. Poulett Thomson, and latterly Lord Palmerston, though in the beginning he liked him very much; Mr. S. Rice he liked pretty well; the Lord Chancellor [1] very much, and always told Lord Melbourne that the Lord Chancellor was " a kind good man "; Lord Dunraven [2] thought the King liked him (Ld. D.), but Lord Melbourne said he thought the King disliked him " at bottom," though he was confidential with him. I asked Lord Melbourne if he did not see the King often ? Lord Melbourne replied not often, and never at Windsor latterly; that he was always very civil to him, though not very open, and always very short. He said (that by the paper which Taylor wrote and gave me, and which Lord Melbourne has read) that the King had intended, in case the Ministry had resigned (which Lord Melbourne said they had declared they would, about the Irish Corporation Bill) to send a paper round to the Duke of Wellington,

[1] Charles Christopher, first Lord Cottenham. On Lord Melbourne forming his second Ministry, the Great Seal was not offered to Brougham, but at first put into Commission. Pepys, Master of the Rolls, was one of the Commissioners, and became a little later Chancellor.

[2] William Henry, second Earl of Dunraven (1782–1850).

Sir Robert Peel and Lord Melbourne calling upon them to form a Ministry. Lord Melbourne added: " He " (the late King) " was not at all a clever man ; he was a very timid man ; very easily frightened ; in fact he was quite in Taylor's hands ; Taylor could turn him any way." This I observed was a wrong thing ; Lord Melbourne said certainly it was, " but considering the King's character, and how difficult it was for him to take a resolution, one cannot say it was an unfortunate thing." I observed that Taylor turned the King to the Tory side ; Lord Melbourne said : " The Tories don't at all consider Taylor a friend." I spoke of the unfortunate day in August '36, when the King came to Windsor (after having prorogued Parliament) in a great passion. Lord Melbourne said this was caused by the King having set his mind upon having a Marine executed who was recommended to mercy ; Lord Minto (whom the King neither liked) came to Lord Melbourne in great distress and said : " The King will have this man hanged." The King hated the Speaker, and told Lord Melbourne that all the time the Speaker was addressing him in the House of Lords: " Shocking voice he has."

Wednesday, 14th February.—Lord M. told me that Lord John had written to him that he would be unable to attend the House of Commons next day, when this *anxious* Ballot Question comes on. Lord Melbourne said he did not think it quite a bad thing that Lord John would be away when this Ballot Question came on, as he thinks there will be less irritation if he is absent, and as Lord John is unwell and " worried about the child," Lord Melbourne observed he " might say something imprudent." I think this all very true. Lord Melbourne was very

funny about caps and bonnets; he looked round
the table and said, "There is an amazing cargo of
bonnets and things come from Paris, I fancy,"
which made us laugh; and he observed Lady Caroline's hat and said he imagined that was something
quite new. He spoke of Mdlle. Laure; we (Lady
Durham and I) laughed very much and asked him -
how he knew about her; "They tell me of her,"
he added, "and I fancy she has beautiful things."
The Duke of Wellington was in very good spirits,
but it strikes me he is a good deal aged, particularly
in appearance. Lady Francis Egerton [1] is a clever,
agreeable little person; and, though much altered,
is still very pretty. I sat on the sofa with Lady
Francis and Lady Durham [2]; Lord Melbourne sitting near me the whole evening; and Lord Francis
not far from him; the other ladies were seated
round the table. We (Lord Melbourne, Lord Francis
and I) spoke about German literature—the weather
—fires, the fire at Paris, &c., &c. Lord Francis is
rather a silent person and it is not easy *de le mettre
en train de parler.* I asked Lord Melbourne what
the Duke of Wellington had told him that made
him (Ld. M.) laugh so much; Lord Melbourne then
told me the following anecdote of George IV., which
caused the laughter. When George IV. returned
from Ireland, he was very sick and suffered a good
deal; and he stopped and rested at Badminton;
upon this the Judge, who was sitting at the Assizes
at Gloucester, imagined that he could not have a
man executed when the King was in the County

---

[1] See *ante,* p. 278.
[2] She was Louisa Elizabeth, daughter of Lord Grey the ex-Premier,
mother of the "Master Lambton" of Lawrence's portrait, who died,
aged fourteen, and grandmother of the present Earl of Durham, K.G.

without asking him about it, came over to Badminton and wished the King to hear the case, which put the King into the greatest passion and he exclaimed, " What! am I to be followed all over the country with the Recorder's report ? " . . . Spoke to Lord Melbourne about Lord John's child, and the anxiety of having one child only. I observed to him however that I did not think having more than one child lessened the anxiety about them ; for if persons loved their children, they would be just as anxious if *one* of the many was ill, and would feel the loss of *one* as much as if he or she had but that one. Lord Melbourne said he thought quite so too ; but that somehow or other " if there are many, they have seldom anything the matter with them." He added " it is not the right affection for a child, if they love them only as being their heir, or for keeping up their name." He said he was going home after he had left the Palace, as he had a great deal to do. He thinks his sister had better go out of town, as she is not well, and out of spirits since she is in London. I spoke of sons-in-law and daughters-in-law and observed that I thought daughters-in-law seldom got on well with their mothers-in-law, in which Lord Melbourne quite agreed ; whereas the sons-in-law they generally were fond of. I asked him how his sister agreed with the young Lady Cowper. " Pretty well," he replied, " but I don't think she forms any exception to the rule." Lady Ashley and Lady Fanny, he said, liked their sister-in-law, but had also a certain feeling about it ; " they don't like to see her in the same place where they used to see their mother." Spoke of the very strange custom in Russia that on Easter Sunday *everybody* who chooses is allowed to *kiss* the Empress, saying at the same

time " Christ is risen." Lord Melbourne told me an
anecdote of the Emperor of Russia. " He said to a
sentinel, ' Christ is risen,' and the man answered, ' No,
he is not '; the Emperor started and repeated, ' Christ
is risen '; the man again said, 'No, he is not, for I
am a Jew.' The Emperor said, ' You are quite
right.' " I was quite happy to see the very amicable
and friendly terms on which the Duke and my excellent friend were ; it is impossible for Lord Melbourne to be otherwise almost with anybody, and
the Duke having behaved very well lately, and being
likewise an open, frank man, it renders it easy for
them to be so. . . .

Thursday, 15th February.—I sat on the sofa with
the Duchess of Sutherland, the Duke of Sutherland
and Lord Durham sitting near us. Lord Durham
spoke of the King of Greece [1]; says he is *remarkably*
plain and mean-looking, very shy and awkward in
society, and *en fin* unable to do *anything*. The Sultan,[2]
whom he also saw, he describes as a fine-looking
but not " thorough-bred " looking man ; short and
dark, with an expression of treachery in his eyes. . . .

Wednesday, 21st February.—At about a $\frac{1}{4}$ p. 2 I
went into the Throne room for the Levee with my
Ladies &c., and all the Household and the Ministers
being in the room. The only person who I was very
anxious to see and whom I was much interested to
have seen, was *O'Connell*, who was presented, and
of course, as everybody does when they are presented,
kissed hands. He was in a full wig as one of the

---

[1] King Otho had accepted the throne of Greece in October 1832,
and ascended it three months later. This was done in virtue of a re-
quest from Greece to Great Britain, France, and Russia.

[2] Mahmud II., Sultan (1808–39), succeeded in the latter year by
Abdul-Medjid.

Queen's Councillors in Ireland, and not in the brown
Brutus wig he generally wears. He is very tall,
rather large, has a remarkably good-humoured
countenance, small features, small clever blue eyes,
and very like his caricatures; there were likewise
two of his sons, Morgan and John O'Connell; his son-
in-law, Mr. Fitzsimon, and his nephew John Morgan
O'Connell. Lord Melbourne told me that one of my
pensioners, a Sir John Lade,[1] one of George IV.'s
associates, was dead; spoke of him, of another called
George Lee; of old Mrs. Fox, who Lord Melbourne
knew formerly; he said of Mr. Fox, "he took great
notice of me." Mr. Fox died on the 13th of September
1806. Spoke of Nelson, &c., &c. He spoke of the
Committee on the Pensions which was going on;
that it was a very fair Committee, and that there
had only been a difficulty about one case, which was
a curious one, and which is a pension given to two
French ladies, Madame de Rohan and Madame de
Longueville, daughters of the Duc de Biron. Lord
Melbourne told me how they came to get it, which
is as follows, and in telling which he became quite
affected and his eyes filled with tears. When Lord
Rodney went to Paris just before he obtained his
great victory, he was arrested for debt, as (Lord
Melbourne said) he was always without a shilling in
the world; and the Duc de Biron said, " Though we
are enemies, still it is too bad that a great English
officer should be arrested for debt here," and he paid
his debts for him. Afterwards when the Duc de
Biron's daughters, Mmes. de Rohan and Longueville, who are the first nobility in France, got into
distress, they sent a statement to George III. of

[1] Of some fame, but little merit. He managed the stables of
George IV., when Prince of Wales.

what their father had done for Lord Rodney, and
George III. gave them a pension. Spoke of O'Connell, and George IV., to whose Levee in Dublin he
(O'Connell) went ; Lord Melbourne said that O'Connell declared he heard George IV. distinctly say
(when he passed) to some one, " God damn him."
Lord Melbourne said that George IV. was in a very
awkward position when he was in Ireland, for that
the whole country was in a ferment of enthusiasm
believing the King to be for the Catholic Emancipation, whereas in his heart he was against it. I said
to Lord Melbourne that there was rather a disagreeable business about Lord Durham's wishing me to
receive Lady —— at Court, which, if she had been
refused at the late Court, it would, I feared, be impossible for me to do. Lord Melbourne said, " It
will not do for you to reverse a sentence passed by
the late Court in the beginning of your reign ; I
quite agree with you that you cannot do this." He
said that in general with respect to receiving people
it was better to go according to what had been
determined by a Court of Justice and if there was
nothing against them there, to receive them and not
to inquire into what their early lives had been.[1] . . .

Friday, 23rd February.—I lamented my being *so*
short, which Lord M. smiled at and thought no misfortune. Spoke to him of the Levée, the place where
I stood which some people objected to, which led him
to speak of the old Court in the time of George III.,
when a Levee and also a Drawing-room was like an

---

[1] This rule was followed with invariable and prudent strictness by
the Queen throughout her reign. She was never swayed in action by
gossip, however subtle or ill-natured—she required proof ; and this rule
governed her decision in regard to disputes as to the eligibility of all
persons to be invited to Court.

Assembly ; the King and Queen used to come into the room where the people were already assembled, and to walk round and speak to the people ; they did not speak to everybody, and it was considered no offence, he said, if they did not. He said Queen Charlotte spoke English with a little accent, but that it was rather pretty. I asked him when he first went to Court ; he said in the year 1803, he thought ; it was at the time when everybody volunteered their services and when he was in a Volunteer Corps. Spoke of Lord Howe, his remaining about the Queen[1]; and when he was made to resign. Lord Melbourne said he (Ld. H.) seldom voted but that when he voted against the Reform Bill, Lord Grey was urged by an outcry from " his people " to press his (Ld. Howe's) removal, which Lord Melbourne said was very unwise ; Lord Grey went down to Windsor, and told the King of it, which alarmed the King a good deal ; they (the King and Lord Grey) discussed with Taylor how it should be done ; Lord Grey proposed his seeing the Queen upon it, which Taylor said never would do, and that the only way was to send for Lord Howe and make him resign, which he (Ld. H.) said he would do. Lord Melbourne said that the Queen had just come home from riding and was half undressed when Lord Howe sent to say he must see the Queen ; she said she would see him when she was dressed ; whereupon Lord Howe sent again to her saying the affair was so urgent that he must see her immediately ; she buttoned up her habit again and saw him ; he gave her the key and said he must resign, which Lord Melbourne said made the Queen very angry and

[1] Lord Howe's attitude was one of hostility to the Government. See *ante*, p. 113.

I—20

rendered her still more hostile to Lord Grey's Government than she already was. . . .

Tuesday, 27th February.—I said to Lord Melbourne that Uncle Leopold was amazingly frightened when the Prince of Orange came over with his sons, as he always imagined that the late King had *some intentions* about that ; (meaning a marriage between me and one of the young Princes.) "And so he had," said Lord Melbourne decidedly. "He sounded me about it," and Lord Melbourne wrote to him (the late King) to say that in a political point of view, he did not think it a desirable thing ; that the country would not like a connection with Holland ; the King was much disappointed at this, Lord Melbourne said ; he (the King) had always a fear about a marriage ; he was afraid Mamma had intentions, which I observed she certainly had ; and that the King therefore thought "he must *dévancer* her" ; that Lord Melbourne told him, if he wished such a thing he had better be sure first if the *Parties* themselves liked it ; for that he never could force such a thing ; of which Lord Melbourne said the King never seemed sensible ; at which I laughed. He said that the Prince of Orange also came to him (Ld. M.) from the King, and asked him if he or the Government had any objection to such a connection. "Personally," Lord Melbourne said to him, "there could be no objection ; no more than to any other Prince in Europe" ; but at the same time he must tell him that his (the Prince's) country was so situated that it would be constantly involved in war if any war was to break out ; "I told him as much as that," Lord Melbourne said, "and that I could not say anything until we saw it in some sort of shape or other." This was all very curious and interesting for me to hear.

H.R.H. The Duchess of Kent

rendered her still more hostile to Lord Grey's Government than she already was. . . .

Tuesday, 27th February.—I said to Lord Melbourne that Uncle Leopold was amazingly frightened when the Prince of Orange came over with his sons, as he always imagined that the late King had *some intentions* about that ; (meaning a marriage between me and one of the young Princes.) "And so he had," said Lord Melbourne decidedly. "He sounded me about it," and Lord Melbourne wrote to him (the late King) to say that in a political point of view, he did not think it a desirable thing ; that the country would not like a connection with Holland ; the King was much disappointed at this, Lord Melbourne said ; he (the King) had always a fear about a marriage ; he was afraid Mamma had intentions, which I observed she certainly had ; and that the King therefore thought "he must *dévancer* her" ; that Lord Melbourne told him, if he wished such a thing he had better be sure first if the *Parties* themselves liked it ; for that he never could force such a thing ; of which Lord Melbourne said the King never seemed sensible ; at which I laughed. He said that the Prince of Orange also came to him (Ld. M.) from the King, and asked him if he or the Government had any objection to such a connection. "Personally," Lord Melbourne said to him, "there could be no objection ; no more than to any other Prince in Europe" ; but at the same time he must tell him that his (the Prince's) country was so situated that it would be constantly involved in war if any war was to break out ; "I told him as much as that," Lord Melbourne said, "and that I could not say anything until we saw it in some sort of shape or other." This was all very curious and interesting for me to hear.

H.R.H. The Duchess of Kent
from a portrait by Stone

INTRODUCTORY NOTE TO CHAPTER IX

THE early months of the year 1838 found Lord Melbourne's Government in considerable difficulties. For legislative purposes the Parliamentary majority was impotent. It was just able to keep the Ministry afloat. "The Queen," wrote Lord Palmerston, " is as steady to us as ever, and was in the depth of despair when she thought we were in danger of being turned out."

This was a year of grave trouble in Canada, but, as it turned out, a year full of promise for the subsequent welfare of that great Dominion, and for her connection with the Mother-country. The Queen was undoubtedly attracted by Lord Durham, the Governor-General, who, although impulsive and impatient of restraint, possessed charms of manner and appearance, together with intellectual gifts, which rendered his personality agreeable to those with whom he was brought in contact. The Queen showed great kindness to him and Lady Durham before their departure for Canada. She regretted his return, and was grieved by the quarrel between him and her Ministers.

Although during this year the Queen was in the habit of taking long rides into the country, which were found to be very beneficial to her health, she worked hard, and she laboriously read, under Lord Melbourne's guidance, masses of despatches and correspondence. At no time during her reign was she more persistent in following the course of public business.

She was now brought a good deal into contact with Lord Palmerston, and was undoubtedly attracted by his great gifts, although at a later period of her reign his administrative methods and high-handed independence occasioned her much anxiety and led to strong remonstrance.

In the month of April, King Leopold was engaged in suggesting to the Queen the possibility of a union between her and Prince Albert of Saxe-Coburg. He wrote constantly to her upon this topic, laying stress upon the young Prince's goodness and distinction, and upon his great anxiety to see his intellectual and moral training perfected under the auspices of Baron Stockmar.

In the course of the spring the preparations for the Queen's Coronation were commenced, and she took keen interest in the detail of that ceremonial. It was a somewhat delicate matter to avoid having to invite her Uncle King Leopold and Queen Louise, but a hint having been dropped to the King of the Belgians, he speedily realised that the custom of not including crowned heads in the invitations to a Coronation was sound and worth preserving. "On mature reflection," he wrote, " I think that a King and Queen at your dear Coronation might perhaps be a *hors d'œuvre*." To this view the Queen graciously assented.

CHAPTER IX

1838

Tuesday, 6th March.—It was Mr. Bulwer's play of *The Lady of Lyons* ; and we came in very soon after the beginning. I think the play acts well, and I like it. Macready acted well as Claude Melnotte, Bartley [1] was very good as Damas ; and Meadows [2] as Glavis. Mr. Elton [3] acted fairly enough as the wicked Beauséant.

Wednesday, 7th March.—Dressed for riding. At a few m. p. 12 I *rode* out with Lord Conyngham, Lord Uxbridge, dear Lehzen, Miss Cavendish, Col. Cavendish, and Sir G. Quentin and Mr. Fozard. I mounted in the garden just under the terrace in order that nobody should know I was going to ride out. I rode my dear favourite Tartar who went perfectly and *most delightfully*, never shying, never starting through all the *very* noisy streets, rattling omnibuses —carts—carriages, &c., &c. I quite *love* him. We rode out through the garden, through the gate on Constitution Hill ; round the park by the water, out at the new gate, by Lord Hill's former villa, a good

[1] George Bartley (died in 1858), a Shakespearean actor who could play Orlando as well as Falstaff. For a time stage-manager at Covent Garden.

[2] Drinkwater Meadows (1799–1869), an excellent performer in comedy of the more eccentric type.

[3] Edgar William Elton (1794–1843) created this part of Beauséant ; he also played Romeo, and (with much success) Edgar in *Lear.*

way on the Harrow Road, I should say within 4 or
5 miles of Harrow—then down a pretty narrow lane
where one could fancy oneself 2 or 300 miles from
London, out by Willesden Field (where I had never
been), and Kilburn, down the Edgware Road—Con-
naught Place, through omnibuses, carts, &c., &c., in
at Cumberland Gate, galloped up to Hyde Park
Corner—and in at the same garden gate at Constitution Hill, and safely to the Palace at 10 m. to 3. It
was a lovely day, a beautiful and delicious ride, and
I have come home quite charmed and delighted. I
rode between Lord Conyngham and Col. Cavendish
the whole way. Dearest Lehzen rode Rosa and
felt all the better for the ride. Wrote my journal.
Signed. Walked about. At ½ p. 4 came my kind
and excellent Lord Melbourne and stayed with me
till 20 m. p. 5. He spoke to me about my ride;
said he had just come from the Cabinet, which was
about these Canadian prisoners [1]; viz. what is to be
done with them; the revolt being put down they
cannot be tried by Martial Law, and there is great
difficulty as to what is to be done with them. I
said to Lord Melbourne I hoped he was not tired
from last night; he said not at all. He said: " I
am not quite so sure of to-night; I think we shall
carry it, but you must not be surprised if it should be
the other way." I coloured very much at this
honest, frank avowal of our fears, from this best and
kindest of friends; and tears were nearer than words
to me at that moment. . . .

[1] The disposal of these prisoners was a difficult matter which became acute in the *interregnum* between the departure of Lord Gosford
and the arrival of Lord Durham. Sir John Colborne postponed a
decision of the matter, and ultimately the prisoners were dealt with
according to the gravity of the case, some being merely bound over,
others deported to Bermuda.

Tuesday, 13th March.—I asked Lord Melbourne what was to take place concerning Slavery to-night.[1] Lord Melbourne then pulled out of his pocket the Bill or Act which is to be read to-night ; he read to me the principal Heads of it explaining to me each part in the *most clear and agreeable* manner possible. I shall not have time or space to explain or name *each* head here, but before I do any, I must just observe that the necessity of this Act shows how shockingly cruel and cheating the Masters of the Slaves are, attempting to evade in every possible way what they are told to do, and what, as the Laws cannot be enforced on the spot, must be done by an Act of Parliament here.

Wednesday, 14th March.— . . . I asked Lord Melbourne how he liked my dress. He said he thought it " very pretty " and that " it did very well." He is so natural and funny and nice about *toilette* and has a very good taste I think. . . .

Saturday, 17th March.—Spoke of the Cabinet, which was just over ; he said that they had been speaking about the Coronation in the Cabinet ; and they all thought that it would be best to have it about the 25th or 26th of June, as it would end the Parliament well and make a good break ; that it would be best to have it like William IV.'s, which would be less long. I of course agreed to this. . . .

Wednesday, 21st March.—Heard from Lord Mel-

---

[1] Great complaints were being made of the cruelty of the Jamaica planters to their negro apprentices, and Brougham had put himself at the head of an agitation in favour of immediate emancipation. Accordingly the Government introduced a Bill regulating the hours of labour, erecting arbitration tribunals for appraising the value of apprentices desiring a discharge, and forbidding the whipping or cutting the hair of female apprentices, or their being placed on a treadmill, or in the chair of a penal gang.

bourne that " the House sat till ½ past eleven last night. Lord Stanhope made a long declamatory speech, very violent, but having in it nothing defined or specific, and was answered by Lord Brougham in a most able and triumphant defence and maintenance of the late Act for amending the laws for the relief of the Poor. Lord Melbourne was very sorry to be prevented from waiting upon Your Majesty. He is very grateful for Your Majesty's enquiries and feels very well this morning." . . . Spoke of Portugal ; Lord Melbourne was very much pleased with the good news, and with the Queen's conduct.[1] I then saw Lord Palmerston, who was in high spirits at the good news from Portugal. The Levée was over at 3. I then went for a moment to the dressing-room to ease my head, as my diadem (which Lord Melbourne thought " very handsome ") hurt me so dreadfully. After this I invested (in the Closet) the Marquis of Breadalbane[2] with the Order of the Thistle ; Sir Thomas Bradford[3] with the Grand Cross of the Bath ; and Lord Burghersh[4] and General Donald McLeod were made Knights Commanders of the Order of the Bath. My Ladies, my whole House-

---

[1] Street riots had broken out at Lisbon, but the Queen behaved with great courage, and, after Costa Cabral had been installed as Civil Governor of the city, the insurgent forces were dispersed. The occurrence of Donna Maria's nineteenth birthday on 4th April was marked by an amnesty, purporting to blot out the revolutionary actions of the last eighteen months.

[2] John, second Marquess and fifth Earl of Breadalbane, F.R.S. (1796–1862).

[3] A distinguished Peninsular officer, who had commanded the Portuguese division at Vittoria ; Commander-in-chief at Bombay 1825–9.

[4] John, afterwards eleventh Earl of Westmorland, son of John, tenth Earl and Sarah Anne his wife, only daughter and heir of Robert Child of Osterley Park. His sister, Lady Jersey (who died in 1867), succeeded to the banker's great fortune. See ante, p. 149.

hold and all the Ministers were present at this ceremony.

Thursday, 22nd March.—Lord Melbourne said he
had been to see the Duke of Wellington this morning
about asking him to be at the head of a Commission
to be appointed to inquire into the promotions in
the Army and in the Marines, which were so very
slow in the time of peace and about which they were
being attacked in the House of Commons. Lord
Melbourne said the Duke had consented to it ; and
that his being at the head of it "will give it
authority" ; the Duke wished to know who was to
be in the Commission ; Lord Melbourne named them to
him and he was very well satisfied with them. Lord
Melbourne told me some of them, which are : Lord
Hill, Sir Hussey Vivian, Sir Alexander Dickson,[1] Sir
Thomas Hardy,[2] the First Lord of the Admiralty,[3]
and the Secretary at War.[4] Lord Melbourne said,
with the tears in his eyes (kind, excellent man),
that the Duke was in very good humour, and "a
very pleasant man to do business with, I think ;
he is so plain and speaks to the point." The Duke
had been reviewing the Battalions which are going
to Canada, and praised them very much, and said
"particularly my regiment." The Duke said that
Lord Brougham's speech on the Poor Laws was the
best he ever heard him make. I told Lord Melbourne
that *Diet* was the best physician for him ; he said

---

[1] Major-General Sir A. Dickson, R.A., had been Superintendent of
Artillery Operations in the Peninsula, and fought at Waterloo, and was
Director-General of the Field-train Department.

[2] Vice-Admiral Sir Thomas Hardy (1769–1839), Captain of the
Victory at Trafalgar. In 1830 he was First Sea Lord, and, later,
Governor of Greenwich Hospital, a post he was holding at this time.

[3] Lord Minto. See *ante*, p. 200

[4] Lord Howick. See *ante*, p. 200.

laughing, he drank too much *champagne,* and I added, mixed too many wines ; at which he laughed a good deal. Spoke of the Queen Dowager who he is going to see at ½ p. 1 on Saturday ; spoke of my calling her Queen Adelaide and not Queen Dowager, as it was painful to people to receive that name. Spoke of all changes of that kind ; of the Queen Dowager's having signed " *Subject* " to me the day after the King died.[1]

Friday, 23rd March.—Lord Cowper is very shy and reserved and speaks but little. He really is the image of his mother,[2] and has exactly the same voice and manner of speaking. The cut of the features is so exactly his mother's—he looks delicate and is very thin ; he has a mild and pleasing countenance. Lord Melbourne spoke to me of these Portuguese despatches which he had not yet seen. He said : " I am very glad the Queen has shown courage ; it gives confidence." . . .

Sunday, 25th March.—I said I had heard from Uncle Leopold, who seems a good deal vexed at this recommencement of this Belgian Question ; we spoke of this and Lord Melbourne said : " I don't like it at all ; I think we shall get into a quarrel somehow or other, which is a bad thing." He said Uncle Leopold had written to Lord Palmerston about this and about this Portuguese Affair ; Lord Melbourne said that Uncle wrote that people complained and with truth that Ferdinand did not show himself ; upon which Dietz[3] wrote that a King should not

---

[1] " Your Majesty's most affectionate Friend, Aunt, and Subject, Adelaide."

[2] Lord Melbourne's sister, afterwards Lady Palmerston. See p. 242.

[3] Dietz had been Governor to Prince Ferdinand, and accompanied him to Portugal, where he took a considerable part in political affairs.

show himself when his subjects are spilling their
blood. Whereupon Uncle observed : that was a
very fine German sentiment, but that if Louis
Philippe had followed that principle, he would have
lost his head like Louis xvi. . . . Of the late hurricane in Ireland ; Lord Melbourne said trees never
grew so well in Ireland and were all a little bent from
the wind blowing across the Atlantic. He dislikes
trees near a house, and he is very fond of thinning
trees. Spoke of Claremont and the trees there. We
then spoke of *names* (Xtian names) for a long while,
about which Lord Melbourne was very amusing and
very funny. He said Lady Ashley was always called
Minny. He said : " I think Mary beautiful." We
spoke of Molly ; " Molly is beautiful ; it's such a
soft word, there are more liquids in it than in almost
any word." Then *Bess* he thinks " quite beautiful,"
as also *Jane,* and *Kate,* and *Alice* ; " Jane and
Joan," he said, " are John." " Louisa," he says, " is
a fastidious name." . . .

Tuesday, 27th March.—At ½ p. 12 I rode out with
Lord Conyngham, Lord Uxbridge, Lord Byron,[1]
Lady Mary, dearest Lehzen, Miss Cavendish, Miss
Quentin, Sir F. Stovin and Col. Cavendish, and
came home at ½ p. 3, having ridden 22 MILES ! ! ! We
rode very hard and Tartar went MOST delightfully,
NEVER was there SUCH a dear horse. We rode to
Richmond, through part of the Richmond Park, out
at Robin Hood Gate, and home over Wimbledon
Common and Vauxhall Bridge. It was as hot as
summer, and *going* I thought I should have melted ;
coming over Wimbledon Common there was some
delicious air. It was a heavenly day. At 6 m.

---

[1] George, Lord Byron, succeeded his cousin the poet in 1824. He
was an extra Lord-in-waiting to the Queen.

p. 4 came Lord Melbourne and stayed with me till 20 m. to 5. He seemed well. Spoke a good deal of my ride. The Debate lasted till 11 last night, and he dined and stayed at home. Spoke of the Archbishop's having made a long speech last night about the Indian Worship ; spoke of that. Spoke of the Duke of Sussex and what he told me about the rank a Prime Minister should have, viz. that of Lord High Treasurer ; Lord Melbourne said : " I think it had better remain as it is." [1]

Wednesday, 28th March.—Spoke of my ride ; of Mr. Bulwer's novels, *none* of which Lord Melbourne has read. Lady Durham said it was very odd that so clever a man should be vain about his personal appearance. Lord Melbourne replied : " I think clever people generally have more of those weaknesses than others." Lord Melbourne said : " I always predicted he would be a genius when he was a boy ; and I was sure he would make a figure ; he used to come over to Brocket when he was 17, and show me his poetry." I asked Lord Melbourne if he was fond of novels ; he said " very fond," but that he had no time to read them now. Spoke of Lady Wilhelmina, who Lord Melbourne says is certainly much grown since last year. I said " Everybody grows but me." He laughed and said, " I think you are grown." . . .

Thursday, 29th March.—I showed Lord Melbourne a bracelet with my portrait by Ross in it, which I'm going to give Lady Durham, which he thought very like.

Friday, 30th March.—Got up at 10 m. to 10, and breakfasted at a ¼ to 11. Heard from Lord John

---

[1] It was altered by King Edward in 1905, and the Prime Minister now takes rank immediately after the Archbishop of York

before breakfast, that Sir George Strickland [1] brought on this Motion for emancipating the Apprentices this year, last night, and was seconded by Mr. Pease [2] (the Quaker). Sir George Grey [3] made a speech of 2 hours and fifty minutes, and completely exhausted the subject. The speech was a very able one and Lord John thinks will change many Votes.

Sunday, 1st April.—I told him of the Duke of Cambridge and what he had said about his wish of going to the Emperor of Austria's Coronation ; and also that he said he could not dine with me on Tuesday, but *invited himself* to dine with me another day *without* the Duchess ; Lord Melbourne laughed and said, " That's very odd ; Your Majesty should have said ' That's not right.' " Spoke of Little Holland House, which Lord Melbourne says is quite near Holland House and a very nice place, with a very pretty garden ; spoke of Miss Fox, Lord Holland's sister, who is such an amiable person ; we were not sure of her age ; Lord Melbourne said she was grown up when he was a boy at school ; spoke of Lady Holland, who has been very handsome though he always remembers her very large ; and she has a vulgar mouth and used always to say, " A vulgar ordinary mouth I have." Spoke of her and Lady

[1] Whig M.P. for West Riding of Yorkshire.

[2] Joseph Pease, M.P. for South Durham, had been a pioneer of railway construction, and had assisted his father in forming (upon the persuasion of George Stephenson) the Stockton and Darlington line.

[3] Sir George Grey of Falloden, Northumberland, second Baronet (1799–1882), Under-Secretary for the Colonies. Appointed Judge Advocate-General in 1839, and in 1846 Home Secretary under Lord John Russell, an office which he held for nearly twenty years. He was a man of fine presence and great social charm. His high moral qualities and freedom from personal ambition gained for him the esteem of both political parties and the confidence of his countrymen. He has been worthily succeeded in his title and all else by his grandson, Sir Edward Grey, K.G.

Lilford, who, Lord Melbourne said laughing, " never had the use of her legs." Lady Holland is about 68, he thinks; she was married in 1786 to her 1st husband, Sir Godfrey Webster, when she was only 16. Spoke of Portugal &c. . . .

Monday, 2nd April.—I said to Lord Melbourne I was so stupid that I must beg him to explain to me about Sir William Follett [1] again; he answered very kindly, " It is not stupid, but I daresay you can't understand it," and he explained it to me like a *kind* father would do to his child; he has something so fatherly, and so affectionate and kind in him, that one must love him. . . . I rode Lord Uxbridge's little horse, which I have Christened *Uxbridge*, and which is the most charming, delightful, quiet horse possible. It has a most beautiful little head, is of a dark chestnut colour, if possible quieter than Tartar, for it never takes notice of anything; full of spirit, and very easy and pleasant in its canter which is faster than Tartar's. It is delightful to have two such horses as Tartar and Uxbridge. It was a very warm, bright, clear, pleasant day. We rode to Hanwell through Acton; home by Castle Hill, Acton again, and in at the Victoria Gate, and home by the garden gate; we rode about 19 or 20 miles. When we were near Notting Hill, or rather more at Brookgreen, I sent on a groom to inform Lord Melbourne (who told me last night he would come to me at *four* today), that I should be at home in a few minutes; but when I came home, they said Lord Melbourne had been at the gate a few minutes before,

---

[1] This brilliant advocate, who died at the age of forty-seven, had been Peel's Solicitor-General, and became Attorney-General in 1841. He appeared for Norton in his action for *crim. con.* against Melbourne, without any success, for the charge was triumphantly refuted.

and on hearing I was still out, said " Very well,"
and walked his horse away. I waited in my habit
till 5, the hour for the House of Lords, when I felt
that my good Lord Melbourne could not come, and
I wrote to him. It is my own fault. . . .

Wednesday, 4th April.—Spoke of the Coronation,
and the fuss the Princesses were in about their robes ;
I told Lord Melbourne that the Duchess of Gloucester
had offered to hold the tip of my train when I was
being crowned, as the Duchess of Brunswick had
done for Queen Charlotte, and that I thought this
very kind of the Duchess ; which quite touched my
good friend. Spoke of Hanwell, and rail-roads ; I
said I feared there were so many rail-roads that they
could not all answer ; Lord Melbourne said he feared
they would not, but that he was sorry for it, as he
was engaged in one. " I was fool enough to engage
in one and to take 50 shares ; I have already paid
£1,000, and have lately had a call for £500 more,"
he added. This rail-road is in Nottingham and he
engaged in it about 4 years ago. I asked him if he
liked rail-roads in general ; he replied, " I don't care
about them," which made me laugh ; and he added
that they were bad for the country as they brought
such a shocking set of people " who commit every
horror." " They are picked men, who mind neither
Lord nor laws, and commit every species of violence ;
nothing is safe," he added ; and " it's more like a
country in time of war " than peace. He spoke of
Dorsetshire to Lady Portman, and she said it was
so poor ; he replied, " That's because you don't
give enough wages."

Thursday, 5th April.—Spoke of Lady Burghersh [1] ;
Lord Melbourne said, " She is of a great deal of use to

[1] See *ante,* p. 149.

us, in a quiet way " ; for if he wished to communicate with the Duke of Wellington, he did it through her ; he, of course, does not wish me to mention this ; but I hope I *am* discreet and tell but little of what he tells to me. Lady Burghersh is a sensible, clever woman, and has great influence over the Duke.

Friday, 6th April.—Spoke of my ride ; rail-roads ; that the Steam-Carriage could not be stopped under 150 yards' distance of an object ; I observed that these Steam-Carriages are very dangerous ; Lord Melbourne said, " Oh ! none of these modern inventions consider human life." Spoke of Col. Cavendish and Sir George Quentin ; of horses ; Lord Melbourne said his mare would not be well enough to come down to Windsor, but that he could get a horse from me there, to ride. I observed that Mr. Cowper complained he (Ld. M.) never rode the horses he should ride ; " I don't know, he never got me a horse I liked ; I don't think he is a very good hand at horses." Lord Melbourne said Mr. Fred Byng [1] got him his present black mare ; he hears a horse-dealer has got a horse which he thinks will do for him ; the price is 160 guineas, which he says is nothing if the horse is a good one ; but a good deal if it is a bad one. . . . Spoke of Byron, who Lord Melbourne said would not be 50 if he were alive [2]; he said he was extremely handsome ; had dark hair, was very lame and limped very much ; I asked if the expression of his countenance was agreeable ; he said not ; " he had a sarcastic, sardonic expression ; a contemptuous expression." I asked if he was not agreeable ; he said " He could be excessively so " ;

[1] The Hon. F. G. Byng, sometime Gentleman Usher of the Privy Chamber.

[2] He would have been 50 on January 22, 1838.

" he had a pretty smile " ; " treacherous beyond conception ; I believe he was fond of treachery." Lord Melbourne added, " he dazzled everybody," and deceived them ; " for he could tell his story very well." . . . Lord Melbourne said, " The old King (George III.) had that hurried manner ; but he was a shrewd, acute man, and most scrupulously civil." He added that the King was rather tall, red in the face, large though not a corpulent man ; prejudiced and obstinate beyond conception ; spoke of the old Duke of Gloucester who, he said, was not a clever man but a good-natured man, though very proud ; of the Duchess of Gloucester his wife ; Lord Melbourne said that Horace Walpole tells that one day *he* (I think) gave the Duke of Gloucester a fête at Strawberry Hill ; and the Duchess came over before to see that all was right ; and when she came there she saw that the host had put up her arms with the Duke's ; she said, " God bless me ! this will never do ; you must take this down directly, this will never do ; the Duke would be extremely angry were he to see this." The Duchess was a Walpole by birth [1] ; she was first married to Lord Waldegrave ; her children by that marriage were beautiful ; they were Elizabeth, Lady Waldegrave,[2] Lady Euston,[3] and Lady Hugh Seymour, who was mother to Sir Horace Seymour.[4] " People were very fond of her," Lord Melbourne said. . . .

Sunday, 8th April. —Lord Melbourne looked over

---

[1] She was an illegitimate daughter of Edward Walpole (second son of Sir Robert) by Mary Clement, a sempstress in Pall Mall. Their two other daughters became Countess of Albemarle and Countess of Dysart respectively.

[2] Married her cousin George, seventh Earl Waldegrave.

[3] Wife of George, second Duke of Grafton.

[4] Father of the Admiral, Sir Beauchamp Seymour, Lord Alcester.

one of the Volumes (the sixth) of a Work called "Lodge's Portraits"; there are portraits of all sorts of famous people in it, with short Memoirs of them annexed to them. Lord Melbourne looked carefully over each, reading the accounts of the people and admiring the prints. I wish I had time to write down all the clever observations he made about *all*. It is quite *a delight* for me to hear him speak about all these things; he has such *stores* of knowledge; such a wonderful memory; he knows about everybody and everything; *who* they were, and *what* they did; and he imparts all his knowledge in such a *kind* and agreeable manner; it does me a *world* of good; and his conversations always *improve* one greatly. I shall just name a few of the people he observed upon :—*Raleigh*, which he thought a very handsome head; *Hobbes*, who was "an infidel philosopher"; he had been tutor to one of the Earls of Devonshire,[1] he said; *Knox*—Lord Melbourne observed that those Scotch Reformers were very violent people; but that Knox denied having been so harsh to Mary of Scots as she said he had been; *Lord Mansfield*, who, he said, "was greatuncle" to the present Lord; *Melanchthon*, whose name means Black Earth in Greek, and whose head he admired; *Pitt*, whose print Lord Melbourne said was very like; "he died in 1806 when I came into Parliament." He (Ld. M.) came in for Leominster. *Wesley*; Lord Melbourne said the greatest number of Dissenters were Wesleyans; he read from the book that there were (at his death) 135,000 of his followers; *Porson*,—Lord Melbourne said, "I knew him; he was a great Greek scholar," and looking at the print, "it's very like him." *Leibnitz*, a great

---

[1] To William, second Earl, when Lord Cavendish.

I—21

German philosopher, and a correspondent of Queen Caroline, wife to George II. ; spoke of her being so learned and her whole court too ; " the Tories laughed at it very much " ; and Swift ridiculing the Maids of Honour wrote, " Since they talk to Dr. Clark, They now venture in the Dark." *Addison* ; Lord Melbourne admires his " Spectator," his " Cato " he also admires, but says it's not like a Roman tragedy ; " there is so much love in it." Addison died at Holland House ; he disagreed very much with his wife, Lady Warwick. Holland House was built, he said, by Rich, Lord Holland, in the reign of Charles 1st.[1] *Madame de Staël,* whose print he thought very like ; " she had good eyes, she was very vain of her arms." She was over here in '15, and died in '17, aged 51 ; she disliked dying very much ; Lord Melbourne also knew her daughter the Duchesse de Broglie ; he said, " Louis Philippe dislikes *her* as much as Napoleon did *her Mother.*" Lord Melbourne saw Madame de Broglie for a moment when he was at Paris for the last time in 1825. He read from the book, with great emphasis, the following passage, what Napoleon said of Madame de Staël : " They pretend that she neither talks politics nor mentions me ; but I know not how it happens that people seem to like me less after visiting her." *Queen Elizabeth* ; spoke of her, and that her Mother must have been very handsome. Lady Holland, he told me, has the greatest fear of dying ; spoke of pictures ; Lord Melbourne does not admire Murillo much, nor Rubens ; he so greatly prefers the Italian Masters to any others ; spoke of subjects for painting ; of the Holy Family being

---

[1] Holland House was built by Sir Walter Cope in 1607. His daughter and co-heiress married Henry Rich, first Earl of Holland.

constantly painted ; " After all," he said, " a woman and child is the most beautiful subject one can have." He is going down alone to Brocket ; I told him his sister thought Brocket so cold, and that she wanted him to put up stoves, which he said would " burn down the house." " I reduced the grates," he continued, " because I thought they gave heat enough ; and so they do, if they make large fires ; but they don't know how to make fires." He can't bear Brocket in winter. He was going home and did not feel tired any more. He spoke of my riding very kindly. Stayed up till a ¼ p. 11. It was a most delightful evening.

Monday, 9th April.—I showed him letters of thanks from Lords Fitzwilliam and Dundas and Captain Sykes, relative to my having repaid to the two first-named the debt incurred by my poor father and owing to their late fathers ; and to the latter the debt owing to himself, accompanied by gifts. Lord Melbourne observed my sleeves (which were very long) with astonishment, and said " Amazing sleeves ! " . . .

Monday, 16th April.—Lord Melbourne told me that there were very strange accounts of Lord Brougham and all he was *saying* and *doing* at Paris ; his having gone to see Louis Philippe at 11 o'clock at night, when the Swiss Guard were (as they always are) asleep on the staircase ; they stopped him (Brougham), saying the King was gone to bed ; upon which Brougham observed that their King had " very rustic habits." Spoke of him, his visiting Lady Fitzharris [1] ; Lord Melbourne spoke of Brougham and his oddities ; of this Review which he (B.) has written and which

---

[1] Wife of James Howard, afterwards third Earl of Malmesbury.

Lord Melbourne thinks "well done." He thinks
Queen Charlotte and George III. very harshly
handled in it, and Queen Caroline amazingly puffed
up ; the Duke of York's character he thinks the best
done ; he says there is a great deal which Brougham
seems not to know ; spoke of George IV.'s character,
not being understood ; of Sir William Knighton's
Memoirs which are just published, and which Lord
Melbourne thinks it very wrong in Lady Knighton [1]
to have published ; of George IV. being so completely in the hands of Knighton, &c., &c. I felt
very unhappy at dinner, in spite of my being gay
when I spoke, and I could have cried almost at
every moment ; so much so, that when I got into
bed, my nerves (which had been more shaken by
the loss of *dearest* Louis,[2] than I can express, and by
the struggle when in company to overcome *grief*
which I felt so acutely) could resist no longer, and
more than half an hour elapsed, in tears, before
I fell asleep. And before I was asleep I saw her,
in my imagination, before me, dressed in her neat
white morning gown, sitting at her breakfast in her
room at Claremont ; again, standing in my room
of an evening, dressed in her best, holding herself so
erect, as she always did, and making the low dignified
curtsey so peculiar to herself ; and lastly on her

[1] Sir William Knighton had been physician to George IV., when
Prince of Wales, and was private secretary and Keeper of his Privy
Purse when King. The King employed him in various confidential
matters.

[2] Queen Victoria in 1872 wrote of Louis as "the former faithful
and devoted friend of Princess Charlotte—beloved and respected
by all who knew her—and who doted on the little Princess who was
too much an idol in the House. This dear old lady was visited by
every one, and was the only really devoted attendant of the poor
Princess, whose governesses paid little real attention to her, and
who never left her, and was with her when she died." See p. 62.

death-bed, pale and emaciated, but the expression the same, and the mind vigorous and firm as ever! These were the images I beheld as I lay in bed! Yet, mingled with my grief were feelings of thankfulness that her end was so peaceful—so happy! . . ..

Saturday, 21st April.—I showed Lord Melbourne the plans for changing the Slopes and making a new walk, and we looked over them for some time together. We then spoke of what *might* have happened when the Duke of York married; for who could foretell, Lord Melbourne observed, that the Duchess of York would have no children?—and that the late King should lose the two he had? This led us to speak of the whole Royal Family, their characters, of the Princesses marrying so late; of George III.'s dislike to their marrying, which Lord Melbourne did not know; of their beauty; he always thought Princess Sophia (when young) very pretty, though very like a Gipsy; spoke of the singular instance of both George III.'s and Queen Charlotte's being very plain and all their children very handsome; spoke of all the Princes and Princesses, of the two little Princes, Octavius and Alfred, who died; Lord Melbourne said, George III. said when he felt he was to be unwell (which he always forefelt) he dreamt and thought of Octavius. Lord Melbourne said Queen Charlotte had fine hands and feet, a good bust, and a pretty figure.

Sunday, 22nd April.—I spoke to him of what I was to write to Uncle relative to Soult's nomination[1]; Soult, he told me, is a large, tall man;

---

[1] Marshal Soult, Duke of Dalmatia, was appointed Ambassador of the King of the French at Queen Victoria's Coronation. He had been Wellington's antagonist in the Peninsula, and this added to his popularity with the masses of the London streets.

looks more " like the Purser of a ship '" than an
officer ; a very distinguished officer risen from the
ranks, and a man of great abilities besides. Lord
Melbourne knew him when he was in Paris. I asked
Lord Melbourne when he was first at Paris ; in 1815
he said, which was the first time he was ever on the
Continent. " We went," he said (which " we " im-
plies himself and Lady Caroline, his wife) " to
Brussels immediately after the Battle of Waterloo, to
see Fred. Ponsonby [1] who was desperately wounded."
This was in June 1815, and he went to Paris in
August, and stayed there September and October and
came back in November. He saw Uncle Leopold
there then, and said he was extremely handsome.

Monday, 23rd April.—Lord Melbourne looked into
the newspapers and said there was nothing in them ;
he read (in the papers) a denial from Lady Charlotte
Bury [2] of her having written the book called *Diary
of the Reign* (I think) *of George IV.* ; Lord
Melbourne spoke of Lady Hertford, though he of
course could not remember her in her great beauty ;
he said, " My nurse nursed Lord Hertford,[3] so that

[1] General Sir Frederick Cavendish Ponsonby, K.C.B , G.C.M.G.,
second son of the third Earl of Bessborough, and brother of Lady
Caroline Lamb. He was the father of the late Sir Henry Ponsonby,
Queen Victoria's private secretary and Keeper of her Privy Purse.

[2] Lady Charlotte Campbell, daughter of the fifth Duke of Argyll,
married, first, Colonel Campbell, and second, Rev. E. J. Bury ; was
Lady-in-Waiting to Caroline, Princess of Wales. She was a friend and
patroness of Sir W. Scott, and wrote several novels. In 1838 appeared
A Diary illustrative of the Times of George IV., which was attributed to
her by Lord Brougham—a charge which was never denied. The
work was severely criticised.

[3] Francis Charles, third Marquess (1777–1842), the " Lord Mon-
mouth " of *Coningsby*. His son, here called Lord Yarmouth, succeeded him and died unmarried in 1870. The fourth Marquess was
the founder of the magnificent collections now the property of the
nation at Hertford House.

I used to hear a great deal about her." The present
Lord Hertford's wife, he said, was a natural daughter
of the Duke of Queensberry, called Mme. Fagniani [1];
she is still alive at Paris, but Lord Hertford has
long been separated from her; Lord Yarmouth, he
said, is very clever, but always lives abroad. [2] . . .

Wednesday, 25th April.—In speaking before of
Mrs. Baring, [3] who, I said, from having been the
most affectionate of mothers, latterly never asked
after her children,—Lord Melbourne said with the
tears in his eyes, " That's a sure sign that all is
over; when people intermit what they have been
in the habit of doing." He mentioned that when
William III. was dying they brought him some good
news from abroad, but he took no notice of it whatever, and said, " Je tire à ma fin." . . .

Friday, 27th April.—I showed Lord Melbourne two
pictures of Lord Durham's children; spoke of the
beautiful boy Lord Durham lost, who would now
be 20. Lord Melbourne said, that boy's death was
the cause of a dreadful scene between Durham and
Lord Grey in one of the Cabinets. Spoke of this
Flahaut [4] business, and of the wish at Paris to throw
the blame of the whole on Uncle Leopold; spoke of

[1] Her paternity was in dispute between the Duke of Queensberry
and George Selwyn.

[2] Lord Yarmouth, afterwards fourth Marquess, and his brother
Lord Henry Seymour always lived in Paris. Lord Hertford possessed
a fine apartment at the corner of the Rue Lafite and a country place
called " Bagatelle " in the Bois de Boulogne. Subsequently they
passed to Sir R. Wallace and later to Sir John Murray Scott. Bagatelle
is now the property of the Municipality of Paris.

[3] Hortense Eugenie Claire, daughter of Duc de Bassano, Minister
of Napoleon I., married 1833 to Francis Baring, afterwards third Lord
Ashburton.

[4] Comte de Flahaut, son of Comtesse de Flahaut Adele, who
was afterwards Baronne de Souza, had once been French Ambassador

Flahaut; Lord Melbourne said he (Flahaut) was first
noticed by Napoleon, in the Russian Retreat, when
in all that cold and misery he heard a young officer
singing, and appearing quite gay; that was Flahaut;
Napoleon said, "That is a fine young fellow," and
placed him on his Staff. . . . Spoke of Lady Campbell[1]
(Pamela Fitzgerald) who Lord Melbourne has not seen
again, but from whom he has had a long letter. . . .

Saturday, 28th April.—Lord Melbourne continued,
that those who were about the Prince of Wales[2] were
not liked at Court " and vice versa." And he said
his family quite belonged to Carlton House; still,
he added, the King and Queen were very civil to
him. Speaking of George IV. he said, "He expected those he was fond of to go quite with him;
to dislike those he disliked, and to like those he
liked, and to turn with him." He then mentioned
what he told me before, that his (Ld. M.'s) father and
mother got into disgrace, for I think 3 years, when
Mrs. Fitzherbert was banished, and they continued
seeing her; and when George IV. came back to
Mrs. Fitzherbert he came to dine with them (Lord
Melbourne was there the first day he came) as if
nothing had happened, and as if he had been there
the day before. Lord Melbourne said, before all
this, that " the only thing one learns at a public
school " is *punctuality*, and the value of time; that
he never had a clock in his room, and always called

in London, as Sebastiani now was, but there was a competition between Flahaut and Soult as to which should be specially appointed
to represent the King of the French at the Coronation. His likeness to
Napoleon III. was considered remarkable and significant.

[1] Wife of Major-General Sir Guy Campbell, Bart., and daughter of
Lord Edward Fitzgerald and his wife Pamela, daughter of Madame de
Genlis.

[2] Afterwards George IV.

to somebody to tell him what o'clock it was, which he owned was bad, as it put you in the power of the man to make you late. He "never carried a watch about him" in his life, and yet he thinks he generally knows what o'clock it is. . . .

Monday, 30th April.—I then showed him a little book relating to the Coronations of various of my Ancestors, and amongst others Queen Anne; he looked over parts of it, and glanced at one part which states that Queen Anne said in her first speech to Parliament that "*her heart was entirely* English." Upon which Lord Melbourne told me that when she concluded the Peace of Utrecht, which was supposed to be rather favourable to the French, a Sir Samuel Garth [1] wrote a poem in which he said of Queen Anne : "The Queen this year has lost a part, Of her entirely English heart,"—which is very funny ; Lord Melbourne did not remember what followed. Speaking of Prince George of Denmark, who Lord Melbourne said "was a very stupid fellow," he added that he (G. of Denmark) was always saying, "Est-il possible ?" to everything, and was always saying so whenever he was told of another Lord having left James II. So when James heard that George of Denmark had left him, he said, "So *Est-il possible* is gone at last!" I spoke of the Duchess of Ancaster [2] having been Queen Charlotte's first Mistress of the Robes ; the title of Duke of Ancaster became extinct, Lord Melbourne told me, and the Dowager Lady Cholmondeley [3] and Lord

---

[1] Garth was an eminent physician in the time of William III. and Queen Anne. He wrote occasional verses fluently, and his poem "The Dispensary" had a great vogue for fifty years.

[2] Elizabeth, wife of Peregrine, third Duke of Ancaster.

[3] Georgiana, daughter of the third Duke of Ancaster, and widow of the first Marquess of Cholmondeley.

Willoughby's mother [1] were her co-heiresses. I asked him who was now Lord Fauconberg; he said the title was extinct [2]; he was a descendant of Oliver Cromwell's by Cromwell's daughter Lady Fauconberg; Lady Charlotte Bellasyse married a person called Thomas Wynne, a Welshman. [3] Sir Ed. Desborow, Lord Melbourne told me, is also a descendant of Cromwell's by one of his daughters. I told Lord Melbourne what the Duke of Sussex had told me, viz. that none of his family " could hold their tongue," which is very true; which made Lord Melbourne laugh, and still more so when I told him that the Duke, in speaking of the King of Hanover, called him " that other man." After dinner I sat on the sofa with Lady Isabella and Lady Augusta, Lord Melbourne sitting near me the whole evening, and some of the other ladies being seated round the table. Spoke of Lady Isabella; Henry Fox, [4] of the Apartments at Hampton Court &c.; of this Review of Brougham's of Lady C. Bury's book. Lord Melbourne said again, what he told me the other day, that there was much which Brougham seemed

[1] Priscilla, also daughter of the third Duke of Ancaster. On the death of their brother unmarried, the barony of Willoughby de Eresby fell into abeyance between the sisters, which was terminated by the Crown in favour of Priscilla, the elder, in 1780.

[2] The barony of Fauconberg, of an earlier creation, was revived in 1903 in favour of the present (1912) Countess of Yarborough, daughter and co-heir of the twelfth Lord Conyers.

[3] Cromwell's son-in-law was promoted from Viscount to be Earl Fauconberg. He left no child. His great-nephew was again created Earl, and married a sister of Peniston, first Viscount Melbourne. Their daughters married as follows: Lady Charlotte Bellasyse to Thomas Edward Wynn, Anne to Sir George Wombwell, Elizabeth successively to the Duke of Norfolk and Lord Lucan.

[4] Henry Fox (afterwards fourth and last Lord Holland) married Lady Augusta Coventry; at her death in 1889, Holland House, Kensington, became the property of Lord Ilchester.

to know nothing about ; he (B.) states that Mrs. Fitzherbert did not know when she married the King that a marriage with a Catholic could not be valid ; Lord Melbourne says she must have known that, and that, by what he has heard, she was against the marriage ; he said Lord Holland knows a good deal about it, and that it is known *where* the marriage took place and by whom it was celebrated. Lord Melbourne thinks it took place in 1784 or 5 [1]; the King left her in 1795, when Lady Jersey got into favour, whom he put about the Princess of Wales ; he came back to Mrs. Fitzherbert in 1802, then left her for Lady Hertford, quarrelled with her, and then Lady Conyngham followed ; the last-named, I observed, was very good-natured ; Lord Melbourne said, " She was the most good-natured, but the most rapacious ; she got the most money from him." Spoke of Lady Augusta Fox ; Lord Melbourne said her mother, Lady Coventry, was Lady Mary Beauclerc, daughter of a Duke of St. Albans (uncle to the present Duke). Her (Lady Coventry's) mother was a Miss Moses, a Jewess. Lady Holland, Lord Melbourne says, does not like Lady Augusta Fox. Lord Melbourne told me that the Irish Poor Law Bill would come up to the House of Lords next day, and that there would be probably a good deal next week, in the Committee about it ; a great deal of difference of opinion ; but he thinks they'll pass it. . . .

Friday, 4th May.—Lord Melbourne told me on Wednesday evening that Landseer said of McLise [2]:

---

[1] 21st December, 1785.

[2] Daniel Maclise (1806–70). His first success was a sketch of Sir Walter Scott drawn by him unobserved. His best-known works are the two cartoons in the Royal Gallery of the House of Lords. He was elected to the Royal Academy in 1840.

" He is beating us all; his imagination, grouping, and drawing is wonderful; he must soften his colouring perhaps a little." Two very clever ones of Grant; a portrait of Lord Cowper by Lucas which is excessively like; Lord Melbourne, by Hayter, and my dogs by Landseer looked very well. The latter is too beautiful. There were also two very clever pictures by Landseer's brother; there was also a very good picture by Sir Martin Shee of the late King; it is the likest I've seen; it's so like his figure.

Saturday, 5th May.—We then spoke of my sitting one day to Sir Martin Shee; of Lord Melbourne's having seen an Academician this morning who said the reason why Hayter was not elected one of their Members was because his character was not good; Lord Melbourne asked me about it; I said I did not know much about it, but that I believed he had quarrelled with his wife and had separated from her. " And did he get another ? " said Lord M. I laughed and said I was not sure of that. . . .

Monday, 7th May.—We (that is Lord Melbourne, Lord Holland and I) spoke about the Exhibition, Landseer's picture of my dogs, the origin of the dog in the Arms of the Seal of the Duchy of Lancaster, which Lord Holland said came originally from John of Gaunt, was adopted by Henry VII., abolished by James I., and restored by William IV.; spoke of *Macaws,* and he offered me one which belongs to Lady Holland. Spoke of Nightingales; Lord Melbourne said he could not distinguish its song from that of another bird's; that it could be mistaken for a wood-lark's, which Lord Holland denied, and they went on discussing the different songs of birds; we then spoke of various birds; of nightingales migrating; of how wonderful the migration of birds was; Lord Melbourne did not think it so incredible; they first went to France, he said, and "then they slide along the country." . . .

Wednesday, 9th May.—Lord Melbourne said he was kept in the House of Lords till 8, the night before; that Lord Shrewsbury [1] made rather a good speech, but that his (Ld. M.'s) fear was that some of the Roman Catholic Peers might refuse to take the Oath on account of all this; and then " we should have all this question " (the Roman Catholic) " over again."

Thursday, 10th May.—At $\frac{1}{2}$ p. 10 the doors were opened and I went through the Saloon into the other Ball-room next the Dining-room in which was Strauss's band. I felt a little shy in going in, but soon got over it and went and talked to the people. The rooms I must say looked beautiful, were so well lit up, and everything so well done; and all done in one day. There was no crowd at all; indeed, there might have been more people. The dining-room looked also very handsome as the supper-room. The Throne-room was arranged for the tea-room. I danced (a Quadrille of course, as I only dance quadrilles) first (in the large ball-room) with George [2]; and 2ndly with Prince Nicholas Esterhazy; there was a valse between

---

[1] John, sixteenth Earl of Shrewsbury, Premier Earl of England. This question of the oath to be taken by Roman Catholic peers and members had been repeatedly brought forward by the Bishop of Exeter. It pledged the jurant to do nothing to "disturb or weaken the Protestant Religion or Protestant Government, or to subvert the Church establishment." A gentleman wrote to the Bishop to say that he could not take the oath, as his wish was to upset the Church establishment, and he was therefore excluded from Parliament. See *ante,* p. 56.

[2] Prince George of Cambridge. See *ante,* p. 77.

each quadrille; I never heard anything so *beautiful* in my life as Strauss's band. We then went into the other ball-room where I danced two other quadrilles with Lord Jocelyn[1] and Lord Fitzalan[2]; the first named is very merry and funny. When I did not dance (which was only the case when valzing went on) I sat with Mamma and my Aunts, on a seat raised one step above the floor. Lady Fanny Cowper was my vis-à-vis when I danced with Lord Jocelyn. At 1 (after my quadrille with Lord Fitzalan) we went into the Supper-room. After supper we went into the large Ball-room where we remained till the last quadrille which I danced in Weippert's room. I danced with Lord Cowper (who was much less shy and very agreeable); Lord Uxbridge (who dances remarkably well); Lord Douro; Lord Folkestone[3] (a great ally of mine); Lord Suffield[4]; and lastly with Lord Morpeth. There was a great deal of beauty there, amongst which were Lady Ashley, Lady Fanny Cowper, Lady Wilhelmina Stanhope, Lady Seymour,[5] Lady Clanricarde,[6] Lady Mary Vyner,[7] Lady Norreys,[8] Lady Emma Herbert,[9] Lady

[1] Eldest son of the third Earl of Roden, and died in his father's lifetime. In 1841 he married Lady Fanny Cowper. See *ante*, p. 188.

[2] Grandson of the Duke of Norfolk. See *ante*, p. 190.

[3] Afterwards fourth Earl of Radnor. See *ante*, p. 60.

[4] Edward Vernon, fourth Lord Suffield (1813–53).

[5] Georgiana, Lady Seymour, Queen of Beauty at the Eglinton Tournament. One of the Sheridan sisters. See *ante*, p. 192.

[6] Daughter of Mr. Canning, the Prime Minister, and wife of the first Marquess of Clanricarde. See Vol. II. pp. 75 and 261.

[7] Daughter of the second Earl de Grey, K.G., and sister of Lady Cowper. She was married to Mr. Henry Vyner.

[8] Daughter of G. G. Vernon Harcourt, M.P. Lord Norreys succeeded in 1854 to the earldom of Abingdon. See *ante*, p 132.

[9] Daughter of the eleventh Earl of Pembroke, afterwards wife of Viscount de Vesci. See *ante*, p. 77.

Clanwilliam,[1] Lady Mary Grimston,[2] Lady Powers-court,[3] Miss Maude,[4] Miss Elphinstone.[5] Lady Fanny was twice my vis-à-vis, as was also Lady Adelaide Paget.[6] I did not leave the ball-room till 10 m. to *four* ! ! and was in bed by $\frac{1}{2}$ p. 4,—the sun shining. It was a lovely ball, so gay, so nice,—and I felt so happy and so merry ; I had not danced for *so* long and was so glad to do so again ! One *only* regret I had,—and that was, that my excellent, kind, good friend, Lord Melbourne was not there. I missed him much at this my first ball ; he would have been pleased I think !

Friday, 11th May.—Got up at 20 m. p. 10 and breakfasted at $\frac{1}{2}$ p. 11. Heard from my good Lord Melbourne that he was " extremely concerned " at not having been able to come to the Ball, but that " he felt so unwell and so disturbed " that he was afraid to venture ; which was right of him, though I regret it *so* much. Heard from Lord John that " Sir Thomas Acland [7] gave notice yesterday that he should move on Monday to rescind the resolution of 1835 respecting the Church of Ireland. The De-bate on this Question must lead to one of the most severe struggles of the session both in discussion and in the Division. Both parties have nearly all their

[1] Sister of Lady Emma Herbert, and wife of the third Earl of Clanwilliam.

[2] Daughter of the first Earl of Verulam. She married Lord Folke-stone (see preceding page) in 1840. See *ante*, p. 189.

[3] Sister of Lord Jocelyn (see preceding page) and wife of the sixth Viscount Powerscourt.

[4] Daughter of the third Viscount Hawarden.

[5] Clementina, sister of the fourteenth Lord Elphinstone, afterwards wife of the fourth Viscount Hawarden.

[6] Daughter of Lord Anglesey, and sister of Lord Uxbridge. She married in 1851 Frederick, son of the third Earl Cadogan.

[7] Sir Thomas Acland, tenth Bart.

strength in London. But a majority for Ministers, though a small one, is tolerably certain." This gave me a pang which somewhat damped my very light and high spirits. We spoke for a long time about my Ball—who I danced with, the beauties, and the different persons there ; I said to Lord Melbourne the moment I saw him, how very sorry I was that he had not come last night. We spoke of all this for some time, and he was so kind about it all, and seemed to take quite an interest in it all. He then said, " They are going to make another attack upon us on Monday ; Sir Thomas Acland has given notice that he means to make a motion to rescind the Resolutions about the Irish Church passed in 1835, upon which we came in." I then added that Lord John seemed certain about a majority, though a small one ; Lord Melbourne said Sir Thomas Acland was a conscientious and not very violent man, and consequently well chosen in that respect to make a good effect. There is to be a Cabinet upon it tomorrow at 1 ; and Lord John is going to have a Meeting of the Members at 4. All this distresses me much ; would to God ! none of these Motions, which are so *useless*, were brought on. I fervently trust however that all will do well. Spoke of my ball, and the different people, the rooms ; he asked if I was not tired ; I said not the least, for though I had danced a great deal I did not valze, as I did not think it would do for me to valze. Lord Melbourne said eagerly, " I think you are quite right ; that's quite right." Lord Melbourne dines with me tonight, I'm happy to say. I showed him the letter I meant to write to the King of Hanover, which he quite approved of. Spoke of several people at the Ball and several other things concerning it ; of Lord Duncannon who is rather better but still very poorly; Lord Melbourne does not like his being so long ill, and suffering with so many different things; there is a disease in the sockets of his teeth which become quite loose, the teeth themselves being quite sound. Lord Melbourne said the Ponsonbys were generally strong, and lived to a great age; that the present Lord Bessborough's father lived to a very great age; Lord Melbourne said he was the man of whom the following anecdote is told :—he (*that* Lord Bessborough) was playing at cards, at Picquet, Lord Melbourne thinks, when his partner dropped down dead; and he said to the Waiter, " Remember, if the gentleman recovers, that I've got such and such a thing in my hand." . . . Spoke to him of the Coronation, and of the different people who were to bear the Swords (which he had already spoken to me of, in the morning; for he showed me then a letter from the Duke of Grafton declining to take any part in it, as he only meant to attend as a Peer). He (Ld. Melbourne) will carry the Sword of State; the Duke of Hamilton [1] he *thinks* of proposing to carry the Crown; the Duke of Somerset [2] the Orb; the Dukes of Devonshire and Sutherland the other swords; and the Duke of Roxburgh,[3] something else. But nothing is as yet settled with respect to all this. Spoke of my reading the Despatches, of which there were so many.

Saturday, 12th May.—At a ¼ p. 1 came Lord Melbourne and stayed with me till 10 m. to 2. He said he was, and seemed, much better. He first read me a Petition from the Society of British Artists, wish-

[1] Alexander, tenth Duke (1767-1852).
[2] Edward Adolphus, eleventh Duke. See *ante*, p. 68.
[3] James, sixth Duke (1816-1879).

ing me to go to their Exhibition, which however he
said was quite unnecessary. He then said they were
going to have a Cabinet upon this motion,[1] which is
to take place on Monday, and to see what can be
done upon it. Lord Melbourne then explained to
me in the clearest manner possible all about it. He
told me that :—In 1835, Sir Robert Peel found himself several times in minorities about various things
which I forget ; but he said he would not resign
until he was beat upon a Question relative to the
Irish Church ; when he brought in his Bill for Irish
Tithes, the resolution, to appropriate the surplus
for the benefit of Moral Education, was carried against
him by 37,—and he resigned ; well, the present
Government came in, and Lord Melbourne said,
found this resolution an awkward one, and that there
was less surplus than they had imagined ; they
however brought forward several Acts, and also
awkward ones, Lord Melbourne said, which were
each year rejected by the House of Lords. Well,
this year the following Bill was brought in (which
Lord Melbourne thinks a very good one, as do I,
but which he hears will meet with a great deal of
opposition), which is, leaving out the Appropriation
Clause, and doing away with the surplus, but proposing to pay the Irish Church out of the funds of
the Empire, which is separating the Irish Church
from the Land, and keeping it up, *not* for the people,
as they are almost all Catholics, but for the Protestant feeling in the country. Now, Lord Melbourne
says, the *Church* don't like it, as they think it's
making the Church Stipendiary and is separating it
too much from the Land, and the *violent democrats*
dislike it as they think it is giving the Church too

[1] To rescind the Irish Church resolution of 1835.

much support. Lord Melbourne observes that the opposition will be so considerable from these two Parties that he thinks it will hardly be possible for *us* to carry this measure. *Now,* it is upon this measure being proposed on Monday that this Motion or amendment is to be made : " to rescind the resolution of '35 " ; " that is," as Lord Melbourne said, " to do away with it, to scratch it out of the Journals." Lord Melbourne said that if this *should* be carried against us, it will be almost fatal to the Government ; he added that it is one of those awkward sort of questions in Politics, which it is very difficult to get over, and at the same time hardly possible to resign upon ; " it is not good ground to resign upon," he said, " it would not be understood by the people, they would not sympathise with you." He continued—but that *Lord John* might consider his honour at stake, and might resign upon it, which Lord Melbourne said he almost thought he would, but that he would hear that at the Cabinet today. He added, " If we have a Majority, why then it's all well." I observed that Lord John seemed to think that likely. Lord Melbourne said he certainly thought we should ; but from the nature of the House it made it " ticklish " and " nervous " ; which, God knows ! it does. He says the Irish Poor Law Bill will not meet with much opposition in the House of Lords, except from the Irish Peers ; Lord Londonderry [1] means to oppose it very violently. Sir Robert Peel has a great dinner today, given to him by his followers. Lord Melbourne said he would let me know what took place

[1] Charles William, third Marquess, half-brother of the eminent statesman, better remembered as Lord Castlereagh. Lord Londonderry was a soldier and diplomatist.

at the Cabinet; and if there was anything very particular he would come himself. He dines at the Speaker's tonight. I cannot say (though I feel *confident* of OUR *success*) HOW *low*, HOW *sad* I feel, when I think of the POSSIBILITY of this excellent and truly kind man (Lord Melbourne) not *remaining* my Minister! Yet I trust fervently that *He* who has so wonderfully protected me through such manifold difficulties will not *now* desert me! I should have liked to have expressed to Lord Melbourne my anxiety, but the tears were nearer than words throughout the time I saw him, and I felt I should have choked, had I attempted to say anything.

Sunday, 13*th May*.—In speaking of the singing of birds, which Lord Melbourne said he never could make out one from another, he said, " I never can admire the singing of birds; there's no melody in it; it's so shrill; that's all humbug; it's mere Poetry; it is not pretty." This made us laugh; ʃhe likes the Blackbird's singing best. He said that people say there is no difference between the song of a ground-lark and the nightingale. I observed that Lord Holland said there was. " Oh ! " he said, " I don't think Lord Holland knows anything about it." " It's very odd," he continued, " Mr. Fox, and Lord Holland the same, like the singing of birds, and can't bear music, nor the Human Voice." . . .

Tuesday, 15*th May*.— . . . Heard from Lord John " that he yesterday brought forward the question of Irish Tithes in a speech of two hours, in which he endeavoured to review the whole subject. Sir Thomas Acland then moved to rescind the resolution of 1835. He spoke temperately and well. Lord Stanley made a short speech professing a desire to settle the Question; Lord Morpeth finished the debate for the night with a very vigorous and very effective speech. The division will probably take place tonight, and may be rather early." Lord Melbourne told me yesterday that he thought Sir Robert Peel's speech at the dinner on Saturday very moderate; but that the whole thing seemed to have been " rather flat." . . . Lord Melbourne said he did not know what the Council (today) was to be about; I said neither did I know, but that it was Lord Glenelg who wished for it. " They always run everything so very late in that Colonial Office," he said; that they never thought *when* they would want a Council, and when they did, they said they wanted it immediately, and always upon the most inconvenient days; that to-day was a most inconvenient day for the Members of the House of Commons. . . . Lord Melbourne said that Lord Munster had been to see him this morning, about their (the Fitzclarences') Pensions, on the Civil List, which there was some fear the Committee might make some difficulty about, which Lord Melbourne said would be very hard; Lord Munster came to show Lord Melbourne the letter he meant to write (to Mr. Rice, I think) about it. This pension was granted them by George IV. Lord Munster told Lord Melbourne that the late King always imagined that Lord Egremont [1] would leave Lord Munster a great deal; and whenever he gave Lord Munster anything, he used to write to Lord Egremont to tell him he had done so, which Lord Egremont did not at all

[1] George O'Brien, third Earl of Egremont, died unmarried in November 1837, aged eighty-six. Lady Munster was his illegitimate daughter, but his estates in Sussex and Cumberland were devised to other adopted heirs.

I—22*

like and said, " This is a scheme from the beginning," meaning that the King promoted the match on account of the money. Lord Melbourne said, " Lord Egremont was a very good man but rather suspicious " ; from always having had a very large fortune he fancied people wanted to get it from him. He gave Lord Munster £5,000 about a fortnight before he died. Spoke of this new Election Committee Bill which Sir Robert Peel asked for leave to bring in. He proposes that at the beginning of each session the Speaker should name 6 or 4 Members who should then choose the Committees to try the Elections. Formerly, as Lord Melbourne told me once before, the Elections used to be tried by the whole House, and it was considered such a mark of want of confidence in the Ministers if their Member was unseated, that Sir Robert Walpole resigned when the Member for Chippenham was unseated. When this became " too flagrant " Lord Melbourne said, George Grenville, great-grandfather to the present Duke of Buckingham, made what is called " the Grenville Act," which is as they are tried now ; viz. the Speaker draws 40 names from glasses, with which Lists the different parties retire and strike off names from each list until they get it down to 15 ; and that's the Committee. Now this, Lord Melbourne said, is found to be partial,[1] and a new mode must be devised.

Lord Melbourne said Lord Redesdale [2] brought

[1] An extreme instance of this partiality is described in Warren's *Ten Thousand a Year*. In 1868 the jurisdiction to decide disputed elections was transferred to the Court of Common Pleas.

[2] John Thomas, first and only Earl of Redesdale (1805–86), Chairman of Committees in the House of Lords, 1851–86. Lord Redesdale was one of the last men in England who wore habitu..lly in the daytime the old-fashioned " tail-coat."

*Don Ferdinand —
Prince of Portugal.
from recollection.
Kens: Palace.
April. 1836.*

H.S.H. PRINCE FERDINAND OF SAXE-COBURG,

AFTERWARDS KING CONSORT OF PORTUGAL.

From a sketch by Princess Victoria

him the Duke of Wellington's letter yesterday. Lord Melbourne had seen Lord John this morning, who thinks we shall only have a majority of 11 to-night, and that Mr. Hobhouse said we should have more in order to delude us into security.

Wednesday, 16th May.—Got up at 10 and heard from Lord John that on a Division *we* had a majority of 19, which he said was more than he expected. How thankful I am and feel! Lord Melbourne said he heard that Ferdinand was annoyed at our pressing the Portuguese Government about the Slave Trade; and that it would be well, if I were to state to Ferdinand that the feeling was so strong in this country about Slavery, and we were so pressed about it, that it was impossible for us to do otherwise. I spoke to Lord Melbourne of these Resolutions relative to the Irish Tithe Bill, which I thought excellent, but which he said a very great number of people were against. I observed that Lord John had told me at Windsor that he thought we should not carry it, but that it might be compromised. Lord Melbourne then again repeated that the Established Church was *generally* kept up for the Poor, as the rich could afford that themselves; whereas in Ireland, 700,000 are Roman Catholics, and the Established Church is *only* kept up for the Protestant feeling in the United Kingdom, and not for the Poor who are almost all Roman Catholics. I then asked about who should stand Sponsor in my place at the Christening of Col. and Lady Catharine Buckley's [1] little boy, who is to be christened down in the New Forest where they lived. I said the child was to be called *Victor*, which I

---

[1] Lady Catharine was daughter of the third Earl of Radnor, and Victor was her fifth son. See *ante*, p. 219.

thought an ugly name; he did not, and said laughing that " Sir Victor Buckley " would sound very well. . . .

Friday, 18th May.—We spoke of various things ; I asked him if he liked my headdress which was done in plaits round my ears,[1] for I know *in general* he only likes the hair in front crêpé in 2 puffs. He said, looking at me and making one of his funny faces, " It's pretty ; isn't it rather curious—something new ? "

Saturday, 19th May.—At a little after 2 I rode out with Mamma, Lord Uxbridge, Lord Torrington, Lady Forbes, dearest Lehzen, Lord Alfred, Miss Dillon, Mr. Murray, Lord Headfort, Lady Flora, Miss Quentin, and Col. Cavendish, and came home at 6 m. to 5. I rode dear little Uxbridge who went *perfectly.* We met Lord Melbourne in going out, who was riding his pony. We rode out by the Harrow Road and home by the Uxbridge Road and Park. Heard from Lord John that " he yesterday stated to the House of Commons the course respecting the Irish Bills, which he had the honour to explain to Your Majesty yesterday. Sir Robert Peel asked for a delay till Friday, and appeared much agitated ; but what afterwards fell from him gives every reason to suppose that the Municipal Corporations Bill will not be opposed. Nor is it probable that the Irish Tithe Bill will meet with resistance from the Radical party in the House of Commons. The Chancellor of the Exchequer made a very clear financial statement, and the deficiency of the Revenue being before known, no disappointment was caused by the announcement. Should matters proceed smoothly

---

[1] There is a portrait of the Queen by John Partridge in King George's room at Buckingham Palace showing the hair done in this fashion.

another fortnight will end the chief party questions in the House of Commons." This was *delightful* news. . . . "Very nice party" (my Concert), Lord M. said, "and everybody very much pleased." I smiled and said I feared I had done it very ill; that I was quite angry with myself and thought I had done it so ill; and was not civil enough. He said most kindly, "Oh! no, quite the contrary, for I should have told you if it had been otherwise." I then said I had felt so nervous and shy. "That wasn't at all observed," he said. I said that I often stood before a person not knowing what to say; and Lord Melbourne said that the longer one stood thinking the worse it was; and he really thought the best thing to do was to say anything commonplace and foolish, better than to say nothing.

Sunday, 20th May.—Lord Melbourne was in delightful spirits and *so* talkative and *so* kind and so VERY AGREEABLE throughout the evening. I almost fear therefore (in consequence of our having talked so much) that I may have forgotten some of the things we talked about. I asked him if he had dined at Lord Shrewsbury's the night before; he said no, that it was all a mistake; he went there, was shown upstairs, where he found Lord Shrewsbury alone with his books and papers, who said that all his family were gone to the Opera; Lord Melbourne said, "I came to dine here"; upon which Lord S. told him that it was *next* Saturday; Lord Melbourne said it was very stupid of himself to forget it, as Lord Shrewsbury had put off the dinner on account of him. He walked home, found his people at home, got his dinner in ½ an hour, and went to his sister's. Spoke of the Preachers being so badly appointed at the Chapel Royal, which Lord Melbourne said was

a great pity, as it would have been such " an instrument of good " if it had been the contrary. We
looked at some prints, and amongst others there was
a very clever one of Capt. Macheath with Polly and
Lucy in *The Beggar's Opera* ; Lord Melbourne said
that *The Beggar's Opera* was written by Gay, and
was used by the Tory Party in order to show up
Lord Townshend [1] and Sir Robert Walpole ; was
very clever, and had an immense run ; but is coarse
beyond conception ; it was likewise performed with
great success when Lord Sandwich brought forward
an indictment against Mr. Wilkes for immorality.
Of Lord Teynham [2] wanting to have a Private
Audience of me, which Lord Melbourne stopped ;
he said Peers are only allowed to have these Private
Audiences to speak on Public Affairs, and not on
Private concerns ; that when the Regent wanted to
prevent Lady Jersey going so often to see Princess
Charlotte, Lord Jersey asked for a Private audience ;
and the Regent said to him, " Of course you come
to speak of Public matters, for if you come to speak
about your wife, I cannot speak to you," and he
spoke to him upon ordinary matters and dismissed
him. Talleyrand is dead—at last !

Monday, 21st May.—Spoke of Talleyrand's death,
which Lord Melbourne said he heard was quite like
that of the former French Ministers—like Mazarin—
the house full of people to see him die. He (Ld.
Melbourne) said he had heard that Louis Philippe

[1] Charles, second Viscount Townshend, K.G., married Dorothy,
sister of Sir Robert Walpole. Townshend was President of the Council 1720, and afterwards Secretary of State. There was jealousy
between the brothers-in-law, and Horace Walpole sarcastically observed that things went well or ill according as the style of the firm
was *Townshend and Walpole* or *Walpole and Townshend*.

[2] Henry Francis, fourteenth Baron Teynham (1768–1842).

and Mme. Adelaide had been to see Talleyrand.
Spoke of his fear of dying, which Lord Melbourne
said people always said of persons whose feelings on
religion were rather loose.　Lord Melbourne said he
heard that Talleyrand had signed a sort of recan-
tation to the Pope, for something he had done, at
the time of the Revolution—for having performed
Mass upon some occasion or other.[1] . . .

Thursday, 24th May.—I this day enter my 20th
year, which I think *very* old !(In looking back on
the past year, I feel more grateful than I can express
for ALL the VERY GREAT BLESSINGS I have received
since my last birthday.) I have only ONE VERY dear
affectionate friend less—dearest Louis !　Oh ! if she
could but be still with us ! ! Though I have *lost*
a *dear* friend, I can never be *thankful* enough for
the *true, faithful, honest, kind* one I've GAINED since
last year, which is my *excellent* Lord Melbourne, who
is so kind and good to me ! ! . . . At 25 m. p. 10
I went with the whole Royal Family into the other
Ball-room through the Saloon which was full of
people ; after speaking to a good many I went to
my seat (without sitting down) and then opened the
Ball in a Quadrille with George.[2]　There were about
the same number of people there as at the 1st Ball,
and a great number of Foreigners there.　My good
Lord Melbourne came up to me after my 1st Quadrille, but only stopped one minute, and though I
saw him looking on at 3 of the Quadrilles I danced
afterwards, he never came near me again, which I
was very sorry for ; and when I sent for him after
supper, he was gone. . . . After supper I danced 4

[1] At the festival of the 14th July, 1790, held in the Champ de Mars
he officiated at the altar.　It was his last celebration of the Mass.

[2] Prince George of Cambridge.

Quadrilles in Strauss's room; he was playing most beautifully. I danced with Lord George Paget,[1] Lord Cantelupe,[2] Lord Milton,[3] and Lord Leveson. Count Eugene Zichy (cousin to Countess Zichy's husband) wore a most beautiful uniform all covered with splendid turquoises; he is a handsome man, with a very good-natured expression, as he is too, very unaffected and good-humoured, and a beautiful valzer. We then went into the other room, and danced a regular old English Country Dance of 72 couple, which lasted 1 hour, from 3 till 4! I danced with Lord Uxbridge, Lord Cantelupe and Lady Cowper being next, and the Duke of Devonshire and Lady Lothian[4] on the other side. It was the merriest, most delightful thing possible. I left the Ball room at 10 m. p. 4, and was in bed at 5—broad daylight. It was a *delightful* Ball, and the pleasantest birthday I've spent for *many* years! . . .

Monday, 28th May.—Spoke of writing to George of Hanover,[5] which he said I should do; and also to the King of Hanover for his birthday; spoke of

---

[1] Sixth son of Lord Anglesey. He was second in command, to Lord Cardigan, of the Light Cavalry Brigade in the Crimea; he subsequently became Inspector of Cavalry, and later M.P. for Beaumaris.

[2] Eldest son of the fifth Earl de la Warr. See *ante*, p. 60.

[3] Afterwards sixth Earl Fitzwilliam, K.G., and A.D.C. to the Queen.

[4] She was younger daughter of the second Earl Talbot, and wife of the seventh Marquess of Lothian.

[5] Prince George, born 1819, succeeded his father on the throne of Hanover in 1851. He ultimately suffered from total blindness, caused by swinging a bunch of keys attached to a chain, that struck accidentally one of his eyes. He sided with Austria in 1866 against Prussia, and after Sadowa his kingdom was annexed to Prussia by decree. King George was a Knight of the Garter and Duke of Cumberland. He was a Prince of amiable disposition and simple manners. At his death he was succeeded in the dukedom by his eldest son, who married the younger sister of Queen Alexandra.

the report of poor George's marrying a Russian
Princess. He then continued saying it would raise
a curious question, " his marrying a Greek " (of
the Greek religion it is); for he believed that *only*
marrying *Roman Catholics* was forbidden by *law*
here (George being in the succession here). I said
I thought it was said, *all* who were not of the *Reformed Religion*, without naming specifically (Greek,
he says, he supposes is included under Roman
Catholics) *Roman Catholic*. Lord Melbourne said I
might be right, for that he had not looked at the
Act for some time. He said he believed also that
George could not marry without my leave.[1]

Tuesday, 29th May.—I told him that Lord Glenelg
had made me a present of a Black Swan; Lord
Melbourne said that a *Black Swan* was *not* a Swan;
" It's a Goose." Lady Mulgrave said the Ancients
had Black Swans, and to prove it began quoting the
lines from the Latin Grammar, which Lord Melbourne
then repeated, and which I used to learn : " Rara
avis in terris, nigroque simillima cygno." Lord
Melbourne said, *that* meant to describe something
very rare, and which *did not exist*. I said to Lord
Melbourne I was very glad to hear that he would
come down to Windsor for the Eton Montem. He
said, " It's quite right to go, but I don't think
it's a very pleasant thing, the Montem ; rather
foolish "; and we spoke of the Regatta on the 4th
of June, to which I'm not going. " The Regatta
as you call it," he said to Lady Mulgrave ; " The
Boats " it used always to be called. *That* is in
fact done *without* the consent of the Masters, and
all the boys were generally flogged next day. Lord

---

[1] According to the Royal Marriages Act, none of the Royal Family
can marry without the Sovereign's consent. See *post*, p. 390.

Melbourne has not been to a Montem since 1809. In speaking of the head Colleger who generally is made the Captain, he said he was usually a big boy about 19; "More foolish than a boy," Lord Melbourne said laughing; and that the expenses were generally so great, and the boy so extravagant for some time before, that he seldom *cleared* anything. I said the Montem generally ended in the boys' being sick and drunk; Lord Melbourne said in his funny manner, he thought in these days of education, no boys ever got drunk or sick—which I fear is *not* the case. He said all this eating and drinking, "all the chocolate and tea and coffee" for breakfast, had got up since his time; that when he was at Eton, they used to cut a roll in half and put a pat of butter inside it and give it to you, and that you then might drink a glass of milk and water (for breakfast); "I never could take milk, and therefore I always took water," he said, "and we did very well"; much better he thinks than they do now. He said that he remembered people always gave children what they disliked most; he used (before he went to school) to have *every* day boiled mutton and rice pudding, which he hated; "Children's stomachs are rather squeamish," he said; and boiled mutton is particularly nauseous to a child, he observed; and he hated rice pudding. "Somehow or other,'" he said, "they found out you disliked it, and there it was every day"; this, he thinks (and everybody else almost, I think, ought to do so), a bad system. He added, "Children's stomachs are rather delicate and *queasy*"; which made us all laugh.

Thursday, 31st May.—He said that Lord Mulgrave was very anxious about being made a Marquis at

the Coronation, and that he supposed it must be
done, but that it would offend other Earls ; he added
that there was great difficulty about making these
Peers,—but that he must soon lay the list before
me. " I shall advise Your Majesty to make as few
as possible," he added. It would not do, he said,
to make any Members of the House of Commons
Peers, on account of vacating their seats. Lord
Dundas wishes to be made an Earl, he says, which
he supposes should be granted ; and Lord Barham
wishes to be made Earl of Gainsborough.[1] William IV. made 16 Peers and 24 Baronets at his
Coronation ; and George IV. 15 Peers ; " he was so
clogged with promises," Lord Melbourne said, " he
had made such heaps of promises."

[1] Lord Mulgrave and Lord Dundas were created respectively
Marquis of Normanby and Earl of Zetland, but Lord Barham was
not made Earl of Gainsborough till 1841.

INTRODUCTORY NOTE TO CHAPTER X

THE three summer months of 1838 were eventful in the life of the young Queen. It is not only that she attended an Eton Montem (that quaint ceremony so graphically described in *Coningsby* by one who was in future years to be her Prime Minister), and not only that she held her first Review in Hyde Park (which was somewhat of a disappointment to her owing to Lord Melbourne having dissuaded her from riding on horse-back), but on the 28th June she was crowned in Westminster Abbey. There have been many accounts from eye-witnesses of the Coronation of British Sovereigns. Volumes have been written on the subject from the earliest times. Even the immortal pen of Shakespeare has touched upon this great ceremonial. Queen Victoria's description, however, is unique in this, that the writer is the Sovereign herself, and that the Coronation is painted from the point of view of the central figure in the picture. Owing to the extreme youth of the Queen, her childlike appearance, her fairness and fragility, and the romance attaching to her sex, owing also to her dignity, simplicity, and composure amid that vast concourse in the setting of the great Abbey, surrounded as she was by every circumstance of pomp and splendour, and overweighted, as it seemed, by the tremendous and glittering responsibility of St. Edward's Crown, the ceremony appeared to onlookers extraordinarily moving. The Queen noticed that Lord Melbourne was deeply stirred. He was one of the many who were in tears.

To the thousands who saw her on this occasion for the first time and to the millions who read the story of the Coronation, the 28th June, 1838, appeared to be the opening day of Queen Victoria's reign. Who, among those present in the Abbey or in the streets of the metropolis, could foresee what her reign was to bring forth, and who could measure with any degree of accuracy the progress of the country she was about to rule, or the growth of the Empire over which she was destined to preside, between the day when the Crown was placed upon her head, and the day when it was borne away by her sorrowing servants from the Mausoleum at Frogmore sixty-three years afterwards?

"The guns are just announcing," wrote Queen Adelaide to her niece, "your approach to the Abbey, and as I am not near you, and cannot take part in the sacred ceremony of your Coronation, I must address you in writing to assure you that my thoughts and my whole heart are with you, and my prayers are offered up to heaven for your happiness and the prosperity and glory of your reign." The answer to this prayer for the young Queen is to be found in the story of her reign, and it is written large in golden letters across the face of her Empire.

CHAPTER X

1838 (*continued*)

Friday, 1st June.—I also told Lord Melbourne that I quite approved of what he had written to me (also in the afternoon) about the Homage at the Coronation; namely, that the Peers should *kiss my hand*; Lord Melbourne smiled when I said this. Lord Melbourne had left Lady Holland in a great fright, fearing there would be a thunderstorm, of which she is dreadfully afraid. We spoke of thunderstorms, of people being afraid of them, of there being always a certain degree of danger; of the danger of standing under a tree. I told Lord Melbourne I never could forgive him for having stood under a tree in that violent thunderstorm at Windsor last year; he said, " It's a hundred to one that you're not struck," and then added smiling : " It's a sublime death." Spoke . . . of Lord Durham for some time, of whose arrival we think we must soon hear. Lord Melbourne said, " I'll bet you he'll go by Bermuda," which would be a good deal out of his way; I asked Lord Melbourne what could make Lord Durham wish to go there. He replied, " I'm sure I don't know why he's got it into his head, but I'll bet you he'll go there." Spoke of my fear that Lord Melbourne was right in what he said about Lady Mary Lambton's[1] great regret at leaving England, the other day;

---

[1] Afterwards wife of the eighth Earl of Elgin, Viceroy of India.

namely, her being attached to John Ponsonby,[1] which we think seems likely, as he (J. Ponsonby) is the ONLY person to whom Lady Mary has written since she left England. Spoke of Epsom, and Lord Melbourne said there was scarcely ever " a Derby without somebody killing himself ; generally somebody kills himself ; it is not perfect without that," he said laughing. Spoke of *Don Giovanni*, and the Statue having laughed so much the other night (about which Lablache told him he was so distressed), and Lord Melbourne said the *original* Piece and Music was very old ; and on my observing that I thought *this* music by Mozart old-fashioned, he clasped his hands and looked up in astonishment. . . .

Sunday, 3rd June.—We spoke of Music ; of Lord Melbourne's going to sleep when Thomas Moore was singing, which he would hardly allow. Lord Melbourne quoted some lines to prove that Lydian music used to put people to sleep ; and of Phrygian music, which made people fight. I showed Lord Melbourne the 1st number of a work called, *Portraits of the Female Aristocracy.* Then he, and also I, looked at a new Work called *Sketches of the ;People and Country of the Island of Zealand,* which are very well done. Lord Melbourne said, in opening it, " These are a fine race, but they eat men, and they say it's almost impossible to break them of it." He farther added, " There are no *animals* whatever there, and therefore they are obliged to eat men." Lady Mulgrave observed that she thought they only eat their enemies ; Lord Melbourne said, " I fancy they eat them pretty promiscuously." Lord Melbourne was in excellent spirits, and very funny in his remarks about the different drawings ; it's always

[1] Son of Lord Duncannon, and grandson of the Earl of Bessborough.

my delight to make him look at these sorts of things,
as his remarks are always so clever and funny.   He
again said that it was so difficult to break them (the
New Zealanders) of eating men ; " for they say it's
the very best thing," which made us laugh.   He
added, " There was an old woman who was sick,
and they asked her what she would like to have ;
and she said, ' I think I could eat a little piece of
the small bone of a boy's head,' " and he pointed
laughing to his own head, explaining *what* part of
the head that small bone was. . . . Lord Melbourne
went on speaking of New Zealand, &c., and said,
" The English eat up everything wherever they go ;
they exterminate everything " ; and Lady Mulgrave
and Mr. Murray [1] also said that wherever the English
went, they always would have everything their own
way, and never would accommodate themselves to
other countries.   " A person in a public situation
should write as few private letters as possible " . . . .

Monday, 4th June.—Spoke of the Eton Montem,
and I told Lord Melbourne I was going to the Provost's house, which he said he was very glad of.
There were two Montems while he was at Eton ; he
said no one knows the origin of the Eton Montem.
Formerly there used to be, he said, a Mock Sermon
at Salt Hill ; a boy dressed like a clergyman and
another like a clerk delivered a sort of sermon, and
in the middle of it the other boys kicked them
down the hill ; George III. put a stop to it, as he
thought it very improper.   We spoke of the Montem,
and of giving money, and Lord Melbourne said he
thought he should give £20.   I asked Lord Melbourne what he did when Lady Holland goes down
to Brocket.   " Oh ! I give up the whole house to

[1] Hon. Charles Augustus Murray. See Vol. II., p. 94.

her," he replied.   And he says she twists everything
about ; not only in her own room but in other rooms
downstairs.   Then she swears she has too much
light, and puts out all the candles ; then too little,
and sends for more candles ; then she shuts up
first one window, then another.   I showed him in
the Genealogy of *Lodge's Peerage* how Lord Barham
came to his title and how he was related to the Earl
of Gainsborough.   In looking over it, Lord Melbourne began to speak of Sir Charles Midleton, First
Lord of the Admiralty, made 1st Lord Barham, and
maternal grandfather to Lord Barham.   He said he
was a most distinguished and clever man.   He told
me, with the tears in his eyes, an anecdote of what
he (Sir C. Midleton) did at the time of the Mutiny.[1]
He was very much for those people and said, " I
used always to think those poor fellows very hardly
treated " ; but when he heard of the Mutiny, he
ordered two 74-gun ships to be put broadside of the
ship in which the Mutineers were, and desire her to
surrender, and if she did not, to send her to the
bottom.   So they said to him, " But if the men should
disobey ? "   " Why, then we shall be in a scrape ;
but give your orders steadily and they won't disobey."   " That was very fine," said Lord Melbourne.
Spoke of clothes, about which Lord Melbourne was
very funny ; said the fewer you had the better, and
that he was certain it was very bad to keep things
in *store*, at which we laughed much, and said it
would be impossible for ladies to keep dresses in
store, as the fashions always changed ; and he was
against keeping furs, as he said " The moth doth
corrupt."   Spoke of Miss Chaworth, Byron's first
admiration, about whom Lord Melbourne told a

[1] *I.e.*, Mutiny at the Nore, May 1797.

story on Sunday, which I did not quite understand, and I begged him to repeat it which he did. It was as follows:—Miss Chaworth was told that she would like Lord Byron very much (she *did* admire him) and would in fact marry him. She said, No, she never would; for that if ever she married, it should be a man with two straight legs (Byron having one leg and foot quite deformed[1] from his birth, which made him limp very much); this was told to Byron, whom it shocked most exceedingly, as he was extremely unhappy and conscious of his lameness, and made him quite indignant. He went to her, made her copy a piece of music for him (they had been in the habit of singing together) in order to have a remembrance of her, took it, left the house, and never saw her again. Lord Melbourne told me there was an awkwardness between the two families; as in George II.'s reign Miss Chaworth's ancestor was killed in a duel by a Lord Byron; they quarrelled at a Club, went upstairs, fought and Chaworth was killed[2]; Lord Melbourne said it was always suspected that he had been killed unfairly, as Chaworth was known to be the best fencer there was, and it was thought that Byron passed his sword through him before they fought. Miss Chaworth married afterwards a Mr. Musters and was very unhappy; lived on bad terms with her husband, and at last died deranged. Lord Melbourne said he saw her once,

---

[1] This is now proved not to have been the case. He suffered from infantile paralysis of one leg which was badly treated and developed into permanent lameness. Miss Chaworth's words, which were either overheard by or repeated to Byron, were," Do you think I could care anything for that lame boy ? " He did see her on more than one occasion in later years.

[2] Her grand-uncle was killed as described by William, fifth Lord Byron, in 1765.

I—23*

he went over to her place, Annesley, when he was staying in Nottinghamshire in 1813, and stayed there two days. She was then living on very bad terms with her husband, and everything was in a very uncomfortable state ; but she was very kind to Lord Melbourne. (I asked Lord Melbourne where Lord Byron made the acquaintance of his cousin, Miss Milbanke, now the Dowager Lady Byron; he said at his house, at Whitehall, where Byron used to come.) Spoke of Irish and Italian servants, who Lord Melbourne says are very uncertain and not to be trusted. I asked Lord Melbourne if he had good servants ; he said, " Not very " ; he added, " I'm told that great drunkenness prevails in my house," but that *he* never saw it, and as long as that was the case, he could not much complain ; he, *of course*, can't look after them. The man he always takes about with him, when he comes here, he says is a very steady, exact man, and always ready ; he has risen from being a steward's boy in his house. He told me that he has but few servants ; a butler, this man, an under butler, and one footman ; that's all. He's likewise told that his expenses in comparison to other people's are very great ; that the profuseness in his country house was beyond everything, people told him ; *he* does *not* think the expense very great, in fact he says it *cannot* be, as he is so little at home.

Tuesday, 5th June.—At a ¼ to 11 we got into our carriages for Montem. Mamma and Lady Mulgrave were with me ; Lord Melbourne, Miss Paget, Lord Albemarle and Lady Flora were in the next carriage to mine ; then Lady Theresa, Miss Dillon, Lord Conyngham, and Miss Davys ; and lastly Lord Lilford, Mr. Murray, Colonel Wemyss and Col. Cavendish. These carriages *preceded* us in going to

Eton.   We were stopped on the Bridge for " Salt."
When we reached Eton College we were received
there by the Provost,[1] Dr. Hawtrey,[2] and the other
Fellows ; we went under the Cloisters and saw all
the boys march by, 3 times, which is a pretty sight ;
some of the boys were beautifully dressed.   We then
all went up to one of the rooms in the Provost's
house, where we looked out of the window and saw
the flag flourished ; we then took some luncheon at
the Provost's, I sitting between the Provost and Lord
Melbourne.   The only people besides our own party
there, were, Mrs. Goodall (the Provost's wife), Lady
Braybrooke,[3] Edward of Saxe-Weimar,[4] Mr. Wood,[5]
and two nieces of the Provost's.   The room in which
we lunched is hung round with many portraits of
the young men (now mostly, if indeed not all, old)
who had been at Eton ; amongst which were Lord
Grey's, Lord Holland's, Lord Wellesley's, Mr. Canning's.[6]   Lord Melbourne's was not there, which it
ought to have been.   Lord Melbourne said he had

---

[1] Dr. Goodall.   See *ante*, p. 119.

[2] The Head Master.   See *ante*, p. 119.

[3] She was Jane, daughter of the second Marquess Cornwallis and
wife of the third Lord Braybrooke.

[4] Son of Duke Charles Bernard and Duchess Ida (a sister of Queen
Adelaide).   Prince Edward was A.D.C. to Lord Raglan in the Crimea,
and ultimately Commander of the Forces in Ireland.

[5] Charles Wood (afterwards Lord Halifax).   At this time Secretary
to the Admiralty.   See *ante*, p. 99.

[6] These portraits were among those which by custom were presented to the Headmaster of Eton by certain distinguished Etonians
on leaving school.   The gift of a portrait was usually made by re-
quest.   A boy was considered honoured by being asked to leave his
portrait to the school.   The custom lapsed about forty years since.
This collection was recently overhauled by Mr. Lionel Cust.   It is
now in fine order, carefully arranged in the Provost's Lodge at Eton.
The portraits have been engraved and collected in the form of a
sumptuous volume.

been painted by Hoppner, for Dr. Langford (his
Master, but not the *Head* Master, who was then
Dr. Heath), and had been sold at the sale of his
things when he died.[1] Lord Melbourne said that
Lord Holland had a fine countenance when young,
but always *lame*, there being some ossification in one
of his legs ; he was " very slim " when young ! !
After luncheon we got into our carriages again (the
other carriages *following* mine), and drove to Salt
Hill, where we saw the boy again flourish the flag.
The heat was *quite intense*, and the crowd *enormous* !
We got back to the Castle at 20 m. to 2.   I saw
Lord Melbourne from 7 m. to 2 till 7 m. p. 2, in my
room on my return.   He said he was not tired, and
was very anxious I should not be so.   Spoke of the
Montem, the fine boys ; he thought they looked
" very sheepish " and shy as they marched by ; and
the boy (a great big boy) who held up the bag for
" Salt," very shy, on the bridge.   Lord Melbourne
gave £10 ; and I £100.   Lord Melbourne thought
that the Provost and Mrs. Goodall, knew nobody,
for she took Lord Melbourne for Lord Ebrington.
It is 69 years, Lord Melbourne told me (the Provost
had said) since he (the Provost) walked in a Montem !
Lord Melbourne was going to dine at Lord Anglesey's.
He said he was going away directly.   He had neither
slept well.   At ½ p. 2 I left Windsor (as I came the
day before), and reached Buckingham Palace at ½
p. 4 or 20 m. to 5. . . .

Wednesday, 6th June.—I showed him the letter
from Uncle Leopold which I got yesterday, and in
which he touches upon these unhappy Affairs, wishing *me* to prevent my Government from taking the
lead in these Affairs, &c., &c. ; and saying his posi-

[1] This may be the portrait now in the Corridor at Windsor Castle.

tion is *des plus embarassantes*. Lord Melbourne
read it over with great attention, and then spoke of
it all most *kindly* and sensibly; said he did not see
how we could get out of this Territorial Arrangement; said he felt that Uncle's position was not an
agreeable one, for that he was made to do what his
people disliked and what was extremely unpopular;
" and people and countries never make allowances
for the difficulties Kings are placed in; the King is
made the Instrument of an Act which is extremely
unpopular; and all the blame will fall upon him."
All this is most true; we spoke of this, and of its
being rather hard of Uncle appealing to my feelings
of affection for him. I told him what Uncle had
said of Stockmar to Van de Weyer, and that Stockmar said he did not fear all this, and was sure that
Uncle would give way in a little time. Lord Melbourne said, " He always says that the pressure of
circumstances will make him give way, but I think
he trusts everything to that power"; which Lord
Melbourne does not think always is the case. He
was going to show the letter to Lord Palmerston.
I showed him another letter from Ferdinand in
answer to mine to him about the Slave Trade; he
seems very anxious to do what we wish, but stated
the difficulties are so great; which Lord Melbourne
said was true. . . . Before this, Lord Melbourne
said, " Immense crowd at the Montem; my servant
told me he never saw such a number of people."
Lord Melbourne was in sight of us, in coming to
London, already before Datchet. His servant also
told him that there were 72 pair of Post-horses sent
down the road yesterday, and he (Ld. M.) paid
8 guineas for going; whereas in general he only
pays 4. Spoke of the Montem; and of the boys

there ; the Collegers generally stay longer than the others ; they must stay till there is a vacancy at King's, unless they are past 19 ; he says there are much fewer little boys than there used to be ; the Provost told him " they had only 20 in the lower form." " People don't send their children as early as they used to do." We spoke of the Montem ; the deal of money said to have been collected, more than ever was known. Lord Melbourne spoke of the boy who held the bag and looked so sheepish ; of the Provost, who Lord Melbourne said was an excellent Master ; that nobody could make a lesson so pleasant to the boys ; and that he was " a beautiful scholar " and " a good-natured man." Lord Melbourne said that " A Master should have great spirits ; better spirits than all the boys." He went on saying, " It's now 42 years ago since I left Eton, and I should like very much to be put back to that time." He would not like, he said, to go through all he *had* gone through ; but to go back to that time, with his *present* experience ; " I should manage them all so much better," he said laughing. He spoke of the extreme love of contradiction children have ; of the great deal of disputing there used to be formerly in private Society. Lord Egremont used to say, that Society was not near so amusing as it used to be ; people were all so well educated, that there were no more any originals to be seen. Lord Melbourne said the love of arguing was at an amazing height when he was born ; " People used to argue till they got into a passion and swore at each other." That people always would find the other in the wrong. . . .

Sunday, 10th June.—I told Lord Melbourne that the Queen Dowager had come to me the day before, and had told me that Chambers [1] had told her that she must not pass another winter in England, and wished her to go to Madeira, which she declared was too far off ; he then named Malta, to which she assented, and asked my leave to go, and to have a frigate to go in ; about which Lord Melbourne said there could not be the slightest difficulty. I said she told me she preferred Malta, as being still in *my* dominions. . . . Lady Mulgrave began saying how much mischief the Eton boys committed after the Montem, hacking and cutting things all to pieces. Of the Montem, its origin ; the wish of some to abolish it ; the Provost's declaring he never would. The Provost, he told us, is the son of the butler of Lord Lichfield's grandfather. Spoke of Dr. Hawtrey's introducing much new learning, which the Provost disliked. Spoke of what the boys learn, and many coming away amazingly ignorant. What makes the school one, Lord Melbourne said, is that the most gentlemanly boys are sent there. Lord Melbourne told us that Talleyrand said, " La *meilleure* éducation, c'est l'éducation Publique Anglaise ; et c'est *détestable* ! " There is one Head Master and an Under Master, and eight other Masters at Eton, Lord Melbourne said. The Masters, he says, who are quite young men, often require more keeping in order and are more irregular than the boys. " *My opinion is,*" said Lord Melbourne, " that it does not much signify *what* is taught, if what's taught is *well* taught." Then he added, " People too often confound learning and knowledge with talent and abilities " ; for that the two former could not make the two latter. Lord Melbourne was sent

[1] W. F. Chambers, Physician-in-Ordinary to King William and Queen Adelaide, and afterwards to Queen Victoria and the Duchess of Kent.

to Eton at 9 years old, but had been with a clergy-man before, who taught him on quite a different principle, but very well ; made him work very hard, with a dictionary, by himself, and at Eton they construe it to you first ; " so that when I came to Eton I was infinitely superior to most of the other boys, and I could do my lessons and theirs too." That's because he *always* was cleverer than most other people. He said, " I never was so surprised as when I came there ; I did not know what to do. It was perhaps 12 o'clock, and they said that I might stay out till two. I said, ' What can I do ? Who is to stay with me now ? ' I thought it then very odd, for I had been accustomed to have 2 or 3 nursery-maids after me, not allowing me to wet my heels near the water ; and here you are let into a field alone, with a river running through it, which is 10 feet deep at the bank ; and if you make a false step you're drowned to a certainty." Then he said his father gave him a great deal of money, and he ate such a quantity of tarts, made himself so sick, though he was only there three weeks when he first went—that he was very ill when he went home, with eruptions and spots over his face. This made us laugh much. Spoke of the fighting there, and that the Masters should never allow it to go on long. " I always yielded directly," he said, " if I found the boy too much for me ; after the first round if I found I could not lick the fellow, I gave it up, and said, ' Come, this won't do, I'll go away, it's no use standing to be knocked to pieces.' " All this and a great deal more Lord Melbourne told us in the funniest, most delightful way possible ; he is *so* amusing about himself, and so clever and sensible about education.

Monday, 11th June.—At 20 m. to 2 Lord Palmerston introduced the Prince de Ligne to me, Uncle Leopold's Ambassador to me for the Coronation ; I then went into the Drawing-room where the Prince de Ligne (who is a gentlemanlike and rather young man) introduced five other Belgian gentlemen, who have accompanied him. I hear he came in the most splendid equipage, with four grey horses. At 7 m. to 2 came my good Lord Melbourne and stayed with me till 5 m. to 3. He said he was well, and we spoke of the weather. He then told me of the difficulty of replacing the Chief Baron of Ireland (Joy, of whose death he had told me last Friday), and he said it was wished, and he thought it was best, to make O'Loghlen, now Master of the Rolls, Chief Baron, and to offer the Mastership of the Rolls to O'Connell ; he said O'Connell might possibly refuse it, but that it might likewise satisfy him and his party ; on the other hand, the difficulties are, that O'Connell might not give up his *agitation*, and that " we," as Lord Melbourne says, may be attacked for it by the other party. He then asked me twice over, " Have you any particular feeling about it ? " I said none whatever, and therefore it is left to Ministers to offer it, or not, as they may think fit.[1]

Wednesday, 13th June.—I made Lady Mary Paget[2] sing after dinner which she did beautifully, two songs before the gentlemen came in, the pretty one from *The Ambassadrice*, and one by Alari ; Lady Adelaide[3] accompanying her in the last. The gentle-

---

[1] Sir Michael O'Loghlen did not, however, leave the Rolls. The new Chief Baron was Mr. Stephen Woulfe, the Irish Attorney-General.

[2] She married Lord Sandwich (see p. 191) in the following September.

[3] Lady Adelaide Paget (afterwards Lady Adelaide Cadogan). See *ante,* p. 319.

men then came in ; after this Lady Mary sang the
other song by Alari which she sang at Buckingham
Palace ; and then " Ah ! non giunge " (Lady
Adelaide accompanying her), *most beautifully*, with
all Persiani's ornaments. They, particularly Lord
Anglesey, then insisted on *my* singing ; which I did,
but literally shaking with fear and fright. I sang
" Il superbo vinctor " from *Il Giuramento*. Lord
Melbourne stood opposite me, *listening*, which really
is marvellous, considering he does not care the least
about music. Lady Mary sang a very pretty little
thing from *Beatrice* ; and I then sang " Sogno talor."
We then sat down (at a ¼ p. 10), I sitting on the sofa
with Lady Surrey, Lord Melbourne sitting near me
the whole evening, and several of the other ladies
sitting round the table. I observed to Lord Melbourne how dreadfully frightened I had been ; and
he smiled and said " I can quite understand it."
Talked of Ascot Races ; Lord Melbourne said he had
not been to Ascot Races since he left Eton, *42* years
ago ! ! The Eton boys are now not allowed to
go to Ascot, but in Lord Melbourne's days they
were much less severe than they are now. " My
brother " (Pen Lamb) " was a great man on the
Turf. I used always to go to him ; I always got
leave all the week, and used to go all the week,
and very good fun it used to be," Lord Melbourne
said.

　　Thursday, 14th June.—Spoke of Miss Pitt, and of
our fearing she was attached to her brother-in-law ;
Lord Melbourne said such a marriage could not take
place now [1] ; that the *Law* preventing it was only

---

[1] The Marriage Act of 1835 made null and void all marriages
within the prohibited degrees of consanguinity or affinity. Before
they had only been voidable.

made last year. Till then such a marriage could take place ; but was void, if any of the parties made objections to such marriage. This Bill made good all such marriages which had taken place (like the Duke of Beaufort's[1]) but prevented any others being made. Lord Melbourne said he did not know if it was right or wrong ; we spoke of it for a little while.[2] I then asked him if he thought it would be well, if, on occasions like the Races, I should wear my Star and Ribbon ; he said yes.[3] I said to him also, that, if he did not dislike it, I should be so *very* happy if he would wear the Windsor Uniform when he came down to Windsor ; he replied kindly, " I shall be very happy," and I added I hoped he would often be at Windsor.[4]

Friday, 15th June.—I told him that I had been reading in the morning in Coxe's *Life of Walpole* ; which I found very interesting, but that I had got a good deal puzzled with the South Sea Company, and the *Redeemable* and *Irredeemable* debt ; and that it was very difficult and puzzling, which he said it was, and that I should not trouble or puzzle myself with that part of the book, which is not clearly written ; and he explained to me in a few words and in his clear delightful way, like a father to his child, this difficult South Sea Scheme. We spoke of that

---

[1] In this case the two wives were *half* sisters, daughters of the Duke of Wellington's sister by different husbands.

[2] The Prince Consort was strongly in favour of legalising these marriages, and King Edward (then Prince of Wales) always voted in favour of the Bills introduced for the purpose of amending the law.

[3] This custom has now unfortunately fallen into disuse.

[4] No one has a prescriptive or *ex officio* right to wear the "Windsor uniform. ' It is an honour conferred personally by the Sovereign. Of recent Prime Ministers, this privilege has been enjoyed by Lord Salisbury, Lord Rosebery, and Mr. Balfour.

strange proposition, the Peerage Bill,[1] which is curiously told in Coxe's *Life*. " That was all a party scheme," said Lord Melbourne ; " and done with a view to cripple George II." " If that had been done," he continued, " there would be hardly any peerages left now." Lord Melbourne was speaking of how many peerages, *of that time*, were extinct ; and that there were now 20 peers in the House of Lords without heirs. I likewise told him that the Duke of Wellington had let me know that George IV. and William IV. always wore the *Order of the Bath* on that day—Waterloo Day—as also on the anniversary of the battle of Trafalgar ; and I asked Lord Melbourne if he thought I should do so, or not. He said he thought I should. I observed I did not like giving up my *Blue Ribbon, even* for one night ; but if he wished it I would do so. He said, " If you don't dislike it, I think you should do it ; it will be considered a compliment to the Army."[2] . . .

Monday, 18*th June.*—Lord Melbourne then gave me a list of the Creations and Advancements which are to take place, which are as follows :

[1] Sunderland's Ministry in 1718 introduced a measure to limit the creation of peers, the object being to prevent the Prince of Wales (when King) from swamping the Lords with his partisans. Walpole spoke and wrote vigorously against the Bill, and organised the opposition to it in anticipation of the time when it should reach the Commons. He succeeded in altering the public attitude to the Bill, and it was rejected by a large majority.

[2] After this date, that is to say, the early part of the Queen's reign, the Order of the Bath began to be somewhat neglected. It was partly owing to the creation of new Orders, such as the Star of India and the St. Michael and George. It has, however, recently been ordained by King George V. that the annual service for the Order of the Bath in Westminster Abbey shall be revived, and the banners and shields of the Knights Grand Cross be affixed to their stalls in Henry VIIth.'s chapel.

The Earl of Mulgrave	Marquis of Normanby
Lord Dundas	Earl of Zetland
The Earl of Kintore (Scotch)	Baron Kintore
The Viscount Lismore (Irish)	Baron Lismore of Shanbally Castle in the County of Tipperary
The Lord Rossmore (Irish)	Baron Rossmore of the County of Monaghan
The Lord Carew (Irish)	Baron Carew of Castle Boro in the County of Wexford
The Hon. Wm. S. C. Ponsonby	Baron de Mauley
Sir John Wrottesley, Bart.	Baron Wrottesley of Wrottesley in the County of Stafford
Charles Hanbury Tracy, Esq.	Baron Sudeley
Paul Methuen, Esq., of Corsham in the County of Wilts	Baron Methuen of Corsham.

Lord Melbourne said he wished to add two more, with my consent, namely, Lord King,[2] an Earl; and to call up Lord Carmarthen [3] to the House of Lords. I of course consented to both. Before I say another word, I must not omit to mention that I wrote a letter to Stockmar begging him to mention to Lord Melbourne my anxious wish to give him the *Blue Ribbon* (which I offered to him through Stockmar already last year, immediately upon my acces-

---

[1] See *ante*, p. 205.

[2] Sir Peter King, who became Lord Chancellor, was created Lord King of Ockham in 1725. The present baron (eighth holder of the title) had married in 1835, Ada, the only child of Lord Byron. Lord King now became Earl of Lovelace.

[3] Eldest son of the Duke of Leeds, who died in the following month.

sion, and which he refused in the most noble manner), as I said I felt I owed him so much; and he had been and was so very kind to me that it would grieve me to be giving other people honours whom I cared not about, and him nothing. Stockmar told me this morning he had shown Lord Melbourne my letter and that Lord Melbourne would speak to me on the subject. Accordingly Lord Melbourne said to me, " The Baron showed me your letter, and I feel very grateful, I am very sensible of Your Majesty's kindness "; upon which I assured him he was quite right (having previously heard from Stockmar that he would decline it); " I hope," he continued, "you don't think I've any contempt for these things, but it gives me such a command "; which is most true; "and therefore you'll allow me to decline it." [1]   I added I thought him quite right but that *I* could not do less. This is a fine noble disinterested act, and worthy of Lord Melbourne, and I honour, esteem and admire him the more for it; it only increases my fondness of him.[2] . . .

Friday, 22nd June.—At a $\frac{1}{4}$ p. 2 came Marshal Soult, Duc de Dalmatie, who was introduced by Lord Glenelg. I was very curious to see him; he is not tall, but very broad, and one leg quite crooked from having been severely wounded; his complexion is dark, and he has the appearance of great age; his features are hard, and he speaks slowly

---

[1] In 1847, when the offer was repeated, Lord Melbourne wrote to the Queen that " for a long time he had found himself much straitened in his circumstances " and that " he knows that the expense of accepting the ribbon amounts to £1,000, and there has been of late years no period at which it would not have been seriously inconvenient to him to pay down such a sum."

[2] With the exception of Lord Beaconsfield and Lord Palmerston, no Prime Minister, as such, has accepted the Garter in recent times.

and indistinctly. His eyes are piercing ; he seemed much embarrassed. I then went into the outer room, where he presented his 12 (I think) Attachés to me, amongst whom were the Marquis de Dalmatie (his son), and his son-in-law. Wrote to Aunt Louise. At 3 came Lord Melbourne, and stayed with me till 4. He asked how I was, and was sorry to hear I had so much to do. I told him I had just seen Soult, who was so much embarrassed ; which Lord Melbourne said he was also when he came to him ; and that he never would understand anything, and that he made Lord Melbourne repeat the things over 20 times. He gave me a list of the names to be made Baronets on the occasion of the Coronation ; there are 30 ; amongst whom are Mr. E. Lytton Bulwer and Mr. Micklethwait,[1] which last I must say Lord Melbourne has been most exceedingly kind about. I then begged him to add (to write down) the two following names to the list of Peers which he gave me the other day, and which he did ; Lord King to be Earl of Lovelace, and Viscount Ockham in the County of Surrey ; and the Marquis of Carmarthen to be called up by the title of Baron Osborne. . . .

Wednesday, 27th June.—At 20 m. p. 4 I went with Lady Lansdowne and Lady Barham (the Duchess of Sutherland going in her own carriage, as she feared an open one), and Lord Conyngham and Col. Wemyss to Westminster Abbey to see all the Preparations for to-morrow. The streets were full of people, and preparations of all kinds. I was received at the Abbey by Lord Melbourne, the Duke of

---

[1] Sir Sotherton Peckham-Micklethwait, of Iridge Place, Sussex. Created a baronet " for a personal service rendered to Her Majesty and the Duchess of Kent at St. Leonards in Nov. 1834." See *ante*, p. 104.

Norfolk, Sir William Woods,[1] and Sir Benjamin
Stevenson. The whole thing is beautifully and
splendidly and very conveniently done ; Lord Melbourne made me try the various thrones (that is,
two) which was very fortunate, as they were both
too low. I came home again as I went (crowds in
the streets and all *so* friendly) at 5. The preparations for Fairs, Balloons, &c. in the Parks, quite
changes all, and the encampments of the Artillery,
with all their white tents, has a very pretty effect.
I did not think Lord Melbourne looking well, though
he said he was better. I'm very glad I went to the
Abbey, as I shall now know exactly where I'm to go,
and be. The Duchess of Sutherland came to ask
for further Orders a few minutes after I had got
home, and said she had taken Lord Melbourne in
her carriage to Downing Street which is only one
step from the Abbey. He walked *to* the Abbey.
Wrote my journal. At ½ p. 7 we dined.

Thursday, 28th June !—I was awoke at four
o'clock by the guns in the Park, and could not get
much sleep afterwards on account of the noise of the
people, bands, &c., &c. Got up at 7 feeling strong
and well ; the Park presented a curious spectacle ;
crowds of people up to Constitution Hill, soldiers,
bands, &c. I dressed, having taken a little breakfast before I dressed, and a little after. At ½ p. 9
I went into the next room dressed exactly in my
House of Lords costume ; and met Uncle Ernest,
Charles and Feodore (who had come a few minutes
before into my dressing-room), Lady Lansdowne,
Lady Normanby, the Duchess of Sutherland, and
Lady Barham, all in their robes. At 10 I got into
the State Coach with the Duchess of Sutherland and

---

[1] Clarenceux King-of-Arms, afterwards Garter.

Lord Albemarle, and we began our Progress.   It was a fine day, and the crowds of people exceeded what I have ever seen ; many as there were the day I went to the City, it was nothing—nothing to the multitudes, the millions of my loyal subjects who were assembled in *every spot* to witness the Procession. Their good-humour and excessive loyalty was beyond everything, and I really cannot say *how* proud I feel to be the Queen of *such* a *Nation*.   I was alarmed at times for fear that the people would be crushed and squeezed on account of the tremendous rush and pressure.   I reached the Abbey amid deafening cheers at a little after $\frac{1}{2}$ p. 11 ; I first went into a robing-room quite close to the entrance, where I found my eight Train-bearers : Lady Caroline Lennox, Lady Adelaide Paget, Lady Mary Talbot, Lady Fanny Cowper, Lady Wilhelmina Stanhope, Lady Anne Fitzwilliam, Lady Mary Grimston, and Lady Louisa Jenkinson,—all dressed alike and beautifully, in white satin and silver tissue, with wreaths of silver corn-ears in front, and a small one of pink roses round the plait behind, and pink roses in the trimming of the dresses.   After putting on my Mantle, and the young ladies having properly got hold of it, and Lord Conyngham holding the end of it, I left the robing-room and the Procession began. The sight was splendid ; the bank of Peeresses quite beautiful, all in their robes, and the Peers on the other side.   My young Train-bearers were always near me, and helped me whenever I wanted anything.   The Bishop of Durham [1] stood on one side near me.   At the beginning of the Anthem where I've made a mark, I retired to St. Edward's Chapel, a

[1] Edward Maltby (1770–1859), Bishop of Durham, to which he had been recently translated from Chichester.

small dark place immediately behind the Altar, with my Ladies and Train-bearers ; took off my crimson robe and kirtle and put on the Supertunica of Cloth of Gold, also in the shape of a kirtle, which was put over a singular sort of little gown of linen trimmed with lace ; I also took off my circlet of diamonds, and then proceeded bare-headed into the Abbey ; I was then seated upon St. Edward's chair where the Dalmatic robe was clasped round me by the Lord Great Chamberlain. Then followed all the various things ; and last (of those things) the Crown being placed on my head ;—which was, I must own, a most beautiful impressive moment ; *all* the Peers and Peeresses put on their Coronets at the same instant. My excellent Lord Melbourne, who stood very close to me throughout the whole ceremony, was *completely* overcome at this moment, and very much affected ; he gave me *such* a kind, and I may say *fatherly* look. The shouts, which were very great, the drums, the trumpets, the firing of the guns, all at the same instant, rendered the spectacle most imposing. The Enthronization and the Homage of, 1st all the Bishops, then my Uncles, and lastly of all the Peers, in their respective order, was very fine. The Duke of Norfolk (holding for me the Sceptre with a Cross) with Lord Melbourne, stood close to me on my right, and the Duke of Richmond with the other Sceptre on my left. All my Train-bearers standing behind the Throne. Poor old Lord Rolle, who is 82 and dreadfully infirm, in attempting to ascend the steps, fell and rolled quite down, but was not the least hurt ; when he attempted to reascend them I got up and advanced to the end of the steps, in order to prevent another fall. When Lord Melbourne's turn to do Homage came,

there was loud cheering; they also cheered Lord
Grey and the Duke of Wellington; it's a pretty
ceremony; they first all touch the Crown, and then
kiss my hand. When my good Lord Melbourne
knelt down and kissed my hand, he pressed my hand
and I grasped his with all my heart, at which he
looked up with his eyes filled with tears and seemed
much touched, as he was, I observed, throughout the
whole ceremony. After the Homage was concluded
I left the Throne, took off my Crown and received
the Sacrament; I then put on my Crown again,
and re-ascended the Throne, leaning on Lord Melbourne's arm; at the commencement of the Anthem
I descended from the Throne, and went into St.
Edward's Chapel with my Ladies, Train-bearers,
and Lord Willoughby, where I took off the Dalmatic
robe, Supertunica, and put on the Purple Velvet
Kirtle and Mantle, and proceeded again to the
Throne, which I ascended leaning on Lord Melbourne's hand. There was another present at this
ceremony, in the box immediately above the Royal
Box, and who witnessed all; it was Lehzen, whose
eyes I caught when on the Throne, and we ex-
changed smiles. She and Späth, Lady John Russell
and Mr. Murray saw me leave the Palace, arrive at
the Abbey, leave the Abbey and again return to the
Palace ! ! I then again descended from the Throne,
and repaired with all the Peers bearing the Regalia,
my Ladies and Train-bearers, to St. Edward's Chapel,
as it is called; but which, as Lord Melbourne said,
was more *unlike* a Chapel than anything he had
ever seen; for, what was *called* an *Altar* was covered
with sandwiches, bottles of wine, &c. The Archbishop
came in and *ought* to have delivered the Orb to
me, but I had already got it. There we waited for

some minutes ; Lord Melbourne took a glass of wine, for he seemed completely tired ; the Procession being formed, I replaced my Crown (which I had taken off for a few minutes), took the Orb in my left hand and the Sceptre in my right, and thus *loaded* proceeded through the Abbey, which resounded with cheers, to the first Robing-room, where I found the Duchess of Gloucester, Mamma, and the Duchess of Cambridge with their ladies. And here we waited for at least an hour, with *all* my ladies and Trainbearers ; the Princesses went away about half an hour before I did ; the Archbishop had put the ring on the wrong finger, and the consequence was that I had the greatest difficulty to take it off again,—which I at last did with great pain. Lady Fanny, Lady Wilhelmina, and Lady Mary Grimston looked quite beautiful. At about ½ p. 4 I re-entered my carriage, the Crown on my head and Sceptre and Orb in my hand, and we proceeded the same way as we came—the crowds if possible having increased. The enthusiasm, affection and loyalty was really touching, and I shall ever remember this day as the *proudest* of my life. I came home at a little after 6,—really *not* feeling tired.[1]

At 8 we dined. Besides we 13, Lord Melbourne and Lord Surrey[2] dined here. Lord Melbourne came up to me and said, " I must congratulate you on this most brilliant day," and that all had

[1] The ceremonial as described by the Queen does not compare favourably with those of King Edward or King George, when hardly a mistake was made by any of those officiating. The ritual at the Coronation of King Edward was especially difficult, owing to the age and infirmities of Archbishop Temple.

[2] Lord Surrey was son and heir of the Earl Marshal, the twelfth Duke of Norfolk, whom he succeeded in 1842. He married Charlotte Sophia, daughter of the first Duke of Sutherland.

gone off *so* well. He said he was not tired, and was in high spirits. I sat between Uncle Ernest and Lord Melbourne, and Lord Melbourne between me and Feodore, whom he had led in. My kind Lord Melbourne was much affected in speaking of the whole ceremony. He asked kindly if I was tired ; said the Sword he carried (the 1st, the Sword of State) was excessively heavy. I said that the Crown hurt me a good deal. He was much amused at Uncle Ernest's being astonished at our still having the Litany [1] ; we agreed that the whole thing was a very fine sight. He thought the robes,[2] and particularly the Dalmatic, " looked remarkably well." " And you did it all so well ; excellent ! " said he with the tears in his eyes. He said he thought I looked rather pale, and " moved by all the people " when I arrived ; " and that's natural." The Archbishop's and Dean's Copes (which were remarkably handsome) were from James the 1st's time ; the very same that were worn at his Coronation, Lord Melbourne told me. Spoke of the Duc de Nemours [3] being like his father in face ; of the young ladies' (Train-bearers') dresses which he thought beautiful ; and he said he thought the Duchess of Richmond (who had ordered the make of the dresses, and had been much condemned by some of the young ladies for it) quite right. She said to him, " One thing I was determined about ; that I would have no discussion with their Mammas about it." Spoke of Talleyrand and Soult having been much struck

---

[1] The Litany was omitted at the Coronation of King Edward VII., and reintroduced at the Coronation of King George V.

[2] The robe is exhibited in the London Museum at Kensington Palace.

[3] Second son of Louis Philippe. He was offered two thrones, Belgium in 1831 and Greece in 1832, but declined both. See *ante*, p. 130.

by the ceremony of the Coronation ; of the English being far too generous *not* to be kind to Soult. Lord Melbourne went home the night before, and slept very deeply till he was woke at 6 in the morning. I said I did not sleep well. Spoke of the Illuminations and Uncle Ernest's wish to see them.

After dinner, before we sat down, we—that is, Charles, Lord Melbourne and I—spoke of the numbers of Peers at the Coronation, which Lord Melbourne said was unprecedented. I observed that there were very few Viscounts ; he said, " There are very few Viscounts " [1] ; that they were an odd sort of title, and not really English ; that they came from Vice-Comités ; that Dukes and Barons were the only *real* English titles ; that Marquises were likewise not English ; and that they made people Marquises when they did not wish to make them Dukes. Spoke of Lord Audley who came as the 1st Baron, and who Lord Melbourne said was of a very old family ; his ancestor was a Sir Something Audley [2] in the time of the Black Prince, who with Chandos gained the Battle of Poitiers. I then sat on the sofa for a little while with Lady Barham and then with Charles ; Lord Melbourne sitting near me the whole evening. Mamma and Feodore remained to see the Illuminations, and only came in later, and Mamma went away before I did. Uncle Ernest drove out to see the Illumina-

---

[1] This has been remedied by the recent custom of giving a Viscountcy to any Secretary of State who is raised to the Peerage.

[2] Nicholas, third Baron Audley by writ and tenth by tenure, fought in the wars with France 1359 and 1372. His sister Joan married Sir John Tuchet, killed at Rochelle, 1371, and her grandson succeeded to the title. On the death, in 1872, of the twenty-first Baron (son of George Edward Thicknesse Touchet, twentieth Baron, whom the Queen and Lord Melbourne were discussing), the barony fell into abeyance between his daughters.

by the ceremony of the Coronation ; of the English being far too generous *not* to be kind to Soult. Lord Melbourne went home the night before, and slept very deeply till he was woke at 6 in the morning. I said I did not sleep well. Spoke of the Illuminations and Uncle Ernest's wish to see them.

After dinner, before we sat down, we—that is, Charles, Lord Melbourne and I—spoke of the numbers of Peers at the Coronation, which Lord Melbourne said was unprecedented. I observed that there were very few Viscounts ; he said, " There are very few Viscounts "[1]; that they were an odd sort of title, and not really English ; that they came from Vice-Comités ; that Dukes and Barons were the only *real* English titles ; that Marquises were likewise not English ; and that they made people Marquises when they did not wish to make them Dukes. Spoke of Lord Audley who came as the 1st Baron, and who Lord Melbourne said was of a very old family ; his ancestor was a Sir Something Audley[2] in the time of the Black Prince, who with Chandos gained the Battle of Poitiers. I then sat on the sofa for a little while with Lady Barham and then with Charles Lord Melbourne sitting near me the whole evening. Mamma and Feodore remained to see the Illuminations, and only came in later, and Mamma went away before I did. Uncle Ernest drove out to see the Illumin-

[1] This has been remedied by the recent custom of giving a county to any Secretary of State who is raised to the Peerage.

[2] Nicholas, third Baron Audley by writ and tenth by tenure fought in the wars with France 1359 and 1372. His sister Joan married Sir John Tuchet, killed at Rochelle, 1371, and her grandson succeeded to the title. On the death, in 1872, of the twenty-first Baron (son George Edward Thicknesse Touchet, twentieth Baron, whom the Queen and Lord Melbourne were discussing), the barony fell into abeyance between his daughters.

H. S. H. Feodora
Princess of Hohenlohe-Langenburg
from a portrait by Gutekunst 1830

tions. I said to Lord Melbourne when I first sat
down, I felt a little tired on my feet; " You must
be very tired," he said. Spoke of the weight of
the robes, &c. ; the Coronets ; and he turned round
to me, and said *so* kindly, " And you did it beautifully,—every part of it, with so much taste ; it's a
thing that you can't give a person advice upon ; it
must be left to a person." To hear this, from this
kind impartial friend, gave me great and real pleasure.
Mamma and Feodore came back just after he said
this. Spoke of these Bishops' Copes, about which he
was very funny ; of the Pages, who were such a nice
set of boys and who were so handy, Lord Melbourne
said, that they kept them near them the whole time.
Little Lord Stafford [1] and Slane (Lord Mount-
charles) [2] were Pages to their fathers and looked
lovely ; Lord Paget [3] was Lord Melbourne's Page
and remarkably handy, he said. Spoke again of
the young ladies' dress about which he was very
amusing ; he waited for his carriage with Lady
Mary Talbot and Lady Wilhelmina ; he thinks Lady
Fanny does not make as much show as other girls,
which I would not allow. He set off for the Abbey
from his house at $\frac{1}{2}$ p. 8, and was there long before
anybody else ; he only got home at $\frac{1}{2}$ p. 6, and
had to go round by Kensington. He said there
was a large breakfast in the Jerusalem Chamber,
where they met *before* all began ; he said laughing
that whenever the clergy or a Dean and Chapter
had anything to do with anything, there's sure to
be plenty to eat. Spoke of my intending to go

[1] Eldest son of the Duke of Sutherland, and nine years old. He
succeeded his father as third Duke in 1861.

[2] Eldest son of Lord Conyngham, and thirteen years old. Succeeded as third Marquess in 1876, and died in 1882.

[3] Eldest son of Lord Uxbridge, seventeen years old. Died in 1880.

to bed ; he said, " You may depend upon it, **you**
are more tired than you think you are." I said I
had slept badly the night before ; he said that **was**
my mind, and that nothing kept people more awake
than any consciousness of a great event going to
take place and being agitated. He was not sure if
he was not going to the Duke of Wellington's.

Stayed in the drawing-room till 20 m. p. 11, but
remained till 12 o'clock on Mamma's balcony looking
at the fireworks in Green Park, which were quite
beautiful.

Friday, 29th June.—I told Lord M. that I had been
quarrelling with Feodore about Louis Philippe, whom
she called a Usurper, and that I told her he was not,
and that we disagreed amazingly about it ; he
smiled. That she called our William III. and Mary
Usurpers ; Lord Melbourne said it was that strong
feeling of the divine right of Kings which some
people have ; that many people would not be convinced that Louis Philippe had *not* organised that
Revolution ; but that it did not do, he said, to wish
well to the Family and not to Louis Philippe as
Feodore did ; for that the happiness of the *one*
depended on the *other.* . . .

Sunday, 8th July.—Got up at 20 m. to 10 and
breakfasted at 11. Signed. Heard from Lord Melbourne that, " He finds himself much better this
morning and will wait upon Your Majesty about
three or a little after." At ½ p. 3 came my excellent
Lord Melbourne and stayed with me till a ¼ p. 4.
He looks very thin and pulled as I think, but was in
excellent spirits and as kind as ever. He said he
felt much better today, but that his knee was still
stiff and had been very painful yesterday. It's the
same leg (the left) which was first bad, but the *foot*

was nearly well ; he wore large loose shoes and no straps to his trousers. I showed Lord Melbourne a letter from Lord Glenelg I had got about Lord Durham and a letter from Lady Durham. And Lord Melbourne showed me one from Lord Palmerston about Van de Weyer's being asked, and about the Ladies of the Ambassadors having some seat at the Balls. . . .

Monday, 9th July.—At a ¼ p. 11 I went with Mamma and the Duchess of Sutherland, Feodore, Lady Barham, Lord Conyngham, Lord Albemarle, Miss Pitt, Lady Flora, Späth, Lord Fingall, Miss Spring Rice, and Miss Davys, Lady Harriet Clive and Mr. Murray to a Review in Hyde Park, of which I subjoin an account. I could have cried almost not to have *ridden* and been in *my right* place as I ought ; but Lord Melbourne and Lord Hill thought it more prudent on account of the great crowd that I should not *this* time do so,[1] which however now they all see I might have done, and Lord Anglesey (who had the command of the day, looked so handsome, and did it beautifully and gracefully) regretted much I did not ride. I drove down the lines. All the Foreign Princes and Ambassadors were there, and the various uniforms looked very pretty. The troops never looked handsomer or did better ; and I heard their praises from all the Foreigners and particularly from Soult. There was an immense crowd and all so friendly and kind to me. . . .

Wednesday, 11th July.—Spoke of Soult, and that

---

[1] This was certainly an error of judgment on the part of Lord Melbourne. The Queen's appearance on horseback, in the uniform still to be seen in the London Museum at Kensington Palace, was extraordinarily fascinating, and added greatly to the interest of any Review at which she appeared.

Uncle Ernest said that the Duc de Nemours told him that Soult was in excellent humour here, in better humour than he had ever seen him. Lord Melbourne seemed pleased. He said he was not at all surprised at the manner in which the English received Soult; as they were always curious to see distinguished foreigners. During the War, at the Peace of Amiens when Marshal Orison [1] came over, they took the horses out of his carriage and dragged him through the streets; "and that was in the midst of war," he continued. "Many people were rather annoyed at that; but that was from mere curiosity." I spoke of Feodore, and asked him if he saw any likeness between us; he said, "I see the likeness, though not perhaps very strong." I spoke of her children and of Charles (her eldest) being her favourite, as he was so much the fondest of her. Lord Melbourne said smiling that one must not judge according to that, and to the *manner* in which children *showed* their love; "Children are great dissemblers; remember how Lear was deceived by that. They learn to be the greatest hypocrites," he said.

Thursday, 12th July.—Lord Melbourne said that they were going to have a Cabinet upon what O'Connell and Sir Robert Peel declared in the House of Commons, the day before yesterday, upon the Irish Tithes. They proposed that the sum left from the sum which was voted in 1833 for the distressed

[1] The Queen evidently did not grasp a name unfamiliar to her. The ratification of the Treaty of Amiens was sent over by Napoleon in charge of Colonel Lauriston, his A.D.C. When this officer left the house of M. Otto in London to deliver his credentials to Lord Hawkesbury, the scene occurred which the Queen here describes. The carriage was accompanied to Downing Street by a guard of honour of the Household Cavalry.

Clergy, should be employed to pay the arrears of Tithes due. I asked Lord Melbourne if he thought this a good plan ; he said it would have the effect of quieting the people, but that it was " rather a lavish way of bestowing the Public Money." In general, Lord Melbourne said, when any sum of the kind is voted for a certain class of people, many miss it who ought to get it, and many get it who ought not to get anything.

Friday, 13th July.—Lord Melbourne said Ellice had told him that they cheered Soult amazingly when he went to Eton (that day), and Ellice told him he must ask for a Holiday, which he did, upon which the Boys cheered him much more ; he shook hands with some of the Boys, and then they all wished to shake hands with him, so he shook hands with the whole school. . . .

Tuesday, 17th July.—He (Ld. M.) said that the Sutherlands had a large family ; and asked if the last was a boy or girl, at which I laughed very much, as I said he *ought* to know ; he said boys were much more expensive than girls ; there was only the girl's dress that could be expensive and perhaps Masters ; but nothing to what boys' going to school cost. I said that younger sons were always so poor, and that girls married ; he said certainly that was so, and even if girls did not marry they wanted less money. I said Feodore at one time liked having boys much better than girls, but she did not now, as she thought that boys got into more difficulties and scrapes than girls. " Men certainly get into more scrapes than girls," said Lord Melbourne ; " but there is risk in both." We spoke of other things ; and he said Lord Ebrington had come to him and spoken to him about its being reported that I had so many French things, and that the lace of the Servants' coats came from France ; which I said I knew nothing about, and I assured him I had quantities of English things, but must sometimes have French things. He said he knew quite well it was so, and that it was impossible not to have French things, if one wished to be well dressed. That it was not so much the material, but the make which we English could not do ; he said they never could make a cap or a bonnet ; and that the English women dressed so ill. . . .

Monday, 24th July.—We spoke of Sir Edmund Lyons,[1] who writes such long despatches ; and who Lord Melbourne has never seen before ; he was a Naval Officer and never employed before in the Diplomatic Service. He was the Captain who took out Otho. I then went over to the Closet, where the Prince Royal of Bavaria was introduced by Lord Palmerston and Baron Cetto. Having neither attendants nor uniform, he came in morning attire. He is not quite good-looking, but nearly so,—slim, not very tall, but very gentlemanlike and agreeable and lively. I made him sit down, and he was completely *à son aise* and consequently put *me* at ease. I showed Lord Melbourne Hayter's sketch for his great picture of the Coronation ; which Lord Melbourne liked very much, and which was very generally admired ; Lord Melbourne looked at it for some time observing upon each part ; he said that Hayter would never get it as good in the large

---

[1] Afterwards first Baron Lyons of Christchurch (1790–1858). At this time Minister Plenipotentiary at Athens. In 1853, war with Russia being imminent, he was appointed second in command of the fleet in the Mediterranean, and displayed boldness and initiative in the attack on the sea defences of Sebastopol. He became Commander-in-Chief in 1855, and, on the termination of the war, a Peer.

picture as he had got it here. I then said to Lord
Melbourne that I thought the Coronation made him
ill, and all the worry of it; he said he thought he
would have been ill without it; " It wasn't the
Coronation," he said, " it was all these Peerages ;
but I think that's subsiding a little now." I asked
if Lord Derby expected being made a Duke ; Lord
Melbourne replied, " No, I don't think he did ; I
told him at once that could not be, and that generally satisfies people." Lord Derby has a very good
claim for it, Lord Melbourne said, for the following
reasons :—George III. declared he never would make
any Dukes, and wished to reserve that Title *only*
for the Royal Family ; and he only made 2, Lord
Melbourne thinks—the Duke of Northumberland
and the Duke of Montagu [1] ; Mr. Fox told the late
Lord Derby that if he could ever make the King
waive his objections, *he* should be made a Duke ;
and *this*, Lord Melbourne said, certainly was a strong
pledge for a Whig Government ; but Lord Grey
passed him over (Ld. M. doesn't know why) and
made the Duke of Sutherland and the Duke of
Cleveland ; and Lord Derby said in his letter to
Lord Melbourne, " he did not see why the names of
Vane (D. of Cleveland), Grenville (Duke of Buckingham), and Grosvenor (Ld. Westminster), should be
preferred before him." [2] He did not mention *Gower*,
Lord Melbourne thinks from civility, but that he
feels the same respecting him. I asked *what Duke*
he wished to be ; Lord Melbourne said he supposed

[1] The dukedom of Montagu, created in 1766, become extinct at
the death of the first Duke in 1790.

[2] In later years Edward Geoffrey, fourteenth Earl of Derby, three
times Prime Minister, was reported to have refused a dukedom, on
the ground that he would not exchange his Earl's coronet, which dated
from the fifteenth century, for a set of new strawberry leaves.

Duke of Derby, which was formerly a Royal title, having belonged to the Dukes of Lancaster; he takes his title from Derby, a Hundred of Lancashire —*not* from the C°. of Derby. He thinks, Lord Melbourne continued, that he has a right to be Duke of Hamilton, through his mother, Lady Elizabeth Hamilton, who was daughter to James, 6th Duke of Hamilton, and a very handsome person; I asked who she married afterwards; Lord Melbourne replied, " It was a very awkward business; she *married* nobody; she had a great attachment for the Duke of Dorset " (father to the late), " Lord Derby parted from her, but would not divorce her, in order that she might not marry the Duke of Dorset." " The Duke of Dorset," Lord Melbourne continued, " was a very handsome and agreeable man; with a great deal of gallantry. . . . I asked Lord Melbourne what sort of person Charles Sheridan was; he said an agreeable lively young man; but rather wild. We then spoke for a long time about all the Sheridans. C. Sheridan was in the Admiralty and rose to get £300 a year; but they fancied, he said, that he was in bad health, and made him give it up. There are three sons, Brinsley, Frank (who is with Lord Normanby), and Charles; " They are, like all the Sheridans, clever but careless, and have no application," he said. They plagued Lord Melbourne constantly to give Charles a place; and Lord Melbourne offered him a Clerkship in the Audit Office; but he would not have that, and said it was less than he had had. George Anson [1] told Lord Melbourne it would be quite nonsense to give it to him, as he would never come,

[1] Lord Melbourne's private secretary. He afterwards served Prince Albert in a similar capacity. See Vol. II. p. 37.

and there would be a complaint of him the first
month. Lord Melbourne said that a person who
leaves the situation he has, must not expect to be
put in again in the same place he had. This is a
£100 a year, " which is better than nothing." I
observed that a person who does not wish to submit
to that cannot be very anxious to do much, in which
Lord Melbourne agreed. This Charles Sheridan lives
a good deal with the Chesterfields, and positively
has nothing.[1] Lord Melbourne said, " I know they'll
get ruined, and we shall have to provide for them."
" They all have £60 a year." There is one Charles
Sheridan, an excessively ugly man, who is Uncle to
all these people ; he is Brinsley Sheridan's son by
his 2nd wife ; his 1st wife was a professional singer,
a Miss Linley, whom Lord Melbourne remembers when
he was a boy ; she died in 1794 ; she was excessively handsome [2] ; " The women " (Lady Seymour)
" are very like her ; some of them," he said. Spoke
of young Brinsley Sheridan running away with his
wife ; of Lady Seymour, who, Lord Melbourne said,
" is the most *posée* of them all." " She says those
odd things," Lord Melbourne continued, " as if they
were quite natural." They (the Seymours) are
always teazing Lord Melbourne about *Titles*, and are
so vexed at their boy's having no title ; and they
never will call him anything else but the *Baby* [3] ; I
said that was foolish ; " Very foolish ; and I've told
them so," replied Lord Melbourne, " but I can't

[1] He was for a time *Attaché* to the British Embassy in Paris, and
died in 1847.

[2] A lovely portrait of her by Gainsborough is the property of Lord
Rothschild at Tring Park.

[3] Lord Seymour bore, by courtesy, the only other title of his
father, the Duke of Somerset. So there was not a third title available
for the grandson, as is the case in other families of ducal rank.

convince them." The Sheridan[1] who wrote the Dictionary was Great-Grandfather to all these; his Wife was a very clever woman, Lord Melbourne said, and wrote some very good books; " they have been a very distinguished family for a long time," he added.

Tuesday, 25th July.—At a ¼ to 4 I *rode* out with Lady Portman, Lord Uxbridge, Lord Lilford, Lord Portman, Col. Buckley, Col. Cavendish, and Miss Quentin, &c., and came home at 6. I rode *dear Tartar* who went most beautifully; it was a delightful ride; we rode to Acton, and round by East Acton home. We never rode *harder*. We cantered almost the whole way going out, but coming home we *galloped* at least for *3 miles* without *once* pulling up. We came home through the Park and in at the front entrance of the Palace. It was a charming ride. At 7 we dined. Besides we 13 (Lady Charlemont, Lord Headfort, Lady Caroline Barrington, and Wm. Cowper replacing Lord Byron, Lady Tavistock, Mrs. Campbell, and Sir H. Seton), Lord Conyngham dined here. I sat between Lord Conyngham and Lord Headfort. At a ¼ p. 8 I went to the Opera with Mamma, dear Feo, Lady Charlemont, Lady Caroline, Miss Cavendish, Lord Conyngham, Lord Headfort, Mr. Cowper, Col. Buckley, Col. Cavendish, and Lady Flora. It was *I Puritani*, and Lablache and Grisi were singing their Duo when we came in. Unfortunately poor Grisi was taken ill, quite at the end of the 1st act, and was unable consequently to sing her fine Scene in the 2nd act.

---

[1] Thomas Sheridan, actor and lecturer on elocution. Published in 1780 a General Dictionary of the English Language with a special view to teaching pronunciation. A work of phonetic rather than philological value.

Fanny Elsler danced the Chachucha (at my desire) between the 2nd and 3rd acts.

Wednesday, 26th July.—Lord Melbourne said, "Lord Duncannon tells me he thinks that marriage of Lord Shelburne's[1] is quite off." Lord Melbourne said that somebody said to him (Ld. Shelburne) how handsome Miss Elphinstone was; upon which he replied, "I don't think so; but beauty is not the thing to look to in a Wife.'" Now this may have been repeated to her, Lord Melbourne says, and of course could not please her; and the young lady may have said, Lord Melbourne continued, "Why, you don't seem to show that fondness for me you ought to have, and therefore I think we'd better break it off altogether." Lady Kerry,[2] he said, had told Lord Duncannon that she believed it was all off; I observed, *Why* then had Lord Lansdowne announced it to me, if it was not quite settled?—Lord Melbourne said, "The same thing happened to Lord Duncannon that happened to you"; Lord Lansdowne announced it to him—said it gave him great pleasure—that it was very nearly settled but they did not wish to speak of it for the present; "and two hours afterwards he got a letter from Lansdowne, saying it was not at all settled," and that he should not mention it.[3] Lord Melbourne then asked if I had got the letter he sent me, from the Duchess

---

[1] Eldest surviving son of the third Marquess of Lansdowne, and afterwards fourth Marquess. The elder brother (Lord Kerry) had died without male issue.

[2] Aunt of Lord Shelburne. She was a daughter of the fourth Earl of Bessborough.

[3] Lord Shelburne married in 1840 Lady Georgına Herbert, daughter of the eleventh Earl of Pembroke. She died in the following year. In 1843 he married the Hon. Emily Elphinstone-de-Flahaut, in her own right Baroness Nairne.

of Sutherland to him, saying her sister Lady Burlington [1] gladly accepted the situation of Lady of the Bedchamber; and Lord Melbourne said, " That may now be considered as settled " ; and that Lady Lansdowne had best be spoken to about it all; which I begged him to be kind enough to do, which he said he would. I told Lord Melbourne that Conyngham had told me that he heard from Frederic Byng, that Lord Essex [2] was so *excessively* pleased at my having called up Lady Essex (Miss Stephens, the Singer that was, and married about 2 or 3 months ago to Lord Essex) at the Ball, and having spoken to her; this touched Lord Melbourne; we both agreed she was a very nice person. [3] Wrote my journal. At a ¼ to 8 I went into the Throne room with my Ladies and Gentlemen, Feo and Mamma, where I found the Duchess of Gloucester, the Duke of Sussex, the Duke and Duchess of Cambridge, and Augusta and George. After waiting a little while we went into the green drawing-room, which looked very handsome lit up, and was full of people *all* in uniform. I subjoin an account of all the arrangements and all the people. After remaining for about five minutes in that room, talking to several people, amongst others to good Lord Melbourne, we went in to dinner, which was served in the Gallery, and looked, I must say, most brilliant and beautiful. We sat down *103*, and *might* have been more. The display of plate at one end of the room was really very handsome. I sat between Uncle Sussex and

[1] Formerly Lady Cavendish. Her husband had succeeded as second Earl of Burlington in 1834. See *ante*, p. 53. She died in 1840.

[2] George, fifth Earl of Essex (1757–1839).

[3] Ladies of unblemished character, retired from the stage, were permitted to appear at Court.

Prince Esterhazy. The music was in a small Orchestra in the Saloon, and sounded extremely well. Uncle Sussex seemed in very good spirits, and Esterhazy in high force, and full of fun, and talking so loud. I drank a glass of *stein-wein* with Lord Melbourne who sat a good way down on my left between the Duke of Devonshire and Lord Holland. After dinner we went into the Yellow drawing-room. Princesse Schwartzenberg looked very pretty but tired ; and Mme. Zavadowsky beautiful, and so sweet and placid. About 20 m. after we ladies came in, the gentlemen joined us. I spoke to almost everybody ; Lord Grey looked well[1] ; the Duke of Wellington ill but cheerful and in good spirits. I spoke for some time also with Lord Melbourne, who thought the Gallery looked very handsome, and that the whole " did very well " ; " I don't see how it could do better," he said. He admired the large diadem I had on. At about 11 came some people who (as the Gallery was full of dinner &c.) were obliged to come through the Closet, and of whom I annex a List. Lady Clanricarde I did not think looked very well ; Lady Ashley, Lady Fanny, Lady Wilhelmina, and Lady Mary Grimston looked extremely pretty. Strauss played delightfully the whole evening in the Saloon. After staying a little while in the Saloon, we went and sat down in the further drawing-room, next to the dining-room. I sat on a sofa between Princesse Schwartzenberg and Mme. Stroganoff[2] ; Lord Melbourne sitting next

---

[1] Charles, Earl Grey, the ex-Prime Minister, who rarely came to town at this period of his life, and must have been a novelty for the Queen.

[2] Count Stroganoff was the special representative of the Czar at the Coronation.

Mme. Stroganoff, and in a little while Esterhazy near him, and Furstenberg (who talked amazingly to Lord Melbourne, and made us laugh a good deal) behind him. The Duchess of Sutherland and the Duchess of Northumberland sat near Princess Schwartzenberg, and a good many of the other Ambassadors and Ambassadresses were seated near them. The Duchess of Cambridge and Mamma were opposite to us ; and all the others in different parts of the room. Several gentlemen, foreigners, came up behind the sofa to speak to me. We talked and laughed a good deal together. I stayed up till a ¼ to 1. It was a successful evening. . . .

Wednesday, 1st August.—I asked Lord Melbourne if he saw any likeness in me to the Duke of Gloucester ; he said none whatever ; for that when formerly they wished to make me angry, they always said I was like him. I asked if Lord Melbourne remembered the Duke's father ; he said he did ; that he was a very good man, but also very dull and tiresome. His two brothers were Edward, Duke of York, who died long before Lord Melbourne was born, and Henry, the Duke of Cumberland. " The Duke of Gloucester and the Duke of Cumberland always remained Whigs," Lord Melbourne said, " and never could understand the King's (George III.) change ; they said the Whigs brought their Family to this country ; they went with the King but could not understand it." Lord Melbourne said, " Whenever George IV. took offence at the church, he used to say, ' By God, my Uncle the Duke of Cumberland was right when he told me, The people you must be apprehensive of, are those black-legged gentlemen.' " I said to Lord Melbourne that Princess Sophia Matilda told me that George III. had four illnesses.

Lord Melbourne said they were not all declared illnesses. The 1st, he said, was in 1788 ; the 2nd in 1800, then in 1804, which was not exactly allowed to be so ; and the last in '10' when he never got well again ; it is said, Lord Melbourne told me, that he had been ill in the early part of his reign ; as early as 63 or 4, but no one knows exactly ; he had a very bad fever then. I observed that the Cheltenham Waters, it was said, brought it on the first time. Lord Melbourne said, so it was said, but that he did very odd things when he first went down there. . . . He used to give, Lord Melbourne said, all the orders before his being ill with perfect composure. Whenever he was going to be ill, the King heard—Lord Melbourne continued—perpetually ringing in his ears, one of Handel's oratorios ; and was constantly thinking of Octavius [1] who died, " of whom he (the King) said, ' Heaven will be no Heaven to me if my Octavius isn't there.' " But his " master delusion," as Lord Melbourne expressed it, was thinking that he was married to Lady Pembroke (Lady Elizabeth Spencer that was, and Mother to the late Lord Pembroke, and who only died 7 or 8 years ago), with whom he had been very much in love in his young days, and very near marrying. I told Lord Melbourne I remembered going to see her when she was ninety, and she was very handsome even then. Lord Melbourne then told me how very near George III. was marrying Lady Sarah Lennox,[2] sister to the late Duke of Richmond, who was excessively handsome. Lord

---

[1] His son who died, aged four years, in 1783.

[2] Lady Sarah Lennox, who was a daughter of the second Duke of Richmond, married first, Sir Thomas Charles Bunbury, secondly the Hon. George Napier. George III. was undoubtedly much attracted

Melbourne said he was only prevented from marrying her "by her levity." This was quite early in his reign. He told Lady Susan Strangways, Lord Ilchester's Aunt, "Don't you think I ought to marry a Subject? I think I ought; and that must be your friend" (meaning Lady Sarah Lennox); "and you may tell her so from me." "Then," Lord Melbourne continued, "she" (Lady Sarah) "committed every sort of folly; she entered into a flirtation with the Marquis of Lothian, rode out with him after a masquerade quite early in the morning; this was represented to the King, and *détournée*'d His Majesty a little," said Lord Melbourne laughing. Nothing could equal the beauty of the Women at that time, said Lord Melbourne, from all the accounts he heard, the Duchess of Argyll and Lady Coventry, sisters,[1] &c. . . .

Sunday, 5th August.—Spoke of Lord Alfred's[2] having gone to see his father's leg, which is buried at Waterloo, and of *100 old women* having come to see him get into his carriage when they heard whose son he was. We spoke of all this; of Sir H. Vivian's suffering much now, Lord Melbourne said, in consequence of a severe blow he got at Waterloo "by a spent grape shot." Lord Melbourne went over to Brussels almost immediately *after* the battle of Waterloo, to see Sir Frederic Ponsonby[3] who was dreadfully wounded, stabbed through and through; Lord Melbourne said, though he lived for 20 years

by this lady. By her second marriage she became the "Mother of the Napiers," a designation almost as famous in the British history of the Napoleonic Wars as the "Mother of the Gracchi" in Republican Rome.

[1] Daughters of John Gunning, of Castle Coote. See *ante*, p. 215.
[2] Lord Alfred Paget. See *ante*, p. 226.
[3] See *ante*, p. 310.

afterwards, he certainly died in consequence of these wounds. I asked Lord Melbourne if he didn't think Johnson's Poetry very hard ; he said he did, and that Garrick said, " Hang it, it's as hard as Greek." His Prose he admires, though he said pedantry was to be observed throughout it ; and Lord Melbourne thinks what he *said* superior to what he *wrote*. In spite of all that pedantry, Lord Melbourne said, " a deep feeling and a great knowledge of human nature " pervaded all he said and wrote. . . .

Tuesday, 7th August.—I asked him if he had seen Pozzo, which he told me in the evening he was going to do ; he said he had, and it was about the Pasha of Egypt [1] ; and he said Russia would go quite with England in the whole affair and quite approved of England's intention of sending a Fleet there ; at the same time, Lord Melbourne said, he stated distinctly, that if we didn't send a Fleet, they would be obliged to march an Army into Turkey for its protection ; but, Lord Melbourne said he hoped, from what he saw by the last despatches, that the Pasha had given up the idea of declaring his Independence. " I think he only tried it," Lord Melbourne said, " to see what effect it would make ! " Lord Melbourne said he had also seen Lord Palmerston, and had spoken to him about these Belgian Affairs, which they still hope, in spite of many difficulties, to settle ; and they have now satisfied Sebastiani,[2] who, Lord Melbourne said, was of a jealous disposition and thought they were going on without him

---

[1] Mehemet Ali, the Pasha, having announced his intention to pay no more tribute to the Porte (an action equivalent to a declaration of independence), great efforts were made by the representatives of the Powers to induce him to reconsider his decision.

[2] The French Ambassador in London.

with Bülow [1] ; Lord Palmerston had only got from Van de Weyer a statement of this Debt,[2] Lord Melbourne said ; but that it would be impossible to alter ; I expressed a fear of the Belgians resisting. Lord Melbourne said (which is quite true) that it would be very awkward if Uncle Leopold came over just in the midst of these Conferences, which would have the effect, as if he came for that purpose, and which Lord Melbourne said would prevent their acting as much for his interests as they otherwise might do.

said I quite felt it ; but that Lord Melbourne had best send for Stockmar and get him to settle it with the King. . . .

Sunday, 12th August.—Saw Stockmar for a little while, and then took leave of this good and kind friend, which I was really sorry to do. He told me he had been to see Lord Melbourne, and he said I should have (what *I* have *always* had) the greatest confidence in Lord Melbourne, and ask his advice, not only in Political Matters, but in domestic affairs, —and ask his advice just like a *Father*, which are quite my feelings. Lord Melbourne was very funny about the Statue of the Duke of Wellington which is put up (in wood) only as a Trial, on the Archway on Constitution Hill,[3] and which we think looks dreadful and much too large ; but Lord Melbourne

---

[1] Baron Heinrich von Bülow, many years Prussian representative in London, afterwards Prussian Minister for Foreign Affairs.

[2] The adjustment of the debt between Holland and Belgium.

[3] The equestrian statue of the Duke of Wellington stood on the arch at Hyde Park Corner from 1846 to 1883. It excited much ridicule at the time of its erection. There was a question of its removal, but the Duke of Wellington strongly opposed the suggestion. He said that he never wished his statue to be put upon the Arch, but once there, there it should remain. It was removed nearly forty years later to Aldershot. Recently some prancing horses and a chariot have taken the place of old Copenhagen and the Duke.

said he thought a statue would look well there, and that it should be as large. We then observed what a pity Wyatt should do the statue, as we thought he did them so ill ; and we mentioned George III.'s ; but Lord Melbourne does not dislike that, and says it's exactly like George III., and like his way of bowing.[1] He continued, " I never will have anything to do with Artists ; I wished to keep out of it all ; for they're a waspish set of people." . . .

Tuesday, 14th August.—I went and fetched the Speech, and he read it to me, in his beautiful, clear manner, and with that fine voice of his, and full of fine expression. I always feel that *I* can read it better when I have heard him read it. The Speech is, as Lord Melbourne said, " not long and safe."

Wednesday, 15th August.—Lady Normanby then practised putting on my crown, for to-morrow. After this I read my Speech twice over, in my crown. Played and sang. Wrote. Wrote my journal. I forgot to say that I got in the morning, 2 notes from Lord Melbourne in which it seemed almost certain that the Prorogation could only take place on Friday ; but at a little before 2 I got another note from him, in which he said that he heard from Lord John, it could take place next day, and therefore, that there would be a Council. I asked Lord Melbourne if it ever had been usual for the Sovereign to *read* the Speech *after* the Prime Minister had done so at the Council, as Lord Lansdowne had twice asked that question. Lord Melbourne said, never ; but that the late King had done it once, when he was in a great state of irritation, and had said, " I will read

---

[1] As an illustration of the vagaries of " taste " in Art, it may be mentioned that this statue is now considered one of the most successful in London.

it myself, paragraph by paragraph." This was the last time the late King ever prorogued Parliament in person. I asked if Brougham was in the House; he said no, he was gone. I told him I heard Brougham had asked Lady Cowper down to Brougham Hall; but that she wouldn't go; I asked if she knew him (Brougham) well; Lord Melbourne said very well, and " I've known him all my life; he can't bear me now; he won't speak to me; I've tried to speak to him on ordinary subjects in the House of Lords, but he won't answer, and looks very stern "; Lord Melbourne said, laughing, " Why, we've had several severe set-to's, and I've hit him very hard." I asked if he (**B.**) didn't still sit on the same bench with Lord Melbourne. " Quite on the gangway; only one between," replied Lord Melbourne. Lord Melbourne and I both agreed that it was *since* the King's death that Brougham was so enraged with Lord Melbourne; for, till then, he would have it that it was the *King's* dislike to him (and the King made no objection whatever to him, Lord Melbourne told me) and *not Lord Melbourne*; " he wouldn't believe me," Lord M. said; and *now* he's undeceived. Brougham always, he said, used to make a great many speeches. I observed that I thought if his daughter was to die, he would go mad; but Lord Melbourne doesn't think so; and said, " A man who is always very odd never goes really mad."

Thursday, 16th August.—" You were rather nervous,"[1] said Lord Melbourne; to which I replied, dreadfully so; " More so than any time," he continued. I asked if it was observed; he said, " I don't think anyone else would have observed it, but I could see

---

[1] This refers to the reading by the Queen of her " Speech."

you were.'" Spoke of my fear of reading it too low,
or too loud, or too quick; " I thought you read it
very well," he said kindly. I spoke of my great
nervousness, which I said I feared I never would
get over. " I won't flatter Your Majesty that you
ever will; for I think people scarcely ever get over
it; it belongs to a peculiar temperament, sensitive
and susceptible; that shyness generally accompanies
high and right feelings," said Lord Melbourne
most kindly; he was so kind and paternal to me.
He spoke of my riding, which he thought a very
good thing. " It gives a feeling of ease the day
one has done with Parliament," said Lord Melbourne. He spoke of the people in the Park when
I went to the House; and I said how very civil
the people were—*always*—to me; which touched
him; he said it was a very good thing; it didn't do
to rely too much on those things, but that it was well
it was there. I observed to Lord Melbourne how ill
and out of spirits the Duke of Sussex was; " I have
ended the Session in great charity," said Lord Melbourne, " with the Duke of Wellington, but I don't
end it in charity with those who didn't vote with
the Duke when he voted with us "; we spoke of all
that; " The Duke is a very great and able man,"
said Lord Melbourne, " but he is more often wrong
than right." Lord Holland wouldn't allow this;
" Well, let's throw the balance the other way,"
continued Lord Melbourne, " but when he is wrong
he is *very* wrong."

Friday, 17th August.—I then told Lord Melbourne
that I had so much to do, I didn't think I possibly
could go to Windsor on Monday; he said if I put
off going once for that reason, I should have to put
it off again, which I wouldn't allow; I said there were

so many things to go, and to pack,—and so many useless things; " I wouldn't take those useless things," said Lord Melbourne laughing. I then added that he couldn't have an idea of the number of things women had to pack and take; he said many men had quite as much,—which I said couldn't be, and he continued that Lord Anglesey had *36* trunks; and that many men had 30 or 40 different waistcoats, and neck-cloths, to choose from; which made me laugh; I said a man *couldn't* really want more than 3 or 4 coats for some months. He said in fact 6 were enough for a year,—but that people had often fancies for more. I said our dresses required such smooth packing; " Coats ought to be packed smooth," replied Lord Melbourne. I asked Lord Melbourne if Pozzo had spoken at all about the Belgian affairs. He said he told him he wouldn't meddle with them at all. Spoke of Pozzo's disliking Lord Palmerston, who didn't, he fancied, treat him with enough *égard*; and Lord Melbourne said Palmerston keeps them waiting sometimes for a long while,—which, though they say they don't mind it, they do mind; and we both agreed that he was a little apt to sneer sometimes, and to make it appear absurd what people said. I said, independent of Uncle's coming—hurting his interests in the Conferences—his own country was in too disturbed a state to do so[1]; Lord Melbourne said whatever would be done would be attributed to Uncle's presence; that justice must be done to Belgium; but that there was such a desire in the Cabinet to settle the affair, that they wouldn't be disposed to listen to any unreasonable demands of

---

[1] All this paragraph refers to the disputes between Belgium and Holland over their respective financial responsibilities.

Belgium; I said one felt less anxious reading the Speech at the close than at the beginning of the Session. Lord Melbourne said he didn't know; "The responsibility is so much greater during the Vacations; when Parliament is sitting one comes at once to Parliament; one has that to go to, and hears the worst at once." . . .

Sunday, 19*th August.*—Spoke of the Phœnix Park being considered unwholesome; of its being drained by what they call the Sub-soil-plough. He repeated the anecdote about Lord Talbot; the present Lord Talbot—(I believe I have already noted down the anecdote as he told it me twice before, but am not quite sure)—asked someone why they had never thought of draining the Phœnix Park, and they replied, "Why, your Ancestors were so much employed in draining the *Country,* that they had no time to think of draining the Park." He said Talleyrand told an anecdote of a lady in the time of the Revolution who was speaking of what she would be, and she said, "Paysanne, oui; mais Bourgeoise, jamais." I said to Lord Melbourne I was afraid he disliked the Germans, as he was always laughing at them, which he wouldn't allow at all and laughed much. He said, "I've a great opinion of their talents, but not of their beauty." He asked if I had seen Mr. MacNeill's[1] despatches giving an account of his going into *Herat* at night; I replied, I had not; Lord Melbourne said it was a very curious and even fearful account, his going through these Barbaric Armies at night, 9 o'clock, all the Persians without, prepared for the Attack, and all those within, for Defence; and he gave an interesting account of

[1] Afterwards Sir John MacNeill. He had been sent as Envoy to Teheran to try to prevent the Shah attacking the Afghans.

1—26

one of the principal persons in Herat ; Mr. MacNeill
said he found them quite disposed to negotiate, but
when he returned to the Shah's camp, he found the
Russian Ambassador there, and the Shah would
listen to nothing ; so Mr. MacNeill came away. Spoke
of not liking the Cathedral Service and all that singing, and Lord Melbourne said, " It is inconsistent
with a calm and right devotion ; it's papistical, and
theatrical." [1]

Monday, 20th August.—Spoke of Pozzo's being very
civil to Lord Melbourne ; Lord Melbourne said,
" He's very fond of me," upon which I said, " I
don't wonder at that," which made Lord Melbourne
smile. He continued, that Lord Palmerston gave
Pozzo rather unnecessary offence by not treating
him with respect and *égard,* which those sensitive
Corsicans and Italians expect. I said to Lord Melbourne, I felt often ashamed at being so ignorant
about many things, and at being obliged to ask
him about so many things. He replied MOST KINDLY,
" Oh ! no, you know everything very well ; it's
impossible for anybody to know everything that it
is right for them to know." We spoke of the Archduke Charles, who, as Mr. Macgregor told Lord Melbourne, " and as we know," he said, was a most
able man, but wouldn't take the slightest part in
public affairs. We spoke of how many brothers
there are still alive : Archduke Charles, Archduke
Palatine, Archduke John, Archduke Rainer, and
Archduke Louis. Spoke of Hayter's Picture, and
of his having made the Duchess of Sutherland so like
already. Spoke of the Duchess of Sutherland's
features being large, which he agreed in ; but that

[1] Lord Melbourne was a " low Churchman and an Erastian," like
so many of the Whigs of that day.

he liked large features, for that people with small features and " *Squeeny* noses " never did anything. Spoke of the business of the Army, which Lord Melbourne said he was afraid Lord Howick would bring on, and that there would be a good deal of difficulty about it. Lord Howick, he says, has pledged himself about it, and is displeased with the Horse-Guards. He (Lord Howick) is very indiscreet in the House of Commons, Lord Melbourne said. He has written Lord Melbourne a letter about this Army business, which Lord Melbourne told him he would answer ; but he begged Lord Melbourne not to write to him, as long as he was at Spa,—as the letter would be read. I said I hoped Lord Melbourne had never found me indiscreet, or that I had ever repeated things which I ought not to have done. He said, " Not at all ; no one is so discreet," and that it was impossible sometimes to help letting out things. I then also begged him always to tell me, when he heard anything, might it be agreeable or disagreeable, and that he should never be afraid of telling me so ; which he promised to do.[1]

Tuesday, 21st August.—Lord Melbourne said he had seen Lord Palmerston, who told him he hoped to be able soon to bring this Belgian business [2]

[1] This love of straight dealing and dislike of flattery were lifelong characteristics of the Queen.

[2] In 1815 Belgium and Holland were, by the action of the European Powers at the Congress of Vienna, united into one Kingdom. This led to constant friction and even to open hostilities between the two nations, and in 1831 a Conference of the Powers decreed a dissolution of the Union, and drew up a Treaty, but the division of territory again led to a war which is chiefly notable for the siege of Antwerp in 1832. In 1838 Holland announced for the first time her readiness to accede to the provisions of the Treaty of 1832. The Belgians claimed that this acquiescence came too late, but under pressure of the Powers she had in the end to give her assent. During this excite-

to a sort of conclusion; that he had had several conversations with Bülow, and Senfft,[1] " who seems a very fair man "; and that they think they may settle this Debt, and satisfy the Belgians by this slight change. " Then I talked to him," continued Lord Melbourne, " about the King's coming, and that it would be more for the disadvantage of his Interests." I then spoke of my having received such an odd present of a Kitten in the morning, which made him laugh. (I got a basket, which they said came from Sir Henry Wheatley, and which I thought was full of flowers, and when my Maid opened it, we found a pretty little *Kitten* in it—which some poor people sent me as a present.)

Monday, 27th August.—Of Uncle Leopold; when he married Princess Charlotte; Lord Melbourne hadn't the slightest acquaintance with her, and never had spoken to her. She never came to her father at that time. Lord M. said he never went near the Princess of Wales, for he said considering that he opposed the Regent so much in Parliament, he didn't wish to oppose him in his quarrels with his Wife; for, he said, he had been so much with the Prince of Wales, and was so much attached to him, that he thought that would have been wrong.

Tuesday, 28th August.—Lord Melbourne then read me a letter from Lord John about all this Belgian business; he says that he won't support Belgium in its new claims. Lord Melbourne said, " It's very

ment the failure of the Bank of Brussels produced a financial crisis which caused great distress among the people.

[1] Count von Senfft Pilsach was Austrian Minister at The Hague, and came to England in 1838 as Austrian Plenipotentiary at the Conference which took place in London to settle the Separation of Holland and Belgium. He signed the Treaty of 1839 on behalf of Austria.

well of John saying he won't support,'" and so forth,
but that it would be impossible for us not to take
one side ; our interests would compel us to do so ;
they lay so much with the Low Countries ; England,
he said, could never permit France to have possession
of Antwerp, which was such a great Maritime place.
He then read me a letter from Lord Minto relative
to an alarm which prevails, and which was caused,
Lord Melbourne says, by a speech the Duke of
Wellington made in the House, about the weakness
of our Naval force ; which Lord Minto quite dis-
claims. Lord Melbourne sent him a paper of Sir
Robert Inglis's [1] about the Russian, French, and
American Fleets ; which Lord Minto says is quite
erroneous ; Lord Minto states that in a very few
weeks, he could be quite ready for war ; Lord M. says,
what countries generally ruin themselves with, is,
keeping up their Naval and Military Establishments
during the time of peace ; and he said, " Better be
at War then." [2] He owned that the Russians
sending their fleet to the Black Sea "certainly is
far from pleasant." Then I spoke of Lord Ponsonby's great alarm about Russian Influence, which
Lord Melbourne said always was the case. Spoke
of Queen Charlotte's having been supposed to have
had a great many presents which she was fond of,
from Mrs. Hastings [3] ; and Lord Melbourne said the
King was thought rather to go with Hastings, who
was accused and tried for misdemeanours in India.
There was an ivory bed-stead Queen Charlotte got,

---

[1] Member for Oxford University. He had displaced Sir Robert
Peel at the time of the Tory split on Catholic Emancipation.

[2] This was common Whig doctrine up to the Crimean War, when
the unreadiness of the Military Authorities caused a reaction, which
indirectly led to the fall of the Aberdeen Government.

[3] Wife of Warren Hastings.

I—26*

which Lord M. believed was at Frogmore now. Spoke of Queen Adelaide's having got all those Shawls which the King of Oude sent. This led us to speak of the Crown Jewels; of there not being many, yet more than I ever wished to wear, of my not liking those sort of things. Lord M. said he didn't like a profusion of them, but thought a few fine ones the best. Spoke of the Jewels which Queen Charlotte left to her daughters. Lord Melbourne said the Queen Consort can do with her *own* things what she pleases; can make her own Will, and "is a *femme seule,*" for no other woman can—all is her husband's. Lord Melbourne (in reply to my question when he first knew George IV.) said, as soon as he could remember any one; he was 4 when the King was 21, in '83, when Lord Melbourne's father was first put about the Prince of Wales. "He used to be at Whitehall, or Piccadilly[1] where we then lived, morning, noon and night," Lord Melbourne said; and he used to come down to Brocket; he always was fond of children and took notice of them; I said he took notice of me; I observed how much more submissive we were to him than to the late King; Lord Melbourne said George IV. had more power. Lord Melbourne said *none* of the Royal Family could marry without the Sovereign's leave since the Marriage Act, passed early in George III.'s reign, in consequence, Lord Melbourne believes, of the Duke of Cumberland's marrying a Mrs. Luttrell[2]

---

[1] Melbourne House stood on the site of the Albany. See Vol. II., p. 96.

[2] In 1771 the Duke of Cumberland secretly married Anne, daughter of Lord Irnham (afterwards Earl of Carhampton) and widow of Andrew Horton. Her brother was Colonel Luttrell, the opponent of Wilkes. Not long afterwards, the Duke of Gloucester made public the fact of his marriage to the Dowager Countess Waldegrave. These two marriages led to the passing of the Royal Marriage Act,

which was very much disliked; else the Duke of Sussex might have married Lady Augusta, and the late King Mrs. Jordan, Lord Melbourne said. The member of the Royal Family, Lord Melbourne continued, gives notice to the Privy Council of his intention to marry, and if they don't disapprove, it's supposed the King will consent. Lord Melbourne said it was a difficult subject the marriage of the Royal Family; marrying a subject was inconvenient, and there was inconvenience in foreigners; " It was very often done " (marrying subjects); " Kings did it; and I don't know there was any harm in it," said Lord Melbourne. Anne Hyde was the last who married a Prince who became *King*, and that was considered a dreadful thing. Lord M. said he had been looking at some of those letters [George III.'s] to Lord North which seemed to him very ill written,[1] both as to hand and style, and in bad English. Lord North was a great favourite of George IV.'s, Lord Melbourne said; " Lord North was a very easy, good-natured man," and the King knew him " when he first came in to life." Lord Thurlow, whom Mr. Pitt beat and turned out in '93,[2] turned to George IV. and became also a great favourite of his. He was clever but ill-tempered, Lord Melbourne said.

Wednesday, 29th August.—Lord Melbourne said he had been looking at those letters to Lord North, and found on closer examination that they were written with much more practical knowledge and knowledge of men than he had at first thought. The

which governs (with certain exceptions) the marriages of all descendants of George II. See *ante*, p. 333, and Vol. II., p. 43.

[1] Lord Melbourne modified this opinion next day.

[2] Partly in consequence of his intrigues with the Prince of Wales against Pitt in the matter of the Regency Bill.

letters he has been reading are relative to a Negotiation which the King entered into, with the Opposition, in order to strengthen the Government; and Lord Melbourne related several parts of it, which made him smile and which he said were true enough. Lord Melbourne said he (George III.) couldn't bear Mr. Fox, for that he says in one of these letters that he (Lord North) might offer him any situation which did not bring him in immediate contact with the King, or into the Closet; and as he (Mr. Fox) never had any principles, he wouldn't have any difficulty in changing. These letters prove, Lord Melbourne said, what strong personal dislikes the King had. These letters to Lord North, Lord M. thinks, were returned to George IV. by Mrs. Douglas on the death of her husband, who was the son of Lady Glenbervie, Lord North's daughter; Lord North had three daughters, Lady Glenbervie, Lady Sheffield, and Lady Charlotte Lindsay (whom I know); all very clever, Lord M. says. He had 3 sons, George (who was a very pleasant, lively man and a great bon-vivant, Lord M. says), Frederic, and Frank; who were all in succession Earls of Guilford. The present Lord is son to Lord North's brother [1] who was a Bishop, Lord M. told me. Lord North died in '93, and Lord M. remembers seeing him (when Lord M. was a boy) led into the House of Lords, quite blind, at Hastings' trial; he was Lord Guilford for a very short time.

Lord M. does not think that George III. was very fond of Mr. Pitt. Spoke of the violent dislikes George III. and George IV. had; William IV. had them also, but Lord M. said they were easily got over.

[1] Brownlow North, Bishop successively of Lichfield, Worcester, and Winchester.

Spoke of George III.'s hand-writing ; of mine, which Lord M. thinks very legible and generally very good ; of my inclination to imitate hand-writings, and people,—which Lord M. said, showed quickness, and was in the Family ; of George IV.'s mimickry. I said I kept a journal, which, as Lord Melbourne said, is very laborious, but a very good thing ; for that it was astonishing in transacting business, how much one forgot, and how one forgot *why* one did the things.

Thursday, 30th August. . . . I gave Lord M. this Pamphlet of Sir H. Taylor's which Mamma lent me. We talked about many things, and in going home I asked Lord M. how long Lord North had been Prime Minister to George III. ; " From '70 till '82," he told me. " The Duke of Grafton " (who preceded him, and was the present Duke of Grafton's father) " went away," Lord M. continued, " without telling any body and without telling the King ; they were difficult times, and he went away ; I know why he went away, people are always doing those foolish things ; and the King didn't know what to do ; he sent for Lord Gower "[1] (I forget what he was), who, I think Lord M. said, refused it ; " and then he sent for his Chancellor of the Exchequer " (Lord North) " and made him his Prime Minister." Lord M. spoke of Dr. Keate, and told me an anecdote of him and George III. ; and then he said that Dr. Keate couldn't bear to be reminded of his boyish days at Eton ; somebody, who Lord M. knows, reminded Keate when he was walking across the School-Yard with him, of the window, pointing at it, out of which they had often jumped, upon which Dr. Keate said, " Don't mention it ; it's a very foolish remark."

[1] See note, *post*, p. 397.

Friday, 31*st August*.—Lord M. then said, that the French were going to send out a fleet to Mexico, with which State they have been in a quarrel for some time,—and that they meant to send the Prince de Joinville with it, to ask for reparation, and if not, to attack the fort of Aloa which commands the river, and which it would not be agreeable for us if the French were to possess ; and Lord Palmerston proposes we should send a swift sailing Vessel to Mexico to apprize the Mexicans of what was to take place and to advise them to make reparation. And also, Lord P. proposes sending a Vessel to Guiana, where the French are making great encroachments, and to see what they are about.

Lady Cork[1] is 92, a very strange old woman ; Lord M. knows her ; she was clever, a great favourite of George III. and Queen Charlotte. She was a Miss Monckton, sister to Lord Galway, he said. Lord M. said in returning Dr. Hook's sermon (which I sent him to read) when he came in, that it was eager, but nothing very particular, and able. Lady Holland seems " very fond of Senfft," Lord M. observed ; " she would settle that Embassy too, as she does every thing else," he said laughing. Lord M. said, in speaking of Taylor's pamphlet,[2] " There is no force in it ; it isn't pointed." Taylor is very fond of writing, he says, and fancies he writes well. Spoke of Lady C. Bury's book.[3] Lord M. says these

[1] Mary, daughter of the first Viscount Galway, married, as his second wife, Edmund, seventh Earl of Cork. She died in 1840.

[2] *Remarks on an Article for the " Edinburgh Review " on the Times of George III. and George IV.*, by General Sir Herbert Taylor, who had been Secretary successively to the Duke of York, George III., Queen Charlotte, and William IV.

[3] *A Diary illustrative of the Times of George IV.*, published in 1838. See *ante*, p. 310.

Friday, 31*st August.*—Lord M. then said, that the French were going to send out a fleet to Mexico, with which State they have been in a quarrel for some time,—and that they meant to send the Prince de Joinville with it, to ask for reparation, and if not, to attack the fort of Aloa which commands the river, and which it would not be agreeable for us if the French were to possess ; and Lord Palmerston proposes we should send a swift sailing Vessel to Mexico to apprize the Mexicans of what was to take place and to advise them to make reparation. And also, Lord P. proposes sending a Vessel to Guiana, where the French are making great encroachments, and to see what they are about.

Lady Cork[1] is 92, a very strange old woman ; Lord M. knows her ; she was clever, a great favourite of George III. and Queen Charlotte. She was a Miss Monckton, sister to Lord Galway, he said. Lord M. said in returning Dr. Hook's sermon (which I sent him to read) when he came in, that it was eager, but nothing very particular, and able. Lady Holland seems " very fond of Senfft," Lord M. observed ; " she would settle that Embassy too, as she does every thing else," he said laughing. Lord M. said, in speaking of Taylor's pamphlet,[2] " There is no force in it : it isn't pointed." Taylor is very fond of writing, he says, and fancies he writes well. Spoke of Lady C. Bury's book.[3] Lord M. says these

---

[1] Mary, daughter of the first Viscount Galway, married, as his second wife, Edmund, seventh Earl of Cork. She died in 1840.

[2] *Remarks on an Article for the " Edinburgh Review " on the Times of George III. and George IV.*, by General Sir Herbert Taylor, who had been Secretary successively to the Duke of York, George III., Queen Charlotte, and William IV.

[3] *A Diary illustrative of the Times of George IV.*, published in 1838. See *ante*, p. 310.

H.R.H. The Duc de Nemours
from a portrait by Eugene Lami

things make less impression than people fancy; they " make a day's noise ; but nobody minds them much." Spoke of Lady Anne Hamilton,[1] who attended Queen Caroline at her Trial; Lady Charlotte Lindsay gave evidence. " Lord Egremont said," continued Lord M., " ' As for Guilford,[2] he twaddled like a waiting maid when he gave evidence ; but his Sister lied like a man,' " which made us both laugh very much. Spoke of Kenney,[3] who is Author (Lord M. told me) of *Love, Law, and Physic,* and *Raising the Wind,* and is at Holland House. Spoke of my knowing Rogers and Moore ; having seen Scott and Southey. Lord M. rather admires Southey's works, and thinks his *Life of Nelson* very pretty. Spoke of his *Life of Cowper.* Spoke of a new book lying on the table, sent to me by Granville Penn,[4] which Lord M. looked at and said he thought might be curious ; it is the *Life of Sir William Penn,* Admiral in Cromwell's time, and who, with Venables, took Jamaica. Spoke of Mrs. Hutchinson's *Memoirs of Colonel Hutchinson,* which Lord M. thinks very curious ; spoke of her violence ; spoke of Clarendon's book which Lord M. said " is a fine book." I observed there were few books on the

[1] Lady Anne Hamilton was a lady-in-waiting of Caroline, wife of George IV., whom she accompanied to England in 1820. *The Secret History of the Court* was published without her name, but the authorship was never disputed.

[2] Lord Guilford was the son of Lord North, George III.'s Minister, and his sister, here mentioned, was Lady Charlotte Lindsay, wife of Lieut.-Col. Hon. John Lindsay. See *ante,* p. 392.

[3] James Kenney (1780–1849), a successful dramatist. He was the original Jeremy Diddler in his own *Raising the Wind,* when it was acted by amateurs. The play was subsequently performed at Covent Garden.

[4] Granville Penn (1761–1844), grandson of William Penn, the founder of Pennsylvania.

Parliamentary side; he replied few at the time, but a good many since. He mentioned one by Brodie, a Scotchman; Bishop Burnet's Memoirs of his own time, during Charles II.'s reign; and he said, " There is a book which I think would amuse Your Majesty, and would be of use to you, and which isn't long, which is Guizot's account of the Revolution." It's only in 2 vols., and is a summary of whole thing, he said.

Lord M. said Lady Holland was a great friend of Pozzo's, and that his first acquaintance with Pozzo was at Holland House. I asked if she knew Sebastiani; he said she did, but didn't like him much, except from his connection with Napoleon " whom she adored." She never knew Napoleon, Lord Melbourne added, but saw him at Paris at the Peace of Amiens. She used to send him things she knew he liked, said Lord M.; when he was at St. Helena she sent him *gâteaux* and chocolate, &c. " She was half on his side," Lord M. continued, " if not more." Spoke of Lady E. Wortley's [1] admiration for Napoleon. Soult was no friend of Napoleon, Lord M. said; none of them, he continued, were to be compared to Napoleon himself; the two best after Napoleon, Lord M. said, were Dessaix who was killed at Marengo, and Kleber who was murdered in Egypt.

I asked Lord M. what Lord Gower, whom he mentioned to me before, was; that Lord Gower, he said, was the Duke of Sutherland's grandfather; he was " Lord Privy Seal " when the King sent

---

[1] Lady Emmeline Wortley, daughter of the fifth Duke of Rutland, wife of Charles Stuart Wortley. Her daughter, Victoria, goddaughter of the Duchess of Kent, afterwards Lady Welby-Gregory, was sometime a maid-of-honour to the Queen.

for him.[1] "He did not think himself equal to it" (being Prime Minister); "he was a man who took great part in politics." Lord M. also told me that he believes the present Lord Bute to be the great-grandson of the Minister of George III. "George III. found the Duke of Newcastle and Mr. Pitt, and everything was going on very well, when he was advised to change; he couldn't bear Mr. Pitt; who was afterwards Lord Chatham; and he took Lord Bute in his place; and then followed all that unpopularity." I asked if these letters of George III. showed great confidence in Lord North; Lord M. said "they show a great liking for him, more than a great confidence." That the King never seemed to think him strong enough; Lord North, all along, Lord M. continued, was pursuing a Policy contrary to what he himself approved, but which he was urged to by the King: and Lord North remonstrated very much with the King. The difference, Lord M. observed before, between George IV. and his father, was, that the former (which Knighton's Memoirs show, Lord M. said) always required somebody to lean upon, whereas the latter always wished to act for himself, and only yielded, but said at the same time he disliked doing it. He never would have yielded on the Catholic Question, Lord M. continued, nor would the Duke of York; the late King was for it; but George IV. did it very unwillingly. George III. was deeply hurt at the loss of the American provinces, which I observed was no wonder; I said I thought it was *his* fault. Lord M. said most likely it was;

[1] Granville, Earl Gower (1721–1803), had sat for Westminster before his accession to the Peerage. Thereafter he was Lord Privy Seal, Lord Chamberlain and President of the Council. He was created Marquess of Stafford, and K.G. He married Lady Louisa Egerton, daughter and co-heiress of Scrope, first Duke of Bridgwater.

but that it was impossible any longer to keep up the great Colonial Policy, namely that they should exclusively trade with England and make nothing for themselves ; even Lord Chatham, Lord M. said, who all along advocated their cause, " said they shouldn't drive one hob-nail for themselves." The Separation was easily done, they had nothing to do but to declare it. Lord M. continued that the first settlers were composed of people who left England in discontent,—of dissenters &c., and consequently no loyal people could spring from them. Spoke of the people whom William III. ennobled, which I've no time to enumerate. He told a most absurd anecdote of a very fat little porter at Lansdowne House. " He is a leading man in all the Parish Debates," said Lord M. ; " and somebody told Albemarle, ' He speaks very well ; to tell you the truth he speaks very like my lord.' "

END OF VOL. I

Printed by Hazell, Watson & Viney, Ld., London and Aylesbury